Master of Self-Realization

An Ultimate Understanding

Shri Sadguru Siddharameshwar Maharaj

Master of Self-Realization
An Ultimate Understanding

Spiritual Discourses of His Holiness
Shri Sadguru Siddharameshwar Maharaj

Recorded by Shri Nisargadatta Maharaj

An English Translation of the Marathi Text
"Adhyatma Jnanacha Yogeshwar"

The Spiritual Science of Self-Knowledge

Also included in this book is the spiritual text titled:
Master Key to Self-Realization

© 2023 Sadguru Publishing

ISBN: **978-1-7376607-4-3**

2023, First International Edition

No part of this book may be reproduced or utilized in any form or by any means, electronic or mechanical for commercial usage without written permission from Sadguru Publishing

Contact Information:
sadguru.publishing@gmail.com

This is a follow-up edition of earlier versions of this text published with permission and cooperation of Shri Sadguru Trust – Mumbai, India

Original Cover Design:
Kirti Trivedi &
Shweta Kathe

A Sadguru Publishing Publication

A Note From the Editor:

Contained within the pages of this book you will find the teachings of Shri Siddharameshwar Maharaj. This teaching is identical with that two of His distinguished disciples, Shri Nisargadatta Maharaj, and Shri Ranjit Maharaj.

Disciples of Shri Nisargadatta Maharaj, and Shri Ranjit Maharaj, and the publisher of this book, have decided to include within these pages the most recent edition of the work of great distinction that was authored by Shri Siddharameshwar Maharaj titled ***Master Key to Self-Realization***.

The book ***Master Key to Self-Realization*** provides a foundation for the teaching contained in all of the talks given by Him, as well as those given by Shri Nisargadatta Maharaj and Shri Ranjit Maharaj. This classic text which was overseen by Shri Siddharameshwar Maharaj himself explains the fundamental teaching of Advaita Vedanta in the traditional method used by all of the great Masters of this lineage, or Sampradaya.

Thus, we felt it prudent to include this fundamental text here in these pages as a prelude to the 130 talks given by Shri Siddharameshwar Maharaj that were originally published in the Marathi language under the title of **Adhyatma Jnanacha Yogeshwar** by Shri Nisargadatta Maharaj in 1961 and 1962. It was then republished at the insistence of Shri Ranjit Maharaj in the year 2001 in Marathi, and is now available in English.

Every effort has been made to present this great teaching in fluid, modern English that can be easily comprehensible by spiritual seekers of all backgrounds, as well as those with no prior spiritual exposure.

Great thanks are offered to Mr. Satish Avhad and Mr. Diwakar Ghaisas, without whom this great text may never have come to be made available to English speaking spiritual seekers. Mr. Ghaisas has drawn on his extensive translation experience of advaitic texts including such great classic works as **Dasbodh**, to present mankind with a translation that provides the true impact of the words of Shri Siddharameshwar Maharaj.

This book is being given as an offering to all sincere seekers to whom we say "You Are That." May you realize the meaning of this statement with the aid of the words of the Sadguru contained within these pages. Most especially, this text is being laid as a humble offering of devotion at the feet of Shri Siddharameshwar Maharaj, Shri Ranjit Maharaj, and Shri Nisargadatta Maharaj, to whom we can only say:

Jai Sadguru Parabrahman!

David Moe
Editor and Publisher

A Few Words About This Book...

His Holiness Shri Siddharameshwar Maharaj, the Spiritual Master of Shri Nisargadatta Maharaj and Shri Ranjit Maharaj gave very informal, instructional, and thought-provoking discourses on spiritual wisdom during the period from 1934 to 1936. They were based not only on scriptural texts like **Dasbodh** of Samartha Ramdas, **Yogavasishtha**, etc. but also based on his own realization. During that time while attending these discourses, Shri Nisargadatta Maharaj used to take handwritten notes. Much later in 1961-62 Nisargadatta Maharaj with the help of Shri Khanderao Sabnis, alias Bhainath Maharaj, got them published for the benefit of devotees and other interested readers. This edition was soon out of print and the publication was not available for many years. A new edition was therefore published in 2001 at the insistence of Shri Ranjit Maharaj.

These 130 discourses were originally published in two volumes in Marathi, the language in which they were delivered. Shri Nisargadatta Maharaj and Shri Ranjit Maharaj, both disciples of Shri Siddharameshwar Maharaj became prominently known to non-Marathi Indian, and Western spiritual aspirants through the books **I Am That** (Shri Nisargadatta Maharaj) and **Illusion vs. Reality** (Shri Ranjit Maharaj), which were published in English. Readers of these books became therefore keen to know more about Shri Siddharameshwar Maharaj and his teaching and often requested for publication of an English translation of these discourses. We have therefore thought it fit to accede to these requests and to publish an English translation of these two volumes and thereby acquaint the non-Marathi Indian and Western aspirants with the teachings of Shri Siddharameshwar Maharaj as well. Shri Diwakar Ghaisas offered to undertake the task of English translation in the spirit of service without any reservation.

Shri Diwakar Ghaisas is an accomplished author as well as translator of a number of religious and spiritual publications. He had the good fortune to listen to late Shri J. Krishnamurti for over thirty years and to translate several of Shri J. Krishnamurthi's books into Marathi. He has also translated **Dasbodh** of Samarth Ramdas into lucid English. He is also well known in spiritual circles because of his own accomplishments in that field. We have therefore, entrusted this English translation to his experienced and able hands.

This book contains 130 discourses of Shri Siddharameshwar Maharaj, based on scriptural texts and Self-Realization. These discourses are unique and incomparable in their sweep, clarity, directness, and instruction. Being results oriented, they are a valuable aid to devoted seekers and will help accelerate their progress towards Self-Realization. There are many references to Indian scriptures, mythological and historical characters and events, traditions and practices in these discourses, with which the non Indian reader may not be familiar. Necessary notes have therefore been provided separately to clarify the context and aid understanding and appreciation. We hope that the devotees and other readers will welcome this effort and like it. We crave their indulgence for possible errors through oversight although every effort has been made to present a flawless translation.

Satish Avhad

Translator's Note

To translate into a foreign language, the informal talks given in a very tacit and cryptic manner in Marathi of a dialectic nature by a Spiritual Master to his disciples, who are also well-acquainted with the abstract ideas in metaphysical philosophy and to put the whole contents in a followable, lucid manner is in itself not an easy job. When the publisher of this book, having come to know my experience in translating J. Krishnamurti's books into flowing Marathi requested me to translate the book of talks by Shri Siddharameshwar Maharaj, I most hesitantly consented to try my pen, but when I actually started to put the various broken colloquial sentences into the current English, I found the task both exhausting and enervating.

However, the fact that I could finish this job even to this level of accuracy is only due to the great benevolent grace of the succession of the Masters of this Sampradaya right from Rewanasiddha to Shri Satishji Avhad, who somehow stood by my side and without compulsion or intimidation gave me enthusiasm to complete the whole translation of talks from both the volumes to form one book, which is now being presented to the readers interested in direct experience of Reality to the extent which is possible through printed word. To undertake such a work on the terms of any monetary gain is itself like defeating the very mission of imparting the nectar of the teachings of the Yogic Masters of wisdom so, naturally as expressed in Bhagvadgeeta, no thought of fruit has touched my mind, while doing such a duty towards the Gurus on one hand and the readers on the other.

This work was first tried by Mrs. Dungaji but as it lacked in English phraseology, the rough typed matter was left aside and I was asked to do the job. Whatever efforts were taken by Mrs. Dungaji are laudable and have not gone in vain, because that manuscript gave the skeleton base to me to proceed. Further, the whole matter when typed was shown to Mr. Anavkar from Kalyan, who not only went through it line by line, but also checked the text and gave useful hints for improvements.

I am most humbly requesting the elite readers to connive at any errors of language or grammar which might be there through oversight or lack of expertise and consider the most valuable teaching of the Master in its right spirit.

D. A. Ghaisas.
Thane 12th October 2005

Table of Contents

Master Key to Self-Realization

CHAPTER 1: THE IMPORTANCE OF SELF-KNOWLEDGE.........................1

CHAPTER 2: INVESTIGATION OF THE FOUR BODIES IN SEARCH OF "I"...18
  The First Body - The Physical Gross Body......................................*21*
  The Second Body - The Subtle Body..*27*
  The Third Body - The Causal Body..*31*
  The Fourth Body - The Great-Causal Body (Turya)........................*32*
  Brahman...*33*

CHAPTER 3: INVESTIGATION OF THE FOUR BODIES IN DETAIL............34
  A Methodical Approach to Explanation..*34*
  The Investigation Commences...*38*

CHAPTER 4: THE GREAT-CAUSAL BODY - "I AM"..............................55

CHAPTER 5: THE APPEARANCE OF THE WORLD...................................59
  Experiencing the Castes in a Human Being....................................*63*
  The Three Worlds...*64*
  Understanding the Knowledge of Self..*66*

CHAPTER 6: MAYA AND BRAHMAN..70
  Search for the Lost "I"..*73*

CHAPTER 7: DEVOTION AND DEVOTION AFTER LIBERATION................76

Master of Self-Realization - Volume 1

PREFACE TO MASTER OF SELF-REALIZATION - VOLUME 1
 Written by Shri Nisargadatta Maharaj..........................85
1. THE IMPORTANCE OF DEVOTION..................................89
2. DESIRELESSNESS AND SELF-REALIZATION.........................90
3. GIVING UP THE SENSE OF "MINE"...............................91
4. THE SELF IS THE KNOWER IN ALL BEINGS........................93
5. SELF DISCOVERY..93
6. GOD IS THE SUPREME SELF, PARAMATMAN.........................94
7. OBJECTS OF PERCEPTION CEASE ALONG WITH THE PERCEIVER........95
8. THROW OFF LAZINESS..97
9. SELF AND NON-SELF...97
10. TRUE RENUNCIATION..99
11. THE WAR BETWEEN RAMA AND RAVANA...........................101
12. BE DISINTERESTED IN OBJECTIVE THINGS......................102
13. WHEN THE KNOWLEDGE OF OBJECTS ENDS........................103
14. MEDITATE UPON WHAT YOU HEAR...............................105
15. THERE IS ONLY "ONE" WITHOUT DUALITY.......................107
16. KNOW BY SPEECH, MIND AND ACTION...........................108
17. TRUE RENUNCIATION AND DESIRELESSNESS......................109
18. THE SELF NATURALLY CONTAINS SPIRITUAL POWERS (SIDDHIS)....110
19. THE THOUGHT OF A DREAM IN THE DREAM.......................112
20. SPIRITUAL POWERS ARE NATURAL IN THE SELF..................113
21. TURN THE MIND AWAY FROM OBJECTS...........................115
22. THE SELF IS THE MOST SUBTLE...............................117
23. WHY IS THE WORLD SEEN IF IT IS UNREAL?....................118
24. ATOMS AND SUBATOMIC PARTICLES ARE ONE.....................119
25. YOU ARE THE SELF IN THE HEART OF ALL......................122
26. LISTEN TO THE TRUE NATURE OF THE TEACHING.................123
27. THE SELF IS CONSCIOUSNESS ITSELF..........................125
28. SELF-SURRENDER..126
29. DISSOLVE THE SENSE OF "I".................................128
30. KNOW WHO YOU ARE..130
31. THE SIX VIRTUES OR QUALITIES..............................132
32. GOD IS IN THE FORM OF THE DEVOTEE.........................134

33. The Signs of Desirelessness..135
34. Look at God Through the Eyes of the Devotee...............137
35. The Persistent Wish is Called Desire..................................140
36. One Who Lives as a Body, Suffers as a Body......................142
37. Concentrate on My "Real Nature".....................................143
38. The Glory of Paramatman..145
39. The Self is Free From Worry..149
40. Meditate Upon Me..150
41. Give Up the Addiction to Mundane Worldly Life............152
42. Know That You Are Paramatman.......................................155
43. How to Do Spiritual Practice (Sadhana)............................160
44. Paramatman is All-Pervading..161
45. Remain in the State of Brahman...163
46. Serving at the Feet of the Master..165
47. Serving the Feet of the Master..167
48. The Fire of Knowledge...170
49. Live According to Self-Knowledge.....................................170
50. The Greatness of the Sadguru, and "You Are That".........173
51. Dnyaneshwari..174
52. God is Permeating the World..176
53. The Sadguru is the God of All Gods...................................179
54. The Body is Not "I"...181
55. The Cycle of Maya..183
56. The Nine Faceted Devotion – Navavidha Bhakti..............185
57. Let Us Bow Down to the Mother Veda (Shruti)................189
58. Who is God?..192
59. Formless Brahman..194
60. There is Only One Without a Second................................198
61. The Main Doctrine of Vedanta...201
62. God is Life-Energy (Chaitanya)..205
63. Conceive of Brahman Beyond Conception......................207
64. Self Purification..211
65. Formless Unqualified Brahman..214
66. Seeing the Self-Reality...218
67. Eknathi Bhagwat..223
68. Brahman is Attributeless and Maya has Attributes...........226

Master of Self-Realization - Volume 2

PREFACE TO MASTER OF SELF-REALIZATION - VOLUME 2
Written by Shri Nisargadatta Maharaj..................231
69. LISTEN TO THE SIGNS OF KNOWLEDGE..........................234
70. IN PRAISE OF THE GURU WHO IS SHIVA........................237
71. BE ALERT WITHIN..239
72. THE DOUBTING THOMAS......................................242
73. THE STATE OF VICTORY.....................................246
74. NON-DUAL BRAHMAN EXPLAINED...............................250
75. NARAYANA PLAYS IN ALL FORMS..............................253
76. THE WORLD AS KNOWLEDGE...................................257
77. EVICT "ME" FROM THE HOUSE................................259
78. THE APPEARANCE OF THE WORLD..............................262
79. BE QUIET LIKE GOD..265
80. BRAHMAN IS ALWAYS AWAKE..................................268
81. GIVE UP DOUBT AND DISCRIMINATION.........................272
82. TAKE CARE IN SPIRITUAL LIFE..............................275
83. ATMAN AND PARAMATMAN....................................277
84. OFFER EVERYTHING TO GOD..................................279
85. MEDITATE ON THE DIVINE TREE..............................282
86. THE POWER WHERE "NO KARMA" REMAINS.......................286
87. THE SEED OF KARMA..290
88. THOSE WHO ARE WORTHY OF SPIRITUAL KNOWLEDGE..............293
89. THE SUPERIORITY OF THE PATH OF DEVOTION..................295
90. BRAHMAN IS REALITY.......................................298
91. THE GREATNESS OF DASBODH.................................301
92. THE COMPANY OF THE SAINT.................................303
93. PARABRAHMAN IS NON-PERCEPTIBLE...........................305
94. THE IMPORTANCE OF THE GRACE OF THE GURU..................308
95. FREEDOM AND DEVOTION.....................................310
96. DEVOTION AFTER LIBERATION – BLESSED IS UDDHAVA...........314
97. DEVOTION AND THE BLESSING OF THE SADGURU.................315
98. THE NATURE OF AVATAR.....................................318
99. THE FEARLESS STATE.......................................321
100. THE SUPREME STATE.......................................323

101. Raja Yoga – The Power of God...................................325
102. The Joy of Inner Realization....................................328
103. Transform Clay Into Gold...331
104. The Game of Chess..335
105. Know That You Are Paramatman............................337
106. The Eternal Home (Sayujya Sadan).........................339
107. Self-Surrender..342
108. The State of the Perfected Man..............................345
109. God and Devotee are One.......................................348
110. Enjoy Glory by Dropping Body-Consciousness.......351
111. The Ghost of Worry..353
112. Illusion is Only Visible to the Imagination..............357
113. The City of Brahman...361
114. The Root of Birth..364
115. The Tragedy of Family Life......................................366
116. Drinking the Nectar of Immortality........................367
117. Curing the Disease of Maya....................................370
118. The Duality Broken..372
119. The Golden Day...374
120. The fulfillment of fulfillment..................................376
121. The Third Eye..379
122. The Line of Demarcation..381
123. Saints are Incarnations of God...............................384
124. Conviction in Brahman Through the Path of Knowledge 386
125. God Incarnate...389
126. The Grace of the Guru..392
127. The Comfortable Seat of the Devotee of God.......396
128. The Fruit of Happiness and Joy..............................401
129. My Only Capital (Wealth) is Devotion to All..........404
130. Brahman Consciousness (Chidghana Brahman)....406

Shri Nisargadatta Maharaj

Shri Ranjit Maharaj

**Renowned Disciples of
Shri Sadguru Siddharameshwar Maharaj**

Shri Sadguru Siddharameshwar Maharaj

Master Key
to Self-Realization

The Spiritual Science of Self-Knowledge
as Presented by His Holiness
Shri Siddharameshwar Maharaj

Chapter 1: The Importance of Self-Knowledge

At the beginning of this exposition reverential adoration is offered to Shri Ganesh first, then to Shri Saraswati, and finally to Shri Sadguru. What is the reason for offering salutations in this order? If someone were to ask, "If the sequence of this adoration is changed will there be confusion?" The answer has to be, yes, there will be confusion. This is because Shri Ganesh is the deity for meditation and contemplation, and Shri Saraswati is the deity for the exposition of the teaching through words. With the help of these two deities, the deity in the form of "The Light of the Self," that arises in the heart of the aspirant is none other than the Sadguru. Therefore, the Sadguru necessarily has to be adored after Shri Ganesh and Shri Saraswati. Only when the understanding of the subject becomes firm does "The Grace of the Sadguru" descend. Neither the exposition of this text, nor the contemplation on the contents of this text will by themselves lead the aspirant to the goal. Therefore, one should reverentially adore *both* Shri Ganesh and Shri Saraswati.

There is an ancient method of expounding the teaching of Vedanta that is commonly followed in this tradition (Sampradaya) when presenting the subject matter of this text to the aspirant. According to this method, first the manifest form of the Sadguru is seen by the eyes. Then the knowledge about the teachings of the Vedanta, and the value and significance of these precious teachings is extolled through the words of the Guru. Then, a Mantra (a subtle name of God, or a phrase) is given and the aspirant is instructed to practice meditation on the repetition of the Mantra for a short period of time (usually several weeks) to imprint its significance within. This provides a means for the aspirant to make the mind more subtle so that the teachings to follow can be more easily grasped and realized. This is the seekers initiation to the teaching and invitation to become an aspirant on the path to realization.

In accordance with the method of the Saints that has been outlined above, the Sadguru first explains about the subject that is to follow, then indicates its characteristics, and finally follows by imparting a detailed knowledge of the subject. In most schools of education, when teaching small children about any subject, the teacher first verbally informs the child about the subject matter that will be taught. This is called the kindergarten method of education. Similarly, initially the Sadguru verbally gives you a concept or idea of Reality (such as "You are He" or "Only Brahman Exists," or some other similar form of mantra) that is to be contemplated upon. Through repetition or churning, this idea will be indelibly imprinted on the mind. This is called "The Tradition (Sampradaya) of the Sadguru." Through this preliminary method the aspirant achieves results sooner. So be it.

Afterwards, the Guru expounds the Truth (the subject matter) to an ordinarily intelligent aspirant, and he understands what the Sadguru conveys, and about "That" which He is teaching. However, the main difficulty is in experientially realizing what has been intellectually understood. Through the exposition of the subject by the Sadguru, one understands what the Self (Atman) is. However, the ghost of doubt pops up in the mind of the aspirant in the form of the question "How am I the Self?" and the aspirant's mental attitude does not become free of doubt. There is an intellectual understanding, but no realization. The remedy for this is to study with determination and learn the teaching. Unless there is sustained and repeated study, it will not be fully understood and realized. For example, in the instructional handwriting book, the letters presented are very beautiful. We understand this, but initially we cannot write the letters in the same way. If however the same letters are written repeatedly, then by virtue of that practice or study, the letters are beautifully formed as soon as the pen touches the paper. Here someone might ask, "How much study or practice is required to learn the subject well?" The answer is, "The study and the practice, or effort, must continue relentlessly according to each one's capacity, until it is understood or realized."

A general example can be stated here to impress upon the mind of the aspirant the importance of repeated study. An ordinarily intelligent man can understand something if it is explained to him two or three times. If he repeats it ten or twenty times, it becomes a habit. If he repeats it a hundred times, it becomes like an addiction. Once he becomes familiar with it a thousand times, it becomes inherent nature for the one practicing it. If we look at the fibers of the jute plant, they are so delicate and fine that they become scattered in all directions when blown by the wind. However, when the same fibers are entwined together to form a rope, it is so strong that it can bind even a strong and violent elephant to a small peg. Similarly great is the power of the repetition of the study of this type of practice. It is indeed true that Parabrahman is All-Pervading and Eternally Free. However, the Wind in the form of mind has become so strong in us due to misdirected practice and study through birth after birth that it has imprisoned the eternally free Brahman in the thought of identification with the body. About the tremendous result of repeated practice Saint Tukaram has said, "Whatever is unachievable, becomes achievable only by virtue of repeated study and practice." Recognizing the importance of this study, the aspirant should adore the principles symbolized by Ganesh and Saraswati. This means that one should fulfill himself by continuous meditation, and learn through repeatedly hearing the exposition of Truth.

Now, before one begins this study it will be desirable for the aspirant to know many other things relevant to the subject. Why has the illusion "I am the body" arisen in a human being? What was the condition of the human being when he was born? How did he develop this idea of "me" and "mine"? Is his condition in the world free from fear? If so, by whom and how was he helped to be rid of that fear? All of these things must be taken into consideration.

First, the human being was lying twisted up in a small space inside the mother's womb. When he was born, he came into this boundless world and slightly opened his eyes and looked around. Upon seeing the immense space and tremendous light, he averted his eyes, and he was in shock. "Where is this that I have come alone? Who is going to give me support? What is going to be my fate?" These types of fear arose in his mind. Immediately after birth, with the first shock, he started to cry. After a little while he was given a drop of honey to lick. With this, he felt relieved thinking that all was well, and that he had someone's support. Thus, he pacified himself. However, that first shock of fear was so ingrained in his mind that he became startled at the slightest sound, and then again becomes quiet when given honey or his mother's breast. In this way, taking external support at every step, this human being became dependent on the support of his parents. As he grew older, his parents as well as those who looked after him as a child started giving him knowledge about the world. After that, his school teachers taught him the various physical sciences such as geography, geometry, geology, etc., which are valueless like dust.

As one enters the stage of youth, he again looks for additional props for his life. As it is determined in the world that support for life comes from money, wife, etc., he gathers wealth and takes on a wife. He takes it for granted that he can be sustained on this worldly support alone, and he squanders away his life. With fame, learning, power and authority, wealth, and wife, he gets added prosperity, and becomes entangled more and more. His principle possessions and his entire support, are his wife, wealth, status, youth, beauty, and authority. Taking special pride in all of this, and becoming intoxicated with worldliness, the human being misses knowing his "Real Nature." The pride about money, pride about authority, and pride about beauty absorb the man and he forgets his Real Nature. Eventually, the above possessions start dwindling one by one. When these possessions start to drop off according to the law of nature, the memory of the original shock that he received earlier shakes him to his very roots, and he becomes frustrated. Panicking, he inquires "What shall I do now? I am losing support from all sides. What will happen to me?" However, this ignorant man does not understand that all these possessions had only one solid support, which was his own Existence, or sense of "I Am." It is by that support alone, that money had its value, that his wife appeared charming, that honor received seemed worthwhile, his learning gave him wisdom, his form acquired beauty, and his authority wielded power. Oh, poor man, you yourself are the support of all the above described wealth! Can there be a greater paradox than to feel that wealth gave you support? In addition to this wealth, power, woman, youth, beauty of form, and honor, if one further receives ill-gotten fortune, how strange and perverted would one's actions become?

A poet once wrote (describing the pranks of the human mind), "It is primarily a monkey, in addition to that he gets drunk, and to top that, a scorpion bites him." Even such a poet would put his pen down seeing the ludicrous absurdities of this human being, and would bid goodbye to his poetic talents. The sort of man who considers his body as God, and is absorbed in its worship day and night should be considered to be like a shoemaker. There is an appropriate proverb that says that a chambhar's God should be worshipped only with shoes (in Marathi, the word chambhar means "the one who carries a hide on his back"). This tells us the way in which this "God" (the body) of such a man has to be adored. The devotion of an atheist is the feeding of his body, and his liberation is the death of the body. For such a man whose ultimate goal in life is feeding his body, and his liberation is death, there is no rising above the

"Gross Body" level. This is not surprising in his case. If due to some misfortune, he were to lose all his wealth, he would still borrow money to indulge in his habits of eating, drinking, and enjoying. If creditors were to hound him, he would declare insolvency to be rid of the whole issue. When death strikes him, ultimately he just lies dead. He passes away just as he had come. Could there be anything more tragic or wretched than this sort of life?

Why should the woman who showers praise on her husband for getting her a lovely nose ring think of the Lord who has provided her with a nose to put the nose ring on? In the same way, how can the animalistic human beings who only look to the body as the "be-all" and "end-all" of life, see God? The One whose power gives the Sun its existence as the Sun, the Moon its existence as the Moon, the Gods their existence as Gods, is the One Almighty God. It is He, who is the support of all, who is present in the hearts of all beings, and has become invisible to man. The one whose eyes are trained on external objects sees only that which is external. The word "Aksha" is a synonym for "eye" in Marathi. "A" is the very first letter of the alphabet, and "ksha" is one of the last consonants. It means that whatever the eye sees will lie within the range of these two letters of the alphabet. It will only bring information or knowledge of external objects. Gross objects will be visualized by the gross eye, and the subtle will be sensed by the senses, which are subtle. However, one letter of the alphabet that comes after 'ksha' in Marathi is "gnya." The letter "'gnya" indicates Knowledge that cannot be seen either by the gross external eye, or the subtle eye of the intellect. Therefore, the intellect and the senses together indicate the "eye" with the synonym "aksha." Like the eye, the other sense organs, the ear, nose, and tongue, are all pointing outwards, and continue to exist on the strength of external objects.

The "King of Knowledge" ("I Am") influences all of the senses, and seems to grant these senses the "lordship" over the sense objects. It is because of this externalization that the fact that He is present prior to the senses does not attract anyone's attention. Over many births, the mind and intellect have acquired the habit of only looking outwards. Therefore, to "turn within" has become a very difficult task. This is called "the reverse path" which the Saints follow when they turn in the opposite direction, and behold the mind completely giving up seeing all that is external. Where an ordinary man is asleep, the Saints are awake, and where an ordinary man is awake, the Saints dose off. All beings find themselves awakened to external objects, and have become extremely skillful in this type of awakening. The Saints however, have closed their eyes to external things, and it is the Self, to which other beings are asleep, that keeps the Saints wide awake.

One who gets a million rupees is worried about how to double it the next day. He pushes himself to acquire more and more. However, the Saints warn him, "Turn back, turn back, you may be caught in the whirlpool of Illusion (Maya). This Maya has come in like a full tide, and you might be carried away." The modern technological advances that come to this world with newer and newer innovations, as well as those yet to come, make up a cyclone of "Great Illusion" (Mahamaya). Be certain that you will be held captive by it. Who knows to where the one who is caught by this great cyclone will be carried off? When the Saints see one whose attention is taken up by these modern advances running here and there, struggling in his pursuits, they try their utmost to bring about an awakening of Self-Knowledge in him.

There is a story about when Saint Ramdas and Saint Tukaram met each other while standing on the opposite banks of a river. With a gesture of his hand, Samartha Ramdas asked Saint Tukaram "How much awakening have you brought about among the people?" Saint Tukaram replied with a gesture forming his right hand in a fist and putting the back of it to his lips to indicate that nowhere had he found anybody who cared for awakening to the Self. Then Tukaram Maharaj put the same question back to Samartha Ramdas, who then indicated that there was no one awakening whatsoever. They then continued on their way. Saint Tukaram has said, "How can I describe the obligations of the Saints? They are continuously awakening me." Even though it is true that Saint Tukaram and Samartha Ramdas are no longer with us in bodily form, they have given us all that they wanted to teach in the books **Abhangagatha** and **Dasbodh**. The great wealth that they have handed over to us is the priceless legacy of these books. Whoever makes a claim that he is heir to their legacy will enjoy this priceless inheritance. However, the one who wants this wealth must give up the pride of mundane demonical wealth. In addition, whatever acts that one considers as meritorious, and dear to one's heart, must also be renounced. One must be prepared to take a step on the path that turns inward. These are the conditions for becoming a beneficiary of this legacy.

Man is fully immersed in the pride of his body, his caste, his family, his region, his country, and whatever good or bad is in his nature. All of these various types of pride have possessed him. Until he becomes completely free from these various types of pride, how can he claim to benefit from the legacy of this treasure that the Saints have left behind? Only the one whose heart sincerely relinquishes pride can become the beneficiary of this wealth. There is hope for the man who becomes aware of these various types of pride that he has acquired from birth after birth, which have become his second nature, if he sincerely relinquishes this pride. He need not be frustrated. If a slave is awakened to the knowledge that he is a slave, he instantly starts looking for a way to freedom. A slave who finds joy in his slavery, and makes every effort to continue in that condition, cannot even conceive that a highway to freedom exists, until such time that the knowledge of his slavery dawns on him. Similarly, a lucky man who feels that the ambition of getting ahead of others is actually taking him on a downward path, will get from that day onward a glimpse of the reverse direction shown by the Saints. Slowly, he automatically starts making the effort to step onto a new path.

The various types of pride may not leave one all at once. If the aspirant starts to become completely determined to be aware of the pride that he harbors, and begins to leave them one by one, the infinitely merciful Lord will not fail to give him a helping hand. If one takes pride in vicious or evil acts, this should be counteracted by increasing pride in good acts, thus eradicating all of his bad qualities. The good qualities should be nourished and developed. However, one should not be attached to them, and should slowly begin to abandon the pride arising from good actions. A doubt may arise here that although vices deserve to be left, "Why is it that you tell us to leave good qualities also? After all good qualities are always good." Dear aspirants, although the possession of good qualities in comparison with vices and bad qualities seems to be better with regard to the pursuit of attaining Self Knowledge, the possession of the good qualities which one holds dear to one's heart is really a hundred times worse, and truly needs to be thrown out. Look into this and see. An aspirant tries to leave his bad qualities on the advice of the Saints because of the sense of shame that is created by society or in one's mind, however, the one who possesses good qualities is always getting praise in the world, and is accordingly full of pride about these good qualities. It is very difficult for one to let go of the pride about good qualities.

The pride regarding negative qualities can be left fairly easily, but it is not so in the case of pride regarding good qualities. Nobody wants to admit that he has committed any error, but the pride that one harbors when he has given meals to thousands who have visited the four holy places, or opened lodging for holy people, or worshipped the deity millions of times, becomes so firm in him that it becomes almost impossible to give up. It is when one recognizes one's worldly ways and is ready to relinquish them that he soon finds a Sadguru. However, the one who is sought after by everyone for performing many good deeds, gets so deeply buried in the flattery that is showered upon him, that his way to the Sadguru becomes lost due to his pride. Realizing this, one must conclude that pride about bad qualities is tolerable, but the pride about good qualities is best to be avoided completely. Both the pride about one's good qualities and pride about one's bad qualities are thorns on the path to Self-Knowledge. When one thorn is pulled out with the help of another thorn, there still remains the second thorn (pride of good actions) that one carries around in the shirt pocket. Will this thorn not also prick the chest or rib? If a thief is shackled by iron handcuffs and a king by golden handcuffs, does that mean that the king is not bound?

Take it for granted that while the man in the iron cuffs will thank someone who frees him from them, the man with the golden cuffs will pounce on the throat of anyone who tries to free him. He will try his best to permanently keep the golden cuff on his hands. What is the force behind this? Who is this "friendly enemy" in this example who makes one feel so happy in his bondage? It is the pride one has in good deeds that is the real archenemy of the aspirant. This pride is the enemy who blocks the way to "Ultimate Truth" (Paramartha). Therefore, it is necessary to renounce any pride that one has about good deeds. This may require tremendous effort, but without renouncing all pride, the aspirant can never claim his legacy to the wealth of "Knowledge." It is believed by many that a man's worldly wealth such as money, a beautiful wife, status, etc. is the result of meritorious deeds done in previous births, but these very beliefs act as boulders obstructing the way to finding the "Ultimate Truth." Therefore, it may be said that these things are really the result of body identification (the definition of sin). When a person is infused with pride, he becomes possessed, and therefore becomes incapable of treading the path of Ultimate Truth.

Contrary to the wealthy man, there might be a man who does not have a penny, who is quite ugly, has no wife, no status, and is so poverty stricken that in order to fill his belly, he is willing to eat whatever food he could get from anyone. He may have lost his caste, family, friends, and all who were dear to him. This homeless wanderer may be naked on all fronts, and even believed to be wretched by the whole society, yet he truly may be more worthy of gaining Self-Knowledge, because he is naturally free of pride. The ears of someone like this poor naked man turn towards the Sadguru sooner than one whose ears are filled with flattery. The one who is puffed up with pride has no room for receiving the advice of the Sadguru. Such a person has no time to turn to the Sadguru's advice even for a minute.

The whole of humanity has become entangled in Illusion from birth, and lives in bondage. In addition to this, man creates many types of artificial bondage around him in the form of comforts and attachments resulting from ever newer inventions. If man has to live in modern society, he has to abide by and respect the norms of traditional social conventions, and governmental rules. For example, wearing a necktie in order for one to do one's daily work is supposed to be the proper social etiquette. In these types of ways, to be up to date in society makes one feel that he is getting more and more freedom. In modern society, if one does not indulge in drinking or drugs, or does not shave everyday, he is considered a social outcast. By diving into the bondage of such a society and holding such silly ideas dear to the heart, one only continues binding oneself, only further increasing the pride that one has about worthless things. Unless these types of social bondage and pride are completely thrown off, and unless one is considered to be a madman by the "socially wise" people, there is no hope that one will arrive at such a mental state that allows one to be free from pride, and such social bondage. The Sadguru's only aim is to help one to become completely free of all pride, and to eradicate the identification with the body. If the aspirant finds the renunciation of all pride and social bonds difficult to do, or is unwilling to formally renounce his wife, money, or estate, he can begin with inward renunciation. When this becomes successful, the formal renunciation slowly becomes possible.

Inward renunciation means renunciation that is undertaken with the mind. For example, there may be someone who has the habit of hurting others with harsh words. It does not cost the aspirant anything to replace that habit by saying only kind words to others. As another example, there may be some people who have the habit of telling lies unnecessarily, in their case, they should begin renunciation by stopping the telling of lies, at least until such time that an occasion arises where unless they tell a lie, some great calamity may occur. This type of mental renunciation will also not require any expenditure. While looking at a neighbor's prosperity, one should not be envious of his neighbor. Will making such a decision bring the aspirant any harm? In this way, when one begins to renounce negative qualities, he also begins to gain strength in renouncing external things. This world is like a dream, and in this dream-like world whatever is considered to be good or bad, merit or sin, or anything in the realm of dualistic morality is of no consequence in the process of awakening to the Self. Therefore, renunciation of both sides of duality such as good and bad, or auspicious and inauspicious, is necessary to gain Self-Knowledge. Even though this may be understood, it is still difficult to eradicate pride. No matter how often someone may repeat to himself to "renounce, renounce," it will not make even the slightest dent on pride. However, if the reason why this pride enters one is discovered, it can be eradicated, and renunciation automatically follows. The aspirant must come to understand that the reason why one harbors pride for objects is because he believes the objects to be true.

If one understands that objects are only a temporary appearance, and becomes convinced that objects cannot really provide true happiness, then the apparent reality of the objects automatically fades away. It then becomes possible for one to develop detachment for those objects that were previously held dear to one as true. A wooden toy in the shape of a tamarind pod is not a real tamarind pod. It is made of wood. However, unless one has the discriminative ability to be able to tell the difference, the sight of the wooden tamarind is sure to make one's mouth start watering. The reason for this is the conviction that the thing is real. Once one becomes aware that the tamarind is made of wood, he may appreciate the artistic or aesthetic lines of the toy, but it will not affect his salivary glands. This discriminative knowledge, or the recognition that it is not real, results in true detachment towards the object. This example shows us that the detachment towards objects is brought about by understanding their true nature. Unless the futility of acquiring objects in this world is impressed irrevocably upon the mind, Self-Knowledge is difficult to attain. Unless one understands the false nature of objects, one will never aspire for the "Real Thing." There can be no renunciation of the false as long as the intellect believes it to be true. The day that the wrong knowledge regarding the world is eliminated by virtue of the Sadguru's advice, one becomes convinced that this entire world is only a temporary appearance. When this happens, one becomes able to look at the world and appreciate it as if it were a cinema, or a source of entertainment, and with the detachment that has been achieved, one remains unaffected.

Detachment without Self-Knowledge is like what is experienced when one is watching the activities going on at the cremation grounds. Without Self-Knowledge, there can be no real renunciation, and without renunciation, there can be no Self-Knowledge. This is the paradox. The Saints have given us various methods of getting out of this situation through such means as devotion to the Guru and God, singing the praises of the Guru and God (Bhajans), visiting holy places, giving in charity, etc. In this way, the Saints have given an infinite number of means of salvation to humanity. Human nature is such that if a man is forcibly robbed of a thing, he suffers immensely. He will make persistent efforts to regain that thing. Yet, if he were to part with the same thing out of his own free will, that sacrifice would bring him immense joy. A man who is normally unwilling to spend a dime under compulsion, would out of his own free choice spend thousands in order to feed the people at a religious gathering. However, there are countless examples of how after mixing with Saints, and chanting bhajans, even very proud people have changed. One whose pride previously would not have allowed him to submit to another person's will is now willing to bow in submission to someone even of a much lower standing in society. By his keeping the company of Saints, he naturally and easily completely forgets his pride of caste or social status. That important man who was filled with pride, and felt ashamed to even apply sandalwood paste to his forehead in his own house, now allows Bhuki (a black powder) to be smeared on his face, indicating a total lack of pride. The same person who previously considered singing and dancing obscene, forgets himself and his body, and starts dancing in ecstatic joy with a partner, while chanting the name of God. Understanding how aspirants sacrifice pride in this way, the Saints have given mankind the teachings prescribing Bhajans and Worship (Puja) for daily practice. With this teaching, they have pointed out a progressive step on the path of Self-Knowledge. In this way, they impress upon the aspirant how easy it is to renounce the objects of the world, and how to clear one's mental attitude from pride.

Self-Knowledge is the Knowledge about one's Self. Once we recognize who we really are, then automatically the determination is made regarding what is permanent and what is transient. Then, very naturally the renunciation of the impermanent, and the acceptance of the permanent follows. Because of the transient nature of things, the fear of dissolution is inevitable. The one who is overpowered by this fear of dissolution, or death, continuously strives to see that some particular thing is not taken from him. He takes every precaution to preserve his money, tries hard to see that his wife's youth and beauty does not deteriorate, and struggles to keep his status and authority. However, try as he may, nothing ever happens according to his wishes or desires. No one can escape their destiny, and because death is all-consuming, everything will eventually get crushed in its jaws. Even Gods like Brahma are not free from the fear of death.

Even if such a fear-ridden man were given everything he desired, could he avoid being afraid? If he needs anything at all, it is the gift of fearlessness. The aspirant must find that which will free him from fear permanently. This beggar called man, who has lost his own treasure of the Self, continuously chants "I am the body, I am the body." He is forever discontent saying "I want this, I want that," and wanders around always begging for something in the world. He can only truly be pacified with the gift of the Self. The man who chants "What will happen to me, my wife and children, and the money that I consider to be mine?" is always disturbed and upset. This sort of man needs to be given the gift of fearlessness, and thus be made fearless. Only the Sadguru is generous enough, and capable of bestowing the gift of fearlessness, which is the noblest of all the gifts. Kings and emperors, and even gods are incapable of granting this gift of fearlessness. Although all earthly wealth is at the feet of an emperor, he is restless with fear at the very thought of an enemy attack. Even Lord Indra is anxious day and night with the thought that his status as "King of the Gods" might be shaken by the austerities and practices performed by some sage. Think deeply on this. Can those who have not freed themselves of fear give the gift of fearlessness to others? Only those Great Saints, the "Mahatmas," who have uprooted fear from its very depths by establishing themselves in the Self and destroying the identification with the body are capable of granting the gift of fearlessness. Except for these Mahatmas, the hosts of gods, demons and men are like penniless beggars. They can never get the gift of fearlessness unless they take shelter with a Sadguru. If they are gods, they entertain the pride of godly wealth, if they are demons, they carry the pride of their own vicious wealth on their heads, and human beings are crushed under their own burdens. Gods are no better than servants who carry other people's burdens on their heads. What is the lowly status then of the human beggar? It is only the Sadguru who extends his hand to lift their burden, and blesses them at the same time with the gift of fearlessness.

Out of all the various types of knowledge, Self-Knowledge is the greatest, and of all the paths, or dharmas (dharma is one's religion, or one's nature), Swadharma is the most noble. The Mahatmas spread the "Knowledge of the Self" among mankind and teach them the meaning of Swadharma. In this world, the knowledge of astrology, black magic, public relations, the fourteen types of sciences, and the sixty-four arts are taught. However, all that knowledge except for "Knowledge of the Self" is false knowledge. Saints refuse to recognize these other types of knowledge, and spread only the "Knowledge of the Self." Many missionaries who are competing with one another assert their opinions and start giving advice saying, "My religion is the noblest, and all others will only lead one to ruin." Not only do they just give advice, but also they fulfill their sacred duty of conversion, sometimes through bribes, or threats of burning people's houses, or sometimes even by killing people. Without much change from days of old, this kind of propagation of religion is going on even today. This piracy of religion full of compulsion and tyranny is not useful for accomplishing the well-being of anyone.

Saint Ramdas said, "If there is any one religion in the world that is noblest of all, it is Swadharma." Swadharma means to live in one's "True Nature." To live in one's innate nature is Swadharma even though one may belong to any caste, religion, or nation. To understand Swadharma, one should realize that it is existent in all forms of life, be it an ant, or an insect. One's "True Nature" alone is Swadharma and all other paths or cults parading as religions are "paradharma," meaning that they are religions pertaining to something that is other than the Self. These various cults and religions put down certain rules and methods which are alien to our real nature. This is how we can define Swadharma and paradharma. If we take for granted the currently accepted meaning of Swadharma, it can be considered absurdity. Suppose there is a prostitute. She also has a relevant dharma, her nature, which she follows diligently believing that it is her swadharma, or her true nature, her true religion. She teaches the same to her daughter from the time she is in the cradle, and in the end she dies following her own religion. Who can say, perhaps some "Streetwhore Swami" (a lover of women) may even come forward to include that woman's life story in some book about religious saints.

The Lord has cautioned us in the **Bhagavad Gita**, "It is best to die in Swadharma (the death of body identification, which brings one into the Self). Dharma that is alien, is full of danger. While trying to achieve this, if death comes, it is to be preferred over following some other dharma which is alien to the Self." The aspirant should recognize the importance of the caution that is being imparted in the Lord's words. Eradicating the idea of identification with the body is the sign of the "Knowledge of the Self." Mahatmas experience this type of death while living. This type of death is to be preferred over the death that occurs when following someone else's religion. Saint Tukaram said, "I have seen my own death, how shall I describe that process which is unique?" How can those who live in a religion that is not of the Self, and who die a corpse's death, understand this process of death while living? The unfortunate one only thinks of death in terms of various customs and rites according to one's religion. Those dharmas built on the strong basis of body identification contain the dualities of temptation and fear, heaven and hell, merit and sin, and bondage and liberation. Every human being has the right of following Swadharma, one's own nature where there is no temptation of heavenly enjoyments and no fear of pain in purgatory, and where bondage and liberation have no meaning. There is a cruel but true maxim that states, "Whatever comes has to go." All of the recent "pseudo-religions" are spreading because of their newness, and in some cases even with government patronization. They will definitely sink to the bottom, and there will be nothing but glory and victory to Swadharma alone. (Note - During Shri Siddharameshwar Maharaj's time, the Government in India was in many cases helping to fund religious schools and even missionaries. In this paragraph all religions that are not of the Self are being called "pseudo-religions," not being of our "True Nature," or "Swadharma," and ultimately they will not last)

Lord Krishna advised Arjuna on this. He said, "Leave aside all religions and come seek refuge in Me. Come to Me, and leave off all of those religions which create hindrances on the path to reaching Me. Seek refuge in Paramatman who is of the nature of Self-Knowledge. You will have realized your Self when you attain Me, and there will be nothing more for you to do. All karma (actions) gets exhausted in Self-Knowledge." On the pretext of advising Arjuna, Lord Krishna has given this advice to all human beings that they should fulfill themselves by accepting this advice that he has given. There is nothing in the whole world as sacred as Self-Knowledge. All other work or action is meaningless. In this context one should not think that all other types of knowledge or actions except Self-Knowledge are useless, meaning that they are of no value, or without any result. However, they are of no help in achieving Swadharma. It is not that getting results such as a son, or heaven by means of performing sacrifices. By studying scriptures one becomes proficient, and it is possible for one to appease various deities by worshipping them. Even if this is so, and even if all these actions are supposed to be meritorious in this mundane world, they are still hindrances as long as the Self is not pleased, and does not shower His Grace. The qualities valued as best in the practical world only count as disqualification, and all remedies only turn into obstacles in pursuit of Self-Knowledge. The sages know this well and do not even care in the slightest if they are able to conquer all of the three worlds. They consider Lord Indra's status, that is ridden with jealousies, to be as useless as the droppings of a crow. The Saints harbor only one desire in their hearts, and that is the desire of achieving "Oneness with Brahman." With regard to everything else, they are desireless. Those Saints who are represented by statues of auspiciousness became one with Brahman when their Consciousness became dis-identified from their body. In ordinary cases, the body is viewed only as a corpse, while in the case of those Mahatmas, they became worthy of worship, and they receive adoration from people. Not only this, but also many temples were built around their shrines. Thus, they became immortal by becoming the object of worship and adoration by the whole world.

Rama, Krishna, Siddhartha, Hanuman, Malhari, Jagadamba, were all Mahatmas in the form of Gurus. While they were alive, they did the work of spreading Knowledge and they became gods when they left the body. All the temples on earth belong to these very gods who grant the wishes of devotees according to their vows and desires. They lift the aspirant to their own level and bring them to the achievement of Self-fulfillment. Many people think that the God that one worships meets him (when he sees a vision) and gets his work done, but God is not limited to one point or place as the devotee imagines. He resides in the devotee's heart as well as in every heart, and it is He who inspires one to get one's work done. Nobody should ever entertain the wrong idea that after the Mahatma leaves his body, he assumes the same body again and comes out of his Samadhi (comes back from the dead) and then gets his devotee's work done.

When you wish that a certain person should get ten rupees at Pune (a city in Maharashtra State in India), you give a ten rupee note in cash to the main Post Office at Sholapur. On the second or third day, you get the receipt indicating that the intended person has received the amount that you have sent. Have you ever made inquiries to the effect that the same note, or the same coins that you handed over to the Post Office have reached the intended person? No, this type of question never even arises in your mind. Your attention is centered not on that exact note, but on the value of the note. When the amount sent has reached the person, you do not have any complaints. In the same way, these past Saints and Mahatmas who have turned into gods get the devotees work accomplished through the Mahatmas that are living today, and who are of the same caliber. This is the way their devotees' wishes are fulfilled.

What magical skill did these persons possess who were honored in their lifetime and became immortal, thereby retaining their fame even after their bodily death? What special learning did they have that they should be adored by people even after death? In this world, there are many arts and sciences. Many discoverers and many adventurous heroes are praised during their lifetime. These heroes are congratulated and covered with garlands of flowers, and bouquets. The people even express their admiration for the heroes by carrying them on their shoulders. However, in due time, a hero who had been an object of people's adoration soon becomes a subject of their abuses. Soon people who were pampered as heroes for a few days, are condemned in an assembly. Sometimes, even resolutions condemning them are carried out. It is clear that the greatness of these heroes is artificial and not everlasting because their "greatness" is based on transient learning or adventures. Their greatness is not based on the sacred learning that gives everlasting peace like the "Knowledge of the Self." It is based on some science such as politics with some practical motive. In politics names and faces continue changing with time, and in the physical sciences new discoveries follow one after another. A person who was once proclaimed as great is found to be of no importance and in some other corner of the world some other person starts shining on the horizon. The greatness that is achieved through any learning other than Self-Knowledge eventually takes an opposite direction. Because of this, these "great ones" have to suffer the sweet and sour experiences associated with honor and insult. It is no wonder that no one goes to the trouble of thinking about these "great men" after they are dead.

Out of all the types of Knowledge (Vidya), Self-Knowledge (Atma Vidya) is the only Knowledge that grants everlasting peace. One Saint asked, "What is the use of any knowledge that does not grant peace of mind?" There are many types of courses of learning that are available in the world. Why is there such a proliferation of courses? The reason is that no one has found peace of mind. The struggles in the world have not stopped even a little because the restlessness of the mind has not ceased. Why is this? It is because all of these sciences and arts are centered in Ignorance, and they are useful only for increasing the agitation and restlessness of the human mind. There is no relationship of cause and effect relating learning to peace. The one who evaluates various kinds of gems, and one who examines various sciences and arts, or aesthetics, has lost the happiness that comes from peace of mind because they have no ability to examine themselves.

Why should one search another man's house when he has not searched his own house for something that he lost while he was at home? The man who boldly asserts "This man is like this, and the other man is 'Mr. A' or 'Mr. B,'" while he does not know who he is himself, is never free from restlessness. It would be futile to discover what thing could be extracted from where, or to know many addresses, if one does not know one's own address.

Chapter 2: Investigation of the Four Bodies in Search of "I"

Who is this "I"? Once upon a time, there lived a man named "Gomaji Ganesh" who lived in a town called Andheri. At one point in time, this man established a custom in the Courts of Law that no order or document could be accepted as legal unless it bore a stamp with his name on it, along with the words "The Brass Door." From that point on, all of the officials of that town only accepted a document as being legal if it bore the stamp of "**Gomaji Ganesh, The Brass Door.**" This procedure for making documents legal continued for a long time until eventually the stamp officially became part of the legal system of the city of Andheri, and no one ever enquired as to just whom this "Gomaji Ganesh" was. As time passed, it happened that one day an important document that did not bear the official stamp of "Gomaji Ganesh, The Brass Door" was cited as evidence in a case filed in the Court of Law. Except for the fact that this document did not have the official stamp, it was otherwise completely legal according to all other points of law and ordinary procedure. At one point in the case, an objection was raised that the document should not be accepted as evidence because it did not bear the official stamp of "Gomaji Ganesh, The Brass Door."

At that point, a courageous man who was a party to the lawsuit argued before the judge that the document was perfectly valid because it bore all of the relevant signatures of the current government officials. He argued "Why should the document not be admissible if it is otherwise perfectly legal except that it does not bear the stamp of Mr. Gomaji Ganesh? Thus, he questioned the legality of the stamp itself. Consequently, the legality of the stamp was made an issue of contention. Until that day, no one had ventured to bring this issue before a Court of Law. Since it had now arisen for the first time, it was decided that a decision should be made regarding the legality of this stamp. Out of curiosity about how the procedure of the stamp of "The Brass Door" came to be put in place, the judge himself took the matter in hand for inquiry. When his inquiry was completed, he discovered that many years in the past, a man of no particular status, a Mr. Gomaji Ganesh, had taken advantage of the badly administered government of his day, and put his own name on a stamp that was to be used for all official documents. From that time onward, all government officials simply continued following the tradition blindly. In fact, the judge discovered that Mr. Gomaji Ganesh was a man of no importance whatsoever, who had no authority of any kind. When the judge made this discovery, a decision was made by the Court that the stamp was no longer necessary for legal documents. Since that day, the stamp was looked upon with ridicule. In the same way, we should inquire about the sense of "I," and how it dominates everything with the stamp of "I," and "mine," just like the stamp of Mr. Gomaji Ganesh described in the above story. It is a general rule or principle in nature that if two things are combined, some new third thing is produced.

For example by the contact of a piece of thread with flowers, a garland is produced that did not previously exist. Even the names of the parent objects whose contact was responsible for producing the garland disappear as soon as the garland comes into existence. The garland then comes to be known by its own label. The labels of "flowers" and "thread" become extinct, and the new name of "garland" is used, and with that new name, further action takes place. With the contact of earth and water, mud arises as the labels "earth" and "water" become extinct. In much the same way, stones, bricks, mud, and mason come together, and a third thing called a "wall" stands before our eyes, while the stones, bricks, mud, and the mason simply vanish from our sight. It is by the coming together of Knowledge and Ignorance that a peculiar thing called the "intellect" comes into existence, and it is through this "intellect" that the contact with the world emerges. Gold and goldsmith come together and produce a third thing that appears before our eyes as an ornament. The ornament is seen, and the gold and the goldsmith are forgotten. As a matter of fact, if anyone was to try to find out if there is any such thing as an "ornament" inside the gold, one would see nothing but gold. If we tell someone to bring an ornament without touching the gold, what could he bring? The thing we call an ornament would simply vanish. In the same way, out of the union of Brahman and Maya (Illusion), the thief called "I" has come along proudly saying "I," and raising its head proclaiming sovereignty over both Brahman and Maya. This "I," or ego, is a barren woman's (Maya's) son who tries to establish unlimited sovereignty over the entire universe. If we observe the parents of this "I," it is clear that it is impossible for them to give birth to such a child. The mother of the child is Maya, who does not exist. From the womb of this Maya, the "I" has come forth. It is supposed to have been produced by the "Life-

Energy." Yet, this Life-Energy (Brahman) has no gender, and does not even claim to possess "doership," so the readers can imagine what kind of an "I" this is.

As described above, the existence of "I" is only in name. Yet, like Mr. Gomaji Ganesh, he announces his name everywhere as "I." He goes around saying "I am wise, I am great, I am small," all the while having forgotten from where he came. Instead, he starts glorifying himself as "I," like the cat who laps up milk with its eyes closed, not aware of the stick that is ready to strike him from the rear. As soon as he accepts a right, or a privilege, he must also accept the responsibility that goes along with it. As soon as one says, "I am the doer of a certain act," that "I" must enjoy the fruits of such action. Enjoyment and suffering of the fruits or the results of action are tied to the action itself, and to the identification as the doer. Actually, no such thing as an "I" exists. The entire doership that is the motivating force behind the "I" is contained solely in Brahman. However, Brahman is so brilliant, the moment that he finds someone who takes pride in "doership," he leaves all responsibility for the actions on the head of that "I" and remains unattached. Consequently, the poor "I" is destined to revolve on the wheel of birth and death. In the example of the garland mentioned above, the name "garland" came forward after the names "flowers" and "thread" were forgotten. When the garland dries up, nobody says that the flowers have dried up, they say the garland has dried up, or if the thread snaps, they say the garland has snapped. This indicates that the "doership" of the original object is imposed upon the third object due to the pride, or identification with the object. In the same way, a series of miseries strike the non-existent "I." If one wants to get free from this misery, he must leave the "I." However, before it is left off, one has to find out exactly where this "I" resides. It is only when we find the "I," that we can talk about leaving it off. The aspirant should begin the search for this "I" at his or her own center. It will never be found outside of us. In every human being this sense of "I" or ego, and "mine," the feeling of possession, is filling one up to the brim. All the actions in the world are carried out by the force of this ego, and the sense of "mine." The assumption of "I" is taken for granted by all human beings. However, all actions can be carried out without this ego, or the sense of "mine." How this can be done shall be seen later. Presently we will discuss only this sense of "I" and "mine."In order to trace this "I" let us first examine our own Physical Gross Body that seems so close to us. After analyzing it, let us see if this "I" can be found anywhere in this body.

The First Body - The Physical Gross Body

What is a body? It is a collective assembly of parts (limbs and organs) such as hands, feet, mouth, nose, ears, eyes, etc. The assembly of all these parts is called the "body." Out of these various parts, let us find out which one is "I." We can say that the hand is "I," but if the hand is cut off, nobody says "I have been cut off," or "I have been discarded." Suppose the eyes go blind. No one says, "I am gone," or if the stomach is bloated, no one says, "I am inflated." No, instead one says "my hand is cut off," or "my eyes have gone blind," or "my stomach is expanded." All of these parts are spoken of as "mine." Not only that, but the body itself that is an assembly of all these parts, is also spoken of as "my body." By looking in this way, it can easily be seen that the one who asserts ownership of all the limbs, and even of the body itself, is really someone who is quite different from the body that he calls his own.

We have stated above that the "I" is not any part, or any of the limbs of the Gross Body, and that all the limbs are considered as "mine." There is an established general truth, or maxim, that says, "Where the 'I' does not exist, there cannot exist anything that can be called as 'mine'." From this maxim, it follows that the body and limbs actually do not belong to "me," as there is not any "I" residing there. The same maxim applies if "I" do not reside in the neighbor's house, can the neighbor's house, or its contents or associated parts belong to me? If one wants to verify the truth of the maxim "Where there is no I, there can be nothing of mine," one only has to go to a neighbor's house and say "I am master here, and the wife of this household is also mine." If you try to show your sense of "mine" to the wife in that house, and start making advances towards her, you will quickly see what kind of an experience you will get. The true master of the house would hit you so hard that you would quickly realize "I am not the master here, and she is not mine." In the same way, when the "I" cannot be traced anywhere in the body then how can it be said that the limbs of the body and its tendencies belong to "me". If you still insist upon calling it your own, find out why, and also look closely at the condition of all human beings who look upon their bodies as their own and act accordingly.

The human being forgets his True Self, and does not understand who he really is. Therefore, he has to take many births in numerous species. Sometimes he becomes a worm and passes out in a stool. Sometimes he becomes a bullock and gets yoked, turning around and around in a mill. Sometimes he becomes a donkey and works hard wallowing in a heap of garbage. How many such miseries one has to suffer is almost impossible to describe. After suffering births in all the other species, finally one gets the good fortune to be born as a human being. This birth in the human body is unique as it has the capacity for higher intellect and discrimination so that we can know God, the "Supreme Self." If we look at the body of the human species, it can be compared to a dressed-up character in a vulgar play during the period of the *Shimga* festival. This character can be described thus: The character's face is smeared with black paint, the body is dressed up in rags with a garland of shoes around his neck, and an umbrella made of shoes is held over his head. Then, this character is seated on a donkey and taken in a procession through the streets accompanied by various strange noises. Ironically, this character takes pride in being the center of such a demeaning show, and salutes people on the street. In the same way, one's body is also a peculiar part of this passing show. All the beauty of the face is supposed to be concentrated in the nose and eyes. We say that a man is handsome or a woman is beautiful if they have a good nose and good eyes. However, what is the nose except a tube for nasal discharge?

The mouth is like a spittoon full of saliva and phlegm. The stomach resembles a sewage plant of some city. The body is given some respectable name, but it is only an accumulation of bones, flesh, and blood. It is the intention of the Supreme Self, to awaken the human being by demeaning him and making him miserable with the body. He then makes the human being cry aloud for happiness, and wander about in all directions in search of it. In spite of this, the human being considers the body to be a great gift, and with joy he describes it with flowery language. The nose, which is a tube of mucus, is compared to the bud of some beautiful flower. The eyes, which are the places of abundant discharge are called lotus eyes. The face, with a mouth like a spittoon full of saliva, is called a moon face, and the arms and legs which are like crooked branches of a tree, are referred to as lotus hands and lotus feet! The human being looks upon this type of behavior as normal, and exhibits his foolishness shamelessly.

However, the Great Lord grants a wonderful thing called the "higher intellect" even to this "Shimga" character of a human being that He has not given to any other species. The purpose of that gift of higher intellect is for the human being to be able to realize the "Divine Nature of the Self" and put an end to this demeaning show. However, the human being misuses this great gift of the intellect. He looks upon a gutter as the Ganges, and the body as God, and only spoils it further. The human being spends a lot of his time adorning the Physical Body. Taking this body as "I," he then comes into contact with a female body and begins calling that person as his own. He then begins to place the sense of "mine" or possession on that female body. By virtue of the contact of this "I," with that which is "mine," many children are born and a whole household is brought into existence. The household eventually gets shattered, and the poor man suffers ridicule. This story has been described in great detail in the book **Dasbodh** by Shri Samartha Ramdas. It is recommended that the knowledge in this book be studied and understood.

We have determined that the "I" cannot be traced anywhere in the body. It is also a fact that the body is not "mine." Then to whom does the body belong? Who is the "owner" of the body? The five elements (Earth, Water, Light or Fire, Air or Wind, and Space or Sky) have the right of ownership to this body. After the body falls, each of these elements takes away their own share, thereby destroying the body. The body is a bundle of these five elements. By analogy, it's like clothes that were tied up in a bundle and have now been taken away by their respective owners, and even the cloth in which the bundle was wrapped up has also been taken away. How then, can anything called a "bundle" remain? There is not even anything left that can be seen.

In the same way, once the body that is composed of the five elements is unbundled and dispersed back into those five respective elements, there remains no object such as the body. Examining in this way, we can see that "I" am not in the body, nor does the body belong to me. This type of body consisting of a bundle of the five elements cannot support any pride of "I" or an "ego." Nor can it sustain the relationships that existed due to the identification with the body, such as birth and death, or the six passions (greed, anger, desire, hatred, craving, and pride) that affect the body. These cannot be related to any "me," as being "mine." The body may be in a state of childhood, or youth, or old age, or the body may be dark, fair, beautiful, or ugly. It may be infested with disease, it may be wandering aimlessly, going to holy places for pilgrimages, or it may be motionless in samadhi. All of these attitudes, properties and modifications belong to the body, but the "I" is separate from all of these.

From the analysis of the Physical Body, we have learned that the "I" is separate from all of its qualities. Additionally we can easily see that someone else's beautiful cute bonnie baby is of no value to us, compared to our own dark stocky boy who has pockmarks and a flowing dirty nose. We do not suffer if someone else's sweet child dies as much as we suffer if our worn old shoe gets lost. The reason for this is that we do not have the same sense of "possession" or "mine" for the other person. Once one understands that some particular thing is not "mine," and that it belongs to someone else, he becomes indifferent about that thing. He even gradually starts disliking that thing which belongs to "someone else," or "another," and then it is easily renounced. Understand clearly that the body is not "mine," it belongs to the five elements, and that it is someone else's property. When you understand this, whatever kind of properties the body may possess, how does it affect you? So, let us leave the Physical Body, and let us proceed ahead. However, to leave the body does not mean that it should be pushed into a well, or be hung with a noose around the neck. We leave it by understanding it, and by gaining the factual knowledge about it. When the body is known for what it really is, the obsessive interest in it subsides, we can step beyond it, and it is automatically renounced. If the body is purposefully destroyed physically, then one definitely gets reborn again and again. Complete renunciation of the body is achieved only through discrimination of the Real from the unreal. By using discrimination while one has the human body, one naturally arrives at a state of renunciation, and instead the body becoming a reason for rebirth, it has the capacity to liberate one from the cycle of birth and death altogether.

There are five types of dissolution. Two are at the level of the body, two at the level of the universe, and one through discrimination. They are:
1) Daily dissolution, or the Dissolution of Deep Sleep
2) Dissolution through Death
3) Dissolution of the Creator and Creation (Brahma Pralaya)
4) Dissolution at the time of many Ages or Kalpas (Kalpa Pralaya)
5) Dissolution by Thought, or Discrimination

Out of these five types of dissolution, everyone is familiar with the two types of dissolution associated with the body, or daily dissolution, which are Deep Sleep and the dissolution of Death. In Deep Sleep, the whole world, including our body is dissolved. However, upon awakening, the body and the world are present just as they were before going to sleep, and all actions start again, just as they did before. The dissolution through Death is the same as the dissolution through Deep Sleep, however, after Death, in the absence of Self-Knowledge, the being has to take a new body in accordance with one's actions (karma) and mental disposition. In the new body, the actions such as eating, sleeping, mating, and fear happen according to the impressions remaining from previous lives.

Above the bodily level at the universal level there are two other cosmic types of dissolution. The first is the dissolution at the end of the life of the Creator and his Creation (Brahma Pralaya). The second is the dissolution that takes place at the end of an age or "Kalpa" after many such Creators and their Creations have come and gone (Kalpa Pralaya). With these two types of dissolution, a new "Creator," or a new "Kalpa" starts, and "Creation," which was latent for some time, rises with renewed vigor and activity, and starts all over again. In this way, the wheel continues to revolve, rising and setting at fixed periods. One can see from the descriptions given so far of these four types of dissolutions, that bodies cannot be dissolved finally in all of them. However, the result of the dissolution by discrimination, or thought, is very powerful and unique. In this type of dissolution, the body not only is dissolved while living but also after death, and when it gets finally dissolved it will not rise again.

Suppose there is a toy snake lying around that is made out of rubber. It is only until such time that one understands that it is only made of rubber, that the fear of the snake will completely disappear. Otherwise, by closing ones eyes, or putting the snake away in a basket, the fear subsides. However, in that case, as soon as the eyes open, or the basket is opened again, the fear returns. Suppose someone throws the rubber snake away and some mischievous person again throws it in front of the fearful one. He will again be shaken. In order to escape the snake, the man goes into Deep Sleep, however he will see the snake again as soon as he wakes up. Suppose he gets intoxicated with drink, or is made unconscious by chloroform in order to make the snake go away. Again, as soon as the effect of the drink or anesthesia wears off, the snake is there once again. This shows that the eradication of the fear of the snake by any of the means described is only temporary and not lasting. How is it then that he can be freed from the fear of the snake? The only remedy to be rid of the fear of the snake, is to know for certain that it is only made of rubber.

Once this knowledge dawns, then even if his eyes see the snake, or if somebody wants to frighten him with it, there is no cause for fear. In the same way, when one knows correctly as to exactly what this body is, the pride for it and the sense of "mine" about it vanishes, and it is automatically renounced. This is what is called the "dissolution by thought." One who dies with this certainty of thought is free from the cycle of births and deaths. However, it should be taken for granted that one who dies "thoughtlessly," dies only in order to be reborn. By virtue of the "dissolution by thought," the thing is seen as if it were immaterial, whether it is or is not there. With the other types of dissolution, even if the thing is hidden from sight, it is just as if it still exists. Samartha Ramdas therefore asserts that it is only "thoughtfulness" (Vichara) that makes a human being complete, and brings one to fulfillment in life. After thorough investigation, the "I" could not be found when the Physical Body was dissected with the procedure of "dissolution by thought."

The Second Body - The Subtle Body

Now we will use the same process of "dissolution by thought" in trying to trace the "I" in the Subtle Body. Let us investigate and see if this thief called "I" can be found anywhere in the Subtle Body. First, let us find out what the Subtle Body is.

The Subtle Body is comprised of a committee of seventeen members. These are:

1. The Five Senses of Action (hands, feet, mouth, genitals, and anus),
2. The Five Senses of Knowledge (eyes, ears, nose, tongue, and skin),
3. The Five Pranas or vital breaths (vyana vayu which supplies liquid food materials throughout the body, samana vayu which is found in the navel, udana vayu which is found in the throat, apana vayu which is found in the bowels, and prana vayu which is what we breath in and out),
4. The Mind (Manas), and
5. The Intellect (Buddhi)

Whatever orders that this committee of the Subtle Body puts forth are carried out by the Gross Body. The Subtle Body's "field of authority" is very vast, so in conducting a thorough investigation, it may be possible to find that elusive "I" here because he has a strong passion for asserting authority. When we begin our investigation of the Subtle Body, we find that the "I" puts his stamp of "mine" here also. Whatever is found here is labeled as "my senses," "my pranas," "my mind," "my intellect." However, upon closer examination, no such sound as "I am the intellect" is ever heard. That "I" parades around as the "owner" here in the Subtle Body also, but is nowhere to be found. Thus, according to the same reasoning used previously that "There can be nothing which I can call 'mine' where 'I' am not present," the Subtle Body, nor any of its collective members (the senses, the Pranas, the mind, or the intellect) can be "me."

There is an objection that can be raised to this logic of "Where I am not, there can be nothing which I can call my own." For example, King

George the 5th is not present in Sholapur. Does it then follow that Sholapur is not under his ownership? The answer to this objection is thus: At least there is an individual who is called George the 5th, and even if he is living elsewhere, he can have ownership in Sholapur even though he is presently not there. However, this "I" is a "non-entity," and like "Mr. Gomaji Ganesh" from the example earlier, the proliferation of its arrogance and ignorance has remained unexamined, and this "I" is claiming authority here in the Subtle Body as well. When the "I" cannot be traced, how can there be anything there that can be claimed as "mine" to be sustained by the Subtle Body?

The Subtle Body is like a subtle silk bundle. Even though it is more difficult to untie the subtle silk knot with thought than it was with the Gross Body, it is still necessary for the aspirant to put forth the effort to untie it. Once the bundle is untied and left open for thorough examination, the Subtle Body is automatically renounced. It is important to recognize that the Subtle Body is itself the seed of birth and death, which is of the nature of desire. If that seed is roasted just once in the "Fire of Knowledge," it may appear unchanged, but even if it were ever to be sown, there is no hope of it sprouting.

A doubt may arise here that if both the gross and subtle bodies are renounced, and the attitude of pride such as "I" and "mine" also disappears, is it not possible that the actions of the body may either come to a halt, or might not be executed efficiently? The doubt may be removed thus: Suppose someone keeps a thing in a locker because he is under the impression that it is made of gold. However, at some point, he finds out that instead of gold, it is really made of brass. With that recognition, he can choose to either leave it in the locker or remove it and keep it outside. His attachment to it will either vanish or become greatly diminished, and this is a fact. In the same way, if the pride of possession of the body as "mine" is ignored, nothing of value will be lost.

Saint Tukaram said, "Let the body live or die, I have complete faith in my Self Nature." If an aspirant reaches this level of conviction, the attitude arises, "When one experiences the 'Bliss of Brahman' (Brahmananda) who cares for the body?" When this attitude arises, it is truly praiseworthy. A dog once bit off a piece of flesh from Saint Kabir's calf muscle. Saint Kabir simply said, "Either the dog knows, or the flesh knows. Anything is possible." What could have been the feeling of the people around upon hearing this from Saint Kabir, who was a great devotee? The aspirant can easily see the degree of renunciation that Saint Kabir had reached. He fully understood that it was the flesh that was affected and not his True Nature.

Although this understanding that the Self remains unaffected was experienced by Saint Kabir, and also by Saint Tukaram when he lost his whole household, the aspirant might not get the same sense of unshaken ecstasy within oneself in the beginning when one initially undertakes the search for the "I." If by God's Grace, such bliss does overwhelm you, you might say, "What are all these worldly possessions worth after all?," and you will never feel the need to ask such pointless questions as "Will my house be run properly?" At that point, you will have developed such an indifferent attitude that you will say, "Let whatever is to happen, happen, and let whatever has to go, go."

However, if the aspirant understands intellectually, which is easier than experiencing the Self, he raises the question "After the Knowledge of the Self is attained, and the possessive pride of the body and the mind is left behind, can one's worldly duties still be performed?" To console him, the Sadguru answers "Dear one, of course, even after realizing the utter uselessness of the body and mind one can establish a household and have children without bringing in the pride of the body and the mind. In fact, these things can be looked after very well. All of the relevant duties one did earlier can still be diligently performed."

How is this possible, you may ask? Understand by this example: Look at the behavior of the nurse of a motherless infant. She nurses the child, carries it around, consoles it if he cries, and nurses it back to health if he gets sick, just as she would if she were the child's actual mother. If she likes the child, she even kisses it lovingly. While doing all of this work, she does not even have the feeling that the child is her own! In spite of all that she does for the child, if the father of the child dismisses her, she at once picks up her things and gets out of the house. At the time of quitting her position, she is neither happy if the child was to put on weight, nor sad if the child were to die. The reason for this attitude is that she does not have a sense of "mine" regarding the child. However, it cannot be said that she has not performed her duty properly due to the absence of this sense of "mine."

Let us look at another example. Take the case of a trustee who manages a minor's estate worth many millions of rupees. His lack of the sense of "mine" does not hinder him in his duty, and he has been managing the estate of the minor very efficiently. If the duty is not discharged properly, the trustee is liable, and will surely suffer the consequences. The trustee does not have the feeling that the estate is "mine" and accordingly, is not affected if the estate increases in value, or even if it is decided in a legal suit that the estate does not really even belong to the minor. His duty is to look after the estate carefully as long as it is under his management. In short, in order for one's duties to be performed properly, it is not necessary that one must have the sense of "I" or "mine" while performing them. In exactly the same way, the gross and the subtle bodies form a bundle that is rooted in the five elements, and is given as a "keepsake" which is entrusted to the human being.

As a trustee, you must look after the bundle in the best possible way. If you neglect this responsibility, you will surely suffer consequences in the form of the loss of health of both body and mind. If the trustee manages the minor's estate efficiently, and the nurse looks after the child very well, they are awarded their salaries in return. Likewise, if you look after your body and mind well, and keep them in a healthy condition, you also get a return, in a form of joy. A healthy body is definitely useful in the search for the Ultimate Truth.

All of this carrying out of one's responsibilities has to be achieved without the sense of "mine." With this attitude, even if the body becomes fat or thin, or lives or dies, there is no elation or lament. If a trustee of a minor's estate is led astray by a sense of "mine" and claims ownership and embezzles from that estate, he will be jailed. In the case of spiritual practice, the identification with the body means forgetting the Self, or killing the Self. The hope of liberation recedes for the one who is bound by the idea of being a body, even though in truth, he is only nothing but the Self.

From the above discussion, it can be understood that the usual obligations and actions of the body and mind should be fulfilled in a proper manner, and that it is not necessary to establish a sense of "ownership," or a concept of "mine" in relation to them. The obligations of the trustee and the nurse while carrying out their responsibilities do not require them to have any sense of possession, and their duties are performed quite normally. In the same manner, the duties of a human being can be performed without entertaining the sense of possession, or any concept of "mine" in relation to the Physical or Subtle Bodies

The Third Body - The Causal Body

Suppose we lose the concept of possession for the Gross Body, as well as the Subtle Body, and admit to the fact that the bundle belongs to a stranger. Still, we must find the answer to the question "Who am I?" or, "Where am I?" Let us now go over the definition of the Causal Body. What is the Causal Body? As soon as we step in here, there is pitch darkness everywhere. Is it possible that this dark Ignorance is the place of residence for this "I"? It surely seems this is his main headquarters. Ignorance seems to be the main property or quality that belongs to him. There is certainly some hope of finding the elusive "I" here. Let us see.

Here we move about as if blindfolded searching for it, and the "I" is not to be found anywhere in Causal Body. Here the "I" seems to have even given up his sense of "mine." There seems nothing that can be called "mine" in this place. Everything seems to be absolutely quiet. That "I" who loudly proclaims "I, I" so arrogantly in the gross and subtle bodies, seems to be totally silent here. The "I" seems to be playing hide and seek so that he does not get caught by the one who searches for it. In the Causal Body, the "I" seems to have dug itself into a trench of darkness so that the one making the search might fall in, being forced to end his search.

Dear aspirants, do not be concerned. The Sadguru is standing behind you as well as in front of you, and He will take you safely across this trench of darkness. Many scholars and learned persons have turned their backs at this point and abandoned their search failing to have faith in the guidance of the Sadguru. For you however, there is no reason to abandon your search like them. You have a guide who is a very capable Master, a Samartha Sadguru. (Samartha means "The Powerful One" who knows his own significance, in the highest sense.)

After stabilizing in this darkness of the Causal Body, and firmly planting one's feet therein for some period of time, a voice is softly heard that says, "I am the witness of this Ignorance." With this, there arises some courage offering the hope of catching the thief called "I." With the recognition of this voice who says it is the witness of the Ignorance, there also comes the thought, "This thief is here somewhere. He may be near, or a little further ahead, but he is witnessing the Ignorance from somewhere nearby." Here the searching takes the form of watching persistently. How this is done will be discussed in the next chapter. The witnessing that is going on is happening from beyond the emptiness of the Causal Body, from the position in the Great-Causal Body (Mahakarana Body), or Turya State. When this is understood, the "I" is quickly overjoyed in finding himself. Who can describe that Joy? In that Joy, the "I" cries out "I am Brahman, I am Self-Knowledge."

The Fourth Body - The Great-Causal Body (Turya)

The one who says "I" is really the all-witnessing Brahman. It is He, who is of the nature of Knowledge, the sense of "I Am." When this certainty is established, there arises wave after wave of Bliss. Afterwards, when this bliss ebbs away, look at the miracle that happens. After enquiry and deep thought (Vichara), one arrives at the recognition that, "I am not even of the nature of 'Knowledge,' for just as I am covered with Ignorance, in the same way, I am covered with Knowledge. I was not originally having any Ignorance or Knowledge. Ignorance and Knowledge were born out of 'me,' and were mistakenly taken to be me. With the aid of such deep thought, it can be seen that the arising of both Ignorance and Knowledge within me, points to me as their creator. Therefore Knowledge is my child, and I am its father, and as its father, I am prior to, and different from, that Knowledge."

Brahman

When this sequence of deep discriminative thought dawns within, the sense that "I am Brahman," (Aham Brahmasmi) that is the Self-Knowledge in the Great-Causal Body, or Turya State, also starts ebbing away, only to finally be fully eradicated. Then "I" am absolutely naked, without any covering whatsoever. Arriving here in this nakedness, it cannot be described as to who or what this "I," is. If you want a description of the "I" who is found here, you may utter any word found in any dictionary, but that is not "I." This "I" here, can only be expressed as "Not this, not this." It is the one who throws light on anything called "this." You may utter words and sentences to try to describe it, but those are not it. Whatever meanings come forth, you take those to be the description of "I," but those are not it. If you do not understand what is being told now, you must leave off the words and concepts, and merge in Deep Silence, and see who "I" am.

Chapter 3: Investigation of the Four Bodies in Detail

A Methodical Approach to Explanation

So far, during the search for the "I," we turned the four bodies inside-out and could not find a trace of it. It is true that the "I" disappeared without words beyond the four bodies, where even the ideas of "I" and "you" do not exist. However, it will not do to just keep quiet, and mistake this for Deep Silence. In the exposition thus far, the Gross, the Subtle, the Causal, and the Great-Causal bodies have been superficially described. It is necessary to examine in detail all aspects of the four bodies. Unless these are fully understood correctly and this understanding is made a part of one's nature, an aspirant will not be able to arrive at this Deep Silence, which is Reality. We will therefore examine in detail what the aspects of the four bodies are.

It is necessary to understand that these four bodies are the four steps that one must ascend in order to proceed on to the fifth rung of Deep Silence which is "Nihshabda," where the "word" becomes silent. Going step by step, one can surely reach the end of the journey. However, if some steps are missed, and one puts one's foot on the next step prematurely, there is a likelihood of losing one's balance, and falling back. Therefore it is only when one body is fully understood that the aspirant should continue on to the next body. Without using this methodical approach, if one starts stepping up the steps too hastily, there will be confusion. In this confusion, true understanding will not be gained, and the aspirant will likely misunderstand the subtle differences between Deep Sleep and Samadhi, as well as mistake Ignorance for Knowledge.

By way of comparison, consider the difference between a toy top that is still when it is not moving and when it appears to be still due to intense speed, or the difference between total darkness and the blackout that is caused by intense light. Although these things appear similar from a casual glance or superficial perspective, there is a vast difference between the two states, and their usefulness or capacity is also different. If one works methodically step by step to gain understanding, there will be no confusion as to the subtle differences that are being indicated. Here it is prudent to bring to the attention of the reader the method of exposition of a subject that is provided in the ancient scriptures. This will convince the aspirant that there is no basis for any doubts to arise regarding any apparent contradictions in the method adopted for the exposition of some particular point in the scriptures. Therefore, we must first describe the method of expounding the teaching that has been adopted by the ancient scriptures (This is often referred to as the "primary premise" presented in the Vedas).

When a subject is to be explained to an aspirant, there is first a description of the subject matter, showing its great importance. It is then explained that a great reward will follow if the subject matter is correctly understood. Once the aspirant understands the subject completely, before moving on and explaining the next subject, the instructor using the scriptural method is to first impress upon the aspirant the uselessness of the subject that has already been understood. Only after that can the importance of the subject to be taught next be impressed upon him. The reason for this method is that there is no inclination for one to strive to understand a subject unless its importance is first brought out, with a promise of some reward as a motivation. Next, the uselessness of the subject matter just learned is brought home to the aspirant so that the subject is automatically renounced, and the aspirant becomes eager to understand what is to be presented as the next topic.

The Mother Shruti (the Vedas) takes into consideration the psychological background of an aspirant, and then inspires him to work for food, first telling him that the food is Brahman. She then gives him time to fondle the Gross Body, telling him that the Gross Body is Brahman. Then it is explained that all experiences of joy that come to the Gross Body are actually enjoyed by the Subtle Body. The Gross Body is shown to be merely a corpse, and it is told how the corpse could in no way enjoy anything if it were not for the Subtle Body. Thus, the uselessness of the Gross Body is demonstrated.

Next, the mind, intellect, senses, and the sheath that makes up the Pranas (vital breaths) are described, and this Subtle Body is said to be Brahman. It is shown to be bigger or more expansive than the Gross Body. In this way, the Vedas give importance to the Subtle Body. After that, comes the description of the Causal Body, which is still and even more expansive than the Subtle Body. It swallows the Subtle Body. The Causal Body is then proclaimed to be Brahman and the advice is given to the aspirant that "You yourself have become the expansive Causal Body." However, since the Causal Body is considered to be Ignorance and in total darkness, the final claim of it being the Self cannot really be made here. Accordingly, the aspirant is therefore compelled to investigate further, into the Great-Causal Body. This Great-Causal Body is still more expansive, and it is from here that the voice saying "I am the witness" emanates. Upon arriving here, the Great-Causal Body, or Turya State, is investigated and examined thoroughly.

In this way, the Mother Vedas dismiss each body after having asserted that it was Brahman. When she is finally confronted with the problem of explaining the changeless, attributeless Brahman (Nirguna Brahman) she claims an inability to describe it, and only keeps repeating the sentence, "Not this, Not this. That which is not Ignorance, and that which is not Knowledge is Brahman, and that which you call Brahman, is not Brahman." In such a negative way, Mother Shruti describes Brahman as "That" which is beyond all of the four bodies.

The principle of what has just been described is as follows: When it said that one body is bigger than the previous body it does not mean that it is higher in relation to it, etc. In a comparison of needles for example, the needle used for stitching jute bags is bigger than one used for cotton, but it is not bigger than an iron rod that is used for digging. This indicates that qualities like "bigger" and "smaller" are not inherent in a thing, but are imposed upon it by relating it to or comparing it with some other thing. The same rule applies here. After listing in sequence first food as Brahman, then Gross Body as Brahman, then Subtle Body as Brahman, then the Causal, and finally the Great-Causal Body as Brahman, and in each case, the latter being greater than the former, the intention is to give the instruction and demonstrate the principle that out of all these, ultimately none can be said to be Brahman. Although it is shown that in each case that the latter state is relatively higher or more expansive than the previous one, it is still not Brahman, and moreover, this Parabrahman is absolutely unique and beyond all of these four bodies.

While utilizing the above-mentioned method of explaining a point, it is necessary to understand clearly just what it is that is being described as Brahman. Why is it that it should be described in this way? How far can one go to describe it as being with some particular qualities? Moreover, why is it that what was once called Brahman, is then negated as not being Brahman in the same breath? It is important to understand this correctly. For example, in giving instruction on how to cook rice to a person who is not a proper cook, the person is told to first light a fire under the utensil in which the rice is being cooked. After some time, another instruction is given to the same person to put the fire out now. It is natural that the person may wonder about the contradictory instructions. His teacher explains to him, "Dear one, it is necessary to keep a fire under the utensil until the rice is cooked, but later, the fire has to be put out, otherwise we would get coals instead of rice."

This is the reason why any method to be practiced is necessary only until its goal is achieved. Otherwise, it will only bring on exhaustion and nothing further beneficial will be achieved. Thus, when the Subtle Body being called as Brahman is thoroughly examined and understood, the merit of calling the Subtle Body as Brahman loses its value, and it becomes necessary to move on, and continue the search for "I" by examining the next thing. This demonstrates that sometimes when we offer a price for something, or place some value on it in order to achieve some particular results, that value that we have placed on it may not necessarily be the real value of that thing. For example, some occasion may arise in one's life where you might have to address even a donkey as uncle. In this example, the honor that is given to the donkey is due to some consequence you must endure for some action done.

In the same way, some great calamity that someone may be facing is because he has forgotten his real nature. It is therefore necessary to become liberated from the calamity or obstruction, which is like being caught in the jaws of a crocodile. If you free yourself from the crocodile by flattery saying that her back is very smooth, does it really mean that her back is as soft as a feather mattress? This question should be asked of the man who gets released from the crocodile's jaws. To rid oneself of the crocodile like grip of the four bodies, they are called Brahman for some short period of time. Taking into account that this is the method of explanation that will be used, we will now turn our attention to the actual explanation and description of the four bodies.

The Investigation Commences

The nature of the Gross Body is quite well known. It is a mass of flesh and blood that can be touched with the hand, and all are quite familiar with it. Not only that, but everyone uses it fully. The Gross Body is "I" and therefore all the passions and desires that happen to the body are "mine." Accordingly, the dark or fair complexion of the body, and the stages of childhood, youth, and old age, belong to "me." The relationship of the body to caste, religion, house, land, and wealth, are all "mine." This is a lesson that every human being has learned through many births, and he has learned it very well. In fact, it is so well learned that even while dreaming, someone will tell you that he is "So-and-so." It is therefore not necessary to teach anyone this lesson that has been repeatedly learned over and over, and has been so firmly implanted in one's psyche. The feet of all human beings are resting steadily on the step of this Gross Body. The state of this Gross Body is that of "wakefulness" and in this body, there is partial forgetfulness and partial remembrance. The quality of worldly action, or "Rajoguna," is predominant in the Gross Body. This basic explanation is enough for one to understand the Gross Body. We will now turn to the next step, that of the Subtle Body.

As has been previously stated, the Subtle Body is a committee. It is a collection of the senses, the Pranas, the mind, the intellect, seated on the "Inner-mind" (Antahkarana), which collectively create a type of mental world or "dream world" that is seen when the visible world becomes invisible when closing the eyes. After some thought and investigation, it can be noticed that the Subtle Body is really a very peculiar thing. Upon examination, it can be seen that all of the movements of the Gross Body are according to the dictates of this Subtle Body. The assertion of a concept, such as "something is like this," is called "Sankalpa," and a doubt, or the notion that "something is not like this" is called "Vikalpa." This Subtle Body is such that it is always presenting this perverse type of knowledge of contradictory thoughts, and its state is that of "dreaming." Continuous memory is the indicative quality of the Subtle Body, and the quality of "awareness" or "Sattvaguna" is the quality that is predominant here.

After being introduced to the Subtle Body in this way, the aspirant becomes that body. When one foot is planted firmly on the next step, the other foot is lifted from the previous step, and placed beside the first foot. In this way, one leaves the first step completely. When one crosses the boundaries of a village and puts his foot within the limits of the next village, the first village is left behind, and one becomes a traveler to the next village. Similarly, in order to understand properly the step of the Subtle Body described above, when the aspirant plants his foot firmly on this step he has to lift his foot from the Gross Body in order to bring this understanding into practice. When the Gross Body is left behind, the aspirant then has to sever all connections with it.

However, this work is not so easily done, as it seems that for crossing over these steps, every human being has only two legs. One leg is the leg of learning, and the other is the leg of putting into practice what one has learned. Taking both feet away from the step of the Gross Body and planting them on the step of the Subtle Body means that one has to transcend the Physical Body. When one leaves behind the sense of pride and possession of the Gross Body and takes up the pride of possession in the Subtle Body, he has to say, "I am only the Subtle Body." Only when this is experienced does it mean that the Gross Body has been renounced and the Subtle Body is now accepted as "I." When the aspirant comes to this second step, then the lower step is left behind and one now accepts that the Gross Body is not "I." The "I" has no relationship with the Gross Body. The changes that happen to the Gross Body and its qualities, such as having a dark or fair complexion are no longer considered as "mine." No qualities of the Gross Body belong to me, as I am only the Subtle Body. This means that the qualities of the Subtle Body such as the senses, the Pranas, the mind, the intellect, the sense of "I am," etc. are not endowed with gross physical qualities such as fat or thin, dark or fair, young or old, etc. It is clear that "I" am only the mind and the intellect, etc., with subtle qualities. If the aspirant studies this diligently, then both feet become firmly planted on the second step and he loses the sense of pride in, and identification with, the Gross Body. He becomes indifferent to all qualities and conditions of the Gross Body.

The third step is above and beyond the Subtle Body, and is the Causal Body, or "Ignorance." The Causal Body is a state of "pure forgetfulness" where the quality of Ignorance or "Tamoguna" is predominant. Here in the Causal Body, there is no thought as to the well being of, or any relationship with, either the Gross or the Subtle Bodies. The Causal Body means that there is no knowledge of anything. It is like the state of Deep Sleep, but it is not Deep Sleep. The Causal Body is difficult to understand, however it is very important to understand this state. Those who proclaim to understand the principle of zero (nothingness; the void) came to this state and turned back saying that there was nothing ahead.

The Causal Body is the state of the "unknowable" or "the void" which is presented in the point of view of western philosophers. This state which is devoid of all thoughts, imagination, and doubts, is often mistakenly taken by aspirants to be Samadhi, and thought to be the same as Brahman without concepts or qualities (Nirvikalpa Brahman). When this void or state of emptiness is reached, one is likely to get a false satisfaction and say, "Today I saw Brahman." The interval or pause between where one modification of the mind disappears, and another one does not arise (such as the space between two thoughts, or the intervening pause before sleep sets in and the waking state disappears) is a state of pure forgetfulness. This is what is described as the "Covering of Bliss" (Anandamaya Kosha) in the scriptures. In the Causal Body all chaos, struggle, and the infinite number of waves of thought have ceased. Therefore, there is a sense of peace in this third body that is not found in the other two bodies. It is true that the aspirant experiences a certain joy, but this is not Ultimate Peace, or even true Bliss. One must understand this point very well. This Causal Body is the natural state of all the gods, demons, and every human being. The state of the Causal Body is the state of "Forgetfulness."

The chief sign or indication of the Causal Body is to forget everything. For example, unless one forgets everything he cannot get Deep Sleep. To say "I was asleep, but I remembered something," is to really say, "I never slept." To really have Deep Sleep means not to remember a single thing. Similarly, to forget everything while in an awakened state, is to enter the Causal Body. To be in a state where you do not know anything, is to also come to this state. As previously mentioned, this is the natural state of a human being. Even the most learned scholars do not understand the nature of a human being, let alone the nature of Shiva. In order for one to fully understand this state of human forgetfulness, the method of studying the pause is prescribed. If anything is very difficult, it is to be completely stabilized in the state of forgetfulness, and to know it thoroughly. To achieve this is important in one's spiritual progress, and takes considerable effort on the part of the aspirant. The Saints have put particular emphasis on this point.

The pause between two states is nothing but Pure Consciousness. The state of the "mouni" (a silent one) is such that he does not allow a single word to rise, or even if it did rise, he does not allow its meaning to rise, but simply lets it slip by. When the word rises, and is allowed to impress its meaning on the inner-mind, the world is born. Ignoring the word, and not allowing it to carry any meaning for the mind, is the eradication of the world. When the word does not energize the mind, what remains is the "Pure Energy of Consciousness." To experience this state continuously is called "The State of Silence."

The aspirant who is about to put his foot on the third step after climbing the first and second, is told that this step is the state of Pure Consciousness. He is under the impression that this state is the Pure Void, and taking this void to be Brahman, he is unable to witness the void. However, when the aspirant proceeds to the fourth step, he begins to look back at the third step. Being unable to see anything in the void of the Causal Body he wonders why the Guru has instructed him to put his foot on this step of nothingness which doesn't exist at all. The reason is, that once Pure Consciousness is known, there can be no trace of anything that is called "Ignorance," so one does not come to understand what the state of "Forgetfulness" is. Once known, there does not arise any modification in the aspirant's mind except that of Pure Consciousness.

Knowledge, or Consciousness presents itself to the aspirant in two ways:
1. When there is an object in Consciousness it becomes "Objective Knowledge" and one will experience it as knowledge of objects.
2. When there is no object, it is experienced as objectless Knowledge, or "Pure Consciousness."

When there is an object, that is called "Objective Knowledge." When there is no object, that is simply "Knowledge," which is Pure Awareness, or Consciousness. With the exception of these two (Objective Knowledge and Pure Knowledge), no other modifications are present in the aspirant's mind. In Pure Consciousness, the word "Ignorance" is meaningless from the aspirant's point of view. It is not possible for

Forgetfulness to exist in his case. Whatever is experienced will either be Objective Knowledge, or Pure Consciousness that is without any objects.

Presenting the state of the Causal Body to the aspirant that it is just Ignorance, a void, a state of Forgetfulness, or something where there is nothing to bring home to him, is to lead him to the above fact of Pure Consciousness. By analogy, a teacher will draw on the blackboard a point of great length and breadth in order to teach the student about a point that has neither length nor breadth. Similarly, this is how the point is being illustrated here. If it is not done in this manner, the next step cannot be explained. The aspirant should therefore have full faith in the Sadguru without further argument and take it for granted that there is a state of Forgetfulness. He should thus commence practicing what is being told, and begin the process of forgetting each and every thing. It must be understood that the casual body is the cause of the two previous bodies. Hence the label "Causal Body."

Here the example is given of the side curtain on a theater stage, which is called the wing, from which the actors emerge and where they again disappear back into. The Causal Body, which is the natural state of a human being, is like this wing on the stage, and exists in the state of the form of "Forgetfulness." From behind this curtain, all memories appear and then disappear. When we say that we have forgotten a thing before remembering it, this means that the thing was abiding there in that state of Forgetfulness, and it is proved that it has emerged from that state alone. In opposition to this, when we say that we forgot a certain thing, this means that the thing that was in memory has disappeared behind this curtain of Forgetfulness. A memory before it is forgotten, and something forgotten after it is remembered, are companions in this arena of Forgetfulness. The rising and setting of all ideas are in the womb of this one "Forgetfulness," which is the common ground for all human beings. It is by reason of this Forgetfulness that each human being feels he is ignorant and strives to obtain knowledge. During this struggle, the majority unfortunately only gain worldly knowledge, thus missing the Knowledge of their "True Nature."

When introducing the Causal Body in the manner described above, the Sadguru tells the disciple, "Dear one, you are not the Gross Physical Body, and you are not the Subtle Body, so you should identify yourself with the Causal Body." For an aspirant to be in the state of

"Forgetfulness," it means that he should have the feeling that "I am definitely not the Gross Body, and I am not the Subtle Body. Therefore, all of the dreams and doubts that arise in the Subtle Body, do not reside in me. I am complete 'Forgetfulness,' empty of all concepts and imaginings. The birth and death of the body, the miseries and temptations, the pain and pleasure, as well as the hunger and thirst that arise in the Pranas, cannot touch me. Honor and dishonor are only notions in the mind, and qualities such as fair or dark complexion belong to the Physical Body, but I am none of these. Nothing can attach itself to me. I am Forgetfulness."

Committing oneself to this lesson again and again and becoming firmly established in the state of Forgetfulness without any idea or attachment, it becomes our own nature. In this way, one experiences oneself as being completely empty of all of the qualities of the Gross and the Subtle Bodies. When this practice of experiencing oneself as Forgetfulness is firmly established the aspirant definitely rises to the third step. Becoming steady in this Forgetfulness, the aspirant is worthy of proceeding to the next step, to the Great-Causal Body (Mahakarana Body), the Turya State.

However, before going to the next step, it is necessary to mention that the Causal Body although similar to Deep Sleep, is a state quite distinct from sleep. In Deep Sleep, all of the senses are in complete repose with the complete absence of any activity, and consequently any perception of sense objects. In Deep Sleep, all beings enjoy the bliss of being in their own nature, yet do not really know their True Nature. Upon awakening from Deep Sleep, everyone will say these two sentences: "I slept happily," and "I did not know anything." Like this, everyone conveys the contentment and bliss of their own nature, as well as their ignorance regarding it. In this manner, although one unknowingly conveys their awareness of Ignorance, it also proves the existence of a deeper Awareness. However, this does not mean that one was aware of their true Self, even though they were experiencing it during Deep Sleep. During Deep Sleep, one does not experience the Awareness that is present there. For example, suppose that there is a person who is unknowingly an heir to a treasure of buried gold coins. Everyday he goes to sleep on the ground and does his normal begging in the morning for his livelihood. For him, the treasure is as good as not being there at all. Similarly, each human being goes into and comes out of their true nature, diving deep and experiencing bliss. However the deep ignorance about one's real nature is there as part of that experience. It is for this reason that Deep Sleep cannot be the means of gaining "Self-Knowledge," the Knowledge of one's "True Nature." In Deep Sleep, the aspirant has no ability to study that state. However, this is not the case with regard to the state of "Forgetfulness."

To study Forgetfulness is to enjoy the state of Deep Sleep while being fully awake. The manner in which to enjoy this wakeful Deep Sleep is taught by the Sadguru. How does a fish sleep while living in water? One can only understand this if you get a birth in that species. How can the sleep of a fish not be disturbed by the water entering into its eyes? This secret is known only when one is born as a fish. In the same way, how can one experience and understand this Deep Sleep state while one is fully awake? One can only understand this by becoming a true Son of the Sadguru, a "Guruputra."

The Causal Body, which is of the nature of Forgetfulness is nothing but a very deep sleep. However, that which is described above, is the silence within that is experienced knowingly, or consciously, during the Waking State. It is not the Deep Sleep state that comes "unknowingly," without conscious awareness. Nothing is known in the state of Deep Sleep which comes "unknowingly." However, the nature of the Self can be known by means of employing the method of knowing "Forgetfulness" which is experienced while awake. This is the difference between "Deep Sleep," and Samadhi.

Although it is known that "Forgetfulness" is a state where nothing is known, the fact is, that after everything is forgotten "Knowledge" remains. This "Knowledge" can only be understood through the study of Forgetfulness.

This state of Forgetfulness exists, and must be understood. Deep Sleep and Forgetfulness are both the result of "Tamoguna." By way of analogy, an analysis of coal and diamond shows that both are made of carbon. This means that the coal and the diamond are but two aspects of carbon. Although this is the case, there is a vast difference in their respective values. When the ingredient of carbon is the same in both, how is it that the diamond shines and the coal is black and lusterless? The reason is that the proportion of the same component is different in the two. Likewise, Deep Sleep and Forgetfulness share different proportions of

Ignorance, which explains why in Deep Sleep the immense density of Ignorance is felt, while in Forgetfulness the flimsiness of Ignorance is realized.

As the depth of Deep Sleep decreases, the onset of wakefulness arises. The man who wakes up from Deep Sleep is at first slightly under the fuzzy influence of sleep, and then awakens slowly. This state is the result of the depth of sleep becoming thinner, or more flimsy, as the state of full wakefulness emerges and sleep ends. Deep Sleep is like a pitch black curtain which covers the lamp of the Self, while the Causal Body or the state of Forgetfulness that is being examined is like a thin transparent velvet curtain. This means that the enjoyment of bliss is the same in both Deep Sleep and the Causal Body (Forgetfulness). However, from the point of view of achieving the knowledge of one's True Nature, Deep Sleep is useless. It is like attempting to procreate by having sexual intercourse with a barren woman. The study of this "Sheath of Bliss," (Anandamaya Kosha) in the form of the state of Forgetfulness provides one with joy and is a necessary step in reaching the goal of knowing one's "True Nature."

Having said all of this, we will now observe the Great-Causal Body, or the Turya State, which is endowed with the "Knowledge" that comes after the study of Forgetfulness. Here, let us digress a little. Those aspirants who have taken the traditional Mantra, according to the tradition of Shri Sadguru Bhausaheb Maharaj may have doubts at this point. The study of the Causal Body means that one should learn to forget everything. Does this also mean that repeating the Mantra given by the Guru, and the color or forms that stand before one's half-closed eyes should also be forgotten? The answer is Yes! You have to do this. Before doing this, while repeating the Mantra the colors and whatever forms are present, and the aspirant must check for oneself that the mental noises and chatter cease and die out completely.

When concentrating on the tip of the nose with half-closed eyes in a relaxed manner, with the exception of the repetition of the Mantra and the color form, there should not arise any other word or form. This having been done, even that has to be forgotten. The broom in one's hand that is used to sweep out the rubbish in the house should not be kept in the hand after the rubbish has been cleaned out from every corner of the house. The broom also has to be thrown out in the end.

The Sadguru imparts the Mantra to the aspirant as a discipline. He gives a tool in the form of the Mantra which sweeps clean all rubbish in the form of doubts, fears, imaginings, and concepts that have been accumulated over the infinite number of births. This tool of the Mantra helps the aspirant learn how to concentrate, or focus his attention, and enables the mind to become subtle. How the tool should be utilized, and when it should be left alone has now been clearly explained.

Now, we will see what the fourth body, the Great-Causal Body is. (The Great-Causal Body is also known in the teachings of Vedanta as the Turya State, or SatChitAnanda. It is called Great-Causal because it is above, or beyond the limits of the Causal Body.) It is the father of the other three bodies. In Hindu mythology, King Janaka (Janaka means Creator, or Producer) was one without a body (Videhi). He had a daughter named Janaki (Janaki means Awareness). This mythological story tells us that King Janaka is the same as the fourth body, the Great-Causal Body. This indicates a state of Consciousness that is without a body in spite of the fact that the body still exists. That is the state of "Knowledge" in the fourth body. This is King Janaka. Out of him, the daughter Janaki (Awareness) is created. Compared with the previous three bodies, the fourth body is a state that is without a body, and without any conditions, in the form of "Knowledge." However, this does not mean that there is an absence of Knowledge found in the previous three bodies.

Knowledge is the same whether it is in an agitated condition or in equanimity. It is clean and pure in the state of equanimity as well as in the disturbed condition, even when immersed in the flood of objective knowledge. In all states, Knowledge is One, and the same. However, the knowledge in the first three bodies is adulterated knowledge, or conditional objective knowledge. The Knowledge in the state of the Great-Causal Body is balanced with an intermingling of the three gunas (Rajas, Tamas, and Sattva), and can be experienced as "Pure Knowledge."

Whether Knowledge is in a balanced or an unbalanced state, Knowledge is always Knowledge. However, it is different with respect to its conditioning. Because of the identification with particular conditionings of Knowledge, a human being sees differences, and creates distinctions and separateness in the "One Knowledge." For example, the sweetness that one tastes in the various sweets called laddoos, or jilebis, or basundis, is all sugar. However, because it is in these particular forms we say that the laddoo is sweet, the jilebi is sweet, or the basundi is sweet. If we taste some sugar that is not mixed with any other ingredients, we will say that sugar is sweet. If someone is given a description of what sugar is like, and is given a laddoo and told that the sweetness in the laddoo is sugar, he will never get the knowledge of the true nature of sugar. However, if he is given pure sugar unmixed with any other ingredients he will know exactly what sugar is.

This example illustrates why Knowledge cannot be experienced in its primal state in the first three bodies because it is always in some form of conditioning. In the first three bodies it will always be experienced only as objective knowledge. In the Fourth Body, that Knowledge that is non-objective and Pure, and which is not apparent (visible) in the other three bodies, shines in its "Pure Nature." This is the reason why aspirants have to be taken to the Great-Causal Body. When Pure Knowledge, or Consciousness, is known, then even if it is mixed with objective knowledge, or is in any other state, the aspirant will understand correctly that the entity that is called "the world," is not separate, or different from that which is called "The Knowledge of the Self" (Self-Knowledge).

Even when each state comes and goes, the witness of these states does not come or go anywhere. The one who sees the dark and fair complexion, as well as childhood, youth, and old age, of the Physical Body, is also the one who sees all concepts, imaginings, dreams, and doubts in the Subtle Body. The same witness also sees the Causal Body where there is a complete absence of concepts, imagination, and doubts. The one who witnesses all three of these bodies is forever awake.

There is a story of a woman with a peculiar characteristic who delivered a child. The child died before it knew its mother, and never saw the faces of its brother or sister that were also dead. This woman had many such children who died. The woman however remained where she was after burying all of the children. Not one child saw the face of another child, but the woman had seen all of the faces of the children, and had within her a recognition of all those children. This is exactly like the three bodies that were born of the Great-Causal Body, which is in the form of the Primal Illusion (MoolaMaya). However, none of these three bodies ever had the chance of seeing the face of each other, or the face of their mother.

Even while one state penetrates into the other, the Knowledge present in all these states is never adulterated. Just as in the example of the thread which supports all beads equally where one bead does not penetrate into the other, the Great-Causal Body is like that, as it pervades all the other states like Deep Sleep, Dream, and the Waking State. The state of Awareness, or Consciousness in the Great-Causal Body is the "Self-Luminous Flame" which becomes naked without any covering whatsoever, by making Ignorance forget itself.

Once the nature of the "Witnessing Knowledge" is known, the state of Ignorance vanishes completely. Though it is true that Ignorance vanishes, it is not true that the appearance of "the seen," or "manifestation," also vanishes. It is only the attitude, or the understanding of the aspirant that changes. By virtue of the intensity of the study, we will experience that all that is seen and appears, is in the form of "Knowledge." As soon one gains the understanding that it is only "gold" that is perceived in a piece of jewelry, the piece of jewelry itself is not destroyed. Similarly, when it is known that everything that exists is only "The Lord of the Universe" the visible universe is not destroyed, just as when the light of a lamp destroys darkness, the objects that become known do not vanish. At first there was no light, and nothing was known beyond the fact that there were some objective forms. The nature of the objects simply became clearly known in the light. In the same way, when we were looking at and feeling the world with blind eyes in the darkness of Ignorance, the Sadguru's advice brings correct vision to our sight.

When the Flame of Knowledge is lit in the "Inner-Consciousness," it spreads light all around and the darkness of Ignorance is destroyed, yet the world appearance remains, as its True Nature is uncovered and revealed. In this way, the point of view from which one was viewing the world changes after one acquires "True Knowledge." A mirage is viewed differently from the perspective of a man and that of a deer. The object is the same, but the seeing of it is different in each case. When sand in the desert, or a road stretching out into the distance becomes hot from the sun's rays, the heat waves that rise will appear to be a body of water to someone standing far away. This appearance is called a mirage. In Marathi language, the mirage is called Mrugjala. The meaning of this is "an appearance of water at a distance that entices a deer." The reason for this name is that the deer is deceived by the mirage, and imagines it to really be water, and runs towards it to quench its thirst. Upon realizing the absence of water, the deer becomes disillusioned. It is the limited capacity of the deer's intellect that leads it to believe the appearance of water is true, and although it looks like water, a thirsty man will not run towards it to quench his thirst. The reason for this is that the mirage is not what it appears to be, and the man understands this. He is not deceived into believing that there is the presence of water there. This is the capacity of the human intellect for discerning the True from the untrue. From the point of view of the sun, there is nothing like a mirage. From where does the appearance of a mirage arise? It is similar to this that the attitude of an aspirant who is ignorant and therefore bound, and the attitude of a Siddha, or a "Liberated Man," are different. The one who is bound is driving the cart of practical duties taking it for granted that the world is true. When an aspirant gains the "Knowledge of the Self," he looks at the world with the attitude that it is just a temporary appearance or an illusion. However, the Siddha is one who has become "The Self of All," and does not see the world at all.

At this point, the first part of the exposition of the teaching, and everything regarding the Physical Gross Body up through the Great-Causal Body has been included. The next part of the teaching that is given after the explanation of the Great-Causal Body, is the teaching of the Final Reality. A person cannot be called a Siddha even if he gains Self-Knowledge by becoming identified with the Great-Causal Body (SatChitAnanda) and has realized that state. Even though he is accomplished, he is still looked upon only as an aspirant (sadhaka). The field where the Siddhas rest is in that field of "Supreme Knowledge," or Vijnana (Thoughtless Reality). However, we will not discuss that yet at this point.

At this stage in the exposition, the step under our feet is the Great-Causal Body (Mahakarana Body), also known as the Turya State. First, we must discuss the Great-Causal Body in more detail. We have said that the Great-Causal Body is the state of the annihilation of Ignorance. However, it should be understood that Ignorance, the state of Forgetfulness, comes into consideration only in relation to the Gross and the Subtle Bodies. Actually, it has no real existence that has to be annihilated by acquiring "Knowledge."

It is ridiculous to say that Ignorance, or "that which is not," has to be annihilated. For example, Rama has a ring and Govinda does not have a ring. Does the absence of a ring indicate the state of existence of a certain thing called a ring? No it does not. It is in exactly the same way that the state of 'Forgetfulness," that is non-existent and appears only in relationship to the Gross and Subtle Bodies, is an imagined state. It truly does not exist. Samartha Ramdas points out in his book **Dasbodh** that this state of Ignorance in the form of Forgetfulness is the state in which that which was "not" becomes non-existent. It is natural at this point that the question might arise, "Does the state of Self-Knowledge really exist?" The one who saw the absence of dreams, imaginings, and doubts, in the state of Forgetfulness, and knew of their absence or non-existence, is "The God of Knowledge" (Jnanadeva). It is He who witnesses the dissolution of all the modifications of Knowledge and is the one who presides over the Great-Causal Body. However, it should be clearly understood that this "Witnessing Knowledge" is also a parasite (an unwanted presence) on the "Pure Nature of the Self." This "Witnessing Knowledge" is only needed to be used to annihilate the "Ignorance" of the Causal Body which means having "no knowledge." When the "Witnessing Knowledge" of the Fourth Body is left behind, the state of Forgetfulness is forgotten, and "Knowledge" sees only at itself. Observation of one's Self cannot be called "witnessing." The seer is called a witness when he forgets the Self and sees something objective or different from the Self. When seeing only Himself, he abides in this "Supreme Knowledge," Vijnana, which is of the nature of the "Absolute."

In that "Aloneness" one likes humming to himself "Aham Brahmasmi, I am Brahman." With that sound arising from within, even this "Knowledge" is limited, or bound, and is still caught in the Great-Causal Body. This hum is the Primal Illusion, the original Illusion that is of the nature of the "Three Gunas" (GunaMaya). If one wants to be rid of this Illusion, even this humming sound has to stop for that rumbling Primal Illusion (MoolaMaya) to be permanently left behind. "I am Brahman" is a very subtle sense of "I Am" that is imposed on the Self, which is actually the absence of the ego or a sense of separate self. However, even this subtle type of "I Am" is like a molecule of salt in milk, and therefore has to be eradicated. To take the false as true, is a mistaken concept, but to take the True as True is the absence of any such concept. By virtue of this statement, in the absence of all concepts, the Gross Body is "I," the

Subtle Body is "I," and the Causal Body is also "I." However, as long as one continues to assert oneself to be any of these three bodies, it is certainly a mistaken concept, and a type of pride.

This having been said, the Consciousness that says "I," as "I am Brahman," can be called egolessness, or having no pride, because this "I" is upholding the Truth. Where is the falsehood in it? Actually there is nothing untrue or false in this, yet, if that "True One" goes on announcing, "I am True," or "I am Brahman," there arises a doubt about this truth. If a Brahmin (someone of the priest caste) goes on telling everybody he meets "I am a Brahmin, I am a Brahmin," the listener will say, "If this man is a Brahmin why is he repeating this? He must really be of some lower caste." In the same way, the repeated assertion of the concept "I am Brahman, I am Brahman," shows that this Consciousness, this Knowledge in the Great-Causal Body is not free from doubt about its Real Nature. From this point of view, even the memory of the concept "I am Brahman" that reminds one of the Self, has to be erased. The Consciousness (SatChitAnanda) that is of the Great-Causal Body should be stabilized to such an extent that it is of neither memory, nor forgetfulness. Only then does the aspirant become "The Nature of Pure Knowledge and Bliss."

Even when we consider our usual daily gross experiences, we are in a natural state that is without any remembrance or forgetfulness. Does anyone have an experience like "I have forgotten myself," or "I was remembering myself"? Has anyone ever tried to prove his existence by making such efforts? We do not ever forget ourselves, nor is it necessary to remember ourselves. We are always naturally in a state that is beyond the state of remembrance or forgetfulness. That is really our True Nature. Remembrance or forgetfulness is always of something "else" that is separate from ourselves. From the basis of this truth, one should make a firm mental decision that whatever is remembered or whatever is forgotten is not "I." It should be your firm conviction that whatever is remembered or forgotten is definitely not you. When there is no memory of Self or forgetfulness of Self, there is just being one's Self, which can be recognized as "Self-Illumination." Therefore, know that the Gross Body is not you, the Subtle Body is not you, and the Causal Body is not you. You are of the nature of Self-Knowledge, the Awareness that "I am the SatChitAnanda of the Great-Causal Body." You must constantly remain the same.

Going by the theory of progressive elimination according to the instruction given above, once the conviction of one's True Nature as "Pure Knowledge, or "I Am" is realized, the four bodies have been collectively considered using the ancient method of investigation and deductive elimination. Up until now, it has been explained that you are not the three bodies. At this point, the Vedas again turn back and now announce that all of the visible appearance of the world is the sport or play (Lila) of your own Consciousness. There is a maxim, or statement, that goes like this: "A thing that is produced is like the thing from which it was produced." For example, when water is turned into ice it is still water. For the one who only sees superficially, water has a flowing tendency while ice is solid. Water has no shape and ice has shape. However, when the substance is known, they are known to be one and the same. According to this maxim it can be understood that the world, and its Lord (Brahman), are the same. This is the teaching in the Vedas.

From the gross point of view, Earth, Water, Light (Fire), Wind (Air), and Sky (Space) appear different, but the difference is only in quality. Ice becomes Water after melting, just as the Earth gets dissolved in Water, and Water dries up by the heat of Fire. Fire, or Light, is contained in the Wind, and Wind gets diffused and simply disappears in the Space. Because the Self is the womb of all these five elements, they all disappear in the Self. If these principles were absolutely different from one another, they would never have dissolved into each other as one, without any remnant of difference. Consequently, the five elements, this gross world, and the subtle world, are only the Self. The Self appears as all of the different characters and species. When a painter paints a tree, a stone, cows, buffaloes, a river, the sky, gods, demons, and human beings, they are all painted with a single thing called paint. In the same way, this spectacle appearing as the world in an infinite number of forms, is nothing but Pure Knowledge. This is the bold and convincing deduction that one must conclude.

One thing has to be mentioned at this point. It must be said that the method itself is of secondary importance, whether it is the method of deductive elimination, or some different or contradictory method, the main purpose of a particular method is to impart the Knowledge of the Self. When an example in math is solved by several different boys, using various methods, and their answer is the same, it becomes compulsory to accept the answer as being right. The answer is what is important, and the method of arriving at the answer is of secondary importance. That is how the Vedas view the methods being used to explain to the aspirant the nature of one's True Self. There is a snag in proving the identity of water and ice, the world and God, and gold and jewelry as being the same. Even if the gold and the ornaments are the same, the ornament could not be manufactured unless the goldsmith puts his skill to work on the gold, and water could only turn into ice by virtue of intense cold. Similarly, although the world and God are the same, the rationale still presents itself that this means that some transformation must have occurred in God. He solidified as Earth, or melted and became Water, then He dried up and became Fire, etc. In this argument, first God became the five elements, and then the world was formed out of the five elements. This is a flaw in the method of deduction, and an objection can be raised in this manner. However, Samartha Ramdas has eradicated even this objection by the sentence, "Oh Man why are you asking about a thing which does not exist at all? The world has not come into existence. The Absolute Parabrahman alone exists."

To forget one's Self is the birth of Illusion, or Maya (Ma means "is not," and Ya means "which"). Maya is that "which is not," which means that she is "that which does not exist." How can one describe this non-existent woman? Is the barren woman's son fair or dark? What is his age, his height, his breadth, his caste? How can we answer these questions about that which has not come into being? To keep a child quiet from crying, he is told "the scarecrow has come." He is quieted by the creation of the tale of a scarecrow that is not really there. After the child becomes quiet, he asks his father "Daddy, what did the scarecrow look like? How long was his beard and how long was his mustache? How big were his nose, eyes, and teeth?" What answer can the father give? Until he responds the child is not going to keep quiet. At such time, the father has to stretch the nose of the scarecrow as far as Rameshwara, and his feet up to the Netherworld, and his head has to reach the sky. Thus, saying whatever he likes, he draws a frightening picture of the scarecrow saying, "he is like this, and like that, etc., so do not cry again." This kind of description alone will match the description of Maya.

The non-existent Maya exists, and she has created this world. The Vedas tried to explain to the Jivas, the human beings, how this world was created according to the capacity of their understanding. The Vedas somehow trace the source of Maya and the world. "This is just the way it happened." It can be seen that the reasoning used in the deductive elimination method at times contradicts some other theory or method. Yet, instead of accusing the Vedas that since they tell one thing to A, and another to B, that they are deceptive and telling wrong things, it must be said that the Vedas have explained the "Knowledge of the Self" to all. By using different methods according to the capacity of the aspirant's intellect, the Vedas have eradicated their Illusion, and as to who was deceptive, the aspirants were deceiving themselves as to the real nature of this world. The mother gives wheat porridge to one child and gives roti (a type of flat bread) to another child who is suffering from indigestion. Can you call this mother partial? That mother knows which food is beneficial according to the capacity of each child's digestion. Similarly, with regard to the Vedas, different methods are used for the different types of aspirants. They differ in intellect but they are suffering from the same disease of Samsara (belief in mundane objective existence).

"Bhava Roga" means the disease that created the idea that the world has been created. To treat this disease, the Vedas and various scriptures had to give explanation in different ways according to the aspirant's capability of understanding. Even if a fever is only one symptom, a clever doctor will give different medications according to the physical condition of the patient. The doctor's goal is only the restoration of good health. There might be different medications but there is no difference in the ideology. One medicine suiting one patient may not suit another patient who has a different physical condition. Similarly, spiritual instructions given to one aspirant may not appeal to another. The knowledge or advice given to an aspirant who has a certain background may not be suitable for who another who has a different background. There is no fault regarding the methods that Mother Shruti (the Vedas) gives. The faults are in the mental disposition of the aspirants at the time the exposition is made. Mother Shruti's final goal is to make all children attain Self-Knowledge. Therefore the aspirant should abandon the faultfinding attitude, and fulfill oneself by achieving the goal of acquiring Self-Knowledge.

Chapter 4: The Great-Causal Body - "I Am"

Up to this point in the text, the explanation has focused on the definition of the four bodies. Now we will see how "Knowledge" arises in these four bodies. To gain the knowledge of objects with sight through the Gross Body, it is necessarily implied that all of the four bodies are instrumental in bringing this about. If we take into consideration a pair of eyes that are drawn in a picture, it is obvious to us that those eyes cannot see an object. In the same way, the physical eyes alone cannot see an object without the help of the subtle eye of the intellect. For example, we see a mango, or have the knowledge that "this is a mango," but what would happen if we were only to just see what the physical eyes alone see? Of course, the physical eye should also see the object as a mango. However, it does not happen like that. Behind the physical eye is the subtle eye of the intellect whose help is sought to know the "mango."

However, even this combination of the physical eye and the subtle intellect is not sufficient. If these two do not have the support of the Causal Body, the intellect is dead. The Causal Body functions in various ways, like space, sky, the void, distance, etc. The intellect needs the background of space in order to function. So, now there is the eye, the intellect, and space in the form of the Causal Body, but if there is no witness, in the form of the Great-Causal body (Consciousness; "I Am") to connect these three, there is no knowledge of anything.

Thus, in order to get the knowledge of objects, it is necessary for all four of these bodies to be present. However, if we look progressively from one body to the next, it needs to be pointed out that in order to know the activity or changes in the Subtle Body, the Physical Body is not necessary. Additionally, the activity or changes that occur in the Subtle Body such as attraction and repulsion, thirst and hunger, and pleasure and pain, can be known only with the aid of the Causal and Great-Causal Bodies. However, looking in the other direction, in order for knowledge to arise in the Causal Body, the help of the Gross and the Subtle Bodies is not required. At this stage in the explanation, it must be made clear that knowledge on any level is always dependent upon the Great-Causal Body.

For gaining knowledge in the Causal Body, the elements of the Subtle Body (mind, intellect, thinking, prana, and the senses) are of absolutely no use. The elements of the Subtle Body only have influence over the Gross and Subtle Bodies. The field of the Causal Body is entirely different from the Gross and Subtle Bodies, and nothing from them can ever step into it. The question naturally arises at this point, "If this is the case, how then, can one enter into the Great-Causal Body?" It is a fact that the scope of the mind and intellect is limited only to the Subtle Body and they do not have the capacity to enter the further two bodies, the Causal Body, and the Great-Causal Body.

At this point, it must be stated that the "Knowledge" of the Great-Causal Body (Turya) is absolutely "Self-Sufficient." It stands on its own, and has no dependency or expectation of help from the previous three bodies mentioned earlier. This Knowledge is "Self-Luminous." By way of analogy, even though the eye sees all objects, no object can see the eye. No one feels the need of the light of a lamp to see the sun. Similarly, nobody is capable of seeing this "King of Knowledge," which is the eye of the eye.

This "Knowledge" proves its own existence by its own luminosity. Even though the eye cannot see itself, anyone who has eyes never has doubts as to whether he has eyes or not. He can see because he has eyes. This type of certainty naturally abides in him. Similarly, one has knowledge of oneself while witnessing someone or something other than oneself. In order to see our eyes, we need a mirror in order to see the reflection of the eyes. That objective knowledge is only the "reflected knowledge" of the eyes. However, the "Knowledge" of the Great-Causal Body proves its own existence by witnessing everything other than itself. For its proof of existence, no other evidence is required.

This Knowledge of the Great-Causal Body is "all-pervading," and yet, it is as if it were invisible from the ignorant being's point of view. Instead of seeing the "Knowledge" of the Great-Causal Body, for him the Gross Body, which in proportion is like a poppy seed in the ocean, has become the biggest thing of all. The ways of this world are indeed perverse. It has become our habit that when looking at a smaller thing, that which is objective, we forget the bigger thing, that which is subjective. We abandon that which is "Self-Proving," and "Self-Sufficient," and praise artificial things. It is like when words of praise are given to beautiful electric lights, yet we fail to give the same praise to the light of the sun, or when we look at the pictures painted on a wall and forget the wall itself. The process is such that even when we look at a wall, we forget the house itself, and when we discover objects in the light, we forget about the light, and when we are reading letters written on a piece of paper, we are not conscious of the paper at all.

What actually happens in this process is that in spite of the fact that the pervading substance is infinitely bigger, when we pay attention to the pervaded object we forget the pervading substance. (The examples of gold and the ornaments, or earth and the wall are commonly used to illustrate this point.) The Gross is pervaded by the Subtle, the Subtle is pervaded by the Causal, and the Causal is pervaded by the Great-Causal (Consciousness, or Knowledge). However, even with this being the case, the "Knowledge" of the Great-Causal Body cannot be seen because everyone's attention is focused on the Gross, and that which is objective. When the narrow focus of the aspirant widens, becoming that which is all-pervading, then one will have the vision of Truth, the "Infinite Knowledge" that covers and envelopes the vastness of Space.

Although the Knowledge that abides in the Great-Causal Body is the destroyer of the Causal Body (Ignorance), it cannot destroy the Gross and Subtle Bodies. The ordinary and superficial objective knowledge that is gained through the Gross and Subtle Bodies is not the destroyer of Ignorance. Only that extraordinary unique "Knowledge" of the Great-Causal Body is the opponent of Ignorance. Ignorance is actually sustained by ordinary objective knowledge. It is only after achieving that Knowledge which is original, that Ignorance vanishes. However, at the same time, the functioning of the Gross and Subtle Bodies does not stop.

Just as the Gross and Subtle Body's inherent activities function for an ignorant man, these activities also continue to function for the Jnani after he has gained "Self-Knowledge." It is similar to the analogy of how the objects that are invisible in darkness are seen when the darkness is destroyed by the light of a lamp. The light destroys the darkness, but not the objects themselves. It is by the power of the light that the objects become known. It is only the darkness that is destroyed while the objects are illuminated. In the same way, when one gains Self-Knowledge, the darkness of Ignorance is completely eradicated, yet the Gross and Subtle Bodies continue functioning.

In the natural progression of this exposition, the question arises, "In the Light of the Knowledge of the Great-Causal Body, and with the destruction of Ignorance, will the Causal Body cease functioning? Let us give this point some thought. Ignorance has many forms such as sky, space, point of contact, distance, etc. After gaining Self-Knowledge it is true that Ignorance is destroyed. In this Self-Knowledge, all impulses or activity (movement) appear in space as either subtle or gross desires. These impulses will not arise at all unless the space is first created.

So what happens is this: When one looks at these bodies after gaining Self-Knowledge, the four bodies appear, or are viewed, in reverse order from the sequence that was used when each body was being transcended in the process of arriving at "Self-Knowledge." First Self-Knowledge ("I Am"), then the Causal Body in the form of space, then the Subtle Body, and after that, the Gross Body, all readily appear and take form. However, before the activities and functioning of the Gross and Subtle Bodies become apparent, although the Ignorance in the Causal Body has been destroyed, out of necessity the Causal Body establishes a "step of space" between the Subtle Body, and the Great-Causal Body.

Chapter 5: The Appearance of the World

When "Knowledge" begins to stir, activity or motion arises, and the Causal Body in the form of the "Space of Consciousness," or Chidakash, is simultaneously created. Then in sequence comes the Subtle Body, and then, the Gross Body appears. In the method of gaining Self-Knowledge that has been expounded previously, the four steps that are ascended in sequence are:

1) The Gross Physical Body
2) The Subtle Body
3) The Causal Body
4) The Great-Causal Body

Now the same sequence is reversed:

1) The Great-Causal Body
2) The Causal Body
3) The Subtle Body
4) The Gross Physical Body

Instead of Knowledge abiding peacefully within itself, it begins to stir and begins its downward descent. The last two steps, those of the Subtle Body and the Gross Body, cannot be stepped upon unless the third step, the "Causal Body" is first stepped upon. Stepping down from this "Causal State," the last two steps, the Subtle and Gross Bodies arise, and it is on these steps alone that the appearance of the world is felt.

Ultimately what happens is this: The Knowledge that contains the appearance of the world has not been able to completely destroy Ignorance. Think about how light destroys darkness, thus giving us the knowledge of objects which were previously unknown because of the darkness. Similarly, the world appears only because the Causal Body has sustained it, or preserved it, in Space. As long as the appearance of the world is felt by either the Jnani (one who has realized the Self), or an ignorant one, it must be understood that Ignorance is still lurking in one form or another. The difference being that Ignorance does not appear to a Jnani in that particular form (The Jnani experiences Ignorance as

Knowledge). Unless Knowledge dies, Ignorance does not die. Knowledge and Ignorance are Siamese twins born of Illusion (Maya). They are both born, and both die, at the same time. If one is there, the other lives on, and when one dies the other is no more. Since this is the Truth, we will see how Knowledge itself dies. Before the Knowledge in the Great-Causal Body dies, the bodies that are below it must all die. These four bodies die in sequence. When looking at a dying man, we do nothing but look at him. We do not die with him. In the same way, we can calmly look within ourselves at how these four bodies die.

One principle that can be easily noticed about death, is that when growth stops, dissolution begins. The meaning of this statement is that whenever something stops growing, it starts disintegrating and follows the path of death. It is unnecessary to do any work for death. Destruction is inherent in growth. In birth, there is death, and in death, there is birth. This is the tradition of birth and death. An object that is born dies its own death, even though there may apparently be some other reason. The root cause of death is nothing other than birth. These four bodies have come upon the "Pure Nature" and they have to die. How do they die? We shall see. The death of the Physical Gross Body according to the principle of "where there is growth, there is destruction" can never be avoided. If not today, at least after one hundred years, or some length of time, whatever it may be. The Gross Body grows until the age of twenty-five or so, and after that, the body begins disintegrating and slowly walks along the "Highway of Death," until one day it becomes a victim of death. As the Gross Body is only the physical form of the Subtle Body, it can be said that it has no separate independent existence. A tree in its gross form is nothing but the result of its seed, which is the subtle form. Both forms of this tree automatically die off.

The Subtle Body is the seed of birth and death. This seed does not get destroyed as easily as a tree. Its growth is so enormous that if it is not sought out and destroyed by man's effort, it will keep on growing indefinitely. This growth becomes the cause of an infinite number of gross bodies. This is what puts a being through births in 8.4 million species. When the growth of the Physical Body naturally stops, the Subtle Body does not stop growing. It is here, that one feels the need for a Sadguru in order to understand how to stop the growth of the Subtle Body. Arresting the growth of the Subtle Body of imagination and doubts means giving up dreams and desires. Desires, dreams, worries, imagination, etc. are the products of the mind. The task of breaking them can be done only with one's own mind. Whatever is created by the mind cannot be destroyed by the hand, and conversely whatever is created by the hand cannot be destroyed by the mind. Whenever we try to forcefully break up these dreams and desires, their number only seems to grow. The mind is frivolously disrespectful. When we try to curb it, it becomes more agitated. Therefore, to stop the growth of the mind, the Sadguru gives us the remedy. "If you try to keep quiet, gradually the imagination and doubts dissolve." When a small infant is sleeping, if you observe its eyes for some time you can easily learn a lesson from him how to stay quiet. When going to sleep, you will see how easily the infant slips into sleep, forgetting himself. While you are looking at the baby, you can also slip into the state of forgetfulness devoid of imaginings, dreams, desires, worries, and doubts.

While a thorn can be taken out by the trick of using another thorn, the mind can only be broken with the mind. Birth and death, or appearing and disappearing, are the two opposite sides of the same state of Consciousness. When one comes, the other goes, and conversely when one goes, the other comes. Death dies its own death like the demon Bhasmasura who put his hand on his own head thereby destroying himself. Thus, when the mind is broken the state that is the Causal Body in the form of Forgetfulness gets completely exposed, and the aspirant gets the Knowledge of that state called "Forgetfulness." The remedy is to diligently practice remembering the instruction, or the repetition of the mantra given by the Guru. Once one begins to stop the growth of the mind, the mind slowly goes along the path of death, and can gradually be completely annihilated. Moreover, one's study and putting into practice the teaching learned from the Sadguru have to be persistent. For example, once a tree starts drying up, even if one tries to keep it green, it will in due time start breaking up, then become uprooted, and eventually fall. Even if one puts plasters on the top of it, paints it, and tries to repair it again and again, a time will come when it comes crumbling down. In the same way, if the mind is constantly stopped from growing, one day it will automatically become tired and break up. However, the aspirant should not become tired of practicing.

In this way, by persistent practice, the next body, the Causal Body, becomes exposed after the death of the Subtle Body. Once the curtain of the Subtle Body is destroyed, it ceases functioning as a covering over the

Causal Body, and the Causal Body automatically becomes exposed. Now let us see how the Causal Body dies. The Causal Body is the producer, or the father, of the Subtle Body. Whenever any state comes uninvited (the Causal Body is not invited) it is experienced for a short time, and once the flood of it recedes it is not remembered. The state of it while it is coming is forceful and growing, yet once the flood ebbs away, it is not even remembered. After having submerged everything for a short period of time, it begins to dissipate, and at last it becomes as if it were not there at all and completely disappears. When a human being is getting roasted in the hot sun and then moves under the cool shade of a tree, at that very moment the flood of cool peace comes to him with such force that he lets out "laugh" as an expression of joy. This shows that the flood of peace is overflowing from the inside as well as outside of him. However, after some time, that "laugh" automatically passes and he lies quietly unaware of his surroundings. Similarly, when the subtle qualities of the Subtle Body such as its hurry and its struggle, becomes comparatively less, forgetfulness in the form of the peaceful void of the Causal Body is automatically forgotten. When this negative state is negated, it results only in negation. To kill it does not require a sword of a positive statement of the "I Am." Shri Samartha Ramdas made this clear by the statement, "The negative is negated by its own negation."

When the state of forgetfulness is dissolved, the Fourth Body, the state of Knowledge that is the Turya State becomes exposed automatically (Turyasvastha - consciousness of "Consciousness"). This state of Knowledge comes to a being with the help of what? It comes in relationship with the state of Ignorance. But even this state of Knowledge, although very powerful, also dissolves eventually. When one attains Knowledge, it is necessary that the Knowledge also must be dissolved. That which comes, has to go. As Ignorance comes, likewise, Knowledge comes. Thus when the Knowledge that is the Great-Causal Body dies, Parabrahman, which is inherent in all of the four bodies, is exposed. This Parabrahman, is "That" which is never born, and never ever dies. After each respective body dies, "That One" who sees the death of all of these bodies, yet remains, is your Real Nature.

Experiencing the Castes in a Human Being

Lord Krishna said in the Bhagavad Gita, "I have created four types of castes." This can be a subject of experience for any human being in his own self. "My creation is divided into four parts and these parts are divided according to their quality and Karma (activity). The four castes are Brahmana (Brahmin; Priest), Kshatriya (Warrior), Vaishya (Merchant), and Shudra (Laborer)." The four bodies can be viewed along the same lines. The Great-Causal Body is of the Brahmin Caste, the Causal Body is of the Warrior Caste, the Subtle Body is of the Merchant Caste, and the Gross Body is of the Laborer Caste. In this way, Paramatman was dispersed into these parts within Himself. The Gross Body is heavy and is an instrument used for service and labor, and therefore it is the Shudra (laborer) Caste. Sitting on a mattress in the Gross Body, taking a balance in hand, and managing the business of the whole world, is the intellect (Buddhi) who compares things as good and bad, big and small, and employs the "laborer" (Gross Body) as a servant to gets things done as he likes, because he is the master. For this reason, this Subtle Body is the Vaishya (merchant) Caste. Now look at the brave actions of the Causal Body. The Causal Body establishes his kingdom by swallowing up the entire wealth in the form of the world that was accumulated on the strength of the capital of desires, imagination, dreams, and doubts. It also swallows up the servants in the form of the Gross and Subtle Bodies. This causality which is one of total destruction is the attitude of a warrior, and therefore the state of the Causal Body is that of the Kshatriya (warrior) Caste.

Now, what remains is only the Great-Causal Body (Brahmin caste). In this body, there is a complete neglect of all the other three bodies. "I have nothing to do with the Gross Body, which puts in hard labor and dies. Neither do I have anything to do with that merchant in the form of intellect, who trades in ideas and dreams, and spreads the vast panorama of the world. I have also nothing to do with the warrior in the form of the Causal Body who sits quietly as if nothing has happened after killing both the subtle and gross bodies. They all may do nothing, or let the Gross Body groan under hard labor, and let the Subtle Body do business with the world, and let the Causal Body wage war against these two. What have I do to with any of these?" There is a saying, "Think of the

Self (Rama) and let the world fight." Knowing this very well, the Great-Causal Body went on announcing the Vedic words "I am Brahman, Aham Brahmasmi," and sat quietly on his own ground, reaching the high stage of Brahmanhood. This Brahmana (Brahmin) is very orthodox about the touch of another caste and cannot tolerate the touch of another body. The other bodies hold the Great-Causal Body in high esteem and smear their heads with the dust of his feet. From the point of view of Vijnana (Supreme Knowledge, or Final Reality), even if this Great-Causal Body becomes polluted by being in contact with the other bodies, it is still the most sacred and highest in all the three worlds (the three bodies, the states of Waking, Deep Sleep, and Ignorance).

The Three Worlds

The Gross Body is the "Material World" (Swarga Loka), the Subtle Body is the "World of Birth and Death" (Mrityu Loka), and the Causal Body is the "Nether World" (Patala Loka). The Great-Causal Body is Brahman. These bodies are divided according to their qualities and these worlds are known by these qualities. The Gross Body is the Swarga Loka and sits on top of, or covers the other worlds. All sorts of external enjoyments and activities are experienced in this world. The wonderful gardens, and the beautiful forests, are created for this world only, and the presiding deity here is Brahma Deva, the Creator, whose main quality is activity, or the Rajas guna. The world below this is the world of death and birth, called Mrityu Loka. In this Loka is a big factory of birth and death where the qualities of appearing and disappearing are continuously being processed. This continuous process is nothing but the rising (birth) and setting (death) of mental modifications. In this way, one is born many times and dies many times during the same day. Everyone should keep for himself an account of his births and rebirths. Every idea produces a visible appearance, and when that idea sets, the appearance also sets. In this way when ideas stop, it is the end of and era, or Kalpanta (the final dissolution of concepts). This is experienced continuously in the Subtle Body. The scriptural writers have accepted the principle of creation and appearance. They stated that as soon as an idea rises, the world rises, and when the idea sets, the world sets. Unless the Subtle Body in the form of Mrityu loka is permanently destroyed and buried, hundreds of eras are sure to rise and set. Therefore, one should die such a death that eliminates the further necessity of being born at all, and live in one's

"True Nature" in such a way that there is no fear of any further experience of dying. Let this be so. Whatever has to happen will happen, but until then, it is certain that this Mrityu Loka keeps its mouth wide open for entry. The abode of the Subtle Body is the "Inner-Mind," which is known as the "Antahkarana," or Consciousness. The presiding deity here is Vishnu, and He nourishes the world. (Note - Antahkarana is a word that has no English equivalent, and is difficult to define. Shri Siddharameshwar used this word frequently in many of his talks, so it warrants some basic explanation. It is generally considered to be the "Seat of Consciousness" that is the spark, or genesis of subtle manifestation arising out of Formless Existence. It is characterized by the motion of the attributes arising out of the attributeless Consciousness. One could say it is the source of the mind, or one's innermost mind, or innermost heart. It is the origin of the assertion of objectivity. It is the mind at its most subtle. Shri Siddharameshwar Maharaj has said about it, "The Inner-Mind of all is the same, while their minds are different." Throughout this text it is translated as "Inner-Mind" for consistency)

The world below that Knowledge of the Inner-Mind is Patala Loka (The Nether World), which is the Causal Body in the form of forgetfulness. In Patala Loka, there is the pitch darkness of Ignorance. The destroyer, "Rudra" (Shiva) who is of the quality of Ignorance, or Tamas, is the presiding deity here. Above these three is the Great-Causal Body, which is the highest body and is therefore higher than these three worlds. The presiding deity here is "Pure Knowledge." That Knowledge rules here and is the God of all gods. From this God, all the worlds are produced, and He is called "The Lord of the three worlds," (Trailokyanath). The Brahmana (Knower of Brahman; Brahmin caste) is the Guru of all the castes and therefore is placed most highly among them. This gives him the status of a Master. This Brahmana does not allow even the shadow of Ignorance to fall on Him. What's more is that he refuses to even become polluted by the mind and intellect. So, give up the idea that He will ever embrace the corpse of the Gross Body. This orthodox clean Brahmin in the form of "Pure Consciousness," or "Universal Cosmic Consciousness" does not allow even a single entrant into his Great-Causal Body. Therefore, it should be understood that none of these bodies, or castes (Warrior/Causal Body; Trader/Subtle Body; Laborer/Gross Body), can ever enter into His abode. This means that the Gross and Subtle Bodies can never enter the Great-Causal Body. These bodies (castes) cannot do anything without the help of this Brahmana, the Primal Knowledge "I

Am." All of their good and bad actions or works only go on the support and strength of this Brahmana. At this time, the Brahmana comes out of his dwelling and accomplishes the work of these three castes. As soon as the work is done, he cleans himself of any traces of them right in front of their doorstep, and only then enters back into His "Own Abode."

Understanding the Knowledge of Self

Brahman is rich with Knowledge. That is why he is called Vedo Narayana (Knowledge that is God residing in All). He knows all the three times (the beginning, the middle, and the end), and He has a characteristic of Sandhya, which is the space between any two thoughts. He is worshipped by all people and therefore is also called the Lord of the World. The people of all castes and creeds worship this God whether they are aware of it or not. The worshipper may be a Hindu, a Muslim, a Christian, a Jain, a Parsee, or a Buddhist. He may be from any country such as Iran, Turkey, etc., yet he only worships this One God, whoever he may be. He cannot help it. When this God is hungry, all types of food and drink are offered to Him. There are mattresses with cushions made into beds ready for Him to sleep upon. If He feels like traveling, there are cars, airplanes, and many other types of transportation ready for him. To supply Him with fragrant garlands, there are many trees and vines that blossom forth laden with flowers. All servants and attendants are ready to obey Him with folded hands. The wife, children, and palaces are for His entertainment, and they are also His dwelling place. God is dwelling in the innermost heart of all beings, and receiving all of the different kinds of service that are rendered unto Himself. Yet, in spite of His greatness and omnipresence, we consider the body as God, and offer all kinds of services to it. The ignorant people have accepted this wrong idea, and have misunderstood the whole affair. It is this idea that has separated God from His devotee. What is there to be amazed about?

Those who are doing any actions are doing it for no other reason than out of worship rendered to Him. This Great God (Mahadeva) is constantly enjoying the shower of all the objects of the senses in the form of sound, forms, touch, taste, and smell. He receives everything that is of the nature the five instruments of senses of action and the five instruments of knowledge. That devotee is indeed glorious who understands the secret of this Great God, Mahadeva. All acts of such a devotee are naturally dedicated to Brahman. The bees, birds, insects, and even the ants, are performing worship to this God. However, they don't have the intellect to understand this so they cannot be blamed for their ignorance. However, it is unfortunate indeed that the intelligent human being does not understand that all of his daily and occasional actions, are but for the sake of this One God, alone. How very unfortunate this is.

This God is the same as the "King of Knowledge" who while swallowing a mouthful of food, tastes and enjoys it. It is He, who discriminates between fragrance and stench. It is He, who understands which sound is pleasant to the ear and which sound is harsh. It is He who observes the difference between a beautiful, or a fierce and ugly form. It is He who understands the soft or hard touch. He is always present, reigning supreme in every being's heart. How utterly misguided is the idea that we worship any other God than this One. Just think of which God is worshipped when the Christians worship Christ, the Hindus worship Vishnu or Shiva, the Parsees worship their Zoroaster, or the Buddhists their Buddha? Are they not merely worshipping the corpses of these mentioned Gods? However, what is the feeling of the devotee who is worshipping? Ask anyone from any religion "Describe your God," and they will answer "My God is Conscious, Luminous, Solid, Omniscient, Omnipresent, and Omnipotent. He animates all, and owns all. He is without birth, and without death." Will anyone say that his God is a stone, or a rock, or mud, or metal, or heavy, dull, and vacant without Consciousness, or that he is weak, blind, or deaf?

From this, it is clear that whether it is Christ, Vishnu, Buddha, Zoroaster, or whatever God it may be, His nature will be full of Consciousness, and He is full of the "Qualities of God." If anyone possesses all of these qualities, then the indication is that He is the Absolute Paramatman. He is God in the form of "Knowledge" that is present in everyone's heart. This God alone dwelled in Mohammed, and Christ's heart was pervaded by this One God as well. It is only by this God that the quality of Vishnu (The Protector) has been sustained, and not by any other God. For any devotee whomever he may be that worships any God, that worship is the worship of this "One Inner-Self." The obeisance made to any other gods, go to this One God, (Our Own Self Nature), alone. This is the "Absolute Truth."

The forms of all the above-mentioned Gods, are only temples of this "One God." All the names belong to His temples (bodies). He is present in the innermost region of all these forms. He sits in all of the forms of all beings and accepts all of their worship. Whatever actions are done by the Gross Body, and whatever imagination or desires, or concepts and doubts that have crossed the mind happen for the sake of this God, in order to please Him. If you recognize this much, your work is done. All of you are doing something through your body or mind. If you say, "We do not want to do it," you cannot stop from doing it. However, whatever you do, the doer, and enjoyer of your deeds is only God (The Self). This fact alone must be recognized in every movement. All auspicious and inauspicious acts thus become dedicated to Brahman, and the aspirant remains absolutely free. This is what is called the "Sacrifice through Knowledge" (Jnana Yadnya).

When you come and go, speak or swallow, when you give or take, stand or sit, do any action at home or outside, or are in bed enjoying sex, leave off all sense of shame or doership, and think only of God. It is the "One Knowledge" alone is playing at each point. To contemplate on this, means contemplating on God. The body-consciousness has to be turned into Self-Consciousness. The decision that the Self alone is doing all, is itself the state of Liberation. This is the advice given by Samartha Ramdas. Even Saint Tukaram asked for this gift from God. "May I never, never, forget you." Likewise, we also must never forget the Self. Then surely salvation is at your feet. As this rope, in the form of the mind, was twisted in the direction of body-consciousness, it now has to be twisted in the opposite direction of Self-Consciousness. When the rope gets untwisted, the strings will be blown about in the wind, and there will be nothing left to call "rope."

When a screw is screwed in, it has to be turned in the opposite direction to come out. Similarly, with regard to body-consciousness, if the mind which is guided by the intellect is directed towards the Self, it becomes absorbed in the Self. As the mind is directed towards the One God, Lord Rama, it gets absorbed in Rama. The mind itself becomes Rama, and there is nothing left in the form of the mind, inside or out, or anywhere, and it becomes one with the form of Rama. Take this advice, and you will see this for yourself. To better understand just how the "One Pure Knowledge" is playing about, you have only to come out of the house, and look at the moon. With what speed does the Pure Consciousness rush towards the moon out from the window of your mind? See how it pervades the whole sky in a fraction of a second. Try this.

Does the mind have this much speed? The mind received the speed of awareness of the moon, only through the help of this "Knowledge." Wherever the mind goes, Consciousness is already there. What a wonder it is then that the movement of the mind seems stuck in this Consciousness. You only have to open the eyelids, and the "Knowledge" (Consciousness) simultaneously pervades the entire sky, the vastness that contains the multitude of stars, and the moon. Instead of saying that it pervades, it is better to say that it has already pervaded the whole, which is now experienced.

When Consciousness travels from the eye to the moon and one recognizes it to be the moon, this is the objective knowledge. In this example, the moon is the object, and the Consciousness takes its shape immediately upon knowing that it is the moon. If there is a cloud in front of the moon, the Consciousness takes the shape of the cloud, and is viewed as that object. Thus, Consciousness pervades the cloud and knows the cloud to be an object.

Chapter 6: Maya and Brahman

Now, try to notice the "crust" of Consciousness that is without an object, the "Pure Knowledge" without the mixture of any objects. That space, which is lying between the eye and the moon, had not come to your notice, yet still it was there pervading, existing in its own nature. That is the pure form of Knowledge. When empty space that is not noticed previously, is purposefully made an object of attention, it becomes the object of attention, as "Space." What can be noticed is Maya, and whatever cannot be seen is "Brahman." While looking at the moon, the space in between did not come to your attention. Therefore, it is Consciousness without an object. If this space is separated, and is made an object of sight this Pure Knowledge is transformed into a zero, because if Space is seen separately, the modification of the mind becomes a void. If there is any difference between Space and Pure Knowledge it is this: To separately look at one's own nature is Space, and when the "looking" is abandoned, it is "Pure Knowledge." Once Pure Knowledge is recognized properly in this manner, even when mixed with any object, it can be selected and recognized. Once pure water is known, even when it is mixed with something else, its existence can be recognized within that mixture. Water is a fluid that can become condensed into ice. Even when water gives up its fluidity and assumes the density of ice, it is still recognized as water in the form of ice. It is not difficult to recognize the wetness in mud as water. Similarly, once Pure Knowledge is known, its steady existence in this moving world in the form of Sat-Chit-Ananda (Being, Consciousness, and Bliss) can also be recognized.

Pure water is devoid of any color, form, taste, or smell. Once this is properly understood, even when water is condensed to assume a dense form, or takes on a hot flavor by adding chilies, or a sweet flavor by adding sugar, or if it becomes fragrant, or takes on a color such as rose, or is used as water in paint, it is quite unmistakably still recognized as pure water, or water minus the form, the taste, the smell, and the color. Thus, by the same method of elimination, even when this Pure Knowledge is conditioned, by subtracting the conditioning and by dividing the form into its respective elements, it will be recognized as absolutely Pure Knowledge alone that fills all form everywhere to the brim. However, before attaining this Pure Knowledge by the method of elimination, if someone accepts the method of enumeration (listing the qualities of God), and goes on chattering about how God alone pervades all beings, and all forms, and that there is nothing else but Rama, and that "the world, and the Lord of the world, are but one," etc., etc., then such babble can never be useful. In contrast to this type of chatter, if one speaks only empty words without having the experience behind them, such as, "I am Brahman," or "the senses do their job, yet I am not the doer," or "there is no sin or virtue at my doorstep," etc., instead of gaining the Self, he will only deceive the Self. In this way, these so-called "Self-discoverers" lose the joy of this world, as well as that of the other world. Saint Kabir said; "He went away as he came." This means that these people die in the same state of consciousness as that in which they were born. They get no benefit from life other than this.

Such worldly scholars take words to be true Self-Knowledge, but has that Truth which is beyond speech ever dawned on an ignorant man? Anyone can say "The senses do the work of the senses, but I am not the senses," or "The mind's qualities are with the mind, and body's qualities are with the body, but what have I to do with them? I am different from these." What is untrue about these utterances? Who is it that understands the Truth? Who is it that has the experience of Truth? Only the one who knows who he is. Of what use are such statements to another? Each one enjoys his own pleasures and bliss. Tukaram said "Each one for himself." Even a parrot can be taught to repeatedly say the words "Brahman is Truth, the world is only an appearance." However, one cannot say that the parrot has understood the Truth of what Brahman is, or what the world is, or even what a statement of Truth is. Where there is no understanding there cannot be the "Bliss of Self-Knowledge."

Let that be as it is. However, an aspirant should not follow the example of one who is an expert with words, yet is a hypocrite. With persistent study, and by applying the method of elimination, one must first come to know what Pure Knowledge is. Knowledge is of different types, such as general, particular, objective knowledge of imagination and doubts, and the Knowledge that is without any thought. The particular, objective, imagining, and doubting types of knowledge are contradictory to Pure Knowledge. When the Pure Consciousness through process of sight takes the shape of an object, one gets objective knowledge, or knowledge which can be of a particular type, or an imagination type, or of a doubt type of knowledge. If the object is gross, it is objective knowledge. If it is only an idea that is subtle, it is idea knowledge, or Savikalpa. This means that when Pure Knowledge takes the shape of an object, an idea, or a thought, it then becomes categorized as particular knowledge. Particular knowledge, being artificial, is by nature transient and lasts only for a very short period of time. It is inherently transient and of an unsteady nature. However, the rule is that particular knowledge must return back into general knowledge, the knowledge that "I Am."

As an example, when we walk, this is considered the common or general speed, and when we increase the speed and start running, it becomes a particular speed. Yet, how long can we run? After sometime the running stops, and soon one assumes the natural speed again. Similar to this, we are naturally very loving and blissful within, and this love within oneself is the general type of love common to all. However, when love is for a son, a friend, or a house, etc., it is an objective and a particular kind of love. Thus, a love that comes, must also go. The love that comes, is of a particular kind which is transient and destructible. The happiness that one gets from objects, also falls into the category of being of a "particular" kind of happiness which only lasts for a very short period of time. A small thing brings in an experience of "particular" type, but while our attention is focused on that, the "One Thing" that pervades it cannot be experienced. The reason is, is that the pervading thing is big and infinite, and in reality we are that same "All-Pervading Brahman." The particular thing is Maya, and the general or common thing is Brahman, and we are "That." When we are focused on the experience of a "particular type" we do not experience the "Love of Our Own Self," nor do we enjoy the "Happiness of the Bliss of the Self."

We will now observe what is called "general knowledge" which is devoid of an object or an idea. There is a slight distance between an outside gross object and the eye, or the mind. That void or space although unknowingly observed, is as if it were not seen, and therefore we have no knowledge or acknowledgment of that space. This intervening knowledge (the space) being "Knowledge" itself, cannot become the object of its own knowledge. How can sugar taste its own sweetness? In the same way, Knowledge does not experience itself as an object. This Knowledge is naturally spread out between the eye and the object, as well as between the intellect and an idea or thought. One should repeatedly take notice of how this general "Pure Knowledge" naturally pervades everywhere before it acknowledges or recognizes an object. This noticing, or "seeing," is not the same as seeing an object such as, "I am the seer of an object," or "I am the thinker, of an idea." It is only seen when one gives up both the seeing as well as the thought that "I am the seer." The instrument of seeing is the eye, and the instrument of knowing a thought is the intellect. "Knowledge" itself can only be seen by setting aside both of these instruments. The instruments of sight and the intellect are of no value here. Any attempt to know Pure Knowledge by means of the eye or intellect is to forget that Pure Knowledge (the unadulterated sense of "I Am) by allowing these instruments to step in. To know Pure Knowledge really means not to know it, and once "known" in this way, the "knower" himself becomes Pure Knowledge.

Samartha Ramdas has said "In trying to meet Pure Knowledge one becomes separated from it. But there is always union with it without trying to meet it." This puzzle is very difficult. Wise men, yogis, and renunciates make a mistake and misinterpret the seen as the seer, when saying "Paramatman is like 'this.' He has four hands. He is like the light of a million suns. He is lustrous. He is dark complexioned. He is like a point, and He is like this and He is like that." etc. They say whatever they like, but by whose knowledge is it that it is stated that "This one is like this, and the other is like that"? That "One" is forgotten completely while they talk of the great things of Realization. However, when the seer is forgotten whatever is seen is "I," which is Brahman. One does not know what to say of this. The brave one sets out to find Brahman but the obstacle in the form of the seen gets in his way. This is the state of the majority of seekers.

Search for the Lost "I"

In a crowd during a pilgrimage, I lost myself and could not find myself even when I tried searching within. Then, I went to the police station and gave them the information that I was lost. At that time a constable came and slapped my cheeks hard until they were red and asked me, "Who is this fellow?" Only then did I become conscious of myself, and was very happy that I was found. This is the very condition of the one that is himself Brahman and yet is in search of Brahman. Where and how can He find Himself? His exact position is such that He is the one who knows everyone but is not known by anyone. The one who tries to know

Him does not know that his own true nature is "Pure Consciousness" so he wanders about in the forest and jungle (searching for that which has never been lost). How amazing this is! How can He, the one who is known only after "the capacity of knowing" has been transcended, be known? Unless one becomes steady within oneself, leaving behind having the desire to know, one cannot have the "Knowledge of Brahman.

There is a story of one foolish fellow who wanted to know what sleep was. Whenever he would start to doze off, he immediately would remember "Aha, now I will catch sleep." With that thought, he would clap his hands and suddenly become completely awake. Repeatedly doing this, the poor fellow became tired and entirely gave up his efforts of trying to catch sleep. Similarly, trying to know Brahman is the same thing. When one gives up trying to "know" Brahman, one becomes Brahman itself. When the Gross and Subtle Bodies are negated the instruments of the mind and intellect are broken up. The aspirant then goes to the state of the Causal Body which is the state of "Forgetfulness." This itself is the Ignorance of the human being. To eradicate this Ignorance, it is necessary to acquire the "Knowledge of Brahman." Therefore, the aspirant tries to get the Knowledge of Brahman with the help of the subtle intellect and that part of Consciousness that is "Pure Knowledge." Saint Shankaracharya (Shri Shankara) has called such a man a great fool. If one tries to know Brahman in this manner with the subtle intellect the Subtle Body will only go on increasing.

When the Subtle Body gets destroyed and one comes to the Causal Body, the one who is trying to know Brahman with the subtle intellect does not become steadied in the Causal Body. Instead he gets pushed back to the Subtle Body with force from the Causal Body and once again comes under the sway of imaginings, concepts, desires, and doubts. If an aspirant dreams, employing the use of words or the mind, he will never progress to where speech and mind cannot enter. Instead, he will go to a lower plane. The aspirant cannot remain as an aspirant, but has to become "One who is Accomplished" (a Siddha). For this, one has to cross over the steps of all of the four bodies. By constant study, one has to enter on the platforms of the four bodies, and clean and clarify them through thorough investigation and deduction. Only then can "The Truth of the Self" be invoked and become fully established. Once this is done, it is certain that the aspirant will become a Siddha.

Up to this point in the text, the exposition regarding the four bodies and the method of study has been explained. The aspirants must also have understood what has been presented. By way of analogy, if a wooden stool with four legs made in the form of the bodies has been constructed, it still is very crude. In order to make it shine properly, more effort has to be made. It is necessary to polish it in order to make it shine so that it can throw off its own light. The procedure for making something is quite different from the procedure of scrubbing and cleaning thereby making it absolutely smooth and appealing. Unless it has been manufactured in that finished condition, it will be not considered finished, nor will it return a fair price. Therefore, before becoming a Siddha, we must be aspirants for some time, persistently polishing the "Pure Knowledge" of the Great-Causal Body. It must be made completely clean.

Chapter 7: Devotion and Devotion After Liberation

We know that the Pure Knowledge in the form of Paramatman pervades every form. After knowing the Self intellectually, the best way of studying it and realizing it fully, is to try to make everyone happy. It is with this practice alone that the Self is seen to be pervading in everything. The whole world is only "Knowledge." Since everything is the Self, by making everyone happy the Self is pleased. In this way, the Truth of the Vedas will be proven and experienced, and Self-Knowledge will become firmly established. The worship of Paramatman with form (Saguna) is the worship of the manifest. Brahmananda (The Bliss of Brahman) manifests in all forms such as that of an insect, ant, dog, or pig. It is the "Supreme Self," Paramatman alone, that pervades everything. Paramatman, which is formless, without any attributes, and not manifest, has become manifest with qualities in the form of the Universe. He is present in those things that are inert, but is experienced clearly in all moving beings. Instead of worshipping lifeless gross objects such as stone and metal idols, it is better to worship the moving, walking, talking God in whom the quality of "Knowledge" is clearly experienced. This is Saguna worship, or worship of the manifest God. What are the qualities in a stone idol? Out of the three qualities, Sattva, Rajas, and Tamas, none of these qualities is found in inert inanimate idols made of stone or metal. However, there is one or more of these qualities found in those manifestations of God who are moving. Therefore, all beings are forms of God.

If one prays sincerely to the Saints or to a good man who is full of Sattva Guna (Knowledge and an inclination towards spiritual understanding), he becomes pleased and grants us our wishes. Yet, if we censure his Tamo Guna, he slaps our face and gives us an experience of a jolt. Therefore, worship the God who is walking and talking. For gaining Knowledge, a stone is of no use. Saint Kabir gave this warning in clear words. He advised all to worship a walking talking God, alone. As soon as the word "worship" is uttered, sandalwood paste, incense, flowers, kumkum, and other various articles of worship come to mind. However, to really worship God means to please and make every being happy. Although Paramatman is "One," existing everywhere, the methods used by devotees to worship Him are different according to their conditioning and how they conceive of Him. A donkey also has God in it, yet if you fold your hands before it in obeisance, it would be like a joke or mischief played on Paramatman. Does it get pleased if you fold your hands before him? If not, then according to what is said above about worship, the worship that is pleasing to another form of God, would not really be the appropriate worship of the donkey. If the donkey were given green grass and clean water to drink, that would be proper worship to God in the form of the donkey. However, worshipping the God who has taken a human form is not just offering it food with the hands, but by pleasing him in a manner that suits him. This would be the proper worship of Paramatman. By giving someone whatever he wants, his heart is pleased, and he feels blessed.

The snake and a scorpion are also forms of God (Narayana), but to worship them consists of making obeisance to them from a distance. This means that they should be left alone to live their own lives. Instead of doing this, if you start embracing them out of devotion, that serpent God will bite you and prove to you that embracing him is not worshipping him. Here someone may raise a doubt, "How could allowing the snake and scorpion to escape alive mean that you are worshipping them? Those beings are wicked and they must be killed." I would say to them that snakes or scorpions do not bite unnecessarily unless they are touched or hurt. However, man is always ready to kill them even if they are off at a considerable distance. Is not the nature of man more wicked than the nature of a snake or a scorpion? Yes, it is, because man has the desire to kill them needlessly. Let the feeling of "The snake and scorpion are of my own nature" be firm, and then see the miracle that happens. The "Self" of a snake or a scorpion is not a stone. When your understanding becomes firm that your Self is the same as the Self in a snake or a scorpion, you will see the Self of the snake is truly one with your own Self, and there will arise no desire in the snake or scorpion to bite you. If one sees a snake as a snake, it also sees an embodied man as an enemy. You will see the same facial expression in the mirror as you have on your face. If you see a bad expression in the reflection in the mirror, is it the fault of the mirror? If you make a smiling face and look in the mirror, you do not need to order the mirror to make a smiling face. Why does the thief rob our house? It is because we also have a continuous desire to rob people in many ways and fill our house. As we develop the feeling of complete renunciation, then that feeling will be reflected in whatever comes before us. Even if you refuse to ask for anything, people are prepared to give up heaps of whatever they have for you. But the one who begs for it, does not get it.

From this discussion a reader may get confused and say, "Maharaj your way of thinking does not seem right. To leave a snake alone after sighting it, or to accept as God the one who pickpockets a bundle of notes and do nothing is something we can never do." Agreed! I would say agreed, a hundred times! Oh aspirant, this cannot be possible because of the habit of many, many, births. This type of worship cannot be achieved all at once. Yet, a beginning can be made in small steps, for example, from the small bugs in the house, instead of the scorpions and snakes. From a petty action like not killing the bugs in the house, one should study the "Oneness of All." See the "Oneness of the Self" in every thing, and every being, and then see what a wondrous experience that you will get. You will then come to have the feeling of the Oneness in all beings, even with those who are more troublesome than the bugs, and gradually "Self-Confidence" and "Self-Experience" increase. This means that one should not proceed with the feeling, "Bugs should not be killed, they should be left alone," but instead the feeling should be that "They are of my own nature, and they are my own forms. Their happiness is my happiness." A mother experiences the feeling of joy by pleasing her child when it suckles at her breast. With that same attitude, one should experience the feeling of satisfaction by allowing the bugs to suck the blood from one's own body. This idea may be difficult to accept, but it is the beginning, or the first lesson on feeling Oneness with all beings.

Gradually and persistently studying this, the earth will be without an enemy, and fearlessness will come your way. In this way, you shall be free from all fear. When an aspirant is free from all doubts and achieves "The Knowledge of the Self," he becomes free. Although this is true, he still cannot experience the "Full Glory of Real Liberation." For example, the achieving of wealth is one thing, while enjoying the status after becoming wealthy, is quite another thing. In the same way, unless a feeling of "The Oneness with All" comes to the Jnani, his Self-Knowledge does not develop or spread. He is like a stingy rich man with his wealth, and he cannot get the "Complete Bliss of Liberation" while alive. Even if one achieves Self-Knowledge, unless he experiences a feeling of "Oneness with All," fearlessness does not come his way. "Complete Bliss" is Fearlessness. Fear is an indication of duality. Fear is a very great impediment in the way of Bliss arising out of Liberation. After achieving

Self-Knowledge, the aspirant should worship Paramatman in the method explained previously. In this manner, dry Self-Knowledge will be moistened with Devotion. A jalebi, which is a kind of sweet that has been fried in ghee, becomes juicy and sweet only after it is fried and then put into syrup. In the same way, the Jnani gets the "Fullness of Life" through "Devotion after Self-Knowledge."

In the game called "Surfati" a player slides first from the lower to the higher house, and then brings back home all that he gets from the other houses. Only then is the game over. By gaining the knowledge all the way from the Gross to the Great-Causal Body, one has to bring this gift of Self-Knowledge back to the lower body in the same way. The factual experience that "The world is nothing but Knowledge" is itself Knowledge becoming the "Final Reality" (Vijnana). It is because of the feeling that there is someone else in the world who is not "I," that we go around night and day with a feeling of anxiety that we should protect our wife, our wealth, and our belongings from the clutches of someone else. In this way, we turn into a "Gasti" or watchman due to the feeling of possessiveness and ownership. However, when one realizes a feeling of "Oneness with Everyone," and the feeling that "I am present everywhere, I am pervading everything." On that day, the "Gasti" becomes "Agasti," the sage who drank the ocean in one sip. This ocean, which is the five elements that make up the entire universe, may not even be enough for one sip.

This is the way in which the devotee who knows the Self becomes fearless while in the body, and enjoys the "Full Celebration" of what is called "Liberation." Now, at this point, we have given the exposition about Self-Knowledge and the "Devotion after Self-Knowledge." We have reached a stage where an aspirant has become the "Self-Knowing Jnani." The end of all of the Knowledge of the Great-Causal Body bears fruit in the seeing of the whole world as oneself. This being true, Saint Ramdas still has called this Knowledge of the Great-Causal Body as being unsteady Brahman when compared with that of Paramatman. Paramatman is steady. It is different from the "Manifest Brahman" (Saguna Brahman), and the "Invisible Brahman" (Nirguna Brahman) associated with the four bodies, and therefore it is "No-Knowledge." So finally the Vedas have said, "Neti, Neti," meaning "not this, not this." "Not this" means it is neither Knowledge nor Ignorance. Unmoving Paramatman is the "Only Truth," it is the "Essence." Nothing else is true.

Saint Samartha Ramdas has expounded upon this conclusion very nicely in **Dasbodh**.

Why is this Knowledge unsteady? Because it is given many names and attributes of masculine, feminine, and neuter gender. It is called Satchitananda, Ishwara, Omkara, Shesha, Narayana, the Primordial Being, and Shiva, etc. These are some of the masculine names. It is called Shakti, Prakriti, Shruti, Shambhavi, Chitkakla, Narayani, etc., and these are some of the feminine names. It is called Nija Rupam (one's own nature), the Great-Causal Body, Pure Knowledge, Brahman, the Empire of Bliss (Anandayatnam), etc., and these are names of the neuter gender. These neuter gender names have come to be known as this "Self-Knowledge." The One who is not any of these, is the Steady, the Immovable, the Essence, the "Real Brahman." The great quality of the Knowledge of the Great-Causal Body is much greater in comparison than the Knowledge in the Gross Body, and by the process of elimination it can be gleaned, and after having been deduced, it can once again be mixed with (as it is all-permeating). However, it cannot be interpreted that the aspirant has achieved the Parabrahman stage by virtue of expertise with the process of elimination, and once again consciously permeating everything.

Parabrahman is "That" from where no one can return. Knowledge has been labeled as "Knowledge," but Brahman really has no name. In the Knowledge of "I Am," there is the mixture of activity or changes in the form of the world. As the mind, called "chitta," undergoes this modification, Knowledge also undergoes modification. Modifications (changes) are a state, or stage. Parabrahman is beyond all modifications. Thus, there is as much difference between "Self-Knowledge," or "I Am" (Jnana), and the Absolute (Vijnana; Parabrahman), as there is a difference between darkness and light. "Where there is a contact between the steady and the unsteady, the intellect is confused," says Shri Samartha Ramdas. According to this statement, the last misunderstanding comes in here. (Contact between the steady and unsteady indicates the presence of a very subtle duality still intact.)

Before the Knowledge ("I Am") dawns, "Forgetfulness" is misunderstood as Knowledge. In the same way, when Jnana, or Knowledge, is under-developed it is misunderstood as Vijnana which is the last stage of the "Absence of modifications" of Parabrahman. When the aspirant mistakes Self-Knowledge, or "I Am" (Jnana) for Vijnana, his progress is arrested there. Samartha Ramdas has compared this type of an undeveloped Jnani to a man who is awakened in a dream, and thinks he is awake. Yet, he is still snoring! "You think that this is wakefulness, but your Illusion has not gone," is the warning given by Shri Samartha to this type of Jnani. That Great-Causal Body, or Turya state in which the Gross and Subtle Bodies are like a dream, is itself like a dream in Vijnana. There is bondage in Ignorance, and liberation in Knowledge, but when both Ignorance and Knowledge are not there, how could the idea of bondage or liberation exist?

The Vedas and scriptures talk up to the point of the Great-Causal Body. Until then, it is the primary premise, or the theory. In the field of Knowledge beyond the Great-Causal Body is the proven final conclusion, or Siddhanta, and the canceling of all that has been laid down is right there. When all phenomena is destroyed, or annihilated, whatever remains is your "Real Nature." It is impossible to describe it in words. Where "the knowledge of words" proves to be Ignorance, where Consciousness becomes non-Consciousness, and where all remedies recommended by the scriptures are only hindrances, you will see for yourself how you reach that highest point. The Sadguru brought you to the threshold and pushed you inside, but the Sadguru cannot show you the beauty, or the panorama within. You have to seize the treasure, the trophy, yourself. Now, after all this has been said, there remains nothing that can be conveyed through words. Words were used for whatever had to be told. That which cannot be conveyed by words has now been entrusted to you. We can only inspire you to be an aspirant, but you have to become a Siddha by yourself. We have reached the end of the book. Words are redundant. One thing is clearly enunciated here, and that is Sadguru Bhajana (All Praises to the Sadguru).

Hari Om Tat Sat.

The End
of
Master Key to Self-Realization

Shri Sadguru Siddharameshwar Maharaj

Master of Self-Realization
An Ultimate Understanding
Volume 1

Spiritual Discourses of His Holiness

Shri Sadguru Siddharameshwar Maharaj

Recorded by Shri Nisargadatta Maharaj

An English Translation of the Marathi Text

"Adhyatma Jnanacha Yogeshwar"

The Spiritual Science of Self-Knowledge

Preface to Master of Self-Realization - Volume 1

Written by Shri Nisargadatta Maharaj

These are discourses, the words being those of my Master. I cannot explain His words and therefore I keep quiet about that. When ego, the "me," becomes silent, "Soham" ("I am He") automatically starts functioning. Soham is endless, limitless, measureless, and is the messenger of Truth, who is self-evident. The message and the messenger are not separate in Him. This messenger is himself the joy that is the enjoyment of the endless. The description of the enjoyment of the Self is called "discourse" in this world, which is really a commentary. The voice of the Master is also called the "Divine Word." His speech, the utterances, are the word, sentences, and the sayings.

The sky is the space, and space is the vast expanse of speech that is the word. Word is the natural quality of the sky as is well known from the days of the Vedas. First there is vibration in the space that is sky (wind), then there is the sound, and then the words appear. The words then become the base of the subsistence of all creatures and things. The sky is the ocean of words of the measureless. That ocean sings in praise to the immeasurable. The purpose of singing in praise of anything is to shed all bad qualities. This "Divine Speech" is doing the work of discarding the duality, or sense of separateness, from the essential "Unity of Existence," through the medium of the mouth of the Master.

At the very moment and in the very place where all reverence towards the Master arises in our heart, the separateness disappears like an insignificant tiny insect. But alas, such things rarely happen! It is seldom that one among billions of people comes to the realization that the Master is Truth itself, Parabrahman, the Ultimate Reality incarnate. When the teaching of the Master is dear to one, and totally acceptable, and when one understands that the feet of the Master (his teachings) are the source of the spontaneous experience of the divine Self within which directs and performs all the actions and functions of the body, and when one holds fast to the feet of the Master within one's heart without a speck of doubt, then unfailingly the stream of the blessings and the bliss of the revered Master flow very naturally from within, which is the movement of the "Life All-Pervading." Where complete trust in the divine feet of the Master is active, the grace of the Bliss of the Master comes to reside in the nature of Spiritual Joy, called "Pralhad." Then, non-duality without the blemish of the separateness of "You" and "I" in the Consciousness flows unhindered. There is no satisfaction other than the Grace of the Master, which is total Self-bliss that is solid and impenetrable.

At the time when the Master (Shri Siddharameshwar Maharaj) was giving his discourses, the writer of this preface was a fresh entrant of the path, and was but a novice. The only acquaintance was that he was introduced to Maharaj and had the opportunity to see Him. The work of listening to the discourses of Maharaj and taking them down in broken sentences was being done by the writer. He was not even knowing whether what he wrote down was correct or not, but the capacity to take down all that he heard was growing, and it can be said that almost all that was heard has been noted in His presence. There were other co-disciples who were learned and had the opportunity of being in the company of Maharaj for many years. They were also taking down the teachings of Maharaj. There are many discourses of Maharaj written by them in their possession. Even then, the writer of this preface has not compared his notes with those of others to verify their accuracy. The writings are as they were heard and written down.

It is now 25 years since Maharaj has left his physical body. During the last two or three years, the writings were read out and correctly re-written. It was intended to publish them but the efforts made for it were not so far successful. However, today, on the 25th death anniversary of Shri Maharaj, this is becoming possible by the good grace of auspicious time. My senior co-disciples who are great and spiritually well experienced, will also publish the lectures of the Master that are in their possession. I say from my conviction of Self-Knowledge that such a Master and such teachings are very rare in this world. I say this out of my faith in the wisdom of our Teacher and my own Self-confidence. These words are expression of my faith. As is one's achievement, so is his experience, so is his contentment and his peace, and so is his satisfaction. All this is the result of one's loyalty. Since my acquaintance with my senior co-disciples, I have always been humble before them and I pray to my Master that I will continue to be so humble before them in the future also.

The reason why I have total reverence for my senior co-disciples is that they somehow managed to keep our Master in Bombay for a long time by offering Him the sweet dish of their devotion and I could have the opportunity to meet the Master who is the "Ocean of Knowledge." They not only had the benefit of seeing Him and serving Him with devotion, but having been liberated through Self-Knowledge, they themselves became the saviors for others. The Cosmos that is the Universal Spirit and Form, abides in Him. It takes refuge in Him, and the senior co-disciples were able to have intimate relationship with Him, and thereby they were saved and became liberators for others. That was and is the imperishable power of having the glimpse (Darshan) of the Master and his teachings. Even those who are simple souls without much learning are purified by having seen only once the "Great Master" who is "The Ocean of Light and Merit," "The Embodiment of Knowledge," "The Knower of Science" and "The Ocean of Wisdom." The sayings and discourses of such a Great Master form the contents of this book. Those who will read them again and again, learn them by heart, and deeply think upon the truthful meaning of his teachings, will become the meaning incarnate, and will themselves become full of the meaning of the Self.

I am putting these words before you as a preface to this book. Every sentence in this book has the potency of giving you the fruit of Self-Realization. One who will read regularly and ponder over these discourses will himself become the channel for the expression of the inherent spirit of these words. The heavenly records contain the imprints of all the Saints and the bevy of Self-Realized "Godmen," their projected schemes, their utterances, their meanings, and the very Life within. The "Realized Ones" truly speak from the fountain of their own experience and there is great conviction in their speech. Their speech has the capacity to discard the ignorance of the ego, and every line in this book has the power to eradicate the reader's ignorance about his True Self and bring forth the True Nature of his Being.

Nisargadatta
Saturday, 4th November, 1961.
Nisargadatta Ashram, Vanamali Bhuvan,
Khetwadi, 10th Lane, Mumbai

1. The Importance of Devotion

Ignorance does not compare to "Enlightened Vision." Ignorance is related to the physical perception. The great statement "Sarvam Khalu Idam Brahma," means "All Things are Brahman." Friends and foes are all Brahman (Reality). Thus, good is Brahman and bad is also Brahman. All the people in the world are slaves of circumstances. Circumstances can compel a man to even pick up dung. Only Devotion (Bhakti) can do away with circumstances. Through "Devotion to God," Knowledge (Jnana) is achieved. A king is bound by the law that he enforces on his subjects. Law should govern our minds. We ourselves should decide whether we should be bound or not. Devotion is the "inner-vision" of wisdom. One who does not have Self-Realization while living is truly lost. One who is ensnared by worldly things is lost in the stream of mundane life. Walk with firm determination on the spiritual path that you have accepted.

Do not be tempted by Illusion (Maya). You must destroy Illusion. Maya dispenses with all people with the same disregard. Only the aspirant whose spiritual practice has remained unfinished gets the human birth and human qualities again. Maya is not afraid of anyone except the one who knows Brahman. Many are the members of the cult of Maya, and very few followers belong to "The Path of Knowledge." You are in essence the "Incarnation of the Divine," and to destroy Illusion is your ordained purpose. Remember that Maya is always keeping watch on you and remain always on guard. Do not lose sight of your origin, your true home. If you want to become beasts like the elephants, the horses, etc., then you may consider this world as your home. Be proud of your "True Nature." Our birth has only the aim of breaking the backbone of worldliness. We have not only to achieve our own Liberation, but we have also to liberate others. If you live with the conviction that you are God, then you will certainly be God.

The one who is without devotion cannot achieve his own good. If you do not follow the "Path of Devotion" while living, you will never achieve freedom. "The one who is awake, achieves, the one who sleeps, loses," is an appropriate saying. Even if you die as a good and pious person, there is no Liberation without devotion. Life without devotion is nothing but deterioration. Saints make their life meaningful while they are living. The one who is liberated while he is living does not worry where his physical body falls at the time of death. The Saint is not born, so he does not die. One who dies while living has transcended birth and death. The "Son of the Guru" (Guru-Putra; one whose consciousness is always connected to that of the Guru) should always use proper discrimination. Live in non-duality. Become aspirants for Truth.

2. Desirelessness and Self-Realization

One who is "steadfast" means one who does not know separateness. To surrender means to give up ego and be humble. In the word "Sharana," "shara" means "arrow," and "na" means "no." The arrow is denoted by shara, which also means the unbending ego. Thus, one who is "Sharana," or who has surrendered, is one who has given up hardness and is devoid of ego. The company of Saints is a very helpful instrument for Liberation. What is heaven? To be born in the company of wise people is itself the attainment of heaven. Consider yourself lucky if your mind becomes fed up with worldly objects. The "Goddess of Sensuality" is very fond of the human sacrifice, and she likes it fried alive! The slaves of the belly cannot have the Glimpse (Darshan) of God. Truly blessed is the one who is completely desireless.

Always remember that we are from the "Abode of God" (Vaikuntha), and that we are Gods entitled to enjoy the Nectar of Immortality. We are but visitors to this foreign town that is this illusory life for just a few days. The only instrument for Liberation is the state of "Desirelessness." Consider it an offering to the all-devouring Death if you have many children. When the crop of Illusion is ripe, Death devours it. Devotion to the "True Guru," the Sadguru, is the birthplace of spirituality. Treat your body as Illusion and thereby fulfill your life. When the disciple escapes from Illusion, the Master is happy. One should satisfy the Master with Devotion (Bhajan; praising the Master). The man who has been illumined by the "Light of Brahman" should be treated as great, even though he may be young or lowly. One who constantly craves after sense objects is immersed in those objects, and one who meditates on the Self (Atman) becomes the Self. Do not say, "I will meditate on God later. I will do it some time later." You should constantly meditate, contemplate, and let your mind dwell on the Self with great love for it. This is the sign of "Self-attainment."

To have no liking for anything other than the Self is the sign of Self-attainment. Meditation on anything other than the Self, is bondage. Always meditate on the "Divine Nature" of your Self. All other things are unreal. Any other concentration except on the Self, who is the Lord, is bondage. Any meditation or thinking except that which is on the very nature of your own being, becomes a tight binding. The "world" by its nature, is the separateness of species. It will never function smoothly. Any fruit except for the Self, is futile. Please think this over deeply. You are attracted to that which is objective because the ego sense never thinks of the true contentment which is found only in the Self. If one truly does something for their own welfare, the sense that "I am an individual" dies because that which exists afterwards is not the individual (Jiva). The individual turns towards sense objects, and in doing so, turns towards sorrow. The objects that appear to be pleasant are really unpleasant. The objects that appear attractive, are actually very destructive and give pain, yet the individual always runs after these objects. Therefore, stop thinking about sense objects and turn to the Path of Devotion.

One must conceive of oneself as a Saint and one who is ready to sacrifice. When the teaching of the Master is assimilated, worldliness is cut away and though such a one may be in the world, he is not a slave to the world. The Sage Shuka said that one should not chase after sense objects, but should remain unattached. Pursuing sense objects hinders spiritual Devotion, even if such Devotion is done with proper attention. One who aspires for Self-Realization should drop the desire for sensual gratification. It is by craving sensual gratification that the Jiva is in a way, "hanged." Meditate only on God who is in your heart. To be devoted to the "One Self" is the real "Alone-ness."

Morning, 18-11-1934

3. Giving Up the Sense of "Mine"

This Knowledge (Jnana) is such that it cannot be understood by merely describing it. To tell someone that sugar is sweet does not enable one to experience its sweetness. One must eat it. Brahman can be understood only by experiencing it, and this is possible only by the Grace of the Sadguru. Only in the right fertile land, the mind of the seeker, can the Grace of the Master come to fruition. One who is a seeker of his own

Self reaps the fruit of the Blessings of the Master. One who understands himself, really "understands," and by Self-Knowledge is "Liberated." He who has understood himself does not need anything, nor does he wish to possess anything.

He who is the "Supreme Self," Paramatman, has no use for Illusion. You are at present very arrogant due to the sense of "mine." You are having two wives who are "wealth" and "woman." The one who says that nothing is possible without money, will not meet God. Money and spouse are meant for the ego, or the individual (Jiva), and not for God (Shiva), because God is formless. He is Pure Spirit. There is a prevailing wrong notion that without having money, devotion for God Almighty is not possible. Really, spirituality has no need for money. When we search ourselves, the Higher Self can be met, and that is where you realize that the Illusion is worthless. Leave behind the ideas of "I" and "mine." To realize that "Nothing is mine" is the very essence of the Grace of the Master. You must think, "I am not my body. The children and the family belong to the body, not to me, the pure unqualified Self." Those who live by the ideas of "I" and "mine" are slaves of Illusion. How can they know the true value of a Saint?

The Saint does not allow Illusion to stand near him. The "Riches of Illusion" do not even compare to the "Riches of Freedom." The Goddess of Prosperity, Laxmi, makes a beggar of the one who seeks after her, but humbly serves the one who does not care for her. The honor is in not demanding anything from the Illusion. To say "I want, I want" is an insult. To demand, is to insult. Not to demand, is to honor. Knowledge (Jnana) does not require anything except renunciation. Make a habit of renouncing everything. Saint Kabir has said, "The mind dies, Illusion dies, and the body also dies, but hope and desire do not die." If hope and desire die, you yourself will be Saint Kabir. When the poison of desire drops away from the mind, then you will drink the Nectar of Immortality. "Let there not be desire for sense objects," says Saint Ramdas. Give up the sense of "mine" and you are free.

Evening, 18-11-1934

4. The Self is the Knower in All Beings

Beingness means "Consciousness," or "Knowledge." The mind attending to other things is what is meant by bondage. The mind when not attending to anything else, is Brahman. When there is no thinking about the objects in the mind, the mind is clean, it is still. That is the state of Brahman. When you are happily asleep, it is natural joy, or Brahman without any emotion. "That" which does not have any state, or attitude, is beyond emotion. It is "You" who is the knower of the entire world, the body, the mind, and the sense organs. That "You" is the "Supreme Self" (Paramatman). To realize Paramatman is the final achievement. This "knowing" is itself a mystery. Drop the desire to pursue sense objects. One who ceases to desire wealth automatically becomes very powerful.

To meditate on Me (the Master) is Freedom. Then you are free from all the sorrow of the mundane and the spiritual life. When the individual (Jiva) leaves the habit of projecting desires, he himself becomes God (Shiva). I give My status to the one who meditates on Me. I send to hell, the one who instead of meditating on Me, thinks only of family and money. Those who desire to have My Power should meditate on Me. I bestow upon them all of My Powers, My Status, and My Selfhood.

Morning, 19-11-1934

5. Self Discovery

One who searches within oneself, achieves Self-Knowledge. You, who are the "Knower of All," are yourself Brahman. Do not hold on to the concept that you are the body. Always think of yourself as Brahman. One who lives as a body will have to suffer the pains of the body. The Sun that is the Self is eclipsed by desires for worldly objects. Be identified with the Sun, the Self, and let go of whatever you have been accumulating up to now. If you give up your attachment to worldly objects while the eclipse is there, and also give up your lust for sensual gratification, then the eclipse will be over. You cannot experience Brahman without you yourself becoming Brahman. (Note - It is a custom among Hindus to give donations to charities and make sacrifices during the time of eclipses.)

Golden is the day for a man when his conceptual images about himself die away. This means that your ego should die. The Master will bless the one who endeavors to search for one's Self. One should not take back what is once given. This means that one should not accept the objects of the senses, after they are renounced. The Supreme Self, Paramatman, is beyond even the state of omni-perception, or being "All-Seeing." If the doer of actions has no sense of being the actor, he is free of the action. He becomes That which is beyond all states. When the knowing of objects, or differentiation, comes to an end, the false pride of "Me," the ego, is destroyed.

Evening, 19-11-1934

6. God is the Supreme Self, Paramatman

If you aspire to be with God, discard Illusion (Maya). The hope that is hidden deep in the innermost layers of your heart and mind is only Illusion. Illusion puts a veil on the Self. The Self is within, and on it, Illusion puts a covering. Brahman is only "Pure Consciousness." The human mind by nature is normally extroverted, focusing objectively. When the mind becomes desireless, and remains so, it is Brahman. However, do not consider the mind to be Brahman. To be constantly thinking about the objects of the senses is to eclipse the Self. When attention is diverted from the Self towards objects, that is called the beginning of the eclipse. That is the Illusion. That is mind.

To remain without thought is Brahman. Naturalness is the sign of Brahman. There is no worry, no lust, and no desire there. In this naturalness, even if one's whole kingdom is lost, the mind does not feel anxiety. When the objective functioning of the mind is over, the natural state comes into being and one becomes steady in the Self. When the worry and concern about worldly life ceases, the eclipse of the Self is over. The Illusion is then seen as the play of God (Vishnu), and is seen to be only Him. The Illusion when seen as only the play of God, makes the mind desireless and free of all worry. The illusion of the individual (Jiva) remains full of cravings and desire. The desire of the individual ego goes even to the level of expecting that one must get a drop of water in the mouth at the time of death. Meanwhile, the Consciousness which is the Self, never cares for the body. Of what use then is the repetition of a name of God or a Mantra at the time of death, for the Self? This is the key of Desirelessness.

How long is this earthly life? One foot is in the grave while the other foot is in the house. What is the use of this family life? This attitude is the sign of Desirelessness. However, for a man who is attached to worldly life, though it is possible that he may die tomorrow, he carries on all his activities as if his life span will be for hundreds of years. The man without desire considers the life span of a hundred thousand years as if but one moment. The attachment in the heart that takes the form of pity towards all the beings is only the illusory play of God, and is nothing but worldliness and worry. We should live for the Supreme Self, Paramatman, and our time should be utilized in the service to Paramatman.

Morning, 20-11-1934

7. Objects of Perception Cease Along With the Perceiver

Seeing with wisdom is to feel that "All is Brahman." You have heard this, but this is not meant to be merely heard. It is meant to be experienced. All beings are essentially of the nature of Brahman. If you start analyzing others, you become one of the analyzed, a separate entity, and this is bondage for you. When you think of another person as a thief, the content of your mind is "thief" because you are thinking of a thief. When you speak about worldly objects you take everything as real, and behave and act accordingly. Yet, when you listen to spiritual instructions, or come to understand them, you rarely keep them in your mind as true. Maintain the attitude that "All is Brahman," and act with the conviction that it is true. Do not keep it dormant in your life by merely saying, "I have heard it." Test it in your life, and see if it is true or not! If you look at everything as being only Paramatman, then you become God (Shiva), but if you see everything as being merely the phenomenal mundane world, then you remain only as an individual (Jiva).

The world appears according to how you look at it. If you look at it as Brahman in various forms, you will see everywhere only Brahman. If you do this, the fever of "me," the pride of ego, dissolves. For example, if there is a wife, then there is a husband, but if there is no wife, whose husband can be there? Because there is the seen, there is the seer. If there is nothing to be seen, how can the seer come into being? If you discard the seen, there is only Brahman. If all of the things in your possession are destroyed, what can the mind think of? When the sense of "I" is immersed, or is drowned, then only Brahman is. The sign of Pure Brahman is that there is no such thing as "Me," or "I," in that state. Whatever is, is only Brahman. What you perceive of objectively as a person, by some name or label, such as Mr. "So-and-so," is not Brahman. If you have not seen who you are yourself, what is the use of going to sacred places of pilgrimage such as Varanasi or some other place? If there is no awakening within to the spiritual nature of one's Self, what is the use of talking about Brahman like a parrot would?

Remove the poison that has affected your mind. You become more experienced according to what you do repeatedly over and over. Everyone has the habit of speaking about sense objects. Drop that habit and speak about the wisdom of Brahman. In that way, by constantly thinking of "That," you become Brahman. You should spend your time discussing Spiritual Knowledge. When you talk of sense objects over and over again, you only become more worldly. The aspirant for Self-Realization should keep relatives and friends close who are interested in these subjects. Do not waste your life talking with others.

It is rare luck to have relatives who are devotees. If you have no Self-Knowledge, what is the use of all worldly activities? The advice given by Saints, who are our "real relatives," is directly applicable to daily living because that advice is a dialogue in Oneness. The Master who shows us "The Path of Liberation" is our real relative. One should tune oneself, like tightening the strings of a Veena (an Indian musical instrument). If the instrument is rightly tuned, its sound will be resonant. Your relationship with the Master should be of that kind. He who helps himself is the truly lucky one.

Evening - 20-11-1934

8. Throw Off Laziness

We are in essence formless, without qualities or form, and full of "Conscious Intelligence" like the sky. This state is called "non-laziness." The body-consciousness, the concept that "I am the body," is the real laziness. You should drop it permanently. Leaving this laziness behind, you should have devotion towards God Hari (Vishnu), and you should be "The Formless God," Shiva, and remain as Shiva.

When you walk on the path for some distance you can see the writing on the signpost and get guidance to further your journey. If you do many various activities for millions of years as an individual (Jiva), you will not get any benefit, but if you become God (Shiva), and then worship God, you will get the fruits of your worship. Be a king and rule. Be God yourself, and worship God. Sometimes, the aspirant becomes lazy while worshipping. Laziness here means falling back to the level of body-consciousness. Worship God by leaving this laziness of body-consciousness. This is required to be done again and again with firm determination. Do not give in to laziness.

Morning, 21-11-1934

9. Self and Non-Self

Anxiety accompanies desire. As long as the mind is full of desire, anxiety will be there. When desire ceases, anxiety is no more. While walking on the street many things are visible, yet we have no attachment to them. However, once the sense of "mine" is conceived, desire arises and one immediately becomes pre-occupied with objects. To feel that something is "mine" is itself bondage. What is truly ours in the physical body? For the body, the air that is inside goes out and the air outside comes in. What belongs to you in this process? In the area of about two feet around the body, there are continuous currents of air. One who can see subtly can be aware of this.

Many special days and festivals are coming and going, and you think that the things in the world are permanent and yours, but you do not see that you really exist prior to all of these objective things. When the perception of objects ends, the desire for the objects also ends, and it does not matter whether objects are existing or not. If you think that is only made from dust is yours, you immediately become worldly. The mind when dwelling on the Self, is desireless, and when focusing on the physical body as "me" or "mine," is full of desire.

Strange indeed is this creation consisting of the five elements. The "One Being" that plays in all bodies is the all-pervading "Universal Self." Understand that "All is Brahman." The example of the ring and the gold is commonly used. If you consider the ring as gold, then only the gold is seen as the substance, but if you look at it as a ring, it is considered as a separate object. Water is water, both in the ocean and the pitcher, but water in the pitcher is separate if you keep the pitcher separate, so do not keep it separate. Know that "All is Brahman."

Consider all to be your friends so that there is no duality or dislike in the mind. When you repeat the statement that "All is Brahman," then why does your attitude not change accordingly? That is because your thinking is warped by the notions of virtue and vice, and you adopt a critical or dualistic attitude. One who pleases you is considered a good person, and the other you consider as bad. However, are there not many others who call that so-called "bad" person, as good? Moreover, to what extent are you yourself good? Are there not some people who take you to be a bad person? Even God is considered in terms of good or bad by many people.

The wise man says that since all are slaves of circumstances (living according to the destiny of the body), how can we differentiate between good and bad people. Circumstances have created the various castes such as carpenters and cobblers, etc. The labels of various occupations have made us think of people as separate. Otherwise, where is the distinction of castes, etc.? Nobody is bad or good. All bodies are subject to circumstances. The stages of childhood, youth, and old-age are there for everyone. The young man will have a black mustache and not a white one, while the old toothless man cannot gulp down morsels of hard food, etc. In short, do not ridicule others. All are subject to circumstances. One may keep long hair on the head, or wear a beard, it is all a matter of one's preference. Why should you hate anyone because of such things? Consider the one who criticizes you, or blames you, as a kind person. Keep an open loving attitude towards those who give you a lot of trouble, and remain without enmity. Only then, will you be as Brahman.

Anxiety kills us very early. The one who worries dies with that worry, and hatred is a very heavy burden to bear. Vishwamitra, who was a bachelor and had done a great amount of spiritual practice, became ready even to murder when he went to kill the Sage Vasishtha out of envy and jealousy. It is said that the bag of saffron (a precious delicate tasting spice) become Asafoetida (a pungent spice with strong taste and odor), only because of being in its vicinity. When pride disappears, the thorn that irritates you drops away. Kill pride and then you will yourself become the "Divine Sage," or "Brahmarishi." Prostrate before the one who hates you. If you decide that someone is bad, then you yourself become bad. One who has no enmity is himself Brahman. To quarrel indicates misunderstanding. The duality of differentiating between sense objects must end. Do not think in terms of hatred or enmity, or good and bad. It is only then that you become as Brahman. Have no enmity towards anyone.

Evening, 21-11-1934

10. True Renunciation

Attachment to pleasure is bondage. If you say, "I don't need anything," all problems come to an end. He who says, "I want" does not get anything. He who says, "I don't want" gets everything. The lion is trapped due to attachment, and the elephant is also bound due to its attachment to food. This is Illusion (Maya). This is what is called bondage. A man becomes pitiable due to his attachment to woman. He is trapped in the snare of attraction because for days he is longing for pleasure, and it becomes his need. When the fascination with his attachment is increased, he becomes a slave, just as if he is chained. One becomes tied down as if handcuffed only because desire is increased. If that desire is replaced by "Desirelessness," then the bondage is broken.

This is the nature of the instruction that Lord Krishna gave to His disciple Uddhava. Then, Uddhava asked Krishna as to how one could be completely desireless. He wanted to have "Pure Desirelessness" born out of the Sattva quality. If one becomes desireless upon hearing from others the bad effects of attachment, this detachment is called "Tamasic Desirelessness." If something is sacrificed for the purpose of gaining Self-Knowledge then that state of detachment is "Rajasic Desirelessness" born out of the Rajas quality. When the mind is convinced that all objects are illusory, this is what is call "Sattvic Desirelessness." With pure "Sattvic

Desirelessness," one feels like laughing at the idea of relinquishing anything. Where was there really ever any bondage to relinquish? You have tied yourself up with ropes that are non-existent. You may say that you have dropped the shackles, but you were only holding fast to that which was not even yours. What was ever yours? What have you dropped? This is what is called the true, "Pure Sattvic Renunciation." If there was nothing ever there to be dropped, then what is there to be let go of?

A rat can very well say that he has relinquished the article of food which is in front of a cat, but his boasting is useless because the moment that he tries to go for the food, he is sure to die. But still, he says that it is renounced. There was death in trying to eat it. He is alive because he did not try. Not to be proud of renunciation is also an important aspect of renunciation. If you act according to your natural state, then what sacrifice have you made? Who was this "I," and how was this "I" ever related to "whom"? Who was "mine," and what was ever "mine"? It was all only Illusion. A story is told about a person who once heard that there is great merit in giving dinner to one thousand priests (Brahmins), but he had not sufficient money for that purpose. So, in order to earn merit, he gave an amount of ten rupees to only one Brahmin and did not arrange for the dinner for one thousand people. In this way, he satisfied only one Brahmin with those 10 rupees. Now, what kind of sacrifice was this since he avoided making the one thousand-dinner offering?

Take note that those who make declarations about the renunciation that they have done are really only hypocrites. There was once a king named Bhartruhari who was thinking that he had renounced everything. Instead of concentrating his mind upon God, he started to concentrate on having done the action of renunciation. Such sacrifice is not true sacrifice. Let there not be any pride that you have renounced. One who says that he has renounced, is not the real renunciate.

Morning - 22-11-1934

11. The War Between Rama and Ravana

In the Hindu epic tale, the ***Ramayana***, Rama is the Self (Atman). The name of the demon king from the story, "Ravana," means ten mouths, which symbolizes the ten sense organs (5 organs of knowledge; eyes, ears, nose, tongue, and skin, and the 5 organs of action; hands, feet, mouth, genitals, and anus), and all of the objects in the world are the demons making up the army of the demon king. All of these objects try to defeat the Self, Rama. The mind is the monkey Hanuman. "Right thoughts" are Rama's army, and "Peace," or Sita, is his devoted wife. Ravana has taken Sita away and kept her captive by force. When the knowledge of sense objects disappears, then the army of Ravana dies and one acquires Peace, or Sita. All of the various sense objects make up the army of Ravana. Ravana intended to wage a war with the strength of his army and defeat Rama.

Rama's brother, Laxman, is the chief of the army of Rama. "Laksh" means attention, and "mana" means mind. Meditation should be done with full attention of the mind. Laxman is the father-in-law of Indrajit (the ego), and in his last birth, Lakshaman was the helper of Ravana. Indrajit had received a special favor from Ravana that he would meet his death only at the hands of his in-law, and not in any other way. Indrajit is the "I," the ego. When your mind desires to gain the "Knowledge of Brahman," then the ego, Indrajit, dies. When fixing the attention of the mind towards Brahman, the ego dies, and when fixing the attention of the mind towards the sense objects, one remains the servant of the senses, or Ravana.

Ravana was deathless. Shiva had endowed him with the power of dying only by his own wish. When all of his army was destroyed, he thought, "What is the purpose of imprisoning Sita here? If I die at the hands of Rama, I will be liberated. I have not imprisoned Sita in order to save my life, I have imprisoned her so that I will attain Liberation. I will not rule over my kingdom by simply surrendering to Rama. I must die."

Ravana said to Rama, "I aim my arrow at you in order to tease and provoke you." He did so and as he did, he died. By analogy, pride is Ravana, who will only die by his own will. This is the individual, the Jiva. By listening to Vedanta (non-dual spiritual teaching), the individual becomes ready to die. The real nature of the Self is covered over by the sense of "I Am," which is subtle pride. This pride is like Rahu who has eclipsed everything (In Vedic astrology, Rahu eclipses the Sun. In this example, the Sun is symbolic of the Self). When pride says, "I am Brahman," all that this is referring to is the body, which has a name. This is what is called the eclipsing of the "True Self." While it is the body with a name that is born, the individual thinks that it is he, the jiva, who is born. If you were only your body, you would die when it dies. You are the knower of the body, you are not the body. The body dies. You do not.

Laxman destroyed the army of Ravana with the help of Hanuman's army. Through correct thinking, the mind comes to understand that what appears to be real, is not real. Laxman (correctly focusing the attention of the mind) understood this, and the army of Ravana was destroyed. The word Satya-nash means destruction. The meaning of this is that it does not exist, although it appears to be real. Correct thoughts are like monkeys. Hanuman's (the mind's) monkey army of "right thoughts" destroyed the army of Ravana (the sense objects).

When Ravana died, the "Kingdom of Rama" became possible. The peace personified by Sita came back home. You should keep fighting by wielding the sword of wisdom (of spiritual instruction) and by repeating the name of Rama (meditation). All of the gods had run away due to their fear of Ravana. Ravana was thereby enjoying supreme power. The epic Ramayana is written in order to impart "Spiritual Knowledge." There is neither anger nor lust in the Kingdom of Rama, there is only peace and happiness. The Self is the Kingdom of Rama. By understanding correctly all becomes Rama. If Rama is victorious, the gods shower flowers, and if Ravana is victorious, all of the demons start dancing. Objects in the world are the demons, and the state of mind without a single object in it is the "Self who is God," or Atmaram.

Evening, 22-11-1934

12. Be Disinterested in Objective Things

We are our own worst enemies. It is we who hinder our own happiness. You are the cause of your own conceptual knowledge. Whatever you do will only be achieved in this "World Illusion." Desire is bondage, and the absence of desire is Brahman. Meditate on the Self in order to do away with attachment. If we continually remain in our True

Nature, desire for objects in the Illusion drops off. The Supreme Self, Paramatman, has no need for anything. He does not need any kicking. It is your body that deserves that. You should live with this fact in mind.

One must learn to discriminate between Self (Atman; the seer) and non-Self (transient appearances). Once you are convinced that your nature is bliss and that all objects are also only bliss, then you are naturally disinterested in pursuing objective things. You then have a mind that says "I don't want anything." You become ashamed to desire anything from this world, much in the same way that a woman will not desire a mustache. "I am always formless and beyond the three qualities (Gunas). What do I have to do with the objects of the world?" If you remain with this attitude, the affection for objects disappears, just as a prostitute is not liked by a priest. This should be your attitude with regard to your "True Nature" (Swaroopa).

Morning, 23-11-1934

13. When the Knowledge of Objects Ends

The individual (Jiva) exists according to its faith. Your perception of things is according to your faith or belief. Understand that everything is false. The house is only made of clay. The entire city of Mumbai is made only of clay. It is all only earth, but we call it "Mumbai." It is only a concept, the imagination of one who speaks, who says "Mumbai." If you say this is a chair, it is a chair. If you say it is wood, it is wood. All of this is conceptual. If there is a woman, she has many relatives. One person calls a woman "wife," and someone else calls her "sister," another says she is his "mother." Actually, she is but a collection of flesh and bones. How is this? Because the experience of something depends upon what one conceives.

The individual is having some qualities according to his imagination and faith. The pride of being "Me," is called Ravana. Really, everything is only Brahman. The ones who possess this home that is called the body should let go of it. The emotionally entangled owners of the body are so many. They must vacate the body-consciousness, and it is He (Brahman) alone, who should remain. It is the sense objects that are the demons. Since you worship them, you also become like demons. Ravana (the world of the senses) is not the real king. He has become a king in imagination only. Taking the knowledge of the outer world as true, he seems to have become king. If you want to escape from his slavery, you have to give up the false importance of the knowledge of objects. Know that all conceptual knowledge is false.

Ravana, who is the ego, can be killed only in human birth. He will not die at the hands of any other species. He is going to remain alive throughout hundreds of thousands of reincarnations. The five sense organs and five organs of action, and the four inner principles that are mind (manas), intellect (buddhi), thinking (chitta), and the sense of "I am" or the ego (aham), together -make the fourteen fields where Ravana rules. When the rule of gods is established on the Earth, the demons go to the netherworld (where the objects of the world are forgotten). When the demons rule the Earth, the gods go into hiding for spiritual practice (they remain as they are, but seem to be hidden). When one is convinced that all things that appear are false, death disappears automatically.

Take up the attitude that "I am not. This person does not exist. There is nobody." When the one who has the Knowledge of Brahman sits for dinner, everything connected with the dinner is Brahman. The seat is Brahman, the food is Brahman, the eater is Brahman, and the one who serves the food is also Brahman. If he sleeps, he will not forget that the bed is Brahman, and even the cot is only Brahman. One should practice with the concept that "All is Brahman." Then the "knowing," or being in contact with objects ends, and the "Kingdom of God" prevails. Whatever is seen is all only Brahman. It is not that one thing is Brahman, and another thing is not. All things are Brahman. It is like ice, which is water, and water, which is ice. If the ice becomes liquid, its former shape disappears, but the whole time it is only water.

You are gaining understanding, but you are still interested in having pleasures for your body. Except for this attraction to sense pleasures, you are understanding everything. Because you have some pride about your body (identification with it), you believe that you are an individual (Jiva). Otherwise, you are Brahman. The "manifest" and the "formless" are only One, which we call God. Without making any modification in the form, you are truly only Brahman. When this concept is truly understood, you become Brahman. At that point, the Kingdom of God comes, and the rule of demons is gone. The demons disappear. All animate and inanimate things are one "Unity." The Illusion persists only because of sentimental concepts. When that Illusion disappears, all is known to be Brahman. One who takes his food with faith that it is Brahman, has observed a fast, although he dines. Whatever such a person speaks, is

Vedic Truth. When he walks and talks, it is Brahman, and when he sleeps, his sleep is Samadhi. He is only Brahman.

A king may move about anywhere, and he remains a king. If he gives orders while he is having a stomachache, it does not affect his authority. He is still the king. Brahman is the Life-Force, Chaitanya. A "Realized-One," the Jnani, is only Brahman although he may be in any situation. The one who has realization of his True Nature, is always in the kingdom of the Supreme Self, Paramatman. The body is but the mill of shit. You may put any type of good food in it, and it only turns into shit. The body is thus only a shit-producing machine. The great wonder of this is that the same body is useful as an instrument for the realization of Brahman.

Vishnu, who is the "Inner-Principle," or Consciousness, gave nectar (immortality) to the gods, and wine (the sensual world) to the demons. It is in our power to drink nectar and become gods, and it is equally in our power to drink wine. What should the wise do? They should keep their sights on "Godliness," or see only Brahman with respect to everything and everyone. Water the seedling until it becomes a big tree. Once the tree is strong and fully-grown, then there is no need to take all of the trouble of tending to it any longer.

Evening, 23-11-1934

14. Meditate Upon What You Hear

Sages like Shuka, Valmiki, and Narada all reached spiritual attainment with Self-Knowledge. That high status is attainable by listening to spiritual instruction and meditation upon it. One must practice according to what one has heard. Only then is Self-Knowledge possible. Only one who is not attracted to the objects of the world can gain Self-Knowledge through listening and meditation. By simply verbally describing a sweet dish, that food does not become prepared. You must prepare it first, and only then can you eat it. Only then, does one get the benefit. The study of the Self is to remain with an attitude of (being in) unity with the Self, or with one's True Nature (Swaroopa). No one becomes a sage by just putting on the crimson or saffron colored clothes of a renunciate.

Your mind should accept what it listens to. The mind should be attuned to what it hears. The attention of the mind should be as smooth and constant as the steady flow of oil from one pot to another, in a fine thin stream. You must read again and again what is written because you do not remember. This forgetfulness is why you do not experience your unity with the Self. Everyone builds their houses on the Wind. They build castles in the air. In the world, everything is taking place because of the "word." First the concept of a tall building is spoken about in so many words, and then the building is erected. Someone who is ignorant becomes wise only through words. If you do not hear the words, how can listening take place? Trying to teach you is like pouring water on a buffalo. All of the water is wasted. That is because your attention is focused on objects and does not loosen its interest from them. If it frees itself, then the job is over, and you have become Brahman. Your "Being" should remain constantly as Brahman.

All of the five elements are finely mixed in each other. The Self(Atman) also dwells in them, but it is aloof. All of the houses are built only out of earth, but their shapes and their owners are different. Similarly, although people are many in number, the Inner-Self in all(God) and the Wind are one. However, there is some factor, which calls itself as "I." That factor is false. It need not be there. If you separate yourself and become proud of that separateness, then you suffer sorrow. Then, listening becomes futile because the mind is attracted to sense objects and identifies with thoughts (subtle objects).

Attaining the "Knowledge of Brahman" (Brahmavidya) is difficult because our attention is turned towards sense-objects. If one has a liking for listening to spiritual teachings, something seems to be missing if one does not get the experience. The mind's disposition changes by continuous good company. There should be constant thinking and meditating day and night on the spiritual instruction that one has received. Talk about it and listen to it, but what is even more important, is putting the good advice that one has received into practice. Just the act of merely listening to the teaching is not so important. One must get the actual experience of what is being indicated, and feel united with it. If one can do this, he attains all of the spiritual powers (Siddhis). What is the meaning of the attainment of spiritual powers? This means that one very naturally gets all of the good things and comforts of life. This occurs because he is desireless. All people insist that they should receive something in return for whatever they offer. Do not be swept away by the desire for riches. You must maintain desirelessness, and then you will be of the "Nature of Brahman."

Morning- 24-11-1934

15. There is Only "One" Without Duality

There is only Oneness. There is nothing other. Then what is this that appears to us as the world? All is Gold, nothing else. The various ornaments, or objects that we perceive are false. The names are not of any consequence. All names and forms are unreal. One and only one Brahman exists. "To see," means appearance, however Brahman is pervading all that is seen as the objects of the world. When your state of Consciousness becomes such, then the idea of yourself as one entity, and me as another entity, disappears. The duality of "you" and "me" disappears. Conceive of all as Brahman without doing any analyzing or separating. When "All is one," do not hold to the concept that "I am a separate being."

The Sun is so brilliant that it does not need a bath. Do you cleanse and wash the fire because it is from the house of a so-called "untouchable"? The Self is eternally shining. If the sense of "I" does not enter in it, it is pure Self only. When the sense of "me" goes, the Self remains as brilliantly pure as ever. There is the same Consciousness in all. It is the Oneness in all things. A drop of sea water is essentially of the nature of the sea, but it does not remain separate from the sea. There is no death in the five elements of earth, water, fire, air, and space. Death is related only to desire, and the subtle "I," with its attributes of thoughts and emotions. Living and dying are applicable only to this separate existence.

When you say that a certain person by some name is dead, it is only the concept of that person that separates itself and calls itself by that label which has died. The state of Realization is where the sense of the "me" has ended. This stranger, who calls himself Tom, Dick, or Harry has wrongly become the owner of the body. Banish him, and then "You Are Brahman." Bear the brand "I Am Brahman" (Ahambrahmasmi) and proceed further without hesitation to the next great meeting. If only One is there, then everything has value. As soon as there are two, there is friction and conflict. Therefore, live in Unity, as One, Alone. One who discards completely the sense of the "you" and "me" is the real Son of the Sadguru (Guruputra).

Evening, 24-11-1934

16. Know by Speech, Mind and Action

One who recognizes Brahman with speech, mind, and in the physical body, is "My Devotee." One should do as he professes. Forget about the body as a body, and consider the body to be Brahman. By having the feeling that the "All-Pervading God" is within everything, thereby making the mind one with Brahman, one feels unified with one's Essential Being. One then naturally acquires all of the spiritual powers (Siddhis). These powers are eighteen in number. There are eight greater Siddhis and ten lesser ones. Eight of these relate to your Being. The subtlest is the power of "Entering into the Consciousness of All." In fact, you are already in the hearts of all. To be invisible is to remain unseen in your own Being and to relinquish all the tendencies of the mind and the body.

King Bharat said, "The whole Earth is mine, but when I die, I will belong to the Earth." This means that because of attachments, one again becomes bound. It is therefore better to surrender everything from the beginning. The object before the mind at the time of death decides what will be the nature of next birth. The desire directs the next progression after death. Do not get involved in the world even with the good intentions to help others, because as soon as you deviate from your own Being, you will fall into the trap. Don't forget your true Self. Your own body is sure to fall one day so why fear its death even today? One who is free from the slavery of the world is the real Saint. Recognize that the entire world is perishable. Let it perish today instead of tomorrow! Don't care for it! Don't bother about this world of the five elements. Only if you live like this, will all of the eight Siddhis be pleased with you.

The nature of the powers of your Being is eight-fold. (1) The Power to become minute like an atom, (2) Power to become huge, (3) Power to be very light in weight, (4) Power to get whatever is desired, (5) Power to have control upon animate and inanimate things, (6) Power to wield tremendous strength, (7) Power to enjoy any pleasure of the senses as wished, and (8) the Power to make anybody do as you wish, are the eight powers.

Your life as it is, is very petty. However, if you remain in unity with your Being, you will get everything as soon as the will arises in the mind. Those who do not deviate from their Being are "My True Devotees." Therefore, remain so, with all of your mind, body, and speech.

Morning, 25-11-1934

17. True Renunciation and Desirelessness

Should one relinquish the family or not? Even if you perform your daily functions, the sum total of your life is the same. If you are not alert within, what is the use of putting on garlands and applying sandalwood paste (conducting spiritual rituals)? There should be inward conviction that the world is Illusion. If that is not achieved, what is the use of becoming a renunciate (Sanyasi)? If you are fully aware that this illusory world is false, and you function in this world with detachment, what is wrong with that? That is really the greatest thing. You may be anywhere, at anytime, and you remain untainted by the world. Is it the case that only if you remain secluded in a room, or in the forest, you are a sage, and if you go out, you are not a sage? No, this is not the case. You must be inwardly detached.

Even for those who are ready to do this, there is the possibility of delusion. With the utmost care, you must treat the five elements with respect, for they will ensnare you. Do not think that the five elements are benign. They will create an impression of gentleness on your mind, but do not be deceived by their facade, and put your trust in them. Do not forget that they are only putting on an act of being docile. Even though the field occupied by the five elements, and the scenery presented by them may be attractive, do not trust in this. These scenes are deceptive. Always remember that they are like ghosts in various disguises. Whatever disguise the ghosts may wear, they are still only ghosts. You are not like the ghosts.

Illusion (Maya) always tries to make you forget your True Nature by adopting various tricks. You must always be on your guard. You may be living in comfort, but be mentally detached. One should remain in a state of "Desirelessness" in one's mind, speech, and actions. Live in Brahman, as Brahman. A man once said to a Sage who had realized Brahman, "Sir, I have seen you once." The Sage said, "You could not have seen me. I am not as you see me. I am not as I appear to you, I am quite different." Even if you leave the worldly life and go away into seclusion, what are you going to gain? There is no need for you to do that. Just change your attitude, or state of mind. Do not lose the sense that you are Brahman. When we give a vaccine, we do not need to consider whether the patient is small or big, thin or fat; all should be vaccinated. The appearance of the person makes no difference. In deep sleep, both the king and the pauper are equal. That is called equanimity. To be in the world is painful. Come to the understanding that the world is an Illusion, then you will experience joy and contentment, even in this world appearance.

You always were, and are, the "Highest Joy." One who harbors desire is but a laborer who is always playing the role of an employee. One who has no desire is the owner. Unless desire is despised, one does not become desireless. It was only for the purpose of attaining Desirelessness, that the Sage Shuka took to the forest while King Janaka achieved the same while ruling over a kingdom. If you truly want to study, I dare say that it can be done anywhere. There is an easy way. It is really immaterial where you are. Whether in a house, or in a forest, you can be leading a spiritual life. You need not run away. The Sage Pralhad could be in the state of Brahman even though he was constantly being harassed. If you say that you cannot do spiritual practice (Sadhana) while you are living in a family, take it for granted that you are not really interested in true spiritual practice. He who really wants to be spiritual will unfailingly do so, wherever he may be.

Evening, 25-11-1934

18. The Self Naturally Contains Spiritual Powers (Siddhis)

The Self (Atman) naturally contains the Eight Greater Spiritual Powers or Siddhis. So long as an individual (Jiva) is dominated by Illusion (Maya), the original nature of the Self remains hidden. When one gives no value to spiritual powers, those Siddhis automatically become his servant (when one is desireless). The eight-fold nature of the Self is essentially the eight-fold power. Pearls are given to the one who does not demand them, but if one has demands things, he does not even get the necessary thing. One who has become void of any wish gets all of the eight powers. The eight powers are identical with My Nature. One who is united with Me gets these powers automatically.

There are six energies, or passions, which are desire, anger, greed, pride, jealousy, and hatred.[1] Hunger and thirst are natural for the body. It is necessary to take food and water to remain alive. Happiness and sorrow are the afflictions of the mind. If you get what you want, it is

---

1. The six attributes arising from Space or the sky; desire, anger, greed, pride, jealousy, and hatred.

happiness, if you do not get it, it is sorrow. What the mind feels is good, is good, and what it feels is not good, is not good. "I" is a concept that is without location or shape. "I am Shiva. I am Shiva," (Shivoham) is a useful concept.

There are six powers, or Siddhis that are specifically related to the body. Not to be aware of hunger or thirst is the first power. To know the meaning of Vedanta is real clairaudience, or the capacity to listen to far off sounds, which is the second power. Clairvoyance is the third power. Victory over the mind is the fourth power. Ability to go anywhere is the fifth power. Ability to adopt any form of body is the sixth power. To be able to enter the body of others is the seventh power. Ability to leave the body, or to die, according to one's will is the same power. To be able to see Gods is the eighth power. To be successful according to one's wish is the ninth power, and the power by which all people obey your orders is the tenth power. All these powers are related to the mind.

There are five lesser powers. To know the past and future is the first. Not to be affected by wind and rain is the second. To know what another man is thinking is the third power. To be able to stop wind and fire is the fourth power, and to always be victorious over others, or not to be conquered is the fifth power.

Morning, 26-11-1934

19. The Thought of a Dream in the Dream

The Self (Atman) who is birthless and deathless slept, and in his dream, he had a dream. What kind of dream was this? The appearance of the world was the dream, and in this dream, he dreamed that he became an individual (Jiva). Then the Illusion only increased. The appearance of this worldly life as real, is a dream. The One who was God, became a servant. To conceive as real all people such as mother, father, brother and others, along with the whole world, is the dream. All the beings in the world are reveling in this dream. It is very rare and important that one among all of them should think very far. To have trust in a Saint is a very rare thing. Such an aspirant acts in a selfless manner. One who is full of ego will not even throw a piece of bread to a dog. After doing some selfless charitable deed, there is often the experience of selflessness, or pure intelligence, that arises. It is a great thing to feel respect for the Saints. Great is the fruit of the blessings of our forefathers, the Saints who have come before.

Discrimination (Viveka) between the Essence and non-essential during this dream life is rare. Wealth is a kind of intoxicant like wine. Because of the merits from the last birth, one turns towards the Guru, and is inquisitive about him. This is one who can truly utilize the power of discrimination. Such a person goes to the Guru and thinks about what is Essence and what is non-essential, and comes to the understanding that "I Am Brahman." Only then can one realize that the world is Illusion, and become awake from one dream. He experiences the pure Essence of the Teaching, and understands that the entire world is an Illusion, and that "The Supreme Self (Paramatman) is the only Truth." One then becomes that "Truth, Consciousness, and Bliss (SatChitAnanda) Incarnate," and One with Brahman.

When you come to know the meaning, and when you think about it, and say "Now, I have got the experience, and now, I am awake," who is this "I" who has gained experience? When you say that you have experienced something, there is the ego, or "I Am" (Aham). The thing that says "I," or "You" is nothing. You say that you know, but that is only ego. It is delusion in Illusion. For example you may think that, "he is," or "you are," the same old entity whom people call Mr. Smith, but now "Mr. Smith" has become Brahman. If you decide that the former Mr. Smith was only Illusion and that "non-entity" has now become

Reality, then your illusion is not yet dissipated. What is naturally your Being, is the Reality as it is. There is no "I" there, even in the most subtle form. So long as it is felt in the slightest, that there is any need to protect the body, "I" is not gone. There should be the actual feeling, the experiencing, that the entire universe is within you. This is the understanding that "All is He, and I Am He."

The silk worm builds its own house, a cocoon, and then dies in it. You are also binding yourself similarly. You consider yourself to be the physical body. This itself is captivity. You have yourself become like the cocoon of the silk worm. Lukewarm water is poured on the cocoon, the worm is killed, and then the silk is taken. If you hold on to the feeling, that the entire universe, and the Wind and Space that it is contained in, is your body, then you are automatically Brahman. There is only Brahman, which is one without a second. He who knows that there is nothing else is himself Brahman. The one whose craving after the objects of the senses is gone, whose sense of "I" as separate from everything else is gone, and whose pride is gone, is the one who has truly realized Brahman.

Evening, 26-11-1934

20. Spiritual Powers are Natural in the Self

All of the "Spiritual Powers" (Siddhis) are of My Own Nature. The study of the Eight Greater Siddhis and the study of Myself, is the same. Even though the Eight Siddhis are different, they are all of My Own Nature, the Self. When the Self is attained, the purpose of life is achieved. Knowledge and Power are one. This is my essential nature. Only "My Devotee" attains this. These powers are not achievable for anybody else. Once a challenge was put before the people: "Who will pull the King's beard?" One wise man said, "I will show you." When the King was seated on the throne, his sons who were sitting on his lap, pulled at his beard. Similarly, the Eight Siddhis that are of the nature of the Self, are attainable by My Devotee.

The first power is the power of the "Inner Life" or Anima. The Atom, or Anu is the ultimate smallest particle that is not further divisible. The small dust particles which are in the air are called Renu. And the subtlest particle of air is called "Paramanu." A letter in the alphabet is formed by the continuation of an original point, and then the figure or line when increased, becomes the whole letter, then words follow, and sentences are formed. Unless the "Anu" becomes "Renu," a line is not formed. The world has come into being out of the "Life-Force," Chaitanya. A Shepherd once said to a well versed scholar, that "All the Vedas and the eighteen Mythological Epics are in my pocket." This meant that he had realized that he is nothing but an infinitely small atom, and to realize this is the Anima, or "Inner Life" Siddhi. He was experiencing that he was abiding in the heart of all creatures. He was the tiniest of the tiny, and the Self of the smallest insect. "I am more thin than the thinnest thing in the world and the purest of the pure." One who realizes this achieves the Anima Siddhi.

All of the physical and subtle bodies are like chariots, and it is God, Shri Ram, who is the Self (Atman) that is the charioteer in the chariot. Turn your face towards Him and become one with Him. When the sense of "I" and "you" is gone, only He remains. The individual (Jiva) has the habit of differentiating things. God (Shiva) likes to be One. When you separate, and make distinctions in the mind, you become petty. When you are unified, you become vast. Where there is no "me," there is no world, no five elements, and the Truth is understood that "All is One, All is only the Self." When one is sure that he is Anu, he achieves the Anima Siddhi.

Consider how minute the taste buds are while you taste something sweet on your tongue. It is the Self that is aware of even in which roots of hair there is some itching. There is nothing that He does not know. He is that Inner-Consciousness, which is called the Self, "Atman." When a man has full conviction that the true "I" is the one who is the innermost dweller of all beings, this itself becomes the great accomplishment, or Siddhi. When a warrior has the conviction that he is a brave fighter of noble descent, accordingly, he very naturally exhibits great courage in battle. The very feeling that "I am brave" makes a man valiant. In order to make Illusion disappear, forget all things from the past. Whatever is in the past has to be invited back by us in order to follow us, otherwise it is gone. The slate is something that is to be written on, and then always wiped clean.

Illusion is not in the background, nor is it in the front, or in the future, but it is only in the present. Its existence is not real. It is only Illusion, a fleeting appearance. Wipe it out from the mind. Forget even the mind itself. In Illusion there are only six principles, the five elements and the Self, or Knowledge. There is nothing else. Do not bother to put forth the effort to think of anything. You are saying and thinking about things because they were said sometime in the past, otherwise what would be there for you to understand? Nothing. Illusion is strange. If you think about and see everybody as fools or donkeys, then they appear as such. Really, all is only Brahman.

Morning, 27-11-1934

21. Turn the Mind Away From Objects

Everything is objective, including this body. So long as the mind is turned toward objective things, Illusion prevails. The pupils and the teacher are interrelated. If pupils are not there, the teacher is not there. Where there is no teacher, there are no pupils. In the body where there is the sense of "I," how can the light of the Self shine? Where is there room for God if "you" are occupying the body? What is the use of even obtaining the "Kingdom of the Fourteen Worlds"? For one who intends to become Brahman, what value is found in objects? Therefore, do not harbor any desires for objective things.

In the great battle told about in the Bhagavad Gita, Lord Krishna said, "On one side, I will be there, and on the other side will be my army. If anybody wants me on their side, I will be alone to fight by his side. On the other side, the whole world is my army. Duryodhan thought, "Of what use is this lone Krishna to me? I will be better off in this battle to take His army." Arjuna accepted Lord Krishna to be on his side. Without God, or Krishna, whatever riches of the world may be there without the Self are all in vain, and if you want to have Him, you must not allow worldly riches, mundane possessions, or selfishness, to even come near you. Otherwise, He will not come near you.

The sense of "I" is the mother, and all the things that come after are her children. If the children go away, the mother does not have existence, and if the mother goes, the children also go. One gets sound sleep because you forget everything in deep sleep. Is there any difference between a king's sleep and a poor man's sleep? Is the enjoyment of sleep somehow less for the poor man? Relinquish all of the things that the "I" desires, and then the mind is automatically slain. To say or assert something is the mind. That is also gone when the "I" goes. The egotistic intellect becomes pacified. The mind says only that which it remembers. If you consider all of this appearance as false, the mind dies. Ask me if it rises again. It may even be possible to fold the sky, but it is difficult to control the mind. However, if you let go of all objects, then what job does the mind have to perform? If a man who is in deep sleep says, "I am sleeping, please awaken me," how are we to awaken him?

If day and night, one's thinking is on the Reality, then all objects are automatically proved to be false. If a seeker wants recognition that he is great, or wants honor, his progress becomes stalled. The one who cannot contain within himself the intention or desire to possess spiritual powers becomes entangled by these powers, because what he wants is a false greatness. Only when the inherent persistent desire for worldly life is truly snapped, will the "Supreme Self," Paramatman, be met. The individual (Jiva) desires to eat the fruits of this tree of worldly life. When that eating of worldly life stops, he becomes God (Shiva) automatically. Leave the enjoyment of objects. Don't take the touch of objective things, and cease craving them. Then immediately you are Shiva. Do all actions like eating food and drinking water, etc. but do not take these things to be real. Do not live as a slave to objects. Maintain the feeling "I am Brahman." There should not be any sorrow or concern about things that come and go. One who does not become arrogant by riches, does not blame the one who blames him, and one who does not whimper due to any pain, is God himself.

One who does not become affected by poverty is god-like. Illusion says, "I will give you whatever you want. Do whatever you like, but you will remain under my dominance." Illusion cannot come near a "Realized-One," a Jnani. The one who has Self-Knowledge is the "True Brahmin" (knower of Brahman). Illusion is always in pursuit. Those who make demands from it are like hanged men. Spiritual life is as soft as butter but as hard as diamond. You have to turn the life around. Turn your life in the opposite direction away from worldliness. Spoil it and it will be destroyed. You are only going to turn into waste whatever you eat, so what is the use of looting from other people?

One who is fed up with mundane life will not think about it even if he is entreated. One who has realized Brahman will not think about this killer who is Illusion (Maya). This Maya herself is mortal. Objective things never remain forever, no matter how much you may endear yourself to them. If you light a lamp and tell it not to throw off light, will it obey you? The lamp that is lit will of course give off light. Giving away everything to God, including all of the inner bodies, is called Bali. The body-consciousness says not to give, but Bali did not pay heed to it. In Hindu mythology, Bali is the name of a king who surrendered everything to the Lord in the incarnation of "Waman," at His biding. He gave everything, the physical body, the subtle body, and the causal body.

These three bodies are the three worlds contained in the three steps that Vishnu conquered, then Bali went to Pataal.

The Goddess Laxmi seeks the man who makes himself dear to Lord Narayana. However, do not even let her stand before you. You see, you should not employ her, or try to possess her even in order to help others, as this only brings in many entanglements. The meaning of cleansing the mind is to let all of the thinking about objects fall away. The mind that is thus purified always shines. Then it does not like anything other than the Reality, which is Pure Being. It has no need of meditation and contemplation. That One, is Pure Brahman.

Evening, 27-11-1934

22. The Self is the Most Subtle

The Self (Atman) is more subtle than the most subtle. That which is matter is perishable. That which is the most subtle is the most powerful. Water is many times more powerful than earth. We can carry on without food if such a time comes, but we cannot live without water. Likewise, heat, or fire is even more useful and essential than water. Without heat we cannot live. When the heat in the body goes, the body dies. Air, or wind, is even still more powerful than heat. Without breathing air, the body cannot live.

In the world, there are ten digits. The number 10 is formed by 1 and 0. However, how many numbers are there in the world? Only one. Only 1, and that one goes on increasing. This 1 is the outcome of Zero (0). Water is ten times subtler than Earth. 1 and 0 is 10. From 10, the figures again change. Wind is ten times more subtle than Fire. If Fire would have been equal to Wind, it would have eaten up the Wind. Whether there is Wind or not can be known by observing the flame. Just as we need Water, Fire needs Wind to live. The Space, or Sky, is ten times more subtle than Wind. Moreover, it is impossible to measure the subtlety of Brahman by comparing it with Space. If Space were not there, our Existence would not be there even for a moment. Unless there is Space, or Sky, there is no place for Wind. God has created that element sufficiently on a vast scale, without which creatures could not live. The Self is totally formless. That which is most subtle and most powerful knows all, yet all of the five elements do not know Him. The Self knows all. He is the knower. The Self is self-existent, and is not supported by anything.

Because of a lamp all objects are seen. The objects do not make us see the lamp. Therefore, the lamp is superior. The one who has the awareness of the lamp is more superior, and the superiority of the intellect is even greater still, than this awareness. An elephant is very big, but a man rides upon him. The elephant does not ride upon a man. Like this, Knowledge is very valuable. It is because of the Sun that all objects are seen. The lamp, as well as all of the various objects of the world, are seen because of the Sun. The Sun is not seen because of them. Moreover, by whose light is it that all objects including the Sun are seen? It is by the light of the Self that they are seen. The Self is the most valuable and the most powerful, and is the only knower of all. Nobody knows Him. It is the Supreme Self, Paramatman, that gives the power of movement to all. It is He who gives the "Power of Life." The Self is the "King of All." The Self is supremely subtle like this.

At the root of the world, there is "no thing," a void. It is a fundamental premise that one who knows this void is older than the void. For example, who is it that witnesses that "I was having a sound dreamless sleep?" It is Paramatman. He is the atom, the very substance of all atoms. What is the meaning of dying? It means that the body is turned into earth. Whatever is gross matter, returns into the earth. One who knows this undying, most subtle Self, obtains the "Power of Life," Anima. Meditate that "I am that subtle, self-luminant Brahman, which is of the Nature of Consciousness, the state of Knowing itself." This "God Self," Atmaram, is "self-evident." It is the Self who is God (Atmadev) who is the seer behind the eye, the listener in the ear, the smeller in the nose, and the taster in the tongue.

Morning, 28-11-1934

23. Why is the World Seen if it is Unreal?

Whatever is seen, is unreal. Only the seer is real. There are two things in the world, the "seer," and the "seen." That which is seen is Illusion. The seer is Brahman. The seen, is unreal, and only the seer is real. One who takes the seen to be real, gets destroyed. One who discards the real and considers the false as real, perishes. By recognizing "That" which is innermost, you attain "That." One who meditates on any object, becomes that object. One who worships the "All-Seeing," becomes "All-Knowing."

If that which is "seen" is unreal, why do we see it with our eyes? Understand it to be unreal *because* we see it with our eyes. Take it for granted that all the things that are seen by our eyes are false. They are unreal. The Self, who is invisible, is the only Reality. If two mirrors are held face to face, the object between these mirrors appears to be many objects. Is this line of objects that stretches out one next to the other, real? Will anybody pay good money to purchase the reflection of an elephant that is seen in the water in front of the elephant? There are many such creations in the world that are all false. Is the image that a painter draws real? One who is intelligent is busy creating his own world. All of this world is the play of imagination. If you are hypnotized by the false appearances in the Illusion, you become as fleeting as they are, and if you know Brahman, the Seer, you are the Supreme Self, Paramatman.

There is a saying in Hindi, (attributed to Saint Kabir) "I went and resided in that country where nobody can go. I was a crow, but I became a swan by losing my ancestral caste and family." All of the various appearances in life are made of earth, and it is only earth that they eat. Therefore, this world is called the region of death (Mrityuloka). One who takes this earth to be real, returns to the earth. Even after death, you have to spend money for disposal of the dead body. Nobody will pay anything to purchase a dead body. Is there any Guru who can show me my own face? When such a Guru is present, he says to the earth, "I am your death, and the time that eats you up in the end. I am indestructible by my own nature. There is no annihilation for me."

People eat the inner parts of fruit, one who will eat the hard outer cover will lose his teeth. Know the Supreme Self, Paramatman, and be Paramatman.

Evening, 28-11-1934

24. Atoms and Subatomic Particles are One.

Atoms and subatomic particles are one. The particles that make up the atoms of Water, Fire, and Air, are called subatomic particles, or Paramanu. The Self (Atman) however is one totality. It is the same throughout. It has no parts such as atoms, or subatomic particles. All atoms and particles are perishable. They perish, yet the Supreme Self, Paramatman, is One and cannot be destroyed. It is a unitary whole. Fire can enter all things and therefore it can burn. Wind, or air is also capable of entering things. These elements are porous, but the Self is spread out evenly everywhere. It creates hundreds of skies. By its Consciousness and capacity "to know," it creates dreams. It creates Space, and within the Space, it creates the world. Wherever there is Space, it creates the world. Where there is the sense of "knowing," the world is created.

The eyes have water in them yet they do not constantly ooze. If one understands that the Self is everywhere, and becomes One with it, he becomes the Supreme Self, Paramatman. I am in the donkey, but I am not the donkey. One who understands that he is in everything obtains the "Power of Omnipresence," or "Mahima." Whatever number of species may be there, life as such, is only One, and the same for all. The Self is the same in all creatures. Nature, the entirety of creation, is the same for all. If all wished to destroy it, then it would perish. However, one can remain aloof from creation, but this is possible only if he has full realization that the world is Illusion, and is fully aware that he is God. The world is seen with the "Eye of Illusion." The Self is without that eye. It only sees itself. The world is as you see it. If the mind thinks that it is false or true, or that someone is a thief, it takes that form. Experience depends upon your concepts. The bed bug does not bite a corpse for feeding. Every creature has his own world. If you call it real, it is real. If you call it false, it is false. There is no sin or merit in the world.

What is a woman to you before your marriage with her? She is nobody. You call her your wife and therefore she became your wife. Otherwise, what relationship does she have with you? You are responsible for creating the world around you. What a man says becomes a source of bondage for him. What you have said has become your restraint. You are bound by your desires. That is the nature of the world created by you. If you say that all is false, you are freed. You are bound only by your own concepts, so free yourself from them. You must think correctly. Everything is dynamic, and the Self dwells in every form. The Self is common to all the five elements. That is "My Real Being," which is very vast.

The Sun is millions of miles away from the Earth. It is also by size, many times larger, but it is seen from earth as a small ball. We see it as appearing to be very small. It would take years of traveling to see it up close. From this example, you can imagine how vast and great you yourself are. The Self is very vast. Sound and light are created at the same time, but they travel at different speeds so you see the light first, and then hear the sound afterwards. However, the Self is so vast that as soon as you open your eyes, it does not take more than an instant to see the Sun, while to see the Sun up close in its actual size would require many years of travel. In a dream with a duration of only 15 minutes, you can experience a lapse of millions of years. However far away a dream world may be located, the Self is at its own place. The Self is so vast it contains all of the dream world, and the waking world within it. The Self is endless and limitless. This means that it really has no end or limit.

Illusion, or Maya, is called the "Mahat" principle. It is the Self that knows Maya. The Self is more vast than all of Illusion. It looks out in all directions at once as soon as you open your eyes. When you say that you are that Self, you automatically become vast. The Self is the vastest of all, but the body does not become vast upon the realization of the Self, because the body is false. When a villager goes to live in a city, he identifies with the big city. Then he does not say that he is from the village. He becomes someone bigger. He no longer says that he belongs to the village. He has now become someone bigger.

A single thread of cotton is very weak, but if it is united with other threads, it becomes very strong. Likewise, if you become separate, you become weak, so be vast in Oneness. If a grain of salt goes to meet the sea, what happens? It is merged into the sea. It becomes the sea. You do service to your body, and forget to serve the Self. It is what you give to the man of Self-Knowledge, the Jnani, that is truly what God receives. The cat that is your body, is eating what belongs to the Self. It does not reach up to the Self. When you bow before the man of Self-Knowledge, it is like bowing before yourself. You are living the family life because you want pleasure. You are not doing it for your wife and children. When you worship the man of Self-Knowledge, you are doing that for your own upliftment. The one who understands these things obtains the "Power of Omnipresence," or Mahima. One then becomes Omnipresent, "All-Pervading."

Morning, 29-11-1934

25. You are the Self in the Heart of All

It is the ego (aham) that motivates the sense organs of all people. The three hundred and thirty million deities preside over the sense organs. They are hidden, invisible principles. One "Lakh" (the number 100,000) is "Laksha," which means "attention." When the attention of the individual (Jiva) is focused objectively, it turns into the one hundred thousand things. The Life-Force of all of these deities of the senses is the Self (Atman) who is different from them. Accordingly, He is their "True Owner." The entity that says "My mind" and "My intellect" is different from the mind and intellect. You must realize that you are the Self that animates and is the "Life-Force" behind all of the sense organs. Only He, the Self, knows Himself. He is not known by the senses.

When you are sure that you have the "Power," then your orders are obeyed. Your "Power" is accepted by all beings, the tigers, serpents, ghosts, and even the five elements. If you hold to the concept that you are this Life-Energy, the Life-Force (Chaitanya), then you get the Power, which gives Life to all of the sense organs. When you understand yourself as the One dwelling in the hearts of all, you are the one who walks, you are the one who eats food, speaks, etc. Your experience is that you are that Power, and you have that "Authority." Realize that you are the Self, the Life-Force in all. You and the sun, moon, and stars are One. Your Life-Energy gives life to all. All move because of Your Power of Movement, they walk because of Your Life-Energy. You must be sure of this Power.

To appear and exist for some duration, and then to subsequently disappear are the two qualities of the world. Whenever things exist and are perceptible, it is from, and because of, "Me," the Self. Be convinced that you are all of the phenomenon in the world appearance. Live that Realization. Although the daily cash is collected by your employees, it still belongs to you. Just as you are sure that you are the owner of that cash, similarly, you also must have the conviction that it is only you who is existing and appearing in and as all beings. Just as someone is very worried and concerned if their child becomes sick, because he feels that it is he who is going to suffer a loss, similarly, your feeling should be such that you have the feeling that all of the activities in the world are your own, and that you are pervading everything.

Morning, 30-11-1934

26. Listen to the True Nature of the Teaching

Just as there is the right method of teaching, there is also the right method of listening. That method of teaching by which one understands the spiritual life is real teaching. Otherwise, people are only endlessly chattering away with each other. Even a rubber doll can be made to talk. You should talk of such things and listen to such things that will help you realize your total unity with God. Otherwise, you can listen to birds that are twittering away, but that is not spirituality. The real subject of dialogue is spirituality, which is possible only for human beings. Ancestors of more than 72 earlier generations are waiting with a hope that someone from their progeny will lead a realized life and uplift their fame. You should not therefore get enticed in the film show that is your mundane life.

The spiritual life is a wish-fulfilling tree (Kalpataru). Whatever you wish for, it is ready. This spiritual life is the wish-fulfilling stone (Chintamani), and the wish-fulfilling cow (Kamadhenu). Make the best of this human birth that you have attained because of great merit in the past. Let that which you aspire for become possible, and let that which is lost, be lost. Once you realize your own Self, anything may happen, but nothing will worry you. One must have Self-Realization and that which helps achieve it, is called *the Teaching*. Talking continuously about various philosophical systems is futile. Is it of any use? You do not eat the husk and throw away the grain. The one who being born here in human form, listens to spiritual teaching and follows it, has really caught the core of life.

Who are the real "wise men"? Those who enjoy the peace and wisdom of Self-Realization are the real people worth congratulating. Please listen attentively to the explanation of what Self-Realization is. The ever-changing mind can never have peace. In the game of chess, the King is not to be over-powered by other men. Similarly, if you are over-powered, you are surely trapped, and your mind is useless. The one who has realized Brahman is not overpowered by anything. To renounce all activities is called meditation, and when the activities of the mind are stopped, it is Brahman. To empty the house means to take out everything that is in it. The house then will remain as it is. The King should not be over-powered. Illusion as a rule gives something, and then takes it back. We must learn to be free always. Somebody falls at my feet. All right, he did it to the feet. How am I concerned with it? Somebody walks awkwardly, or behaves strangely. Let him do so! How am I concerned with it? We may only watch.

The Self must not be subjected to checkmate. Illusion (Maya) has as its purpose to subjugate you by any means. Even simply by emitting a foul smell in front of your nose, she only wants to put you to shame. So make yourself invulnerable. Always be aware. One way or another, Maya will try to dethrone you, but do not give her the chance. Be peaceful in the Self at all times, even if hundreds of calamities may be falling upon the body. When you have the wish for all of life's pleasures, that desire is a checkmate. It is your defeat. It is also your defeat to say, "I don't want any pain or sorrow." When King Shivaji gave a lot of money to Tukaram, he felt that having it was a calamity and was not feeling peaceful until he sent everything away. The heavy sorrow he felt with the burden of money was the sign of his Inner Peace.

When one devotes the mind to the Supreme Self, Paramatman, it becomes pure. Otherwise, what can one with an ever-changing mind attain? The man of real Self-Knowledge is not affected by anything. Keep your mind always peaceful. The entirety of nature is made up of five elements. Everything in the Illusion is perishing everyday. Only Brahman is eternal. You should meditate on That, and strive only for It. All of the idols made of gold and silver, stone or clay, and all of the world's money, are perishable. The individual is also perishable just like an element. Except for Self-Knowledge, everything is perishable. If you believe God to be an idol, this is a sin. You think God to be made of stone or clay, how great a sin is this! Saint Ramdas said this emphatically.

Those who have Self-Knowledge can make anything out of anything. That is their power. They can glorify anyone or dishonor anyone. There is a saying, "The faithful wife goes to hell, and the prostitute to heaven. Such is the power of the Saint." The Saints are the Masters, the Siddhas. They are wielding the power to do, and undo things. There is nothing that is impossible for them. Truly saved is the one who serves them.

Evening, 30-11-1934

27. The Self is Consciousness Itself

The Self (Atman) is Consciousness. It is life itself. It is who we are ourselves. Who is God? The meaning of "I Am That" is: When I wake up from sleep, does the body wake up or does the Self? God does everything like eating and drinking. Had the tongue been eating, it could have eaten even shoes, because on its own it does not know what to eat. All of the actions of one who has the "Realization of Self-Knowledge," are offerings to God. One who knows this, knows that he is not the doer of any action. He knows his position, and this is his secret. Saint Tukaram says, "The confusion is for others." With this same understanding, the Sage Durwasa said, "The river provides the way across, because I have not taken food," even though he had just then taken heaps of food. He had the faith that he had not taken the food, that he was not the doer, and it was the river that provided the way to reach the other shore.

Lord Krishna remained a bachelor though he had sixteen thousand wives. One who acts, receives the fruits of his actions. Understand the meaning of "I am not doing anything." He who is in everybody's heart does all things, and conducts all the movements of the body. That is why He is called the "Mover of all beings." All bad names you call anyone are addressed to Him only. If a wise man is criticized he takes it as a compliment, while an ignorant person gets angry. The word Shivya is a negative name in Marathi, yet, is the plural of Shiva, which means "auspicious." The donkey has the same Self inside as you. You must gain the conviction that you are the Self, directing, leading, and guiding all of the sense organs, and act accordingly. When the sense organs function after they are conquered, you will have the experience that you, the Self, are the doer.

When Illusion with activity, or movement, as the predominant function begins to stir, the powers of Activity, Consciousness, and Beingness are created. There was no appearance of the three attributes (Rajas, Tamas, Sattva) in the beginning. There was only Objectless Consciousness. Then recognition was developed. This is called "Pure Active Awareness." When you first wake up in the morning, only "I am Brahman" is the first utterance, and then you begin to recognize the things around you. Go to sleep with the feeling of being Brahman, and get up with the same feeling. The security that one feels in the knowledge of "I Am Brahman," is the only real happiness. To worry, or be concerned for the things in the world, is sorrow.

The objectless existence, which is Brahman, is called, "Pure Consciousness." That is the Primal Illusion (MoolaMaya). It means that you were pure, formless, and alone. Then, when the awareness of "I Am" arises, understand that this is the active feeling of the ego, which says "I." The one who believes that "I am the One who illumines everything" and realizes this, is himself called "The Power of Illumination." It is He, who by constant meditation on the Self, creates the innumerable cosmic eggs (universes). This is called the cosmic egg of God the Creator (Brahma), because this is what causes the universe to come into existence. One who knows this is the "Illuminator," and has attained the power of illuminating everything. He has achieved "That State."

Morning, 1-12-1934

28. Self-Surrender

You should think about "Who am I?" The mundane life is like a treadmill. It may go round and round, but still you are in the same place. Please do not live this mundane life simply waiting for death. Do not let your life be mortal. Life is for being "Immortal." Do not lead your life only to be burnt down like a heap of grass. In Hindu mythology, the Queen Mother, "Mainavati" advised her son Gopichand that his body, which was so beautiful, was going to be burnt one day, and that he must live wisely so that he would attain immortality during his lifetime. One can do this if one makes right effort. When the bull was given a very energetic beating by the farmer, the bull suffered tremendously, and the skin of its back was peeled away. If he had used his life wisely while in the life of a man, he would not have received that beating. Do not waste the short period of your life. Attain the state of God Almighty (Narayana). The dead flesh of the body is not useful for anything, so use the body for spiritual endeavors.

At least the guts of a buffalo are used to prepare strings of musical instruments. The sound that is made by that string is "Tuhi, Tuhi," which means, "Only you are, only you are." Yet, what do you say? "Me, me," or "I, I"! Do not live for simply dying one day! Live in order to be lively and immortal in life. You work hard and toil your life away, and then at last you die. Your thinking should be from the state of Self-Knowledge. Who are we? Are we only human beings? Priests (Brahmins) should only perform the functions of priests. Their behavior should be in accordance with divine wisdom, which is the "Knowledge of Brahman." A priest will not sew shoes. He will not do other ordinary work although he may be poor. First, we must decide on the qualities by which we can attain Self-Knowledge. Then, our behavior should be in accordance with that standard that has been established, and we must not forget what is required. Then we will readily come to know that we are the Supreme Self, Paramatman.

God is an ancient devotee who is unified with God. From mythological times God has been a devotee, and the devotee has been God. God should be worshipped by becoming God (Shiva). When you become a human being you feel like worshipping man. People pray to the idol of a goddess mother and say, "Oh Goddess! Please come to protect my wife and children. I am exhausted. Please, could you help me further?" The Saint has no anxiety about anybody or anything in any of the 24 hours of day and night. If you become Shiva, you will be like Shiva. I am already the king, so who will make me king? Only one who is actually the king, is really king.

Call yourself Brahman. If you paint yourself like a tiger, you have to act like a tiger. Similarly, you have to attain the state of Shiva by force of your effort. When the spotless and pure Sadguru is met, everything is finished. Otherwise, you may continue reciting the name of God for many durations of reincarnations in the 8.4 million species, and nothing will happen, nothing will be gained. That repetition of mantra alone will not enable you to attain the state of Shiva. Only by becoming Shiva, can you attain the state of Shiva. Then "That State" itself will come and put a garland around your neck.

Evening, 1-12-1934

29. Dissolve the Sense of "I"

The dissolution of the sense of "I" (the ego) is the sign of Realization. The one who does this is a true Yogi who attains the "Power of Illumination." In Brahman, there is no experience. That which has no duality in Consciousness is Brahman. To do something is the sign of awareness of the apparent world. The Self is the "Energizer of Illusion," and of the three qualities (Gunas). There were three things in the world at the beginning; Time, Space, and the Elements. In order to feel that "I Am," there is the necessity of a tremor, or quake. "Quake" here means motion or vibration. When there is some movement, the sense of "I" is created. When there is movement, there is the arising of Consciousness. The Self is neither small or big. There is definitely duality when experience takes place. Where there is only One, there is no experience. For experience to take place, some other object is necessary. Brahman is non-dual.

A Mother said, "I feel affection for my son." The son said, "You feel affection for me, but why don't I feel that for myself?" You get that experience because you feel "I am separate from you." Even if people get a small glimpse of Knowledge, they become puffed up. When there is the attainment of the "Unity with All Beings" within oneself, some powers (Siddhis) spontaneously arise. The Sage who becomes entangled in them does not make further progress and gets caught up in Illusion. Likewise, the progress of one who is elated by achieving some virtue, also becomes stalled. The five elements are always in some degree of opposition to each other. If cats would have never eaten rats, rats would have become so powerful that they would have eaten human beings. That which is created out of any element, eventually gets dissolved back into that element. Otherwise, if it remained unchecked it would go on increasing, and would spell disaster.

Illusion has taken care to put difficulties in the way of happiness. In spiritual life, spiritual powers become entrapments. One who accepts them is trapped. We should not allow that acceptance to touch us. Do not become entangled with powers. Remain with the knowledge that the Self is the same everywhere. In the Reality, there is no place for evil, just as there is none for good. The word Brahmanda means "Cosmic Egg." The entire universe and all of the space in it, is this "Cosmic Egg." Our actions should not defeat their own purpose. If your mind is focused in the wrong direction, all will be in vain. That is why there are instructions being given on this subject matter. This is being said in order to reduce the emphasis on spiritual powers. These powers create a fascination in Illusion, and one becomes entangled there. This is why I gave you this advice. Vishnu is the "Knower of the Age, and of the Time." He is the creator and the destroyer of both. He is Consciousness itself. One who meditates on His Consciousness, can see the invisible, the concepts in the minds of all. Chess is a game that is nothing but conceptual make believe. Nevertheless, people play it. The players control the movements of the pawns and men in the game. Similarly, when one has the understanding that he is not the mover, but that the Supreme Self, Paramatman, is the mover, *this* is the real art of "Knowing." When you adopt the position of "I," you are subject to the limits of the "I." You then become small, and limited, but Brahman is vast. The creator, Lord Brahma, works his art of "Creation," which is beyond our understanding. Where the sense of "I" increases, every arrangement becomes topsy-turvy. The cheeks of the one who likes to eat ghee and sugar, tell the story. This means that bliss is never hidden.

Actually, a strange way of living is going on, in which one declares that the world is false, and at the same time he continues to behave as if the world is true. When one has faith that he is God residing in the hearts of all (Narayana), he attains extraordinary power. However, spiritual powers create hurdles in the way of Self-Realization. Paramatman is beyond the individual with attributes (Jiva), the formless God (Shiva), and even beyond "Prakriti," the basic root of manifestation. God (Narayana) is the fourth state beyond the three states of Waking, Dreaming, and Deep Sleep. The one who has given up seeing, and the things that are seen, is Narayana. The fourth state of being considers the other three states as unreal. The fourth state is the intelligent state of Knowledge. "I am the One in All, the Gods of Gods. I am Narayana who bestows godhood upon the Gods." This is the fourth state, the Turya State. He is called "The Lord of the Three Worlds," because this state is beyond the other three states, or worlds. The word "Trikoota" means the three states that are within. The one who is in all three states and still knows himself as separate from all of these, is Narayana. One who does not understand and know these three states is but a slave, or servant in the three worlds. Being a servant, he is an individual, or Jiva. The One who knows all three of these states is Paramatman.

Morning, 2-12-1934

30. Know Who You Are

One should first know, "Who am I?" This is easy. If there is total inward renunciation, the "I" is Brahman, and then Brahman alone is. However, first there should be renunciation of objects. If we do not know the Self, we only live as individuals (jivas). We should get up in the morning very nicely. What does that mean? If at the time you wake up, you tell yourself that you are Brahman, you become Brahman. We should wake up as a king, and live like a king. If you wake up with a feeling of being a beggar, then you will continue begging. One behaves according to the attitude and feeling one adopts. We are the "knowingness" itself and therefore we become a king or a soldier in no time. We ourselves decide what we want to become.

Work is always going on for millions of years. It will never be complete. We will never say that it is enough. The feelings of "my wife" and "my children" are the riches of the individual. The riches of God are such that there is no need for anything. Adopt the attitude that "Nobody belongs to me, I am the Self, alone." The "Goddess of the Jiva" is actually the "eclipse of misfortune." The Power of Shiva, is the "Goddess of Liberation." Now, whom to wed is in your hands. You may choose whom you wish. Hunger, thirst, desire, and anger may be with you for hundreds of thousands of births. You will get that which you choose (Jiva or Liberation).

It is difficult at the beginning to aspire for the state of Brahman, but it becomes easier afterwards. You should learn to educate your mind to be your own Guru, your own Master. Day and night, you should think of Brahman, and meditate on it. The mind must be helpful. When the mind has a habit, it is doing the same thing again and again. Once there is the attitude or state that one is the all-pervading Brahman, the mind becomes purified, in repose in the Self. It becomes the Guru, and then you will have no difficulty at all. If we think of the devotee and God, that the devotee himself is God, the individual is Brahman and nothing else. However, as soon as there is attachment to objects, you become the individual, the Jiva. When the attachment to objects ends, you are Brahman. When you begin to demand something, you become smaller and smaller. One who has no desire is great. To clap is dependent on two hands. Unless the two meet, there is no clapping.

What has priority, the attachment to objects, or the "Awareness of Reality"? One must meditate on this. Think along the lines that objects are unreal, and detachment from objects is itself awakening to Reality. You should study like this. The disciple asks, "For how many days should this be done? The answer is "Just do it to such an extent that Reality is not forgotten." It should never be forgotten, that is all. There is no separate "I." According to scriptures, "There is only Freedom." You can be free only because you are already free. You *should* feel that you are free, because you are not bound. If you go to the root of God and the devotee, duality disappears. Everything is One.

If essentially everything in the world is made of earth, what separation is there? Then who is this "I"? There exists only the five elements and the one Self. That is your "Existential Reality." The five elements and "You," means that you yourself are the entire universe. The one Paramatman is separate from all that is seen. One who is united with "That," will not remain separate. The principle that is established as soon as self-surrender happens is itself "Undivided Devotion," or Final Liberation (Sayujya Mukti). That which is gained in the Illusion is like a small harvest of corn. The small crop bears a small amount of corn. The feeling that "I am Brahman" causes the harvest of the corn of Brahman. Now, the corn is of the "Freedom of Liberation." The clay lion knows that it is nothing but clay. Similarly, everywhere there is only Brahman. If there is no individual, there is no Illusion.

As the river does not keep its identity once it is merged into the sea, likewise, when a devotee merges into God, he does not remain separate. Once the devotee becomes God, he does not exist as a separate devotee any longer. One who is aware of the unity of the devotee and God, realizes Brahman. Know that you are Brahman, and you will live full of Glory as the all-powerful Supreme Self, Paramatman. If you fall into the realm of Illusion, you will only have the company of anger, attachment, pain and sorrow, which means you that will not get peace. Therefore, you must live as Brahman.

Evening, 2-12-1934

31. The Six Virtues or Qualities

Success, Riches, Glory, Desirelessness, Charity and Wisdom, are the six virtues, or good qualities. The word "Yash," means success, or victory. Whom should we call a successful person? One who is victorious over Illusion should be called successful. It is difficult to conquer Maya, the Illusion. To call her Illusion and to still employ her to serve, is quite difficult. One who conquers her is victorious. Only then can one be called "successful." Then there is "desirelessness," which simply means not to have any desire for anything. However, "charity" is more important. It is possible to be desireless, but it is difficult to be charitable. This means to give in charity that which you possess. However, you are not willing to give up the hold that you have on your possessions. How can you be willing to give up what you possess on one hand, when on the other hand, you deceive others? You give two dimes when you should give four. There is a story of a person was not guarding his field. Someone asked him, "Why don't you guard the crops in your field?" He answered, "I have kept it open so that it may be useful for others. Let people take away what they want." But the experience was completely opposite. Robbers said, "Let us not rob from his field, we will rob from the fields of those who protect their possessions zealously." The sign of the Supreme Self, Paramatman, is charity. Paramatman is One in All. The enemy is Paramatman, children are Paramatman, and the wife is Paramatman. One should never be jealous or envious of anybody. One should never find fault with others. One who behaves like this is Paramatman. He is the "Beloved Lord" (Bhagavan).

In the Bhagavad Gita, Lord Krishna says, "I am That, and nothing else! Yet, while I am Paramatman, people think that I am an individual (jiva), and they insult me. So, I give them many hardships. While they are enjoying their so-called happiness, I put them in a very painful situation. Why? Because they think that I am an individual (in other words, they believe themselves to be an individual). I tolerate this because it is my nature to forgive. Nevertheless, they lift me from the king's throne and throw me into the fire! They put themselves into very painful experiments, like undergoing tests by fire on all sides of the body, or inhaling smoke while hanging upside-down (these are austere practices undertaken to gain spiritual experiences). While I am very simply and naturally One and Alone, "Total in Myself," they imagine strange things, and try to give me pain in all kinds of ways. That is why I do not give liberation even to those who have undergone very austere spiritual practices. On the contrary, I send them to many more births because of their adamant mind. Therefore, 'Devotion to Me' should be free of any desire for sensory enjoyment, devoid of all wishes or demands, and free from imagination."

Look at the strange attitude of the individual (jiva). Although he is the Supreme Self, Paramatman, he thinks himself to be a jiva. This is the great sin that he commits and thereby wastes his life. There is a story about a group of fishermen. One day they were late in returning to their homes. It soon became dark, and they could not travel any further. Nearby was a house of a rich man, who was purely vegetarian. They went to his house for shelter. He welcomed them, received them with respect, and made a suitable arrangement for sleeping in the outer corridor. As the rich man had a good flower garden, there were fragrant flowers stored in some baskets in that corridor and the smell of the flowers was everywhere. The night air was also pleasantly cool. However, the fishermen could not get proper sleep because of the heavy fragrance of flowers. Since they could not stand the fragrance of the flowers, they took the pieces of cloth that they use to cover their fish, and tied them around their heads so that their noses could only smell the odor of fish. It was only then that they could get some sleep. In short, the mind of the individual is similarly addicted to sense objects. It likes to live in the same ignorant way all the time.

It is very difficult to break the habits of the mind and lift it to a higher level. Why does one become a body? It is because of the false egotistical tendencies. To be the body means to be identified with, and limited and shaped by a particular form, like a clay pot. It is to be identified with a limited intellect, limited enjoyment, and a limited consciousness. The jiva does not wish to have no form, no sensation, or to be extremely vast and spread out everywhere. We presume that it is death if we become like that. Thus, there is a liking for a particular form. This is what is called "body-consciousness," and because of it, the desire for objects increases. You are Brahman, so do not harbor desire for objective things. Desirelessness means to let go of that which only disappears anyway. Charity means to say, "Nothing is mine. As I am not the body, how can anything belong to me? I am the Supreme Self, Paramatman, beyond the body."

Morning, 3-12-1934

32. God is in the Form of the Devotee

When we see God in his devotee, only then do we attain godhood, or God's Blessing. If you think that you are God, the Self (Atman), you become God. If you call yourself as an individual (Jiva), you become an individual, and if you say that you are God (Shiva), you become and actually are, God. The poverty of the individual is first pleasure, secondly pain, and thirdly hunger and thirst. You have to suffer all of this because of your identification with the body. When your parents gave birth to you and you are their child, the worldly life is your fate. However, if you become the "Son of the Guru," Guruputra, you perform the last rites of your parents (you cease having the identification of being their son), and are free of that debt. Then, for you, the Guru is your mother and your father. You are to obey the orders of the Guru.

If after surrendering yourself to the Guru, you do not attain His status, then your becoming the Guruputra, the "Son of the Guru," makes no difference. If a person is adopted, he has to cut his relationship with his former parents. If he does not do so, he is not a true son. If one becomes a "Guruputra" only for name's sake, yet remains as the same old member of his family and native place, then his becoming the son of the Guru is meaningless. How can one then attain "divine wisdom," and how can one attain liberation in this way? No, it cannot be so. One who becomes the "Son of the Guru" must act accordingly. If the son starts to come out of the sea of mundane life, the parents will try to pull him back and put him in the dungeon of family life. This is how parents teach their children. Parents will never help one to be free and attain liberation. They will only try to expand your attachments. To merge the child into the ocean of worldliness is the task of parents, while the duty of the Guru is to free one from the worldly life, and endow one with the "Glory of Liberation." Brahman is truly one's Glory, one's Riches, and one's Kingdom.

Let there be constant "Awareness of Brahman." Consciousness should never be thought to be bound by the body. When a person, through the "Realization of Brahman" becomes the Self, "Complete Happiness" itself, he has an aversion to the money of the world. Kamal, the son of Saint Kabir saw a diamond but thought it to be only hardened shit. To one who is successful in reaching beyond the mind, all of the pleasures that money can buy, are false. They are but trivial. The glory of the "Son of the Guru" is such that the three great gods, Brahma, Vishnu, and Shiva, envy him. Those who realize the state beyond the mind do not wish for worldly life. They raise their flags on the "City of Brahman" and give shouts of victory. This state is attained only by the Guruputras. One becomes a Guruputra only by discarding the limitations of the body. Only when body-consciousness is gone does one become the true Guruputra. He has no use for the body. This body is for the enjoyment of the multitude of sense objects. By leaving it, one becomes Brahman. One attains the constant, eternal, pure, intelligent, beginningless state, the origin of all things that is all-pervading. He becomes the Absolute, Parabrahman. You should yourself be God and then see God. To be a "Devotee of God" is to be beyond all objects, and to empower oneself to attain that state is the duty of the Guruputra.

Evening, 3-12-1934

33. The Signs of Desirelessness

The word Vairagya means desirelessness, or "renunciation." This quality of mind comes to one who understands that the world is illusory. When one's attention is diverted from wealth (Laxmi) to God (Narayana), it becomes desireless. Desire that which is the bliss of your "Essential Being." To feel the happiness that is naturally abiding within oneself, to feel an increase in that happiness, to have interest and an urge to know it increasingly, and to not like anything else except that inner happiness; these are the signs of desirelessness. With this desirelessness, comes the quality of charity. With charity, there is wisdom. In Hindu mythology, there was a great Sage by the name of Agasti. Agasti means the one who does not wander, and "Gasti" is the one who wanders. This is the individual, or jiva. To go beyond birth and death is to become Agasti.

The story is told that in the monastery of a great sage, there was silverware and many other articles of gold and sliver useful for the worship of God. This sage told his disciples, "The one who will bring and give, let him give. The one who will take away, let him take away. Do not prevent anybody." One day robbers came and stole some of the objects from the temple and ran out, but there were two people there with bow and arrow, ready at the gate. The robbers tried to escape by every door of the monastery, but at each door, the same two people were there. In the end the robbers left all of the objects, and fell at the feet of the sage. At that time, the sage felt sorry for the robbers, because they could not take any of the things away. This is charity. This means that you may have valuable things but you have no desire to protect them. If a man puts a huge amount of money in a bank in his name, and says that he has renounced, that is not a real sacrifice. And, if a man has simply taken care to behave righteously in society, this is not charity either. The signs that are mentioned above indicate the state of Brahman. The individual is truly none other than Brahman. As long as the conviction that "I am the body" is not gone, wisdom will not come. As long as the desire to pile up more and more money is felt in the heart of the aspirant, it must be known for sure that the body identification, the sense that "I am the body" is not gone.

If Discrimination (Viveka) and Desirelessness (Vairagya) are not present, there is no Self-Knowledge. When these qualities are there, what does one need or demand? One will have no place for God also. God says that such a one is invincible. He says, "He does not want anything. What can I do? He is fearless. He is a renunciate. He has no fear of anyone or anything." One who wants something should worship gods or dead ancestors. While one still has some desire, he has fear. One who does not need anything is the real renunciate. No one can hinder him. He has no bondage at all. He does not care for anything. One who wants everything has fear of everything. Such a one is a beggar, and has great fear. There are many that try to entice a man who says he does not want anything. Do not accept anything from anybody. There is a story of a priest (a Brahmin) who found that nobody was ready to give their daughter's hand in marriage to him, so the Brahmin decided not to marry at all. However, he found that when he did not wish to marry, people began to compete among themselves to offer him proposals of marriage, and eventually one man succeeded in marrying his daughter to this Brahmin, providing him with a great many things. This story indicates that if you are greedy you will be sorry, and that the one who is not greedy gets peace and happiness. Even Death is afraid of the one who has no desire. He is really God. Even the gods are not as happy as He is.

Many sages find it a great burden if they take on many disciples. Saint Ramdas says, "Lucky is that yogi who is imbibed with desirelessness." Consider the one who has no desires greatly lucky. Sometimes one says, "I will let it go if I cannot get it," but still the anxiety in the mind does not diminish. What is the use of this type of desirelessness? One's attitude should be such that one is free of desire. Renunciation should be natural. He is happy whose sorrow has ended. He attains Knowledge based in experience. Otherwise, if one only has verbal knowledge one cannot get the happiness that true Knowledge brings. One whose nature is free of greed becomes bored by even the sight of diamonds, rubies, and stacks of money. Such a man cannot be attracted to money, to house, or property. While it is only when he is left with no other options that a greedy man will be forced to relinquish his possessions.

The sage nullifies all actions by renouncing them from the beginning. He knows that renunciation must not be kept for the last day, because some attachment may creep in that may catch one unaware, and be a cause for rebirth. The one who has become completely unattached, does not have to make any last minute haste. Sages always live in freedom. There is a saying that Saint Muktabai offers all of the five kinds of vital air (Pancha-pranas, or five pranas) in the light of the Aarati. This means that you should not consider things to be yours that do not belong to you. Take the utmost care, as surely an arrest warrant will be given. Know that all of the things in the world are the property of another. One who is living in his house, yet is desireless, is the real forest dweller. He is the true monk. He attains the "Wisdom of God." The main key to spiritual life is the state of "Total Desirelessness." There is a saying: "There is no happiness that compares with Desirelessness."

Morning, 4-12-1934

34. Look at God Through the Eyes of the Devotee

The devotee himself is God. Never think that God is different from his devotee. It is not correct to imagine that someone will come to you, and he will do something to turn you into God. Whatever you have done is simply only what has been done, that much is true. However, do not suppose that you can by some effort, somehow become God. Illusion will try to unsettle you in your decisions, but never presume that Illusion will give you the status of God. The individual has come into existence by your own free will, and you will be able to be God, by your own free will. Your decision will be final and you can be successful if you put forth the effort. If you yourself do not say that you are God, how will others say so?

When you feel that when you are taking yourself to be a human being you are committing a great sin and creating a big chaos, then you will be as God. When you feel like that, you should understand that you are becoming like God, and that "godliness" is developing. Truly, you were already God. Just as a man does not like wearing a sari (an Indian woman's dress), similarly, when one becomes God, he does not like to lead a worldly life. The devotee must have the conviction that he is Pure, he is Truth, and he is Free. You should be ashamed of being an individual. You must develop the attitude that, "I am not the body. I am Brahman. What need do I have for the objects of the senses?" Take note of all the thoughts that come into the mind. These should be examined every day. You should observe how the feeling of your own nature has changed from that which you were experiencing before coming into contact with a Saint. You should observe in what way you were behaving before, and how your consciousness is changed while you are working throughout your day.

What did the mind like before, and what kind of satisfaction did it give to you, prior to this contact? What does it like now? What is the meaning of your life? What is its nature? What is its quality? Gradually as you develop greater understanding of your True Nature, the faculties like eating, protection, development, and the desire for things conducive to realizing that True Nature will change, and your actions will be such that they will be helpful for fulfilling those needs. All beings act according to their nature and species. The knowledge of our nature and our species, causes us to collect things, or to give up things, accordingly. Our mind, our intellect, our consciousness, our ego with the sense of its rights, all function in accordance with our nature, our species, our position, and our circumstances. To know Reality is to look and to be sure about our True Nature. When you are sure about that, it is called steady Self-Knowledge. Only when we definitely know how and what our life is, can we decide what we need, and what we do not need.

Examine daily what kind of thoughts you project. Are they about spiritual life or are they about worldly life? One who examines in this way, gains an inner richness. For one whose attention is turned towards the Reality, the first effect is desirelessness. Then, one experiences that whatever may be given to him or taken away from him, does not matter, as he does not need anything. Charity means that there is no desire to maintain even that which one possesses. Then there is Knowledge.

Afterwards there is success as one becomes victorious over Illusion. There is no sorrow for that which is gone. The fourteen senses are emissaries of the God of Death, Yama. The function of the senses is to increase their activities and invite punishment. To escape from this is extremely difficult. First of all, *you must have the urge* to free yourself from this. Such an aspirant is truly benefited when the Guru meets him. The Guru points the way, only to the one who is ready, and the teaching is useful only when one is ready. After meeting the Guru, you must be disciplined and study hard. Only then will the path become easy for you. The departed forefathers will shower flowers on the one who is able to beat the drums of victory in spiritual life. Only one who remains in the state of "Brahman Consciousness" becomes successful. Only he achieves his goal. Only his boat has reached the other shore. Only He is the victor! Then there is liberation. This One dwells in everyone's heart, all-pervading, everywhere. Then only, is there life in freedom, without any touch of worry, without any desire, the life that is free from all actions. Such a one is God. If one becomes God, all praise Him, and like to have a glimpse of Him (Darshan; to see Him). If one attains liberation while still living, it is considered to be the "Glory of God."

Examine your behavior everyday, and you will know for yourself what virtues you have developed. If you identify yourself with God, you will also gain "His charity." If you come to the realization that "You Are Brahman," you will be Brahman. Then you will not desire anything else. If a lamp is lit in a house, the light shines out through the window, similarly, if Brahman shines within, its signs are evident on the outside. Consider "desirelessness" as a great profit that is gained. What does it mean to you if some other aspirant behaves in a certain way? What do you lose if he goes astray? We must free ourselves from the concept of "you." Otherwise, that also becomes a bondage, a source of worry. Therefore, you should not worry about anybody. Only then are you free, and your fame will have no bounds. Great Saints, like Rama, Krishna, Vasishtha, and Tukaram are very famous. The older the fame, the greater the Glory! The renown and dignity only go on increasing. The one who has escaped from this Illusion is the truly brave one. Without concern for fame, such a one becomes famous, and people sing his praises.

Evening, 4-12-1934

35. The Persistent Wish is Called Desire

When there is a wish in the mind day and night, that is called "desire," or "kama." When the mind constantly runs from one object to another, that is called desire. One who has no desire is mute. Mecca and Madeena (holy places of pilgrimage) are far away but it is necessary to go there in one's life. The one who pursues the fulfilling of desire is the individual (Jiva). One who has no desire is God (Shiva). Fire is fire, cotton is cotton. Knowledge is fire, as it destroys all action (karma). The six qualities that arise in space; Desire, Anger, Greed, Enticement, Pride, and Sorrow are in the nature of the individual. When we get something, we feel increased desire, and if we don't get it, we feel sorrow. These qualities are intermixed with each other. Therefore, desirelessness is the sign of godliness. To have desire is the sign of the individual.

All worldly pleasures are related to the individual. They are not of the Self. One who knows oneself to be beyond all attributes (Gunas), becomes free from sense object enjoyments. Enjoyment of objects makes for the limiting of the Self. To think of objects is the Rajas Guna, while to think of the Self is the Sattva Guna. When one realizes that Brahman is the only true pleasure or joy in life, he becomes Brahman. One then dislikes sense pleasures derived from objects.

Previously, I told you of the eight spiritual powers. Those who practice devotion as told by Me, get all of these powers naturally. I am all-pervading. I am the Space beyond the Sky. I am the listening in all, and the mind of the minds of all. To know this is called clairaudience. I am the eye of the eyes of all. When one realizes this, he gets clairvoyance. One who knows that he is the inner urge of all the minds, that he is mind itself, gets the power of control over mind with his conviction. The realization that "I am Brahman," is itself the conquest of the mind. To think that it is the body that acts, is ego. The concept, "I am the body, I am acting as a body," is ego. To realize that "I am without a body" is the state of Brahman.

One who knows that he is the essence of all forms, and the destroyer of all forms, is truly the occupier of all forms, and gains My (God's) Power. One who stands separate from Me, and thinks "I am God," is my devotee, but those who know that they are one with Me, like Rama and Krishna, become Gods. Vasishtha and other sages thought of themselves as devotees, and remained devotees. Rama, Krishna, and others, conceived of themselves as God, and they were God, by their firm decision. They attained the state of the Supreme Self, Paramatman. Those who come to know Brahman should remain as Brahman. They should feel unity with all the atoms and sub-atoms of the world, which are made up of the five elements, without any reference to a particular entity. The "Realized One" does not feel separate from his Existence. To have the desire of knowing what is in another man's mind, and to have such a capacity is as if to go away from one's Self. When you are in all beings, where is the need to know the thoughts in another's mind? When there is no "other," and there is only one undivided Self, Brahman is spread out everywhere, so what "other" is there to know?

There is the imagined person in you, and you (the Self) are there. Do not become that person projected by your imagination. It is not that "I" should be Brahman, but that the "I" should be dead. Actually, the "I" is itself an illusory imagined entity. "I" is the essence of what is called sin. It demands more and more sensory enjoyments which only kindles more and more desire for sensual pleasures. It is very greedy. Give up this "I." It cannot be slain by any weapon but it dies as soon as you understand it very subtly. This understanding is not so easy to come by. Your task is to make into Brahman that which is already Brahman. You cannot turn that which does not exist, the "I," into Brahman. This is the subtle difference. This does not require spiritual powers. As Brahman is pervading everywhere without division, spread out with no separate parts, who is to search whom, and where? Who is to know whom? Where is the sense of "other-ness" to be found? How can there be anything that is called "second," separate from the One, and how can it know another? There is only Brahman everywhere without any movement. Then what can be known as "other," the second? You should know this subtle difference. Here, there is no more knowing and not knowing. That "One Brahman" is all-pervading. There is none other to know, or not to know.

Lord Krishna says, "By steadfast concentration on Me, one gets strength like Me. He attains the power of taking any form by concentrating on any form. When a yogi takes the form of Vayu or Prana, the vital air, and goes anywhere, in any body, he is said to have the power of "consciousness entering an other body." However, the one who has very strong faith in "My Form," "My True Nature," sees only Me everywhere. If a man realizes that he is in everyone, where else can he go, to be in another's body? Whose mind does he need to read when it is confirmed that there is none other than one's own Self?

Morning, 5-12-1934

36. One Who Lives as a Body, Suffers as a Body

The devotee actually is God. What do you mean when you say that he has "become" God? The concept of "one's self" is an illusion. There is only one Self in the world. Regardless of whether you say serpent or scorpion, all are only Brahman. The world appearance consists of the five elements and the one Self, and all of this is only God. This gives us the Glory of non-division, non-duality, and the non-worrying state. All of this virtue is one, and it comes totally suddenly. Illusion has taken our possession (that of knowing our true identity). Therefore, we have become unhappy. The signs of the "Realization of Brahman" are the sense of peace, absence of anxiety, full contentment, and an extraordinary feeling of Bliss. What is being experienced as Joy, or Bliss within becomes evident in the organs, skin, and face. The peace and contentment which completely fills Consciousness will be expressed outwardly. In other words, the spreading of light out through the windows, from the lamp that is lit inside. This "Glory" is the absence of anxiety in the mental field.

When we live as a physical body, the pains and sufferings of the body are our fate. For one who holds on to the physical body, there is a lack of well being in the mind, as well as the troubles associated with pride, ego, and anxiety. The one who lives in transcendence of body-consciousness gains the Supreme Reality, Parabrahman. To adopt the position of an individual after knowing that one is Brahman, is like a king doing some service like a servant. To become junior in such a way when one is actually senior is akin to committing suicide. This is what is meant by "to fall." Illusion shows her power and even though you know that the play of Maya is only illusion, you think her to be real. This is because you are in the habit of thinking in this way. You must give up this habit. Otherwise, you will remain a slave to Illusion. How can you be free while retaining this type of habitual thinking?

Remain with the "Realization of Brahman." Only then are you identified with Brahman. Otherwise, you again become the individual, the jiva. When only the "Glory of Brahman" gives true happiness, and it is only That which is truly beneficial, why are you again becoming entangled in Illusion? Why do you fall into the prison of your own desires? Do you want to be living in prison? Can you say that you are pleased with your condition, and that you want to remain in prison? All of the virtues of desirelessness, non-attachment, fearlessness, etc., will be accrued to you simultaneously and automatically, when you give up the notion that you are the body. See what a great injustice you are doing to your Self. Being Brahman, you are very adamantly becoming an individual. To call one's Self the body is the very root of what is called sin. Give up this habit, and be free of sin.

Evening, 5-12-1934

37. Concentrate on My "Real Nature"

You are the Self, the dweller in all bodies. We are the Self in all bodies, the Reality in all bodies. You are in all bodies without actually entering into them. The Self is the sense of "Me" that dwells in all bodies, and that "Me" is eternally free. One who meditates upon "Me" in this way, understands "I am the Omnipresent God." Even the three greater gods (Brahma, Vishnu, and Shiva) do not disobey the orders of the one who properly understands that "I am Paramatman." The animate and inanimate things obey the orders of the one who recognizes one's Self as the "Almighty Lord," Ishwara. When one realizes that He is myself, he becomes powerful enough to make all obey his orders.

Now, I will tell you about the five spiritual powers. If one meditates upon Me as the one who controls the creation and dissolution of the universe, his mind becomes pure. This is called "the power of the knowledge of all the three times." The one who is merged into My Being in this way, does not suffer from cold and heat. He is not disturbed by happiness or sorrow, or pleasure and pain. This is called "the power of being without duality." Now I will tell you "the power of blockage." When one realizes that all the things in the world are all his forms, he can ride upon wind, walk on waters, come and go by his own will, and the flames of fire do not touch him. For the one who is enchanted and seduced by objective things after attaining these powers (siddhis), his pride only increases, and he falls into duality and suffers loss. Now listen about "the power of recognition." One who is meditating on God and knows that "I am the all-witnessing Paramatman," gets "the power of recognizing what is in other people's minds." Such a one comes to know the thoughts and proposals in the minds of others, and can impose his thoughts upon their minds. This is called the Apara Siddhi. One who knows his true Self, obtains the power called Vijaya Siddhi.

The one who worships Me according to the type of yogic concentration that I have just now described, gets all of these powers. Those who worship me according to the instruction given, obtain all of the siddhis according to faith. I will tell you this in another way. If one who is desireless keeps a wakeful watch on his intellect, and conquers his mind, he obtains all of these powers. This is the main principle that I have told you. If a man leaves all other paths, and worships Me alone, he does not give any value to these spiritual powers. Such a one devotes himself only to Me because of his real love, meditates on Me, yearns only for Me, has no desire for anything else, and only desires an intimate abiding in Me. Nevertheless, all the spiritual powers are at his bidding, yet "My Devotee," pure of heart, does not use these powers. One who has attained My Feet, becomes very pure and is a very strong devotee, who never resorts to using siddhis. One who worships Me without keeping in mind any other motive, attains My Presence. But, if one is caught in these powers, when they happen to be in his command, and wishes that he should gain fame and righteous dignity due to them, he again recedes to the state of an individual, a jiva. One who has Me does not need siddhis.

There is a story that illustrates this principle quite well. Once a man was going to Kashi as a pilgrim. On his way, he stopped at the house of a prostitute. He was rich, but he spent all his money on that prostitute, and even though he became poor, he did not leave that place. Eventually, that prostitute left him. He lamented his loss for the rest of his life. He was lost, and he could not even go to Kashi any longer. Spiritual powers are like this. They hinder the attainment of Reality. They throw you again into the realm of Illusion. Don't give them any respect or interest. These powers are a hindrance to your reaching Me. Do not be deluded by them. You will only lose that which you have gained. I am purposely giving you this useful instruction. Be particular in remembering this. These spiritual powers appear exactly at the time of your reaching and realizing Me, and they deceive My devotees. These are but another diversion in the shape of pleasure. You feel very good when you enjoy this pleasure. One who keeps on taking pleasures offered to them, becomes estranged from Me. Illusion knows very well where the aspirant will be trapped. Pride about youth, pride about being educated, pride about riches, pride about art, these are all the mischief of the game of Illusion, aimed at turning the seeker away from the correct path, and putting him into the chains of birth and death. Be on guard.

There is a story about a poor man. He worked hard as a construction laborer and could save the sum twenty paise, or one fifth of a Rupee. He was very puffed up by the saving of that little sum of a fifth of a Rupee. It happened that he was arrested by the police and in court, he was fined the amount of one fifth of a Rupee. To hear that sentence given to him was such a blow, he was speechless. His pride was gone as soon as that sum was taken away. Similarly, you have some pride that you are earning something, or gaining something. Give up that pride. Give up the habit of being puffed up. Pride must surely be given up. That laborer only got the sum of a fifth of a Rupee, but even that proved bad for him. I have told you this so that you will come to know the cause of your being deceived. Don't become deceived by powers.

Morning, 6-12-1934

38. The Glory of Paramatman

If one is fully absorbed in the "Glory of the Supreme Self," Paramatman, the individual (Jiva) becomes God (Shiva). One must give up the pride of the body, and only then does one become Paramatman. If one is proud of the physical body, Shiva becomes Jiva. This is called regression or downfall. The difference is slight but it is of great importance. One should give up the desire for public recognition. There is nothing that is impossible for one to achieve. Effort must be made in spiritual practice, but it must be "right effort." Only then does one become the "All-permeating God" (Narayana). You are the owner of the world. Descent means to fall down. If you use a little discernment, you become the owner of the world, you become happy, and you even obtain all of the spiritual powers.

One who takes the medicine named Vitthala (God) must observe certain precautions. The precaution is to give up contact with the objective world. One must be in constant awareness of the Self. You should say, "I am not the body, I am the all-pervading God. Not a single thing in the objective world is useful for me." All objective things should be considered as trash and thrown away. You should tell people, "Even if all things are real for you, I don't want anything, even if it is free." You should treat all objects of this world as disposable. Be as if dead in the eyes of the world. Saints are asleep to those things for which the people of the world are very much awake and concerned about. Moreover, the Saints are awake where the world is asleep. That means that the Saints have no taste for the things that the world likes. That which the Saints give up, the whole world desires and does not want to give up. This is a fact that is clearly seen. One who sleeps with regard to worldly pursuits, becomes awake in the spiritual world. However, in the beginning you have to apply some effort, and willfully forget the objects of the world.

Do not harbor desire for recognition and honor from people, or worldly pleasures, or sense objects, or riches. Continue to simply give up everything. The things of the world are desired by worldly people, but the Saint does not want any thing. He does not even look at them. The one who has truly renounced everything does not want either late-sleeping or early awakening. There is no desire for either kingship, nor any wish to be a beggar. Even the three gods, Brahma, Vishnu and Shiva, are afraid of such a one because he does not demand anything in the Illusion. He does not want anything. If there were to be anything that was to be given, he should be given the blessing that there be no need for anything. Let the wish to demand anything from the Illusion die. Give up all desire, and in return everything is received. The true renunciate, or Sadhu, does not need sense objects or riches by way of alms. That is how the Sadhu becomes victorious. Therefore, shift your attention away from this world. In the beginning, it is okay to keep up the attitude that you are a Saint or a wise man. Vasishtha was thinking of himself as a Saint and a wise man, while Rama, and Krishna, were thinking themselves as Gods, and were acting as the Supreme Self, Paramatman. This is the subtle difference between the Saint and Paramatman.

In the beginning, you must have some pride in your renunciation. One who adopts the behavior that he is a Saint and that he does not want anything from this world, is called the "Son of the Guru," a Guruputra. This is the teaching of the Guru. The sentiments that are there in you from earlier days should be cut away. The concept that the world is real is of a very low stage, it is downward movement. You are deprived of your highest status only because of that concept. Do not question the statements of the Saint. If you do not abide by his teaching, you will have to go repeatedly into the cycle of births and deaths. Truly, you are the creator of all the riches that you demand. Your real status is so high that even the gods Hari (Vishnu) and Hara (Shiva) will obey your orders. You will become "That" if you hold on to the teaching of the Saint. The seekers to whom this teaching is to be given should gradually and silently increase their efforts daily. If you try to break out the news (seek recognition from others), your situation becomes as difficult as dealing with the carcass of an elephant. That carcass is not easily removed from the street, and the street does not become free from traffic for a long time.

The teacher likes the one who follows his teaching and understands it. What is the meaning of the statement that the teacher likes someone and does not like someone else? The question is not one of rich or poor. The teacher is fond of the one who is truly spiritual. This means that the one who holds to the spiritual life as the highest life, becomes the closest disciple or real devotee. When the awareness of being a disciple and a devotee is constantly on the increase, and one makes the firm decision to value the spiritual life as the highest way of living, this is what makes a seeker beloved to the Guru. It is not that the Guru does not love other disciples who are with him, but it is best that you are understanding his teaching. The Guru does not care about the financial prosperity or poverty of the disciple. He loves the great urge in the disciple's mind towards the attainment of the Reality. The disciple should study and attain Reality secretly. He may grow his hair long or not, his physical appearance is not important. He should steadily, keep progressing quietly on the path, on the basis of personally experiencing the Truth. This should be done very patiently, and secretly. If you ask for the opinions of others, you will find that they will try to pull you back.

Study well, but be very much on guard. Do not get caught up in anyone's cult. Only when you stop trying to catch a dog, will it be quiet. Maya (Illusion) says to the gods, "Give me some alms. I am ugly! Who will accept me! Give me some boon!" It was with this anxiety that Illusion came to the mortal world, and what happened? Even though she is ugly, people are devoted to her. They are not ready to let go of her even though she kicks them. Maya got this experience, and she was very pleased. She was successful beyond her expectations. The fear that she used to have previously was automatically lifted. She plays as many games as she likes. All of the people in the world are such that they dance by putting her on their heads (take up the burden of Illusion). Nobody leaves the Illusion even if one may be facing the greatest sorrow. They only love her more. Though her goods are bad, there is only an increase in the number of customers. She on her part is making all efforts to see that not a soul leaves her. You must continue your practice very subtly to consider yourself to be Brahman. Even if there is someone who relinquishes everything, she is always trying to keep him within her field of her control by offering him many things such as powers, etc. She is always offering enticements. Therefore, you should remain alert. Remain unattached. Beware, do not fall prey to the traps of Maya. Those who have thus far been liberated have made it their religion not to pay heed to Maya. We cannot give up our religion. To be one with our Real Nature, the Reality, is our only religion, the one true religion. This is our day of observing a fast, the Ekadashi. Only fruit should be taken. You should deeply enjoy the fruit that is Truth, which the Master has given you. Don't take any other fruit. "I am Brahman" is the food of that fruit-diet. Even if you eat a lot of it, still you will observe the fast of Ekadashi. That is called Ekadashi, which has only one place, the Reality. Don't leave that place which is your own Self-hood. One who observes this Ekadashi should go to the pilgrimage of Pandharpur. But it is only our body that is that Pandharpur. You need not buy any railway ticket. In this body, the Self is the King of Pandhari, the God Vitthala himself. This is the true pilgrimage.

You should increase your devotion like this, and give satisfaction to the heart of your Master. You should get angry if somebody calls you worldly. The true "Knowledgeable-ones," the Jnanis, are not worldly. Do they behave like worldly people? Their daily life becomes spiritual. All of this world appearance is Brahman. There is only this One, without a second. If you behave like this and increase your devotion, you will reach the goal. This is the upward journey. If you go beyond this Illusion, this Maya, then you are saved. Otherwise, Maya rides upon you. Even the Vedas have accepted defeat! If your desirelessness increases, Maya will simply run away and leave you. She will of course try to attract you, but you should pay no attention. Remain with the feeling that you are Brahman. That is what makes Maya run away. When one always remembers God, what can Maya do? Live in the understanding of the "One Truth." Then you will experience that Laxmi (fortune) is the slave to the one who does not care for her, and she will make a beggar of the one who runs after her.

Evening, 6-12-1934

39. The Self is Free From Worry

You are the Self (Atman), and that is the "Essence of Bliss." Happiness is the nature of our own Inner Being. If your mind is content, then that contentment will be present in all outward circumstances. However, we get deluded when we think that we get happiness from sense objects. This is a mistake that all are making. How can you have sorrow if you are convinced that you are not a body but only the Self? What will happen? No matter what you say or do, only that which is destined to happen will happen. So, why should we worry? A man was worrying that his house was about to collapse. A sage said to him, "What are you losing if the house collapses? Have trust in me, and do not worry." He followed the advice of the sage, and within a few days, he unexpectedly received hundreds of thousands of rupees. Then he toppled down his old house himself, and built a new one. The house was sure to fall and it fell, but something good came out of it. He built a new house. That which is destined to happen, will surely happen. Don't worry for anything.

Everybody is anxious about what will happen in the future. Will bad things come to everyone in the future? Everyone is anxious. Don't worry. Your father was worrying about you, and then he passed away. Are you now dying of hunger without him? Don't worry in vain! This is what is called Ignorance. Let whatever happens happen, and don't be anxious about anything. Have steadfast conviction that you are the Self. One who worries will never be happy. Children are happy. Why is this? This is because children do not worry. One who inspite of having the "Knowledge of Brahman," worries, will not enjoy inner happiness. One who worries will never be happy. One who aims at the "Bliss of Brahman," must give up all anxiety and worry. One who gives up anxiety is supremely happy. There is only one way. One must have the willingness to renounce. There should be no desire even if a kingdom is given, and there should be no care, even if the world is drowned. If anxiety increases there is only chaos. When one calls this entire world false, how can anxiety affect him? Don't feel the need for any thing that is in itself false. Just as there is only gold in the ring, yet we call gold by the name of "ring," similarly the world is only Brahman. There is only Brahman in this world. It will appear to you as you look at it. The sages say that you are not mortal, you are Brahman. If you remain confident, you will be without anxiety. Have trust and faith in this.

You are without birth and death. What does it mean when one says that the body is dead? The elements have returned to their own substance, so who has died? Only that which was given some name after birth, is what is dead. Only the name is dead. You never die. You are without parts but at the same time, you are a part. From particle to cosmos, from cosmos to particle, you are permeating everything, yet you are still more. You feel sorrow when taking on the sorrow of others. You should not worry about others. Let the body be glorified, but remain larger and greater than even the earth. Be complete. The space, or sky does not move. You also do not move. If you remain with this wisdom, you are Brahman, the Absolute. The word "Karna" means the one who listens. Listen to spiritual teachings, but do not keep them confined only to the ear. Act accordingly. Only one who acts will benefit. One who puts into practice the teachings of the Sadguru, will attain Brahman. One must listen to and understand the science of life, and then you will be happy. You will get experience according to your faith. If you meditate on God as the Life-Force, as the Life-Energy, then you will be the Life-Energy. We are not worldly. Discard the concept that you are an individual. If you actually live as a sage, you will attain the state of Brahman. If you live as the Self, you will be one with the Almighty God, Narayana.

Evening, 7-12-1934

40. Meditate Upon Me

The Self is without anxiety. Once your ever-changing fascination with Illusion goes and the mind becomes still, you will experience that you are Brahman. Spiritual powers (siddhis) are dependent upon a body. They create enthusiasm for the Illusion and the mind again starts vibrating. Where there is an enthusiastic joy for the sense pleasures, there is the urge toward Illusion. Even extraordinary "Joy," the "Covering of Bliss" (Anandamaya), is also only an inspiration in Illusion. The Self is what is common in both joys. Illusion gives pleasure and pleasure brings in pain. To be agitated and then become tired is like a chain of alternating states.

Please, listen now to how and when this attitude appears. When your attention increasingly becomes concentrated on the Self, the appearance of spiritual powers is incidental, but to use this power is to lose the one-pointed concentration. That enticement is only deception. It is but the bait of Illusion. The main purpose of spiritual power is to deceive one and ensnare him in Illusion. There are four types, or four classes of spiritual powers. (1) Inborn power, (2) Power induced by medicine, (3) Power induced by mantras, (4) Power attained by various yogic practices. One kind of power is gained by unifying the Prana (vital airs or winds) and Apana (eliminative airs or gases from the body). Some power is inborn. A fish swims in water. That is something that is natural, and instinctive for it. This is called inborn power. Some powers or faculties are awakened by drugs. Some are gained by performing some austerities or rituals, by taking up some physical efforts. Some powers are attained by repetition of mantras. The quality of fish swimming in water and birds flying in the air are the inborn powers. The cuckoo sings melodiously very naturally. Such powers are called inborn. By use of medicines, the protection of the physical body in various ways is possible. For example, by habit of continuous ingestion, people can tolerate poison in increasing quantity.

The power attained by austerities or ritual is such that one may undergo some ordeal by fire, take up the practices of Hathayoga, or some may even sit on a dead body and repeat certain mantras or phrases. Some can relieve people from the poison of serpents. Some can do voodoo. However, if one does not do anything in this manner, but only concentrates on the Self, all powers are naturally endowed upon him. The Apana Vayu (Vayu translates as "wind") is very powerful, but it is also very heavy. It is because of this that the body is steady and does not fly away, but it is also so forceful that it can move and throw away even a big house. However, when the Consciousness is contained, the Apana and Prana (Apana is the eliminative wind and Prana is the breath) become unified, and peace prevails. The objects of the senses are in the world appearance and by focusing on them the attention goes outward. Brahman is innermost. By focusing the attention of the mind on Brahman, it becomes introverted, and the Prana and Apana become naturally united in that way. When they become so united, Consciousness loses its duality and one attains Brahman. One attains the Self and gains the four types of Liberation.

God says, "If a man concentrates on attaining various powers, he does not come to Me. My devotees do not desire spiritual powers, and I bestow honor upon them. I worship them. All worship them. The true possessor of all powers is Myself, and My devotee is only Me. I am Myself, the 'Almighty.' All powers are My Nature, so I am called "All-Powerful." When I am attained by the devotee, he becomes one with Me. He is himself God. He has attained the Essence, the Self of all powers. Then nothing is wanted by him. He is the King, and the Glory of the entire kingdom is his. Many servants serve him. That king is truly "The Monarch of All." There are many powers, many siddhis, but for their existence to become possible, the Self must be there in them. Nothing can exist without the Self. So, it is the Self of all powers, of all strengths, and all arts, that is the devotee, who therefore is God. I am one with "My Devotee." There is no other Self except Me in any being. This is Oneness without a second. This is known only by Me, or by My devotee. Others will not know this mystery. When a man becomes the owner of all powers, he relinquishes worldly wealth, or Laxmi (the Goddess of Prosperity), yet, he still becomes the husband of Laxmi. One who kicks away all spiritual powers, all siddhis, becomes the true "Siddha." There is only the "one siddha," the Self, "AtmaSiddha." This One, is the Master, by way of his "True Nature" (Swaroopa)."

Morning, 8-12-1934

41. Give Up the Addiction to Mundane Worldly Life

The Master tells you that you are Brahman. However, Illusion is so enticing that even knowing that one is Brahman, the aspirant still thinks that he is an individual. This is because of one's greed for objects. Greed is itself Illusion. If greed ends, Illusion also ends. When Illusion ends, what remains is Brahman. Such is the way of Illusion. Therefore, do not question the validity of the words of a Saint, otherwise you will be bound to go through the series of millions of births and deaths. In order that the intelligence be in tune with the Self, the Grace of the Master is necessary. It is necessary to have one's intelligence united with the Self. This means that "I Am He" (Soham) should be the concept in the mind.

The worst habit is that of mundane worldly life. It is called the "greatest addiction." By force of this addiction to worldly life, Paramatman is made to believe that He is an individual, and is compelled to live a worldly life as if in prison. All bad habits can be dropped, but the addiction to mundane life is the most difficult to drop. The wife is dear to her husband only so long as she obeys him. The mundane worldly life is called the blind dark life. The greatest enticement of Illusion is this mundane life. However great may be one's sorrow, this addiction cannot be dropped. One is greatly lucky if this addiction is dropped. There is only one person who condemns the worldly life, and that is the Saint. Nobody else does that. One does not even think of leaving this earthly life, even if one suffers utmost difficulties. People try to strengthen their ties with others by speaking to them respectfully and congratulating each other over small things. People compete with each other for earning more honors and status. In this way, they feel that they are happy in life. They act as if this is a respectable bad habit. The "God of Death" is happy to give you many kinds of bodies and various troubles. Give up the sense of "mine." Know that the body is your enemy. Very few are those who have truly understood. Only those who are lucky enough to receive the blessings of the Guru, who is the Self, can escape from this Illusion by right efforts. All others are bound to the treadmill of life in various incarnations, and they make houses of bodies of various shapes and duration.

Blessed is the one who is illumined by the teaching of the Sadguru in this human incarnation. Only with this human body is it possible to have the "Bliss of the Self," and Liberation. The days of your life are very few, so get yourself free while you have the chance. This Liberation is possible only through the teaching of the Sadguru. Therefore, have faith in the Guru and do exactly as told by Him. All people worship the one who turns towards spiritual life. However, those who consider themselves as being very scholarly only raise many various doubts and lead quite a wrong way of spiritual life. They only end up unhappy and make others unhappy as well. The man who is extraordinarily clever is truly of no use. He puts himself and others at a great loss. He suffers because of his own pride.

The one who attains Reality does not suffer from any wants or desires. "God Almighty" looks after his welfare personally. Let such a person be blind or lame, God himself has given a promise, "I look after the welfare of the one who meditates on me." The spiritual person will never be a slave to anybody. Therefore, do not worry. Make God your friend. Who can give trouble to one whom is protected by Lord Rama? There may be as many enemies as there are stars in the sky, but if there is the blessing of the Guru, nobody can touch even a hair. One who has faith in the Guru does not fear anyone. What need is there for anything, if the Guru's blessing is there? Even if one's destiny is the worst, it is the blessing of the Guru that makes all the difference. This is continuously told by the Vedas and Shrutis, very emphatically. Have faith in the Vedas. Conceive of yourself only as Brahman. If your intellect is under your own control, you will have success. Keep your intellect under control and have faith in the Guru. If you do this, you will be easily saved. Put your trust in the Sadguru. He will definitely save you. By remembrance of the Sadguru, Illusion runs away and virtues are developed. Whenever one such as this talks, it is the teaching of the Saints, and it comes so easily.

The things of this world that are cherished by people always breed fear. When some action is done after listening to the opinions of worldly people, it increases many kinds of fear. We get completely exhausted in trying to maintain those things that appear in the Illusion, as those things are ultimately perishable. On the other hand, one becomes fearless by listening to the stories of the Saints. That which is gained by listening to the Saints, "That" which is attained, is not perishable. Spiritual accomplishments are full of happiness. When you get experience in the spiritual life, then you will know the blessing of the Sadguru that you have received. How much happier you will be, and you will witness the pitiable condition of those who had been laughing at you. Blessed is the one who dies while practicing devotion to Lord Hari (Vishnu). Who can describe his fortune? Only he knows his own great fortune. He is Paramatman only. You will, just like Saint Tukaram, be the God of the gods. "I listened to the one Supreme Truth from a Saint and I became the father of the fathers of all. I became God. Otherwise my life was being wasted."

In short, people are like donkeys. They never listen because they are heavily conditioned from birth. However, those who do listen will attain Self-Realization. Take a vow that you will sacrifice in the service of the Sadguru, and you will never stop cherishing the name of God, Hari. Paramatman is near him who has unshakable faith. If you walk along the road of spiritual life already explained, you will be guided and protected by Paramatman, Shri Sadguru Bhausaheb Maharaj. It is He only who is protecting you.

Those who have faith are getting the proof. This is a fact that is well known to devotees. The divine cow (Kamadhenu) will grant all wishes only to the faithful. God abides by your faith. If you think he is with qualities, He is so. If you prefer him to be formless, again He is. If you do not worship him there is no curse. If you worship him there is no reward or special blessing. One will get experience only according to one's faith. To explain clearly, and to clear away doubt, is the job of the Saints. It will be useful to the one who will accept it. For the one who does not accept, there is no compulsion by anybody. Everybody is unto himself what he thinks. God is according to one's faith. A person shaved his head and offered his hair to God. God gave him the birth of a bear. If you offer yourself totally, you will be the Supreme Self, Paramatman. You will attain "That."

Evening, 8-12-1934

42. Know That You Are Paramatman

Any work should be first properly understood and then done. Then, when it is properly done, it becomes beneficial. The individual, or Jiva, is of three qualities. The first is Sattva, the second is Rajas, and the third is Tamas. The meaning of vice is to have a liking for dirty things. That is Tamas. Rajas means to have a liking for grandeur and worldly things, and to have a wish for receiving praise, honor, etc. Being of the quality of Sattva means to do spiritual practice, to practice meditation, to give in charity, to worship and sing devotional songs (bhajans and kirtan), to do formal worship (puja, arati, etc.). What is the purpose of all this? We do this because of the desire to meet the Guru in the future, to be led out of worldly life. As this is very necessary, we give importance to the Sattva quality. When the Guru meets you, he tells you that "You are God." Then, it is up to you to develop that attitude.

When the schoolboy passes his examination and moves to a higher level, he is not expected to sit in the lower level class any longer, because he has already progressed. You are the Supreme Self, Paramatman, yet the state of realizing oneself as Paramatman has yet to be attained. How do you attain it? You have to live according to this goal. For example if you are a lawyer, you have to win the case by doing everything that is necessary. Here, the mind will be the judge. Its judgement is the true judgement. One must be fully convinced that one is God. A mad person was told by a very wise man, "You are not mad. People have wrongly called you mad." He told the madman this and accordingly the madman changed inwardly. Although he was having fits of eccentricity occasionally, he tried hard to believe that he was wise, and soon, his concept changed and his madness disappeared. Each and every person has the right to attain freedom. There is no discrimination such as man, woman, or child. However, everyone must do some type of spiritual practice (sadhana).

Once there was a disciple, who although he had received instruction from his Guru, he had not given up his former attitude. He had a peculiar sense of cleanliness. His concept was such that in order to avoid the touch of the dirty earth, he climbed up a tree. He lived in the tree, drank only rainwater, and continued to believe that the earth was impure. When his Guru came to know about this, he went to see him. The Guru saw that the disciple had become very famous. People had built quite a large round platform around the tree, and had made a lot of decorations with all sorts of pomp and show. The disciple did not like to come down, because to him the earth was impure. When the Guru came to see him, he called to him up in the tree and said, "You come down." The disciple said, "I will not touch the earth." The Guru asked, "Where are you sitting at present?" The disciple said, "On this tree." With this, the Guru said, "The tree is part of earth and you remain on this tree. The tree and the earth are not separate. You have separated them by your imagination, but the tree cannot be separated from the earth. The tree is the offspring of the earth and therefore, it cannot be separated from it. It is in its entirety a part of earth. You are smothered by your imagination and in this way, you yourself have become impure. I gave you a mantra so that you would become pure, in unity with the whole world, but you, by your imagination are holding on to ideas of separateness and of purity and impurity. Because of that you have become impure. You are now unfit for the realization that there is nothing other than Brahman. This is why you have no Self-Knowledge, and you will not be able to realize that everything is only one Absolute Brahman." As the disciple listened to this, he understood his folly and with fear, he climbed down. Then the Guru said, "In order to wipe out your ego, you will have to live in the pen of pigs for six months."

When the Guru gives knowledge, one should leave all former rituals and do only that spiritual practice which is advised by the Guru. One should be completely devoted to the Guru. Do not worship many gods. When you have understood that you are God, why do you think yourself to be an individual? If you are a king and still maintain illusory doubt about it, how can you keep up your kingship or kingdom? Please, bow only before the Sadguru with all your heart. You should not bow down before other gods. Their existence should not even be separately recognized or confirmed. Even if scholars well versed in the Vedas may be present, you should first bow before your Guru, because the Guru has given you the status of God. Worship only your Guru. Consider that the Guru is the Almighty Lord of the universe. Come to the understanding that, "I am Brahman." Do not abandon your godhood and take a step down. Your godliness will be proved by your actions. You must be sure of what you are. If a Hindu declares that he wants to become a Muslim, there are people ready to convert him. As soon as you say that you are an individual, Illusion is very happy to distract you from your real nature and to keep you inside her institution.

Do not lose your godliness by worshiping many gods. Prove your spirituality. As already explained earlier, and commented upon, you are the Supreme Self, Paramatman. Do not step down from that position. Do not worship many other gods. This will make you petty. Even if Brahma, the Creator meets you, you still will not lose your divinity. In the **Bhagavad Gita**, Krishna has advised "Leave all religions and surrender yourself to Me (the Self) alone." Do not indulge in useless activities. It is useless to worship many gods. Do not do it. If others are doing so, let them do it. You should only remember the Self, (Rama), and let the world go on fighting. Those who worship other gods, let them do so. You should become God, Rama. You are Rama. Performing many rituals may give you many things, but these things only overpower you, and subjugate you. The Guru says, "It is you whose authority should be obeyed by all." You must attain the state of Paramatman. If you put before you many lesser gods, how can you be Paramatman? To remain as the Self is to not do any rituals with attachment. You may perform many rituals so long as you are not blessed by the Guru. If you worship lesser gods after that, you become petty. You become that which you worship. Do not degrade yourself and call yourself an individual, a jiva.

Whom will Paramatman worship? You are Paramatman. The lesser deities should be afraid even by seeing you. If anyone is possessed by a ghost, that ghost will run away upon looking at you. If you show respect to a ghost, it will ride upon you. Then where is your divinity? As soon as you become an individual, take it for granted that the ghost will overcome you. It will even eat you. Be very careful not to trade your status as God for that of an individual. Give up meaningless rituals. Be like an emperor. Why are you anxious about the sacredness, or any other conditions of the body? The Self is supremely benevolent, supremely pure. When can you say that the blessings of the Guru have done a great miracle? When you know that you are Paramatman. The lesser deities run away at the sight of the "Son of the Guru," the one who is a truly elevated being. Wine, liquor, and other strong intoxicants should not be taken, because if one is under the influence, there can be great mistakes made. False imagination is just like wine. The lesser gods capture your superstitious imagination and you suffer great loss, because of false imaginings. False imaginings causes harm to others and to yourself. This is done only by you. Only do one thing. Do not lose your own state of being Paramatman. That is most important above all. This is the highest devotion.

To remain in our own Self is the True Religion. There is no other sadhana, and there is no other God. Do not be deceived. Rituals are meant for those who are bound by doctrines such as the Vedas. In daily life keep up the faith that you are Paramatman. Do not forget this. It is necessary to be very observant in this way. There is some danger that something which is incorrect may pass as the right path, and the real path of Knowledge will be lost sight of. Therefore, do not tread too much on the path of rituals. This is futile. You may beg for filling the belly, but do not do anything that will hamper the path of Knowledge. There is no shame for a man of wisdom who begs for alms, but do not allow the worship of lesser deities to prevail. Never allow the mind to fall prey to bad influences. The faith in Brahman must be well maintained. Think before you worship lesser gods. When you yourself are the "Effulgence of Truth," of what use are these petty little deities to you? What will they give you? Will the ocean ask for drinking water from the river? When the Guru declares that you are God, why do you insist upon only being a jiva? This is your own foolishness. Don't do it any longer. Frequently check to see whether you maintain the right concept that you are Paramatman. This means that you should always be conscious of It. Never forget it for a moment. If you go by your own Consciousness, how much time does it take for Self-Realization? It is always there. You should actually live like that. You are that Paramatman, the chariot whose wheels are all of the deities. Don't make any mistake about it. Have no doubt. Remain awake to the fact that you are Paramatman.

They say that if you do some particular thing, you get merit. Why do you want merit? True merit is giving up the state of being a jiva. The following of any religion other than that of the Self is what is called sin. How can the Supreme Self, Paramatman, which you are, follow the religions of "others"? He is the greatest. By virtue of his inherent greatness, He is fully and naturally "Supreme Joy" (Paramananda). If anyone abuses you by a foul word, you hold on to the memory of it, but you do not even notice the Knowledge that it is generously showered upon you. That is the sign of being an individual. Let a person call you that which is most lowly, but be sure that you are God, and see what wonder takes place. Once the inner judge has given the judgement that you are God, that judgement will never be changed. That's all there is to it. Then you really become Paramatman. Suppose that the mind is your wife, and if she does not obey you, where is your bravery? Ask this to yourself each hour. "Are you with me? Are you alert and awake?" The answer must be "Yes!" You must remain awake every moment.

In order to attain "godliness," to attain the conscious awareness of being the Self, you should never do anything for worldly gain that will jeopardize your aspiration for Self-Realization. That act may be desirable from a worldly point of view but anything that undermines the state of Brahman is completely undesirable. This is possible only for one who practices diligently. What will be the accomplishment of one who does not study hard? To develop the sense of being the Self is itself merit. To lose that state is what is called sin. What do you think devotion to the Guru means? By devotion to the Guru, you become the ruler of all the gods. You are re-gaining yourself, you are realizing your True Nature, your Real Being, your Real Power. This is devotion to the Guru. Devotion to the Guru, and devotion to God, means to realize your own Self, your own "Completeness." Even if we practice but a little of devotion to the Guru, we attain Self-Realization. What has happened to those who have had devotion to their Guru? They have become Brahman, they have achieved Reality.

Devotion to the Guru must be very one pointed. Only then is Brahman realized. Some say, "I do service to my Guru. I do devotion to my Guru." To such a man I ask, "What do you do in this devotion? Do you realize your True Nature? Do you gain what is your own "True Possession"? You yourself become the Self, God (Atmaram). This is true devotion to the Sadguru. The Guru is so powerful that all of the lesser deities are afraid of him. Remain as your own Self. Do not lose your dignity. "I Am Brahman" is your dignity. Never forget That.

Morning, 9-12-1934

43. How to Do Spiritual Practice (Sadhana)

One may read various scriptures (Shastras), and mythological books (Puranas), but all of this is useless without Self-Knowledge. In this world, there is really only one path of Liberation. One must study the Self (Atman), and understand that all of the five elements are only one, and that the Supreme Self, Paramatman, is all-pervading. One must gain this experiential understanding.

In the beginning, meditation should be on the Mantra (a name of God, or a statement) that has been given by the Guru. New aspirants may see different colors such as yellow, white, and blue. This is okay in the beginning, but no particular significance should be given to any of these appearances. Meditation should be done in the morning and in the evening with a peaceful mind. After getting up in the morning and having completed the morning toilet, etc., you should take some time to meditate to quiet the mind. The seat where you sit for meditation should be special. If possible, it should not be the same place that is used for your usual sitting or sleeping. It's best that this place should only be used for the practice of meditation. You can sit in the dark at night or in the light during the day and your posture should be natural and comfortable. You should be relaxed, and there should not be any tension in the muscles. You should not do such things as to hold the breath, etc. An easy comfortable lotus position is the best. Those who have gained a better understanding should regularly concentrate the mind on the Self, and peacefully dwell on the real nature of the Essential Brahman that you are. Try to naturally enter samadhi, the "selfless Self."

You will not come to know very easily in the world about this great path to the "Realization of Brahman," to Self-Realization. To serve the Guru is not only to care for him physically, you must regularly do the type of meditation as per your instructions. At least once in a week, you should try to do meditation for one hour more than usual. If it is not possible because of poverty for you to visit the Guru, you can at least do meditation in your home, and concentrate on the Self and sing devotional songs (Bhajans) with love for Guru and God. Understand that it is God Himself who is performing all these things, but do not give up your meditation. Remember and recite what is in the "twelve abhangas" (12 stanzas of poetry containing the essence of the teaching) written by Tukaram every night. Lord Vitthala has himself given the blessing to

Saint Tukaram that whoever recites these abhangas regularly will gain Self-Knowledge.

Even if there is death of somebody in your house, do not stop your meditation. Meditation should be regular. Even if the women have their monthly period, they should meditate. Do not harbor any doubts. Suppose tomorrow you are going to be busy, you should meditate for a little longer time today, but never abandon it. If there is so much work that you have no time even for dinner, then it can't be helped. Consider yourself excused. Even then, you should have in your heart a keen yearning for doing meditation on God. Do meditation in this way, and you will gain Self-Knowledge automatically.

Keep up the memory of God. Never harm anyone, or blame anyone. What is it to you, the deeds that they have done? All will reap the fruit of their deeds. "Deception is nobody's relative." One who harms others, suffers harm himself. Praise the good points in others, and don't criticize their vices. Be deaf to gossip. By gossip, enmity increases, and friendship is cut. Please remember this. You should daily sing devotional songs, offer food to God, study and recite the teaching, and then put the Gods to sleep, and only then, retire to bed. If you live with this desireless devotion, God will bless you.

Evening, 9-12-1934

44. Paramatman is All-Pervading

To fully realize that I am the all-pervading, complete, Supreme Self, Paramatman, enables one to attain all of My Powers. I am the "Master of all Powers." It is because of Me, that everything is seen. I am the Vedas, the very instrument of Knowledge. I am the "Living Spirit," Consciousness, the Self (Atman) in all beings. It is the Self that is the cause of all movement of the body. Otherwise, what is the difference between a corpse and a living man? As the sky is both on the inside and outside of a pot, I am also inside and outside of all. I am the underlying support of all. The Self is at all times spread out evenly everywhere. Being One and undifferentiated, it is always in equilibrium. Not to know the Self is the state of disparity, or separateness. To know completely is parity, or unity. Though this is true, if you do not know it to be true, it is disparity, or a sense of separateness that prevails.

When one says, "I was awake," or "I was asleep," one reiterates and proves that in both states "I existed." It is both the one who says "no" and the one who says "yes." It is the one who says "no," and at the same time, it is only the Self. If the Self is not there, who can confirm or deny? It was there when one said, "I have seen." When one understands, it is automatically known that the Self has understood. Understanding is possible because the Self is there. Had the Self not been there, nothing would have been known. In deep sleep, there is neither pleasure nor pain. It is the Self that is that pleasure and that joy. Everything, whether it be eating, drinking, or sleeping is all only the joy of the Self. It is even joy to pass stools, as it gives much relief and peace. To have a sensation that is conducive to us is joy. To scratch is also a joy. I am that Paramatman, which in its being, moving, and joy, permeates everywhere. The whole world is made up of the five elements, but I am pervading and permeating all of these elements in all places.

When a seeker realizes Me to be complete in this way and by knowing one's nature, becomes That, My spiritual powers (siddhis) come in and misguide him. Know that surely all powers are a hindrance in the way to attaining unity with Me. Do not be deceived by resorting to them. Do not miss your Reality by being attracted to siddhis. Siddhi means power. When there is a sense of pride and dependence on some thing in the world, when you get possession of it and use it, it is a hindrance. Any property or possession, or any experience that you get is only an appearance. The experience of fleeting phenomenon will never be permanent however hard you try to make it last. The one who takes pride in accomplishments or in the objects of the world takes a step downwards. Those who are still not free of Illusion have a liking for spiritual powers. They are weak, and forsake the Self. Please listen to what I am telling you.

One who is completely desireless is not affected by these worldly seductions. He says, "Of what use are these things to me? I am beyond all qualities. I am not a person. I have no use for powers." He realizes that the very nature of spiritual powers is false, and only he attains the highest state of "Complete Knowledge." He who has not left behind all hopes and Illusion, does not attain Brahman. I have explained this so that you will not be deceived by the attainment of spiritual powers. That is why this subject has been presented. One who is happy in giving up everything, gets the blissful joy of one's own Essential Being. The Saint has not any work to do, and has all of the joy of "The Lord of the Three Worlds." This is the joy in renunciation. There are multitudes of attachments which cause pain. To give up all attachments is Liberation. To one who is truly liberated, the siddhis, the spiritual powers, are nothing. He is Paramatman, and "Self-Powerful." Everyone lives according to one's own experience.

No Date Given

45. Remain in the State of Brahman

What can one do after death? Nothing can be done. If people have the custom to burn the dead body, it has to be burnt. If they bury it, it must be buried. Also, know that there is no fixed time of death. When one will die is not known. There is no greater fool than he who postpones spiritual study until tomorrow. No one called the wise King Dharma a fool. It is told how once a brahmin priest came to ask for an audience, and King Dharma told him to come back after eight days. At this point, Bheema, the king's brother, did a strange thing. He beat the big drum, which was meant to denote great joy. As Bheema beat it without any apparent reason, King Dharma asked, "Why did you sound the drum?" Bheema said, "You have told that brahmin to come back after eight days. Do you feel sure that you will live for eight days?" Dharma said, "You got the benefit of being in my company, and you have become wise, but today I have become a complete fool." In short, there is no certainty of any moment, and there is no surety of how long we will live. Whatever you want to accomplish, you should do it while this body is moving about. You must hasten to do your best as soon as possible.

This is why the God of Death, Yama beats the drums of victory. King Dharma, who was well known for his knowledge of religion, was proved to be a fool that day. Your time is also similarly being wasted and misused. You see a lawyer that is serving in a saloon. Why? Because he cannot put his knowledge to proper use. What then, is the use of his education and learning? One who has realized one's own True Being should not behave like one who is ignorant. He must behave according to his wisdom. You must know what you are and what your duty is, and behave accordingly. We have not come only to fill our belly, we have come to emancipate the world. Saint Tukaram has said, "We from Vaikuntha (the abode of God) are here for this one purpose." The great wise men have kept something left over (Prasad). We should partake of it and liberate ourselves. It is the sacred blessed food from their mouth. Actually, what you have understood to be false has benefited you, while what appears to be true is dangerous for you. This is the scepter of Yama. The kingdom of Yama, the God of Death, is this world appearance. If one enters the empire of Self-Knowledge, the kingdom of Yama is no more. The one who has understood the world as false, has properly benefited from life. Otherwise, the high and mighty hand of the Death God is always there. We will clean the path of Knowledge, because there are wild forests filling the whole world. Please think deeply about from where you have come. Why have you come? Is it your work to have children and raise a large family? Do you ever give any thought to this? If you do not think, then who will liberate you, and how?

When one day your body will be taken away and burnt, your game is over, and you are finished. You have to start afresh from a new birth. You have never thought, "What is this all about?" For this, the flame of the Self must be made bright by true desirelessness. Only then will spiritual efforts be possible. If you are not truly desireless, you will never gain Knowledge. To relinquish everything, and to be fed up with Illusion, is the sign of advancement in spirituality, and when this takes place, one definitely becomes happy and peaceful. By discarding Illusion, you attain Brahman. Merge yourself into the reality of your Being. It is for this purpose that we have come here. By being aware of this, practice continuously and attain Self-Knowledge. Attain the "Knowledge of Brahman."

Keep examining everything in daily life. The Guru will not tell you every day, so study with such earnestness that he can give you more Knowledge and be pleased with you. Behave in your life by taking care not to extinguish the inner lamp of Knowledge. Do not wait and say, "I will finish my family duties first and then turn to spiritual life." It is futile to say that you will get the kingdom only after your army is destroyed. You should obtain the kingdom while your army is intact. Similarly, keep on doing spiritual practice (sadhana) as long as you are still breathing. Pay no heed to the criticism of other people. Save your Self from the cycle of endless births. Free it. Let go of ego, then you are saved.

The attitude of pride is a slayer of the Self. Know that "I am not the son of Illusion, I am Paramatman. I am beyond qualities. What does insult or praise have to do with me?" The worldly man gets insult and praise. I am doubtless, formless, and completely detached. What has family life to do with a detached person? There is no bondage for the one who understands this. He is free, although he is physically living in the world. Do not suffer loss in trying to protect the name and fame of your father. Remain with the "Knowledge of Brahman," and stop worrying for the worldly life. Devote yourself to God (Rama) and become God. Remain as Brahman.

Evening, 10-12-1934

46. Serving at the Feet of the Master

One who concentrates in devotion without any expectation, does not feel or see anything except God. He is united with Reality, and attains all of the spiritual powers. However, the one who does not expect anything, who is one with the Lord, whose tentacles of passion are snapped, does not give any value to these powers. In the world, there are five elements and the Self (Atman). These six, and the ignorant individual make seven in all. The individual is two-fold. It is at times an individual (Jiva) and at times God (Shiva). One who clings to the sense of "mine" becomes the individual. When one thinks that "Everything is myself, and I am pervading everywhere" becomes God. The individual is subject to evolution. First, the jiva was a very small atom. In the water on the tip of a needle, there are thousands of jivas (organisms). The jiva is so minute, and even still, it can develop into a big body because of its desires. The lion is more powerful than the elephant, but man is most powerful, yet has more fear. Man fears all other creatures, and because of fear, he has been diminished in size. If there is no fear, he becomes big, but by ignorance he deteriorates and even dies.

If one becomes one with the world through the understanding that the entire world is himself, he becomes Paramatman. Otherwise, even if he is Lord Shiva himself, he becomes a slave. Being a slave, if he gets the advice of the Guru and becomes wise, he becomes vast. All illusion is due to the identification with the body. Let go of the concept that you are the physical body. In this way, you will become vast, and you can be ruler over Time and Death. When the fear of all creatures is gone, this is called Knowledge. Fear is there so long as you remain small. However long their lives may be, even Brahma and Shiva are destined to die. They die after a long period, and human beings die sooner. The gods are also mortal. Man becomes fearless through the teachings of the Sadguru. The body is made up of the five elements. The Self is Life-Energy, it is deathless, imperishable, and it has no birth or beginning.

When the Self looks to life through the eyes of Ignorance, he becomes a jiva, and suffers birth and death. However, looking through the eyes of wisdom, he automatically, without going through births and deaths, becomes Paramatman in the body. Find out how you see when you look at others. If you look with divinity, you will see God. If you look as a human being, you will see a human being. If you see with a concept of "ghost," you see a ghost. You should carefully watch your way of looking at things. How a fish sleeps in water can be known only if you become a fish. You will know the truth of the world when you yourself become the "Preserver" (Vishnu). Today the individual is made up of the elements. That individual which is made up of five elements should become God, Shiva, by attaining the state of Shiva. Similarly, when one knows the nature of Vishnu, he himself becomes Vishnu. The elemental will see only the elements. God will see only God.

The person can see only according to the birth that he takes. Give up the perishable petty concept of being an individual, and then, by the concept of yourself as God, you will become God. You will get the benefit according to your devotion. If you are devoted to worldly life, you will become worldly. If your devotion is to Shiva, you will become Shiva. When you try to concentrate, Illusion tries hard to pull you down by way of offering spiritual powers, which is tantamount to the expansion of mundane life. A dirty thing does not get any dirtier by coming into contact with something dirty, because it is already dirty. That which is of a high quality, whatever it may be, may become impure, but how can that which is already impure, become impure?

God says, "Jivas do not know the happiness that is with Me, and they become enticed by spiritual powers." A person addicted to eating meat left that habit for four days but as the desire was still there, he started it again. Money earned in worldly business is not useful in spiritual attainment. The value is not the same. The value of spiritual attainment is much greater. One who enters spiritual life with ambition will not gain Self-Knowledge. One who concentrates on the Self without any expectation attains Knowledge very easily. If you stand in front of a mirror with your back to it, how can you see your face? You will see your face only if you are facing the mirror. When your attention is diverted towards powers, how can you attain the state of Paramatman?

Do not become a Saint in order to get anything in the world. Be a Saint only for the sake of being a Saint. If devotion is not tainted by any desire, only then can you attain "That." When a devotee is united with Me, he does not care for powers. Only such a devotee attains My State. Inner-bliss is possible only if the service to the Guru is done without any selfish intent. One who has given over his body only for devotion to God, and who is devoted to the Guru, has no need for spiritual powers. The only way of attaining Liberation is through "desirelessness." That is the only way to *true* Liberation. There must not be even an iota of selfishness, or any wish to get anything. The aspirant must be completely desireless. Just as a man has no desire to wear a woman's dress, so it is that when the devotee is without desire, he attains the state of Paramatman.

Morning, 11-12-1934

47. Serving the Feet of the Master

By serving the feet of the Master, one who gives up all other paths and surrenders oneself completely to the Sadguru becomes the true "Accomplished One," or Siddha. One who has the active element of the Almighty God serves the Master. Nobody else will even think of it. For this, the "Pure Sattva" quality is necessary. One who has faith that the Guru is everything attains the state of Paramatman. If you have this feeling, be sure that it is a sign of the desirelessness that brings great inner-bliss. Know for sure that one who is a loyal devotee to the feet of the Master gains Self-Knowledge. Just as a person who is unlucky drives out the sacred cow Kamadhenu (wish-fulfilling cow), those who are dull of intellect never gain higher wisdom. A person who is not lucky suffers from the results of his own vices and would never listen to the Saints. Many have the good luck to meet the Sadguru once in a lifetime, but only the one who has faith is saved and uplifted. As is the faith, so is the result. One who does not like the enjoyments of bodily pleasures easily becomes a person of Vedic wisdom, one who is "supremely intelligent." That is what is called "Great Fortune." What does such a person care for spiritual powers when he has relinquished everything? One whose ego is gone, does not give any value to powers, and therefore Devotion, Liberation, Wealth, and the Powers (Siddhis) are all at his feet. Common people do not understand this. They are all making vain efforts. All powers come to one who expects nothing at all.

A bull is not employed to guard the crop because he would eat it up, and who would put a cat in charge of milk? The one who has no desire gets the fruit. One who does not have any expectations or desire, gets these powers but he has no need for them. They may stay with him even though he says no to them. Actually, the siddhis, the powers, need peace and rest. They are tired after doing all sorts of hard errands for the world. They approach a desireless person in order to get some rest, while they run away from a man who is greedy for pleasures. One who is desireless gains Self-Knowledge and becomes Paramatman in his own right. It is impossible for one who does not have faith in the Guru to attain Brahman. The nature of Brahman is itself like this. Self-Realization is difficult to understand. All of those who have become spiritually knowledgeable have done so only by surrendering to the Guru. How can one gain spiritual knowledge without the Guru? Ordinary school knowledge is learned from a schoolteacher, while what is given by the Guru is higher knowledge that relates to Brahman. To attain the Reality, one's True Nature, the witness is Self-experience. There is that which is witnessed and there must be one who is a witness to it. The religion born out of Brahman is like this. Therefore, one must have devotion to the Sadguru.

Those who are less intelligent are easily seduced by siddhis because without even being aware of it, the mind harbors a subtle sense of ego. The feeling of self importance is very attractive. Even though you may know that you are Paramatman, you still conceive of yourself as an individual, and in vain are willing to suffer pain and sorrow. You know the meaning of the term "in vain," but you don't realize its significance. By looking at the five elements in Ignorance, you become the individual (Jiva), and by seeing with the "Eye of Knowledge" you become God (Shiva). If you look with the concept that "All is Brahman," you become one with Paramatman.

The word "Kumbhaka" means, not so much a retaining of breath, as the realization that "I am filling the entire universe as water fills the earthen pot, or kumbha." To know the world as it is, is the exhalation, or "Rechaka," and the oneness of "me" with "the world" is the taking in of the breath or "Poorak." The word Shwasa means breath, and Vishwasa, or trust, means to have sorrow. This means that sorrow is felt so long as you think that is it you who is breathing. One whose sense of duality is gone is the "Son of the Guru" (Guruputra). When one lives as the sixth element, the Self beyond the five elements, one becomes God who is omnipresent. Then, what one sees is no longer people, or Jana, but one sees all as the "One God," or the "controller in all people," Janardan. If you look in this way, you become God, otherwise you live as a limited individual.

God never even puts a glance towards the person who expects powers. Giving up all desires is the main means for true Liberation. To be without any expectation whatsoever is the highest state. Total Freedom, the "Sayujya State," clings to the feet of one who is desireless, like a lump of clay. Expectation is desire. To be without expectation is itself the state of desirelessness. Faith in the Sadguru is the highest good fortune. There is a story of a cobbler named Basanna. The cobbler once made shoes for the Guru out of his own skin. When the king heard about this, he demanded to have a pair for himself. When the cobbler did not abide by this request, the king forced him to provide the shoes. However, when the king wore the shoes, his body began to have a burning sensation. The king begged to be forgiven. When the Guru told the king to take a dip in the water in the bathroom of the cobbler, the burning sensation was alleviated. God does not tolerate compulsion made on the devotee of the Guru. The Guru said that he himself was also not fit to wear those shoes because it increases pride and that they should be offered to his Guru, Shri Sadguru Linga-Jangam Maharaj. Then through his desirelessness and relinquishing of pride, that devotee of the Guru realized his True Nature. Such is the faith in the Guru. If there is complete faith in the Guru, you can even raise someone who is dead by putting a little earth on him.

I tell you on oath that it is the Guru who gives the fruit that is in your own heart. He knows whatever you do. It is He himself, who gives the correct fruit. The Guru's duty is only to give advice. To have devotion and faith, and to study, is the job of the devotee. You have to study. Do not give up devotion even if any number of calamities fall upon you. How can a devotee and a non-devotee ever agree with each other? Those who have no devotion will only fight. A devotee will have to face tremendous antagonism, and must sustain severe criticism and suffering. In this lies the spirituality of devotion. Such a one is God in the making. Paramatman is waiting for him. The meaning of the centrally important part of the Upanishads is, "Have no expectation." That is the greatest mystery. Eknath Maharaj says that by the blessing of his Guru, Janardan Swami, he attained that state. With inner peace, he became "Desireless" and attained "Inner Joy."

Evening, 11-12-1934

48. The Fire of Knowledge

When the mind and objects of the senses have friction and start to quarrel, the firewood is kindled which burns the forest of Ignorance and destroys it. One who makes friends with and accepts the Sadguru, receives the "Blessing of the Guru." One whose Ignorance is destroyed by the fire of the blessing of the Guru attains Self-Knowledge. When one becomes stirred because of God's Grace, and becomes resolute in attitude, then how much longer can he indulge in mundane life? He gets so fed up with the world that the beasts of the world, the jackals, dogs, and tigers of lust, anger, greed, etc., start running away because the jungle of worldly life is on fire, and the forest of Ignorance is burning up.

When one gives up the attachments of affection and possessions all diseases and calamities run away. The ties of affection and the sense of belonging are the thorns of life. With Self-Knowledge, these thorns of falsehood begin burning. The python of enticement is incinerated. Even the death that is Time, which means the advancing of moments, starts burning and gets burned down. The tiger of egoism cannot find anywhere to run away. The force of the "Fire of Knowledge" is very flammable. It burns down everything in the Illusion, and then itself becomes extinguished after it exhausts its own burning power. Such is the greatness of the Fire of Knowledge.

Morning, 12-12-1934

49. Live According to Self-Knowledge

All of the Air (Wind), and "vital-energy," or Prana, both inner and outer are one. It is part of the body. The sky is only one. Its luminance is one, both inner and outer. If you will not take in the outer air, you cannot live. You may say "it is mine," but if you do not accept it from others, you can't live without it. All of this creation is yours. You are all. The five elements and one Self are the same for all. You have to take from it and release in it. When you write on the surface of water, only the first letter is written, afterwards, it does not remain while you go on to write the second letter. Such is the sequence in creation, the world appearance. This is all undivided Brahman, spread out equally everywhere. If you gain some knowledge, it can be taken with you to any far off places where you go.

You walk simultaneously through the Air (Wind element), the Sky (Space element), and on the Earth. You cannot live by touching only one element, leaving aside another. They are all together forming one body. The five elements make one "Universal Body." The five elements are made up of the one Brahman, and the five elements are one with the Self. All things are one with "This." If Lord Ganapati (Ganesha) rides upon the mouse, the Lord is greater, and if the mouse rides on Ganapati, then the mouse is greater. The entire world is like this. The business of this world, its very function, is like this. If you are Ganapati himself, you are living in the "Inner Existence," the essential part of your being. Be Ganapati and put into practice what you have learned.

A small boy was told to pass stools only when going over to the toilet. He went there and defecated, but he did not remove his trousers, nor did he take sufficient water to clean himself. He was asked why he did this. He said "I did what was told to me. I did not do what was not told." You are doing like this. How can someone tell you everything? You must understand for yourself. A child who reads everyday, who studies everyday, gives a quick reply. He can reply like this because he is continuously studying. One should study like this. You listen, then you go home, and do many other things but forget the teaching. How can you understand fully in this way? That is why everyday you have to be told again. What is taught is not retained. The study should be fully imbibed. Life itself, all atoms, all molecules, and the Self, which is subtler than subtle, "All this, am I." Earth, Water, Fire, Wind, and Sky are One. There is no below, no above, no back, no front. All names and forms are all false. Elephant, horse, whatever; all is Illusion. What is, is one "Pure Spirit," the Self. Name and form are all deception.

The "River of Knowledge" is drowned in name and form. All knowledge is like a river, but the river has become petty, little, and insignificant because of name and form. The great vastness that is the Self is beyond name and form. By name and form, it is as if the river is drowned in the boat. Elephant, horse, and mountains are all drowned in that water, but even a sparrow cannot quench its thirst there. Brahman in the form of a sparrow cannot quench its thirst. Do not be deceived by the illusory ego of name and form. Remain as you are. The mouse should not ride upon Ganapati. Ganapati was seated on a wooden seat. The mouse climbed on his back and stole away the Laddoo (a sweet edible treat) from his hand. He said, "Everyday Ganapati rides upon me but today, I am sitting on his body and eating his Laddoo." When Ganapati rides on the mouse, he gets all of the power, but if the mouse sits on the body of Ganapati, the mouse takes away all of the power. If you conceive of yourself as a petty little creature, you will think of making more and more demands. You are certain to feel like asking for this and that. If you conceive and realize that you are the ancient, always-existing, "Deathless Spirit," then your urge to demand anything diminishes. You no longer want to be a beggar. There is more and more peace, contentment, and health. Automatically you start getting what is sufficient and ample to meet your needs, and there is peace and contentment.

Therefore, take the vow that you yourself are Brahman that is the "inner experiencer" of all experiences. Who is the owner of the field? Is it owned by the king, or the farmer? You have to pay levy, some percentage, to the king. He is the owner. Everything inner and outer belongs only to the king! You are but a villager. You may live in the village, that is your right, but all the authority vests in the king. Whose authority should be recognized? According to custom, a husband should not utter his wife's name, and the wife should not utter the name of her husband, because there is a belief that if you give definite name to that which has no name or form, then some spiritual merit is lost. The main point in this is to recognize that Brahman has no name or form.

Fancy clothes are meant for people who take pride in their appearance. What importance do they have for me? The motive to put on nice clothes is to appear presentable to others, or to indicate that you have many possessions. That is all pride. If the clothes are fine, you have to take care, but if they are ordinary, there is no problem of where to sit. One can sit anywhere. If one takes their clothes and keeps them outside, one need not be anxious about their loss. What is yours is only what you have eaten and put into your stomach. In short, nothing outside is yours. Outer things are for people. All greed is needless. You suffer only because of ego. Give up the ego. A rich man is made happy by the idea that he is rich. Only greed is prevailing in him and nothing else. You should have the attitude that "Everything in the world belongs to me," and give up greed for anything. Will your glory be reduced if you were to say that something is "not mine"? The body is able to move about, and that is your only need. All else may be there or not, what do you lose?

Rama and Krishna were separate, but the mantra "Ramakrishna Hari" is formed by unifying both. Both Rama and Krishna are gone. Drop, the ownership and greed of "Ramakrishna Hari." The wealth of the Son of the Guru all belongs to the Guru. Wind, Water, Light, Night and Day, are all for him only. Everything is his, so where is there any shortage? The one who feeds the creatures inside a rock, and the one who gives food to birds living on the highest mountain peak, is only "He" giving all, with "His Power." On every grain is inscribed the name of the consumer. He is all. The food and He are not two. He is the tiger, and He is the horse. As He is the form, He is also the name.

Even though you call all the limbs of your body by different names, you call all of that as "I." Similarly, be one with all things and all animals. Be your Self. Be your own True Self. Are the Sky, Water, and other elements taking on any attributes such as sitting or sleeping? They are everywhere at all times. Do not keep unity only as a mental thing, put it into practice, and behave accordingly. As Arjuna acted upon what he had heard and learned, he acquired the highest skills. If you live your realization in your daily life, only then do you become "Knowledgeable," a Jnani.

Evening, 12-12-1934

50. The Greatness of the Sadguru, and "You Are That"

The greatness of the "True Master," the Sadguru, is beyond measure. One whose faith in the Guru diminishes after he attains Knowledge, does not get the joy of the "Highest Bliss." The diminishing of faith in the Guru is the cause of failure. One should not even drink water without first offering it to the Guru. All actions and things to be enjoyed should be offered to the Guru and only then, whatever is left over should be taken. The word "Are" in the great statement "You Are That" (Tat Tvam Asi), is only possible to be achieved by the Grace of the Guru. The service to the Sadguru is the highest. That devotion allows you to reach the state that has no equal in the world. At the time of reaching "That," there is a change in the intellect, and an illusory thought enters the mind that asks, "What importance has the Guru?" Never abandon your devotion to the Guru. It is only by having deep faith in the Guru that you are going to achieve realization and see everything happening according to your wish. You must actually feel, and experience the meaning of the word "Are" (Asi). Recognize yourself as Brahman, and arrive at final contentment. Self-Knowledge is felt to be difficult to attain only because devotion is lacking. Devotion to Brahman with quality and form (saguna devotion) in the shape of the Guru, is very difficult. The devotee suffers loss even if there is the slightest laziness in his efforts. Laziness must not be allowed in relation to one's devotion.

To give up all religions has special meaning. It means that you should give up all of your habits that feed your body-consciousness. This will ensure your success in spiritual undertakings. To kill the Kauravas (from the Bhagavad Gita) means to kill the identification with the physical body. To "fight" is what is called religion. That is the path of duty (dharma). We have to fight in order to destroy Ignorance and gain Self-Knowledge. That is called one's natural duty (Swadharma). Therefore, you have to do your duty, to act, and if you don't do your duty, destiny will force some action, and you will experience a down-fall. One's "duty" (dharma) has to be followed, and the fight must be fought. Do as I tell you. You have ample knowledge, but your faith is lacking. Increase the intensity of your faith. Increase your faith in the Sadguru.

You must have conviction about the "Absolute" nature of Brahman. There is nothing other than Brahman. God is according to your feeling. The difference in your feeling is according only to your faith. Those who wish to become God should follow the path of devotion. When your loyalty is proven, the state of Brahman is yours. The veil of countless days has to be removed. If devotion becomes weak after gaining Self-Knowledge, then that Knowledge is not fruitful. By devotion to God you will be famous and influential in the world. He does not need anything. Where is the shortage in His faith? Even though Krishna was a prince, he served his Guru, and did a lot of hard work. His efforts resulted in his earning more riches than his Guru, the wealth of "Divinity." Everyone gets the status as he deserves. The result of real faith is definite and inevitable.

Morning, 19-9-1935

51. Dnyaneshwari

The Sadguru can be compared to the hot Sun. Trouble starts as soon as the Sun has risen. In deep sleep, the king and the beggar enjoy the same happiness. When the "Sun of Knowledge" has risen, there is no longer day or night. As this world appearance is a crude, earthly dream, it appears to be true. When the "Light of Knowledge" spreads, the illusory appearance of the world dissolves. This understanding is the dawn of the "Golden Day" of Knowledge. The birds (Jivas) get the eyes in the form of the Self (Atman). The fear in the minds of those who are travelers on the path of Self-Knowledge is gone. When the light of the Self spreads, the darkness of mundane life is destroyed, and then comes an appearance of the spiritual powers which is nothing but a mirage.

When you understand that you are He, that is noon time when the Sun is at the zenith. Illusion is a night that perpetuates the dream of the existence of the whole world. When that night of Illusion disappears, then the dream of "I" also dissolves. Then the "Great Experience," is fully realized and is our own place. The Sadguru is the Sun that destroys both the rising and setting. That Sun has arisen. To "see," means to see the world. That is Illusion, when the Self is not known. There is a false concept of something that is called "Illusion" in Vedanta, which the Sadguru has wiped out. The greatness of the Guru is such that I have only to praise Him by using his own words. What else can I do?

The Sadguru is beyond both day and night. Who can see Him? He is "The Master of Light," but he himself has no light. Let there be salutations to Him, again and again. The praises of Him are like demoting Him. It is as redundant as if we were to call a king a rich person. No such limited praise is possible for the Sadguru. How can one enumerate all that He has given? It is so vast that words fall short. We cannot say item by item, "Oh Lord, you have given this, you have given that, etc." The more we praise Him, it amounts to having not praised Him at all. The Vedanta is the greatest find. Lucky is one who really studies it. That which can be performed by the body is art, and that which is achieved by mind is Knowledge, or Vidya. The fourteenth type of Vidya is the "Knowledge of Brahman," Brahmavidya. The power by which that Knowledge increases cannot be measured, and the Vedas are the writings which have been written after experiencing this Knowledge. Wherever the seeker has been able to go inside, he has described that experience.

Evening, 19-9-1935

52. God is Permeating the World

Saint Eknath bows to his Guru, Janardan, and says, "The feeling that there is worldly existence was drowned when I gained Self-Knowledge." It is not that he does not see the world, but rather that he realizes the importance of the Guru who knows that there is neither "you" nor "I." So long as "I" is there, all other things are there. What remains when "I" is not? How can God be accommodated where you are occupying the space? There is propriety in salutations so long as you are there. When "I" and "you" are both gone, there is only the Self. One remains separate so long as he does not realize the Knowledge of the unity of all things.

Ganapati (Ganesha) has only one tusk. This means that he is alone by himself. Things are numerous in appearance, but all is one unity. Colors are many but they come out of one color only. The master of all colors is the "Lord of Colors," Ranganath, but he is colorless where he is. All multiplicity starts from Ganapati. Counting begins with him. Everything is contained in the belly of the One. As I have come away, as I am estranged, I am called an individual, a jiva. If, after coming into the human kingdom, we prove our "humanness," only then does one become God, Narayana. Our intellect is not for earning bread, but for Self-Realization. The sign of having used the intellect is that you have become Narayana. This depends on the person employing the intellect. Intellect is an untamed horse. One has to break this horse. This horse, in the human body, makes it possible for you to attain the state of Paramatman, but you must use it for this purpose.

Ganapati is also called the destroyer of calamities, or troubles. His four arms denote the four ideal achievements of Religion, Wealth, Desire, and Liberation. Oh Lord Ganapati, You are the source that gives light to those things that give light. The judgement about true or false is given by you only. Your vision sees all as Brahman. One who understands you becomes the "Voice of Brahman." He becomes happy in the Bliss of Brahman. The belt of the serpent around your belly denotes wisdom. It is called the "Wisdom Belt." One who knows you does not see calamities at all. You pull near you the devotee whom you like, and if there is one who has no expectation of anything, you give him the highest happiness, you give him from your own hand the sweet delight of Joy. The "subtlest place" is your abode. The mouse at your feet is very tiny. When one gets the glimpse of the small mouse, he should not look at the moon. Looking at the moon means that hope and desire should not increase. Ganapati who is formless, has become the "Doer of All Things."

Saraswati means intellect. She discriminates between Essence and the non-essential. Therefore, she is Saraswati. She provokes and activates the sense organs, and is thus called Saraswati. She understands herself by her own light. It is her voice that speaks the Truth, and she says that such speech is good. It is because of her, that Truth can be expressed in words. Who is it that is called a "Saint"? One who is the embodiment of Self-Bliss and who gives satisfaction to those who are in trouble, is called a "Saint." All of the Saints are blissful by nature. Those who are the playful "Joy of Spiritual Wisdom" are called Saints. The Saints give rest to God within themselves. The happiness, the rest, has no other place except with the Saints. They are the "Ocean of Compassion." The Saints do not see any thing lacking in people. The Saints are the very limbs of the Absolute. Contentment resides in the feet of the Saints. One who serves the Saints gets satisfaction and rest. Death never visits you without making you feel sorry for your mistakes. Your next breath may be your last breath. One is always aware of what errors one has made in life when death is imminent. The individual does not die without remembering his mistakes. "Lower your head and put it at the feet of the Saints." One who has fear, has anxiety about death.

Those whom the Saints bless become Brahman. There is no necessity of doing any hard work of acquiring the "Four Achievements" (Purusharth - Religion, Wealth, Desire, and Liberation). The one who emancipates all is Paramatman. He illumines his own intellect and gives full identification with Reality. For this, faith is necessary, and then there is Light everywhere. However, individuals, take the path of doubt and are deceived. Those who harbor doubt will not get the fruit of realization. Even by faith in an idol, it has occurred that one has had the realization of Brahman. If you bow down to a Saint only once with full faith, he will make you just like himself. You may worship him by seeing him, touching his feet, talking to him and listening to what he says, by offering him even a leaf, a flower, a piece of fruit, or only water. Saints are not affected by form, or deformities, or by worldly behavior. A Saint is not affected by enjoyment of objects, or by the relinquishing of everything. If you say someone is purified today, it will mean that yesterday he was impure.

The Saints do not boast of their eccentricity, or their Knowledge. They live in natural simplicity. They live as both the Knowledge and

Ignorance of Selfhood, and they envelope both. The love of the Absolute is fully absorbed in him and the sense of awe is gone. The whole life is one. The worldly life and spiritual life are one. Memory is gone together with forgetfulness. The sense of "I" is gone, and the pride of discarding the sense of "I" is gone. When it was not existing, what was there to discard, and what is it that has come about? The dream and the wakefulness are gone. Ecstasy has become delighted in itself. The seen has gone together with the sense of seeing. The sense of being the witness is also gone. Knowledge has gone along with Ignorance. The recognition of being a "knower" is also gone. All knowledge has gone like a dream. Wisdom has been fully absorbed, but it was always there. It has not come from outside. I bow before those who are wise in this manner. One must have such humility, otherwise the life is wasted in vain. We should bow to the Sadguru. By His grace, we are able to be "All-Witnessing" and we have slain death without actually killing. He is one whose whole body has become beautiful, who is beyond body-consciousness though embodied, and in whom there is no sign of having taken anything. He is one who has no doubt. He has become completely doubtless.

When we lovingly try to become devotees, we gain "Godliness." The duality of the one who devotes oneself, and one who receives the devotion, is gone. "No-mind" has gone to "no-mind." It does not touch the mind. The one to whom we bow, has become ourselves. The observer, that which is observed, and the act of seeing (the observation), are one, and all the distinctions have died. Now, who is God and who is the devotee? Nothing is left. God has lost his identity as God and is now totally permeating in the world without a separate sense of godliness. The duality of God and devotee has been eliminated. Now, immeasurable "Total Freedom" is a servant to him. The bliss of that state cannot be told. Speech has no place there. The sages Narada, Shuka, and many others, have become ecstatic because of this bliss. The river-water and the seawater have become one, while the joy of being "united" is extreme.

Only one who experiences the sense of the loss of duality can know it for oneself. He is the "King of Yogis," and the "Sun of Consciousness" in the human mind. This is the story of Liberation. One who wishes to listen must put his foot down on the head of the mind. You must keep it in check, and verify if what is described is actually part of our Consciousness. Lord Krishna who is separate from Illusion from birth, has liberated even his enemies. He has done extraordinary feats in his incarnation. Being himself the "Totality," he pilfered things, and he was celibate though he was married and had children. All this is very wonderful. Who can praise Him? Who can describe his greatness?

16-9-1935

53. The Sadguru is the God of All Gods

The Sadguru is the God of all gods. Since he makes us God, he is the God of gods. When a poor man is made rich, he values it more. There is no importance in making a rich man richer. The "Universal Self" that dwells in the universe has appeared in a body so that you can call him yours. Unless you have complete trust in the Sadguru, you cannot be as the Universal Self. One who has faith, becomes the Universal Self. Only when that Universal Self actually becomes manifest in the universe does He truly become the Universal Self. The body itself cannot be called faithful. The teaching of Vedanta is primarily practical. The one that is felt even after death, and the one that is beyond the four bodies is this God, the Sadguru. He has been degraded by those who are not faithful and not devoted. This God is "all-powerful" and blesses you by your trust in Him. One who comes to the feet of the Sadguru, receives the sight of Him, his "darshan." The devotee must be able to hold fast to the feet of the Guru. Lord Krishna says that only when the triple aspects of Consciousness (the seen, the seer, and act of seeing), the sense of "me," as well as even the Knowledge of "I Am That" are all dissolved does the devotee merge in Him.

One's parents are related only to the physical body. The Sadguru is the mother of the very essence of your Being. In that sense, the fatherhood is within you. Unfortunate is the one who does not offer devotion to such a Sadguru. I will tell you the sign. Take it from me that one who is not a devotee is already gulped down by Illusion in great sorrow. Lord Shiva is sitting in meditation, in the cemetery. Lord Brahma became his son with a hope to receive Knowledge. Benevolent is the Sadguru who gives such Knowledge to you. Only if one has accumulated great spiritual merit, does the Sadguru then meet him. Saint Eknath says, "Oh my mother and my father, You who are the giver of Self-Bliss have come to my house. I have now fulfilled my life. Advise me in the religion of Bhagwat, and make me free from action as well as inaction."

Illusion is so strong that Hari (Vishnu) and Hara (Shiva) are still afraid of her. This Maya is of three-fold qualities (the three Gunas). For example, the Sun does not have any intention, yet by its rising, the entire world becomes active. When you feel that something is there although there is nothing, that is Illusion. What is there in Reality that says "I"? This is the imagined individual. The body does not only contain that which says "I," there is blood, flesh, semen, and all the other material. However, the entity that is saying "I" is not really there.

In the Absolute Reality, there is no "other," nor is there any doubt or any alternatives. Then, arises the original aspiration that is called the "Original Illusion," Moolamaya. From this, there appears the Bliss that is in the form of the triple aspect of Existence, Consciousness, and Bliss (SatChitAnanda). Then that "One" sees oneself, eats oneself, drinks oneself, and starts wishing to get Self-Bliss, and then begins getting it, according to imagination. All of the four "streams" of beings, are created by imagination. The three gunas, the three worlds, and the five elements are all created by Him. He was many, but He thought himself to be One, and knew that only. In the original pristine "Pure Age," He was alone. Like in dreams, one sees the appearance of many, but one is always only alone.

That which is not moving is Sky or Space (Akash), and that which started moving is Wind (Air). Next, after the Wind comes Fire (Light), then Water, and then the Earth. Wind is that which moves. The "Formless Spirit" is called Purusha, and when it moves, it is called Wind. The five elements are called Prakriti (Manifestation). Purusha is alone, as He is. Prakriti however, is a mixed affair. That is called Harimaya, or the power of Hari, or "God as Illusion." Only He is Self-knowing. One who does not know Illusion, or Maya, is the "Essence of Consciousness," and "Life" is his attribute. All others are dead. The five elements, are primordial. All other is later manifestation. In every element is the self same "I." That same spirit is in the cosmos. It is called "Shiva." When that enters the body, He becomes "Jiva." What we see in sleep is called dream. The dream of God is called the world. Our waking consciousness is the dream of Shiva. In the same way that with knowledge, one knows that the dream is his own thought, when one gains Self-Knowledge, his life becomes an Illusion. That is Maya. While speaking, a man talks because of the power of the Self, but the mistake is made when he thinks himself to be only the body, and it is he who is talking.

When Brahman becomes articulate, the sound OM becomes manifest. A + U + M are its vowels. God here has become a prisoner.

He has come down from his original state." The Jiva is himself Shiva, but the allurement of Maya is there. Although you are Shiva, she makes you conceive of yourself as a body. That is her power. She increases the forgetfulness of the Self and the longing after sensual pleasures. The thinking about sense objects is called mind. The cleverness of ego is called intellect. The same sense of "I," when it thinks that it is the Self, becomes Brahman. The facets of the subtle body (mind, intellect, thinking, and ego) all become one with the singular sound of OM. The ten-fold qualities of the ten sense organs are really lifeless. It is only because God, Narayana, is in all of these that they are able to function. This means that Narayana is the only "One who knows." The sense organs are gross. He conducts all of their activities.

Morning, 17-9-35

54. The Body is Not "I"

Only "One" illuminates the mind, the intellect, and all organs of the senses, and their objects. It is only a false notion that he is "someone." If you maintain an idea that you are a "body," it seems that the body does everything, the eating, drinking, etc. This is called Ignorance. The illusory concept that "I am the body" creates the individual (Jiva), and the sense that, "I am not the body," makes you God (Shiva). The belief that the objects of the senses are full of pleasure, is only a mistaken concept. The sense organs become agitated to take hold of objects. The world of the body is measured. It is only three and a half arm's length (the length of the body). All activities are only for sake of the body. Its enjoyments and its attachments are received only by it. It has given away its true "Glory" in favor of the sense organs, and now it is very difficult to get back to it. The sense organs are addicted, running out of control chasing after imagined enjoyment. That is the wonder! That is what is called pleasure! Pleasure merely indicates the stimulation of sensory nerves.

There is a game of madness, and it was decided that you must keep on playing this game of win or lose, pleasure or pain, and you must keep experiencing it. You call it pleasure, but it is really nothing but a play of imagination. You call it pleasure, but it must be killed. There is real happiness in killing the enjoyment, but people keep up the imagination, which is really only suffering. If you have killed the enjoyment, that is good. However, the killer of the enjoyment, also must die. Objects are imaginary and the enjoyment of them, is also imaginary. Enjoyment is only a thought or feeling that you like. You get enjoyment when everything takes place according to your hopes. God (Shiva) is without any thoughts.

The objects of each sense organ are different. All ten of them pull you in ten directions. Yama, the God of Death, rides upon the "Buffalo of Ignorance" and attacks you. Ignorance is what carries one to the realm of death. The enticement of the senses and being ensnared by pleasure, is nothing but attachment to the body. Everything happens in the grand scheme of things, but the individual says "'I' have done everything." Although he is the Self, he says that he is the body, and bears the burden of merit and sins. This is the disease of body identification called the ego. It's like the dog that is walking below a moving cart and says that he is the one who is driving the cart. Similarly, the individual takes up false pride and claims to do everything. He takes no rest at any time. It is like he is having an uncontrollable seizure of body identification.

There was a law in the town of blind people that said if anybody comes who can see with his eyes, they would take out his eyeballs. One must escape from there with sufficient cunning. Illusion knows that if anybody realizes the Self she would be defamed, so she makes efforts in the opposite direction of Knowledge. Because you are attached to the body and sense pleasures, the cycle of birth and death is continuous. It is only when you see that pleasure is sorrow that you come to real happiness. Action done with expectation of fruit is very detrimental. The desire for fruits, or results, is what compels the Self that is beyond birth, to take birth. Therefore, do not harbor desire for any results. Maya harasses the jiva by imposing upon him the mirage of body identification, but alas, the individual does not get fed up. The jiva takes birth in various bodies and suffers all of his own accord. The jiva that is blindfolding the eyes of Self-hood is wandering all over.

18-9-1935

55. The Cycle of Maya

The sun is stationary, but people say emphatically that it is moving. Similarly, the individual, the jiva, takes the round of births in many various animal forms only because of the play of Illusion. He suffers because he has forgotten himself, and he plucks both the fruits of birth and death. The Self, who is free and complete, has become enslaved because of its identification with body. Over time he has taken the poison of bondage by thinking that there is happiness in objects. A chemical poison kills only in one lifetime, but the poison of the sense objects multiplies, and proves to be a killer for many lifetimes. Sorrow overlaps sorrow. The jiva is thrown into the bottomless pit of desires and sorrows, and while he is there suffering the great wave of destruction washes over the body, and then again there is rebirth.

There are two paths in human life. One is the path of liberation, the second is the path of rebirth. It is rare that one comes upon the path of liberation. Without true "Devotion to God," even one with Knowledge does not become free. The greatest devotion is "Devotion to the Guru." The devotees of the Guru find that their difficulties become opportunities. Illusion is really very strange and awe-inspiring. Those who are simple go beyond her, but those who say that they will escape through their intellect are deceived. The Illusion of God Hari (Vishnu) is really unsurpassable. It is actually a false thing, but it is very strong and very tenacious for one who is attached to the body. Some are thinking that they should be free of this worldly life, but the mind is not under control. Those who have understood that the Guru is himself Paramatman, are able to go beyond Illusion very easily. What is the remedy for Illusion? Only one whose intellect is clear and who recognizes that the Illusion and Brahman are distinctly separate, as if seen in a mirror, alone can tell you the remedy. For such people, to cross over Illusion is as easy as walking on a straight footpath. In order to do this, the attraction towards sense objects must be totally gone.

One who knows what is permanent and what is impermanent is an enlightened person. The pleasure you get from ephemeral things is actually pain. The one who does not want sense objects is already free. Those who feel very ecstatic from the enjoyment of sense objects are only having an animal body. They earn and pile up money until death, only to leave everything for their wife and children at the end. By collecting and accumulating a mountain of merits and sins, the jiva has started on a journey. Only one whose attachment to the worldly life is gone, and who puts faith in the Guru and understands the true spiritual path, is the real spiritual authority. He invariably achieves "True Glory."

The Guru who dispels the ego in his disciples and gives the knowledge about desirelessness, is the real Sadguru. The one who is established as Brahman, who is well-versed in words, and who is not after fame or money is truly a great Guru. He sees all as Brahman and does not put any burden on his disciples to support him. He does not relinquish sense objects nor does he relish them. He is indifferent as to whether his body is being carried on a platform, or is walking on a rough road. The clever pundits do not understand this sign of a good Guru. The knowledgeable scholars are proud of being philosophers and belonging to the great tradition of knowledge. Instead of being merged into the Reality, their minds become very rigid and strong with pride. They do not see that their life is being lost as they continue to increase their learning. Instead of being in complete peace, their ego is running rampant. Peace is the sign of the Sadguru.

The truly learned men do not look at any happenings in the outer world as if they are real. They have no residue of feeling that outer things are real, or that one day they will be useful. Unless one feels that worldly appearances are not true, one's attention will turn towards them. It is only when one feels that the objective world is true, and that today or some other day, it will be useful to oneself or to others, that one is attracted to the world appearance. The one who realizes the Essence and does not have any concept that objective things will be useful today or at any time, is the real Jnani who is truly beneficial. The Jnani does not look at objects and say that they are real. He is retired from them. He is always peaceful without any cause. Without devotion to the Sadguru, you will not achieve such "Spiritual Peace."

The Guru grants "His Own State" to the devotee. Such is the great fruit of devotion to the Guru. One should have such a one pointed decision; "Let death strike, but I will definitely see God. Let the body fall, I will achieve my goal." One who has such strong determination surely gets all the support of the Sadguru. Such people become liberated without delay. One who is ready to put down his life for the sake of the words of the Sadguru, who does not disobey the orders of the Guru, and who is convinced that the Guru is Paramatman, is himself "God Almighty." This is why you should have complete faith in the Sadguru. Truly, He is God.

Morning, 20-9-1935

56. The Nine Faceted Devotion – Navavidha Bhakti

The first type of Devotion is "Listening," or Shravana. Devotion (Bhakti) is the mother of Knowledge (Jnana). Without Devotion, there is no Knowledge. Devotion is the highest path. If you cannot do it in actions, then do it mentally. Listen to how to do worship. Listen to all of the paths explained by the Guru; the "Path of Knowledge" (Jnana), the "Path of Desirelessness" (Vairagya), the "Path of Spiritual Practice" (Sadhana), and the "Path of Final Truth" (Siddhanta). Find out the essence of them all.

The second type of Devotion is "Singing God's Praises," or "Kirtan Bhakti" (Kirtana Bhajana). Kirtan is singing in praise of the God who is embodied. Do the kirtan that you have learned by heart, recognize the many important references, and understand the meaning of them all. The story of God, Lord Hari should be told in kirtan not for any other purpose other than because you feel happy to do so. The entire world is your field for propagating the greatness of the Self, (Atman; God). The "Kirtan Devotion" purifies all.

The third type of Devotion is "Remembrance of God." Remember the Sadguru. This should be done all of the time, morning, noon, and evening. Remember, "I am Brahman," "I am Shiva," "I am He." The remembering should be as constant as the clock that ticks. The heart in which Devotion to God is constant, is the moving, living temple. All can become liberated by the name of Rama. Lord Mahadev (Shiva) himself escaped from the sense objects, through repetition of the sacred name of Rama.

The fourth type of Devotion is "Service to the Guru." The Guru's feet should be worshiped. Serve the Guru in order to be released from birth and death. It is the Sadguru who shows the Reality. That which is not seen by the eyes, and which is not apparent, is achieved because of the blessing of the Guru. Such states of consciousness as non-attachment, surrender, being beyond the body, being beyond the mind, and being in a natural state of complete indifference, are all attained only by the blessing of the Guru. The names are different, but the state is One. If one of these states is attained, all are attained. Non-attachment is to give up the sense of "mine," as well as name and form. There is nobody else capable of forgiving such as the Guru, who is motherly. If you totally depend on the Guru, you will attain God. The devotee should serve at the feet of the Guru. Verification of what we learn should be threefold, the confirmation through the teaching of the Guru, confirmation through the teaching of the scriptures, and verification through one's own experience. The attainment of the "Knowledge of Brahman" is dependent upon oneself, but without the Sadguru, you will not get real contentment. By study only, you will not get that which is learned through the words of the Guru. That which is unattainable becomes possible to attain, only by the "Grace of the Guru." The attainment of the Absolute Reality, Parabrahman, is not possible without the company of Saints. This is the sign of the fourth type of Devotion.

The fifth type of Devotion is "Worship" (Archan). The various Gods are really Gurus who have existed in the past. All of the temples are of these Gods. How can we build a temple to Him who is greater than the world? The "Man of Knowledge" (Jnani), the wise man, is God. The body of the wise man, the form that he bears as his body, is itself an image of Knowledge, an idol of wisdom. He is divine wisdom incarnate. That is the "Knowledge" possessed by the Sadguru, yet the Sadguru is different from these. So long as you have not met the Sadguru, you can only worship the past Gurus, the ancient men of wisdom. However, when one does meet Him, "Devotion to the Sadguru" should be done with one's physical body, speech, and mind. Devotion to the Sadguru is the highest action we can do unto our Self. This is the best action that we can do for our own welfare, the action that makes all achievement and contentment possible. All other actions only become useless, and perish.

The sixth type of Devotion is "To Bow Down" (Vandanam). One should bow down to God, and to the Sadguru. By bowing down, blemishes in our character go away, blessings are given, and the Guru is pleased. By bowing, you gain humility and happiness, and by this happiness, you achieve a state where there is no animosity, only Bliss.

The seventh type of Devotion is "The Path of Service" (Dasyam). One should always be available at the door of God or the Guru. One should rebuild dilapidated temples, reconstruct water tanks and temples, and always increase the glory of God,. The meaning of being always at the door of the Guru or God is to be always concentrating on the Self (Atman) within, the awareness that "I Am." The attention to the "I Am," the sense of our existence, is the door of the Guru, the door of God. The inner side is the place of the Guru, the place of God. Our awareness, our attention, is the path of entering into the temple of that God. We have to enter the inner recesses by this door. By constant Self-awareness, you can go to the state where the Guru exists. We should rebuild old dilapidated temples. This means the bodies of all people. We have to try by various means to make healthy and strong the bodies of devotees that are harassed and troubled by various calamities and difficulties, for which we should give verbal advice, or actually help them. We should reconstruct water tanks. The water tanks of mind are broken by adverse happenings and repeated shocks, as there is a lot of dirt accumulated in them because of wrong thinking, as well as a lot of weeds and moss in these tanks. We should remove all of this dirt, and clean the tank water. The walls around this mind tank should be strong and built to last, and we should so arrange it that the water of this tank will be always useful to others. We should like what the Sadguru likes. The Sadguru likes that we should keep away from sense objects, that we should be content without enjoyment through the sense organs, and that we should remain constantly in the immortal and blissful state of the Self. We should give up anxiety about family life, and recite stories about the greatness of God, as well as sing his praises in kirtan. We should not have any dislike for lesser, more menial types of work. We should even be content to work as a slave for Him. We should do little jobs with enjoyment and enthusiasm so that we lose the pride of our body. We should perform service with pleasure. If we cannot physically do these things, we should mentally think along these lines.

The eighth type of Devotion is "Friendship with God" (Sakhyam). We should be friendly with God. The Self (Atman) is the Sadguru. We should bind ourselves to the Sadguru by our deep love. As there is service in this worldly life, so in spiritual life there is the Ninefold Devotion. We should try to do new things all the time. While offering devotion we should do some novel things using our imagination. This gives our mind happiness and new energy, and joy. We should act in such a way that the Sadguru will be happy. We should behave in that fashion which is loved by God. Only then is there friendship and affection. As soon as things happen according to our liking, there is spontaneous friendliness. We should like what the Sadguru likes. We should praise the Sadguru. We may even have to be aloof from all, in order to be friendly with God. One who acts with such a feeling that God is his "Real Life-Force" is capable to become his "True Devotee." The Sadguru is the Life-Force. He is the Supreme Self. This is called the "Devotion of Friendship." In Hindu mythology, there was a house built out of lacquer and other flammable things, called Lakshagriha. The meaning of Laksha is spiritually somewhat different. God in the form of Lord Krishna could bring out the Pandava family from the Lakshagriha through a tunnel.

Lakshagriha can be said to be our attention to objects. We are tied to objects and we will free ourselves only by focusing our attention on, and remembering the Lord. (Lakshya - object of attention; remembering that "I" am "I".) Remembering that "we are" is called Lakshya. We start from the state of not knowing anything, and by listening and paying attention to our mother and father, and also listening to many things which are told by many other people, we are filled up with ideas that we have heard and our attention is conditioned by that listening. Kauravas means individuals, the Jivas, who have turned their back on the Self, the Atman. By their conceptual imagination, the object of attention is jailed in the house of their attention. Desires are going to burn these individuals by kindling the fuel of objects. By putting our whole attention to remembering the Sadguru, and by remembering the name of God, we free ourselves from this flammable house of objects which brings only the flames of sorrow. Those who free themselves of this enjoy total happiness. Others, by failing to choose the right thing, remain in the same flammable house and suffer from burns again and again. This is the opportunity for you to free yourselves. If you worry about yourself, what necessity has the Guru to worry about you? Give up your worry and take care of your Guru. Then the Sadguru will surely take care of you. The Sadguru is the Supreme Self, Paramatman. He is without any form or blemish. Our faith is so often lost as soon as something happens which is not desirable to us, but we should never worry. Let God do what he likes. You say that you are not superior to God, but your mind does not feel like that. You should behave in accordance with His will, and never be sorry. If a man puts his trust in the Sadguru, it is the Sadguru whose heart suffers even if the man is but slightly hurt, or if but even a hair on his head is touched. The Sadguru is always taking the side of the destitute. He will never rest before giving you the highest place, which is not fallible. Those whom you think to be yours, will accompany you up to the cemetery. They will lament loudly upon your death, but God will never let down those who have surrendered themselves to Him. Therefore, you should have friendship with God.

The ninth type of Devotion is "Self-Surrender". If you feel that All is Brahman, then you must have the conviction that you are also Brahman. The state of non-duality comes naturally. When you get the mantra from the Guru, you are a Royal King. Out of five, only one succeeds. Goddess Laxmi came to put a mark (Tilak) on the forehead of five men, but four of them said that they have not washed their faces. They then rushed off to wash their faces. The fifth man however, stood where he was. Laxmi put the mark on his forehead and he became rich. The very inaction of the faithful devotee became the act of Brahman. This is what is called the "State of Purity." Spiritual practice should be intense. This means that we should leave off all wrong thinking and our Devotion should be all consuming. To hold dear to our heart the image of our Sadguru at all times is the practice and that is this State of Purity. "That" which is always clean, always sacred, and always pure, is the most powerful, indestructible, and deathless True Nature (Swaroopa) of the Sadguru. Not to forget this, is itself spiritual practice.

Evening, 20-9-1935

57. Let Us Bow Down to the Mother Veda (Shruti)

The Veda is the "Mother of All." Just as a mother gives shelter to all, so does this mother called Veda give shelter for all. He who has not taken refuge in this mother is surely sorrowful however strong he may be otherwise. One's ordinary mother is eager to marry her sons to some woman and thus puts them to the treadmill of family life. However, this "Veda-Mother" is not like that at all. Marriage is really a calamity that puts man into bondage. He who is taking shelter with this Mother-Veda is free, and becomes the Primordial Self. Only a Sadguru throws open the great storehouse of the Vedas and gives freely the "Cream of Knowledge" to all. The Sadguru transforms the miserable life into a thing of joy. Saint Tukaram based his allegory on this fact when he said that, "The Golden Sun has risen, which partakes of nectar."

The Sadguru has the power to bestow Total Freedom, and "The Absolute" on his disciple. The compassion of the Sadguru is itself the vast sky. The Sadguru is the ferry across the ocean of life. He is the anchor that ties his devotees to Reality. The Sadguru is the controller of Time that does not spare even the "Three Gods" (Brahma, Vishnu, and Shiva). He himself is the Reality, the support beyond this world that is the home of contentment. One who surrenders himself to such a Sadguru loses all sense of separateness. You should bow to Him by being beyond body-consciousness. This worldly life is an extended dream in which people are babbling their way through Illusion. They think, "I have become a fish in the dream and my wife has become another fish," while this dream fish is really only a lump of flesh that is uttering "I," again and again. The life within the dream is taken by him to be real. Such a one has become the father of the dream character, the jiva. He does not serve anybody except wife. Worldly people think that the Saints are nothing but calamities in their life. However, it is by having a glimpse of Saints and listening to them that mundane interests are broken, and the confidence in active family life drops away. Therefore those who are traditionally attached to family life, who are slaves to Illusion, speak out vehemently against the Saints.

In the dream, which is full of Ignorance, a man says everything belongs to him, but such men who say so are really like monsters. Those who simply enjoy the objects of senses are merely human beings, while the one who is extreme in relinquishing everything is like God Almighty. To talk without knowing anything is called an overflow of talk. When the "Sun of Knowledge" sets, the universe is filled by the darkness of Ignorance and even the star of piety is not visible. This confused mind does not see who he himself is. He has forgotten completely. The ego, who is a king on the throne of body-consciousness, has had a dream. He was stranded in a dense forest, got tired, and became very sorrowful. There, he married a female. He used to cut wood and sell it to earn his living. He would eat the meat of various beasts and lived very miserably. Suddenly he awoke due to extreme suffering. Similarly, you are experiencing this dream. This world is not real. That king ruled there for seventeen years. The five sense organs, the five active organs, the mind, the intellect, and five life forces (pranas) make up seventeen. These are his seventeen years. The ignorant individual, the jiva, has to suffer due to these. You are asleep, you are not awake. You are born in it, and you die in this sleep. In sleep, you wander indefinitely. Instead of realizing your own greatness, you have become a sufferer. Therefore, you must gain the Knowledge of your own Self. This "Spiritual Knowledge" is the greatest science. It is called Adhyatma-Vidya.

What is existing from the beginning? Who is there from the first? "From the Beginning," and "The First," means before you experience something. "The First" is who we are. To know what it is, how it is, and what its nature is, means to "Know," to have "Understanding." When that "Understanding" becomes fixed and definite, it is called Spiritual Knowledge, or Adhyatma-Vidya. Only the listener who listens with all the senses turned into one, is really worthy of this Spiritual Knowledge. He can understand all of this, while others should not even open this volume, as they will not understand the meaning. Only one who says, "Let all else be lost. I don't care. I wish only to follow the spiritual path," can benefit from this path. Only such a one is considered to be truly spiritual. Lord Krishna says, "One who is totally concerned about Me, gets all that is Mine, with all My Glory. The whole world, all the objects are My Army." The devotees of God, choose only God. Paramatman is attained by his devotees without any discrimination between men or women. The yogi who walks on My path, is surely met by Me. That devotee becomes One with the Supreme Self, Paramatman, and is merged into the Absolute.

What is the duty of the aspirant? One has to follow the instructions of the Guru, and by doing spiritual practice (Sadhana) one is merged into God. It is useless to do any degree of practice if you keep faith in your family life. Faith in Knowledge is what is necessary there. It does not matter what occupation one is in. Only one who has faith in Knowledge can reach the state of Paramatman. Man receives according to his earnest yearning. One who has faith in Knowledge gets inspired when hearing about devotion, and such a person thinks about devotion all the time. Only he gives up the attachment to the body. He does not care whether he has the body or loses it. A salt crystal becomes sea when it meets the sea. One whose faith is in Knowledge may even do a wrong thing, still he is merged into Me. His actions do not affect him. When Saint Chokhamela was driven out of Pandharpur, many people began to fall sick, but when he was brought back to the temple, all people became healthy. God likes devotion, the physical actions do not matter so much. The bad actions of My devotees are also good deeds for Me. In My devotee's case, whether actions are good or bad, all becomes merged into God. Actions only bind one who is proud. The actions of a Saint do not bind him. The word power vested in a devotee of the Sadguru is so great that he can do anything because the Guru's blessing is with him. He is the greatest in the world. Even the God of Death fears the devotee of the Guru.

The wisdom of Brahman is of no use to a man who always blames the Guru. That man must be avoided. As long as there is no brilliant "Light of the Self," there will be bad actions and good actions. When there is the Light of the Self, in that Light, all actions are auspicious. Religion means attainment of "Unity with Me," unity with God Almighty. That is right behavior. If there is unity with God, you may even do something which others normally despise as sin! Stories are told of how Pralhad disobeyed his father, Vibheeshana left his brother, and Bharat despised his mother, all to be only with God. When you meet the Universal God, all actions are good. When the Sun rises, the darkness is gone. My devotee attains a state of being where space and time do not exist. A great yogi is one who gives up the identification with the body. Great is the one who is "One with the Self," and has conviction that he is the Self.

Even if a lot of "spiritual knowledge" is poured upon a worldly person, it is of no use to him. Calamities are there in the lives of my devotee, only to uphold and liberate him. If a man becomes proud of his body and does not pay heed to my teaching, he is bound to go in a downward path. Even though you are deathless in essence, if you do not listen to me, you will suffer. Even though you are beyond birth and death, you will have to die again, and again, if you are attached to your body. "Oh Arjuna, I will give you the 'Fruit of Immortality' if I am pleased with you. Neither birth nor death, will turn their attention towards you." There are two birds; one gives birth and death, and the other gives liberation.

21-1-1935

58. Who is God?

The disciple asked the Master, "Who is God?" His answer was, "The Life-Energy, or Chaitanya, is God." The Life-Energy is your Being, or Existence. Gods of clay and stone are manufactured, or made up gods. The gods created by imagination die when the great cosmic cycle, the Kalpa, ends. Chaitanya is the base, or the root of all the incarnations of Vishnu such as Rama and Krishna, or incarnations of the Mother Prakriti, such as Ambika, or Saraswati. Vishnu is the Life-Energy. That Life-Force is God. Lord Shiva told Parvati that the Life-Force that moves everything is God. That is inherent in all. That is God, which is the Pure Chaitanya. The One who recognizes him is also called God. The Sage Yadnyavalkya was asked by his disciple, "Who is God?" He said to the disciple, "You are God." Think about this fact that you are God.

Two disciples, one God, and one a demon went to a Guru. The Guru advised them, "You Are That." The demon went home and continued his meat eating. The first disciple, who was God, started thinking, "How am I God? He went to his Guru again and said, "Please show me how I am God." The Guru said, "God is that which activates the body. The body is not God. The Life-Energy is God and that is you yourself." What is the difference between the dead and the living? There is Life-Energy moving in the living and not in the dead. That is the difference. There are seven main factors that make a body, such as bones, muscles, blood, etc. These are all called Dhatu, or essential elements of the body. This is the physical body. All these run the mill called the body, and the product of this mill is nothing but shit. I am not the physical body. I am not the subtle body. This body is constantly punishable, which means that everyday the body is receiving punishment. The individual, the jiva, is always suffering punishment. Who is it that should be called a monk? One who gives up external things and calls himself a renunciate (Sanyasi)? No, simply giving up external things does not make you a sanyasi! When I am not the mind, and I am not my intellect, the actions done by the mind and intellect, whether good or bad, are also not mine. One who knows this is liberated.

The "mind" means to say, or assert, something. Not to say anything means the relinquishing of the mind. When the mind is relinquished, everything is forgotten, and "nothing" remains. That nothingness is the causal body (Karana-deha). This is the "Night of Ignorance." Beyond this is the kingdom of Mahadeva. If we study this forgetfulness deeply, we can experience that there is this nothing that is called the causal body. When all is forgotten, and this nothing remains, then you must also give up that very nothing. When all is gone, all is thrown aside, what remains is you, yourself. This Consciousness is Brahman. He is the knower of the three worlds; the waking state, the dream state and the deep sleep state. The waking state is the world of Brahma called Satya-loka, the dream state is the world of Vishnu called Vaikuntha-loka, and the deep sleep state is the world of Shiva called Kailasa-loka. Paramatman is beyond all of these.

In the dream state, there is an entity who dreams, who is someone other than the character in the dream. The dream comes and goes, the deep sleep comes and goes, and even the waking state comes and goes. Knowledge of things comes and goes, and Knowledge itself comes and then goes away. Every thing that comes, goes away, yet you remain. That which is changeless and eternal is "You." You witness all of these states. Any taste that comes is sure to go. Any pleasure enjoyed has gone. You may understand anything, but that which you understand does not remain. It is all in the Illusion and thereby mortal. A child is born and if it dies, we dispose of the body. We do so because the child is dead and gone. So, to know the child, its greatness, its enjoyment, the care given to it, is all mortal. It is in the realm of death, Illusion. Anything that is of this realm, whatever is enjoyed, whatever is experienced, even Knowledge, is not immortal. It is all dead. They say that men who are full of Knowledge enjoy the nectar immortality, but all of their experience, together with the knowledge of Vaikuntha and Kailasa, is dead, as they are not immortal. Only the "Man of Self-Knowledge," the Jnani, enjoys the "Nectar of Immortality."

A child is born. We see it, but it only appears for a short time, then it is dead, thereby becoming useless. Only the Jnanis partake of nectar. You should also partake of nectar. The Guru is the Self who is in all beings. When you say so, and experience it, your duty is over. He is in all. That which is deathless is He. We should realize that He is immortal and we should be devoted to Him only. Only He is trustworthy. We should have trust in Him only. He is in all, He is prior to all, and He is there when all is gone. To realize this is the true worship of God. To know the subtle principle is called Self-Knowledge, and he who knows this is called "One with Self-Knowledge," a Jnani. All experiencing is only God, Shri Hari (Vishnu). To worship Him as being in everything all the time is called "True Worship."

The Lord of the three worlds is dwelling in everything. The Supreme Self, Paramatman, is always there, in his pristine "Original Being." Do not say, "That which is within me is God, but God is not in you." He is in all creatures. Recognize this, and behave with a sense of Oneness with all. He was prior to all creatures, and when there was some movement in Him, He became the Wind. All bodies were created afterwards. The Self (Atman) is God, and you are that Atman. Meditate on this.

22-9-1935

59. Formless Brahman

Just as the Space is formless, Brahman is also formless. Space has no shape, and no qualities, nothing. However, it is conceivable, therefore it exists. Similarly, Brahman is like space. While we are asleep, we are not aware of anything, but still we exist. The space is empty like that. Then comes Consciousness, and with it, comes the quality of "knowing." That Consciousness is the Primal Illusion, Moola-Maya. It is the very beginning. This Consciousness is called God, Ishwara. With this Consciousness, the state of "knowing" comes. With this "knowing" there arises the duality of Purusha and Prakriti (Pure Consciousness without objects, and Consciousness appearing as manifestation). Prakriti is the primordial action, the first "Kruti." That is also called Shiva-Shakti, which means the male-female principles unified. This state is also called the "Illusion with Attributes," or Illusion with the three Gunas (GunaMaya). Vishnu is Consciousness. Brahma is the middle aspect (creation) and then there is Shiva (destruction).

To be awake is a natural phenomenon. You are half-awake while asleep, and then when you awaken, you are fully awake. When you are awake, you create your own world. That power is inherent in you. You can create hundreds of such worlds. The original Consciousness is called the equilibrium of all three gunas, and it is also called the "Mahat Principle." When you do not know yourself and you try to know others, that is the state of the causal body. Ignorance, or Tamoguna, is its quality. It is also called Akash (the space from which the world appears). That which describes it is called the mind. That which thinks about it is called the intellect. To be proud of it is called "ego," or Ahankar.

The primary urge or movement that arises in Brahman is God. That itself, is what is called God, and it is the Primal Illusion (MoolaMaya). The Primal Illusion, which is the subtle elements, and the state of disturbed equilibrium of the Gunas, is a state of inertia. When it becomes a movement, it is called the Wind element (Vayu). There are five oceans. The five elements, Earth, Water, Fire (Light), Air (Wind), and Sky (Space) are these oceans. Consciousness (Mahat) is the sixth ocean, and the "Life-Energy," or Chaitanya is the seventh ocean. So it is said that there are seven seas.

That which is apparent is destructible. What you think it to be, it is not in reality. It is not what you conceive, and you cannot conceive it as it really is. You should see it as it is, naturally, in itself. Then you will not see it with your desire. Your inner sight, the "Vision of the Self," is that Shiva-Shakti, the quality of Shiva, or "Supreme Benevolence." From this "Self-Vision," the creation of the universe takes place. In that creation, desire is of no use to you, because you exist first, and the looking at objects comes afterwards. Don't forget that this entire creation is within your own "Self-Vision."

You may show a house by touching it with your finger, but actually, there is only earth there that you call by the name of "house." Even though you know that it is earth, you call it house. You see earth, and call it your house, but if it is to be eaten, you will say it is earth and you will not eat it. A house is to live in, but not to eat. Similarly, this world is only to be seen, and there is nothing in it to be entangled in through your attraction to it. This creation is no doubt earth, but you cannot show an entire road in a package of only 50 grams or so. "Road" is only a name. What it is, is only earth. If you try to bring the road, you will bring only 50 grams of earth. The name is road, but if you want to fetch it, you will have to fetch a handful of earth.

Your face is also the same. You can not prove that it is a face? That is why it is said that the world is made only of earth. Everything rises out of the earth, sets back into the earth, and is eventually covered up by earth. In ancient legend, Bhasmasura was given a boon that whatever he put his hand upon would become ashes. Ashes means earth. When he put his hand on his own head, he also became earth. He was only earth from the beginning. Everything in this world is only earth in essence. To see that everything becomes earth is to see with the eye of intelligence. When you go deeper, you see that earth is engulfed in wind, and wind becomes diffused in the sky (Space). The space is the Life-Energy. The name and form are all only imagined. The essence is this Life-Energy, or Chaitanya, only. See how when the earth and water are mixed, they create a third article which is called clay. When flowers and a string are woven together, we get a garland. The shape changes and the name changes, but still, all are only earth. An earthen pot when broken is called shards or pieces. All of you are Life-Energy, not bodies. Man, woman, daughter, son, all, are only that Chaitanya. All have come about from the One.

The original figure is "one" (1). One by one, the numbers start increasing. Although the numbers may increase infinitely, the primary number is only one, which remains after all the growth eventually is destroyed. So, only one is there, and there is no second. To see that there is "One" is Knowledge, to see that there are many is Ignorance. The wind, the waters, everything, the Goddess Earth, the Lord of Waters, the Lord of Fire, everything is the one Narayana. In everything, dwells only one Life-Energy. The mind and intellect are only Chaitanya, and there is no "I" who assumes a separate existence. Only that should be taken out. We do not understand it, but we must understand that this "I" is false. "That" who knows that "I am the Life-Energy," is Shiva. When you conceive that what you call "me," as only the body, you are a small creature, a jiva, and that spells the expansion of mundane existence.

The teachers in Illusion who themselves are ignorant have taught us "I Am." This world experience is limited by that boundary. Because of this teaching, this "I" must become a dog or cat. Through this worldly teaching, desire is increased and the individual sets up a household, and when he dies with this body, he wants another body. Thus, again he gets the family life. Because of desire, he gets bodies in succession, and he gets birth in a body according to his desire. If you see through a microscope, you will see that the world is full of minute germs. A family man has more worries, and becomes more afraid. He is afraid even of an ant. He tries to save himself from the nuisance of ants. Please tell me what is in this body that dies. The five elements never die.

Suppose one is born and a name is given to him, but he dies after only 12 days. He is gone. He dies, but people still record his name even though the bearer of that name is gone. (It is an Indian custom to name a baby 12 days after birth.) We cannot meet him, as he was but an imagination. When people give a name to a child, they think a lot. This is all conceptual thinking. They give a name that comes to the surface of their mind. Nobody can say why, but all are very keen about name and fame. Everyone is anxious that they should not be defamed, or that their fame should not be reduced. We try very hard to take care of these things. All of this pride is only about that which is false. To take what is seen as true, is Ignorance. To understand that all that is seen is false, is Knowledge. To classify into different groups is Ignorance, and to see everything as One, is Knowledge. This means that to look with the Guru's point of view, is Knowledge. All is of the nature of Brahman.

What is false? Name and form are false. The "Vision of Knowledge" is seeing with "understanding." One who examines everything, is "a man of discernment," a King. He examines everything. He observes all observation. He observes the "observer" who is observing. He also observes the moment of observation. Observation goes to the final border, and one realizes the exact moment, or the origination of observation. The one who realizes is the true "observer," the *King* (Parikshit). One must examine everything. By examining, you come to know. Where there is no examination there is Ignorance. This Ignorance is the thoughtlessness called Avidya. Correct thought is wisdom, or "Good Knowledge" (Suvidya). To see, and know "as it is" is to speak Truth. People speak of something else, while Reality is quite different, and they become proud, saying that they are speaking Truth. All of the worldly talk is only cunning speech and trickery.

Only men of "Supreme Knowledge" (Vijnana) can speak the Truth. It is very difficult to speak Truth. Only God can digest "Truthful" speech. To behave according to what is actually inside, is possible only for God. People speak falsely swearing they are speaking Truth. All of that is deceptive. Mother, father, children, all, are God, Rama. If you say "dog," it is dog, if you say "God," it is God. The Self is all beings. What is meant by the vision of the "Entire Universe"? To "One Being" are attached all shapes. All faces, an endless number of faces, and endless hands, and all their activities are vested in "One Being." Arjuna saw this when Lord Krishna revealed his true face. The pride of the body is the demon Narakasura. To kill it is difficult as well as easy. There is no death. Nothing in this world is ever totally destroyed. If it were, where would it go? That which is not, from where does it come? In the great battle of the Bhagavad Gita, out of all the Pandavas, only Abhimanyu died. Abhimanyu is pride. However, all of the Kauravas, who were of evil mind and were attached to their body were killed. The "Son of the Guru" (Guruputra) knows that "All is One," without a second.

23-9-1935

60. There is Only One Without a Second

The Self (Atman) is One, alone. He is prior to all, only One, totally "complete." If anything else were to come, from where would it come? It could only come by destroying the One. There is no place for a second thing to enter. The one Self is fully "Totally Existing." No "second" is possible. The Supreme Self, Paramatman says that He is everywhere fully. There is only one "Authority." If any other were even to slightly enter, His power would be reduced to that extent. No second has ever been able to enter. If it is felt that some other has entered, this is only delusion. It is only a doubt. In the totality of doubtlessness, doubt is the second thing. That doubt multiplies and becomes a mind full of doubts, and the Illusion of the world appears. By remembering the Self, the vision of Paramatman is confirmed, doubt is removed, and the oneness of Existence is proved. There is only One Form, One State, and One Power that exists eternally. When you are sure that there is only One, then there is no "second."

In all the three times of the day, the morning, at noon, and in the evening, the Sun is the same. There are three times of day, but the Sun is only one. Really, day and night have no reality. The Sun says, "I do not know either morning or evening. You do not know me as I am, therefore you are measuring me." Where are the seven days? Where do they go? The Sun does not know any day as Monday, etc. Your imagination has decided all these things. The Sun knows neither east nor west. As we have become small, we are experiencing this. There is not even a tiny space that is without Me. All is Consciousness. The occupant and that which is occupied are not different, just as the earth and wall are not different. The "Life-Energy" is called Inner-Mind. There is no power other than it that can say anything. Mind, intellect, consciousness, ego, (elements of the Inner-Mind) are all the play of my "True Nature."

One man came for dinner and said, "We are seventeen people." However, he was only one person. (5 pranas, 5 sense organs, 5 organs of actions, 1 mind, 1 intellect, all together make 17.) Nobody except a Saint recognizes Me. A clever scholar does not recognize Me. All is Myself, One and only One. The organs of the senses have to do their jobs as a natural activity. It is their very nature. Once a brother-in-law of a king was awarded punishment to sleep for 27 days. After 5 days he says, "You may even hang me, but I don't want this punishment. Nobody would like to have a mind without any activity. Only a Saint can do it. To be without activity is not the nature of mind. The mind only remains quiet in the vicinity of Reality. The mind can get the "Joy of Freedom" only in the vicinity of Reality. As long as there are false notions in the mind, or the hope of happiness, the mind suffers a repetition of sorrow. Even the mind that is put under control through Hathayoga becomes victim of sentimentality at the time of breaking the trance of samadhi. The Saints who have realized the Self through the "Path of Devotion" know the nature of the rising of mind itself and therefore their mind is always in a happy state. Unless you know the primary cause of how the mind comes into being, it is not possible either to control the mind or make it stay happy. To know this is a mysterious thing. You will not be able to get hold of the mind if you try to find it. Mind and Brahman are one. Both are of the nature of the Life-Energy, Chaitanya. We have to go along with the mind to understand it, and we have to turn it as we want. If you are adamant with the mind, it becomes doubly arrogant. Saints harness the mind with subtlety. Be devoted to that Life-Energy, Chaitanya. Why are you so arrogant? This is a saying in Hindi, "Worship the Guru, why have arrogance?" Life itself is only He." The mind is an appearance on Myself. It is not mind. It is Myself only. If you use the word "second," that is also only full of Knowledge.

The speaker and the thing about which he speaks, is only Myself. Who is there separate from Me who speaks? God has created the Vedas. The Veda means "to speak." The speaker of the Vedas is Me. Vedanta means, "the end of knowing." Veda means to know. The Pranava, or

Omkar, which knows the Vedas, is only Me, myself. The reply and the response, as well as the "O" (origin of Om) is given by Me alone. I am the speech of the primordial speech. When Paigamber was asked, "Where is Allah?" He said, "He is." This means that He is Om. The entity that gives response is Allah alone. We are not somebody separate from God (Hari). God is One. There are no two things. By His speech, the word, the universe functions. It is His word, which is obeyed. Om is permeating in the whole world. The first syllable of Om is A. Without first uttering A, no speech is possible. A+U+M together, are called the three syllables. Om is three syllables with a half syllable which is God. These three syllables together with God are the base of the world. The three worlds are created from this. From the three worlds, innumerable universes came into existence. Therefore, the primordial Om is myself. I am the subject of all speech. To see with the eyes is myself and at the same time, what is recognized is Knowledge. Without Me, the eyes are but a lump of flesh. Vision means Consciousness, which is the moving Life-Energy, which is Me. There is no other seer than Me in the three worlds.

The three worlds are the waking state, the dream state, and the deep sleep state. I am the Master of the three worlds. I am the knower of pain in the stomach. I know all. The art of seeing is Me. I am the receiver of bad names. The cause or origin is known by Me only. One who understands is aware, and that is Myself. I am the light that is given by the eye because Consciousness is there. It is My own "Being." The tongue without Me is just like a sole of a boot. What does it know? I am the One who enjoys the smelling, and that which is smelled is also only Me, and I am the one who recognizes the smell. It is I who has the knowledge of all things. Nobody except Me knows a thing. Bondage is because of Me, and to know Me is freedom. Not to know Me is the only bondage. Any structure devoid of Me is only a hide, an empty shell. I am the taste. Who else except Me knows what it is to be the knower of taste? I am the enjoyer and the creator of all the senses. I am "The Power of Action," and I am "The Power of Matter." I am "The Power of Knowledge." When I am "The Totality," how can the lump of flesh called the body be separate from me? From where would it come? All is One. Then, what is it that can be called as "other"? What is other than Me? The breath of all is One.

Only people who are confused think that the body is separate from God. One has to die every day. Everyday some heavy matter goes out of the body. Everyday some new matter is put into it. Double of that which goes out, goes into the body. One becomes proud of that which is "dead" (the body) thinking that it is "true." Such a one does not recognize that which does not die. These five elements are like waves of water in a single ocean. Actually, there is nothing separate from Me. All of the animate and inanimate creation is only Me. Different names are given only for convenience of functioning in the society. It is not necessary to behave as an eccentric when you become "Knowledgeable" (a Jnani). There is only one "Universal Self," one Atman.

What are you studying? It is enough that you have an understanding of non-duality (Advaita). Is there any other without the One? When you knew your mother, what is the necessity of shouting her name? When mind is imbibed with the discernment that there is "only One," nothing else remains to be done. For the one who realizes that he is everywhere, no further spiritual practice (sadhana) is necessary. For one who knows Me, the Self, his efforts are ended. I told my dear devotees that the Self is all, that "I am in All," but I told the others to do some sadhana, and I told them to grow long hair on their head. I did not give "My Knowledge" to them. This is "My Own Knowledge." I have removed the sense of separateness in the minds of "My Devotees" but for sages and yogis, I prescribed certain regimens of practice. I gave their body a lifetime of a thousand years, but I gave "My Knowledge" only to "My Devotees." My Knowledge, the Knowledge about "My True Nature" (Swaroopa) is difficult to attain. Unless one is devoid of all sense of ego, all desire, and all pride, it is not realized.

Evening, 24-9-1935

61. The Main Doctrine of Vedanta

All is Brahman. To have the concept that "I am somebody" is the imagined being. That which is without concept is Brahman. Concept is the individual, the Jiva, and Jiva is the ego, Ignorance. There are two principles in Vedanta. These are Reality or "Brahman," and Illusion, or "Maya." Maya means "that which is not." Brahman is "That which is." Maya is a falsehood, a hypocrite. That which is not a falsehood is Brahman. Maya is counterfeit, it is trickery. Where there is no trickery there is no falsehood. When the word Maya is used, it means hypocrisy and falsehood, a deception. That which is hypocrisy can never be Truth.

Maya is false, and Brahman is Truth. It is not hypocrisy. Whatever has an appearance, whatever is perceived, is false. If it has any name, or any form, it is not true, it is not durable. If it has an appearance, it will not last, it is not permanent.

Only Brahman is True and therefore, it will not honor that which is false. That which is false makes much dance and show, but the Truth which is Brahman, makes objection to it. The false is not respected even a little bit, and therefore it does not endure. It is not permitted to remain long. It is very short-lived. Whatever is a make-believe hypocrisy, however great may be its force or its boldness, it cannot be proved true before Brahman. It is not supported or respected by Brahman so it automatically drops away, and becomes invisible. That which has disappeared was false, and because it was false, it has become invisible. It should be called, and is called, as Maya. Maya is a derogatory word. It is a contemptuous term. Brahman is True. No pretext can be useful about it. Truth has no replica. We cannot have a fake pretension about that, of which there is no replica. How can truth have a parallel or similar thing? That which can be imitated is not Truth. Truth is unqualified, absolute, and without any image. To be proud of any kind of high quality fake image is totally useless. Brahman considers Maya very despicable. Any falsehood that is proud of itself is to be despised.

Brahman is completely without pride. Therefore, any little pride in any experience, in any achievement, is worthless. It may even be pride in a great good deed that the doer feels he has done, but Brahman does not touch it and does not respect it. This is the "Real Knowledge" of our True Nature that is called "Self-Knowledge." There is nobody such as "I" to be discovered. By searching and eliminating all the elements and principles in nature, and in man, there is no "I" found remaining at all. The Self is there, and the body may be there, but the third person, this "I," is not there. It is Maya who says "I," and "me." The "me" is the product of some disturbance in Maya. When this third person is dropped out, then the seeker, or aspirant, and that which is achieved, the ideal, and his efforts are all eliminated. Then, Paramatman is alone. So long as the ego-sense is not gone, "Self-Knowledge" is impossible. When the "me" is gone, the concept of being a seeker, the sense of doing something, and the idea of something to be attained are also gone. Paramatman is uncovered without doing anything about it. If you examine all of your thoughts, you will find there is no "I" at all.

There are five elements and the sixth is the Self (Atman). The five elements are themselves the sense organs in the body, and Self is the sixth. There is no "I" to be found anywhere in any of this. When Oneness is understood through Oneness, everything is Brahman. When this "I," or lack thereof, is recognized, its function ends. Only that which is the creator of the world remains. What remains when the "I" and the "you" are eliminated? That which remains, which survives this process of elimination, is "Being." That which "is." When that which "is," has gone, and that which "is not" is also gone, and something which is not a thing remains, there is no necessity of declaring what "is." It is "itself" there. When you know what is "not," then whatever "is," is. What is the necessity to declare as non-existing, that which is not there? It is naturally not there! This is called self-surrender (Atma-Nivedan). The sense of "I" is offered to God, he digested it, and it became God himself and manifestation dissolved. Manifestation is called "Prakruti"(Prakriti), the diverse creation. When it is dissolved, only God remains. There was one. He produced second. Second means the other. He swallowed what was produced. Then only One remained. The Prakriti, the separate creation is wiped out. From where did I, the third entity-which is Illusion, come? When it is not existing, how did it intervene? This God is called "Five Faced." The five elements are his five faces. Naturally, all of these five elements are unified in the one Self. It is all One. "God is five faced," says Saint Dnyanoba. Where is there a "me" as an entity? It is "not." It is like going out to search for darkness by holding a light in our hand. If you search darkness with a lantern in your hand, you will not find it. When the "Sun of Knowledge" rises, the darkness, the proud ego, the Ignorance, will not be seen. Where is the "serpent" in the serpent? Where is the "donkey" in donkey? All is the Self. In the beginning and in the end, there is only the Self. He is Atman. "I" and "you" are not there.

When the state of Self-Knowledge is attained, your own dinner is an offering to God, your walking is making sacred rounds (Pradakshina) around God's image. To speak is to praise Him, and to sleep is his samadhi. To be seated in a casual repose, is his "unbroken samadhi." To "Be" naturally, to "Exist," is Brahman that has become manifest. That is Brahman in human form, which has become visible. There is nothing else except "It." That is how it is said that the Saints are Brahman expressed in manifest form. The bundle exists because you have tied it. We have to loosen this bundle by thinking, then there will be no bundle. The lack of discrimination is the separateness that is the bundle, the Jiva. When the lack of discrimination is gone, there is no duality. Then there is only Brahman. The bundle was put together by accumulating various things. While analyzing and sifting these things, the bundle does not remain. The one who was carrying the load of the bundle becomes stripped of attributes.

When "I" has gone, who is there to do any spiritual practice (sadhana)? Who will do meditation? The greatness of the Saints is that they have given the blessing for me to say that I myself am God. It is very difficult for others to accept the salutations of a person of "Real Knowledge." He is God in person, the Almighty. It is extraordinarily hard to be the recipients of salutations from Him. The sin or merit, heaven and hell, do not effect Him. He is self-evident. He is undivided and unhindered in his straightness. He does not suffer Saturn's bad period (in Vedic astrology, a period of seven years of difficulties). Even the sin of one who remembers the "Knowledgeable One" (Jnani) is wiped clean. By his touch, a person goes beyond birth and death. God says, "My presence, looking upon me, is itself good deed, and auspicious time." The Jnani, does not suffer defamation because he is not an individual. He is unexpressed, and beyond all qualities and all forms. Yogis and munis had in them a sense of pride of their being yogis (performers of various austerities and yoga postures, or vows of silence). Lord Krishna also told them that their status was very high because they were not able to lose their identification with their physical body. They were proudly showing off their hair and beards. He said, "You may have a lifetime of billions of years." They had strange notions of sins in eating and drinking. Lord Krishna however remained pure, even though doing all sorts of things, because He was aware of himself as the highest Paramatman.

One who breaks the ties of the body will be Paramatman and the life is fulfilled. You should continue on with your contemplation. Do not hold to any concepts. Do not simply believe in the concept that if Brahman is everywhere, I will be saved. Even when all of this is Brahman, do not hold on to any concepts. Brahman is without concepts. With this "understanding," you will be liberated. Those who harbor doubts fail. Those who are the devotees of the Guru attain the state of Brahman. First, you have to listen to spiritual sermons, then comes service to the Guru, then comes Self-Realization, and then the attainment of the state of Brahman. Those who are simple souls are the ones who have unshakable faith and trust. When you surrender your self, the only pure thing that remains is Brahman. Do not allow the demon of ego, which is hell.

When you realize that you are Paramatman, then you are Brahman including your body. The former mundane life is destroyed. God has no destiny. Do not keep believing in destiny. Your concepts deceive you. Do not fall prey to doubt. Maya says, "I have tethered many big beasts." The seekers, sadhus, and yogis are these beasts tethered by Maya. The Supreme Self, Lord Krishna, became and remained as Parabrahman. Others only identified themselves as separate egos. The mirror says, "There is nobody in me." The man who looks into the mirror says, "I am in the mirror." The "Knowledgeable Ones" know all of these things. Some elements came together, and that became a body. After understanding this, it is important to live according to this Knowledge. It demands skill. First, Knowledge (Jnana) is necessary in order to gain Self-Knowledge. This Self-Knowledge, or "wisdom" then destroys the Knowledge. One should also throw out all that has happened. The Master Key to what is being said here is that one whose conceptual entity is gone, is the Jnani. The Illusion is gone, the elements are gone, and Knowledge is also gone. Only "Supreme Knowledge" (Vijnana) or Brahman, remains. When one house is emptied, all houses are empty.

The transcendent Brahman, which is beyond qualities, is not affected by anything. It is always undisturbed. When we use discrimination, the unessential goes off, and only "Pure Essence" remains. Only Brahman, which is beyond even the Sattva quality remains. The sense of "I" was only imagined. One whose sense of "I" is wiped out by the blessings of the Guru, remains not as a person, but as Paramatman. The outcome is dependent upon your determination. Whatever you conceive, is what you experience. While looking at God, one becomes God. Paramatman has the power to do, to undo, and then to do something else. He is transcendent to all. He can do anything He wills. There is no bondage for Him who is free from all actions. Have no pride in, or identification with karma. A person was deceiving himself and calling himself as some particular entity, but once the sense of "me" goes, then "I," "Who am I?," and "I Am That," also all go away. Then, even if one dwells in a body, he is free of the body, beyond the body. Only Paramatman Is.

Evening, 25-9-35

62. God is Life-Energy (Chaitanya)

The real God is Sat-Chit-Ananda (Being, Consciousness, and Bliss). The Consciousness in the body is God. It is that Consciousness which protects the body from accident, from a horse, or a serpent, etc., that is God. This has become evident. We must know what we are. In this body, that which says "I," is not really anyone. All of this is only misunderstanding and confusion. We have assumed conceptually that we are a body, but if you take a search throughout the body, there is neither "you" nor "I" in it. The sense of "you" and "me" is not there in "That." We see all of the five elements, but these are all created from the Life-Energy, Chaitanya. All is only that Life-Energy. One who has understood that only "One Thing" is real, is liberated from birth and death. Beard, mustache, and hair on the head, are all only hair. Name, form, shape, etc. are all false. Once you know this Life-Energy, all is fulfilled. In all the innumerable forms, God is the only One, everywhere. By analysis of the five elements, you are shown what this Life-Energy is. By explaining the meaning of the great statement, "You Are That," you have been told that you are Brahman. In "Original Being," the ego (Ahankar) is the Wind.

Surrendering to the Guru should be without any attachment. This must be explained. "Without attachment" here means, without being intimidated, without any other person's personal greatness exercising any kind of pressure, or anything or anyone else putting pressure on us. That is, it cannot be that that person does not actively use it even though some pressure exists. It must be that the pressure does not exist. There is not a single bit of pressure upon our own True Being. Therefore, neither now nor anytime in the future is there anything, or anybody which puts any pressure upon, or competes with our True Being for importance. We should be convinced about this. What prevents us or pressures us at all times and everywhere in various forms is our own confusion or misunderstanding. There is no other distortion at all. The surrender should be like this, without any attachment.

By taking a thoughtful look at things (vichara) the sense of separateness disappears, and when even thought goes, there remains only Chaitanya. Then, only a natural disinterestedness (Nivritti) remains. When the speaker disappears, that state is called unmani, or the "no-mind" state. When there is no accused, who is there to pay the fine? Nobody calls his belly as a toilet. For whom is the past karma, and destiny in effect? Why should one who is the king pay any penalty? Who can fine the one who is the king? How can the inanimate physical body have any past karma? The body is Brahman, and the Self (Atman) is Brahman. By "Absolute Knowledge," or Vidnyana, Knowledge (Jnana) has been nullified. The meditator disappeared with the meditation. The "me," the entity who meditates, has become extinct along with the meditation. The "me," which is the cause of worldly life, has gone with that life.

That life which has disappeared has come with all its glory again, but it has now become Brahman. All appearances are nothing but Brahman. The one who dies is dead because he was a "non-entity." The one "who was not," has died. No sin remains on the face of the earth. That which has no bondage was having bondage, and that bondage is no more. God does not have any bondage or freedom. Those who are servants of the Guru, who is the liberator of the downtrodden, also liberate others. They do not remain servants, they remain as Brahman.

26-9-1935

63. Conceive of Brahman Beyond Conception

Parabrahman is non-dual, and we are "That." It cannot be meditated upon, true, but does that mean that we should give up meditation? Meditation is not there because we are holding on to it. On the contrary, it is natural. The first study is the study of the Self, or Atman. But now what I tell is the study of the Supreme Self, Paramatman. One's natural state is Parameshwara. The primal urge or movement in That is the Life-Energy which is God. Consciousness is the Life-Energy of God. That which remains without "knowing," without being "conscious," is the Supreme Self, Paramatman, Parameshwara.

To come down into this world of visibility is the taking of "Incarnation," or Avatar (Avatar means to come down). This is Avatar. When we think about the permanent and the impermanent, the mind comes to a stage of equilibrium. When you know Paramatman, you become something else. Paramatman is devoid of knowingness. (To "be" or "not to be" is always a question. If we try to become, or be, it always bring in obstacles. Not becoming anything, is key in the accuracy of our effort.) Don't even try to remember what Paramatman is. Have absolutely no thought of "becoming" anything, and keep nothing in memory. Even meditation on the Absolute brings in duality. Do not fall prey to doubt. Do not be apprehensive. Leave all Illusion. Paramatman can never be tarnished or stained, nor does it become new by any effort that you make. People without discriminative intelligence get involved in worldly life. Therefore you must utilize the power of discrimination. What you call the individual (Jiva) is actually God (Shiva). When that which is created by imagination has gone, what remains is only Paramatman. Leave off even the sense that "He Is." When this sense of "you" looking at it goes, it is only "He" which remains. Remain with your Self, as you are. Be very natural. It is unaffected by the threefold Time (past, present, and future). When all the past, present and future go away, that which remains at the end, is your Self, Paramatman.

When you begin to look, the three aspects, that are the observer, the act of observation, and the object that is being observed, come into being. When you try to find out "That" where cause does not have any place, and nothing similar exists, you lose it instead of finding it. "That" which should be observed, which is to be remembered, and which is to be worshipped, is your Self. "You Are That." However, when you go about trying to find it, it becomes something "other." It is not possible for you to forget your Self. The fact that "you exist" is your own direct experience. Who else can convince you that you exist? First, you must exist. Only then is enquiry possible. If you are not there, who will conduct a search? You are there without saying that you are. It is necessary to understand that it is not dependent on your senses to confirm that you exist. There is no doubt about the truth or falsehood in that, because it is the state of Being. This is you. "That" which is not tangible to the senses, which cannot be approached, is the Truth. That is the Sat, or "Being-ness" beyond the effects of the three aspects of time.

How can one practice that which is? What is there to think about the Existence, which is already there? It is called the self-evident state, without any effort being involved. The Self is "self-evident." You cannot distort it by twisting it this way or that. You cannot forget your Self even if you try. That which you feel that you are forgetting is not you. It is the "other." It is only the forgetting of that which has been remembered. Whatever is remembered is destined to be forgotten. Whatever is forgettable is other than the Self. Remembering and forgetting happen about something else. It is not you. As you are not the object of memory, you are also not the object of forgetting. These things, remembering and forgetting, only take place in Consciousness. You are without these. In you, there is no damage whatsoever, as "This" cannot be damaged anytime by anybody.

When you came to me, what have I done, after all? I have just removed the Illusion. I removed the Illusion of a serpent. The rope appeared as a serpent and there was fear. I convinced you that it is not a serpent but only a rope. The rope had never become the serpent. You were only confused. Now, the serpent is forgotten. To forget it is itself the remembrance of Reality. First, you have to gain Knowledge, and then leave the Knowledge. It is enough to know this true "I." You have recognized, that is all. Why must you know again, and again? It is permeating everywhere. It is like gold that is permeating the ornaments. If you try to meet it, it escapes. This is the noble story of speechlessness. It cannot be achieved by any kind of means. If you try to lose it, you cannot. It cannot be lost. It cannot be thrown away if you try. It is always existing. It eludes you if you try to see it, and it is there, even if you do not see it. To try to acquire it becomes a handicap. It is realized without the process of understanding. It is devoid of thought, and without focus of effort anywhere. The "me" that was trying to understand it is dead.

Brahman is not a subject of meditation. While you eat and drink, it is He all the time. This is the only thoughtlessness. The mind is false, so how can the vast Brahman be understood by it? One who says that he knows Brahman has not truly gone to that region at all. Brahman cannot be known by mental attitude or the mind. Who can know that which is the father of all things, the root of all creation? If you try to mentally follow it, you will only be confused. Trying to describe it, even the Vedas have remained silent (saying only Neti, Neti). Only the Sadguru can tell of that which cannot be described. It is not for me to tackle it. Who can describe the indescribable?

All imagination is projected according to the ego, the sense of "I." We have to leave that path of ego altogether. Only then can you reach Paramatman. Snap your doubts in the company of Saints. Compare the Saint and yourself. Reduce and finally completely remove, the ego. Learn, and find out how this can be done. Your words should be kept aligned with his words, the understanding of which, should be aligned with his lessons. The form should be kept in proximity with his form, and your virtue should be like his virtue. Your qualities and actions should be compared with the qualities of the Saint. Then we should see what is better in him. We should check to see if that which is better or best in him, is also in us. Then, with his help, with the power of discernment and wisdom in him, we should look into our short-comings. By comparing our qualities, we should keep what is best. We should eliminate from our character that which is worst. In such a way, all doubt should be wiped out totally. All of this investigation and observation belongs to the "inner region." This is the relationship among knowing, not knowing, and

Supreme Knowledge. The one who aligns himself along these lines becomes one of "Direct Knowledge."

The sense of ego is difficult to get rid of. Only the teaching of the Sadguru can do it. Devotion is destroyed by an egotistic attitude. By the ego, the Self, which is self-evident, is shrouded. Because of ego, many have roamed around naked, many have taken a topsy-turvy approach to yoga, many have gone hidden in the mountains, and many have enshrouded themselves with long beards and tresses (dreadlocks) hardened by neglect. All of this so-called spirituality is based on ego. One cannot say what havoc ego will play. Because of ego, there is no spiritual life. On the contrary, it is damaged. In God Consciousness, ego cannot be tolerated. The devotee of the Sadguru drops ego. How is ego to be dropped? It is dropped by being aware of it. It is only by understanding that it is going to be dropped. When you know the Reality, you can be rid of ego. We have to be Brahman, and then we can have direct experience.

Be happy in non-attachment. The one who puts in spiritual effort without pride, is truly worthy of praise. God says, "Rama, Krishna, and the like, are my worshippers. The sages Narada, Sanaka, and others were all praising Me. I am the God of all. All the Saints who have lived up to now were doing my worship (Puja). They were worshipping Me, who is formless, flawless, fully joyous, beyond sentiments, beyond all qualities, without any residue, complete, Atmaram, Paramatman. I am God, the enjoyer of all the works, and offerings given by them. Only your own mind is responsible for your bondage and liberation. There is no hindrance to you from Me."

We have to experience Brahman by being Brahman. The experience should be without "me," the experiencer. Only then is that experience possible. There should not be any "I-consciousness" at all. You should not be aware that you as "ego" are experiencing Brahman. So many tried to be experiencers of Brahman, but they did not enjoy its Glory. Only Lord Krishna could enjoy it. We should be the doer but without the sense that we are doing. The actions should be without the sense of "I" as doer. The state of being aloof should be correctly understood. Only then does one become Paramatman.

Evening, 27-9-35

64. Self Purification

You cannot describe contentment, or that which you call happiness. When a mute man eats sugar, he cannot describe its sweetness. Listen with extreme eagerness. It cannot be understood, and cannot be known, even if it is explained. It cannot be imagined. Words cannot communicate it. The Supreme Self, Paramatman, is absolutely hidden. It can be understood only through being near Saints, by being in their company. That happiness of Paramatman, that contentment, is very deep. If the experience is to be told about by any sign or indication, it is unutterable. It cannot be described. Hand or facial symbolic signs are only the qualities of those limbs, and they are therefore limited, and inadequate. Even the deepest power of speech, which is called the "Para" speech, or the original energy, cannot show it by any indication, as it is indescribable. It cannot be known without the help of the Sadguru. Only one who searches oneself can receive the blessings of the Sadguru.

What is the experience of the one who receives the blessing of the Sadguru? That one experiences that he himself is Paramatman. That is the result of one's Self-search. When you understand that you are nothing, then what remains is only one Brahman. This is called the "Natural State of Samadhi" or Sahaja Samadhi. If he walks and talks, it is called "Sairat Samadhi," this is a state of seemingly insane activities, but a resting in inner contentment. He is completely happy without doubt. People think that he behaves abnormally, but he is not aware that he is behaving at all. The contention of some is that Paramatman is witness to all, but those who know the Reality, the Siddhas, say that "witnessing all," is but a state of mind, and the Reality is devoid of any such state or hypothetical position. Paramatman is beyond all the four bodies and beyond the four sheaths of consciousness (mind, intellect, thinking, and "I" or ego). When you realize that what you perceive is not an objective thing or any material, but that all is Brahman, the complex of "I," the ego, will vanish. When the notion of "I" is dropped, then the idea of "you" also drops away. The disappearance of "I" is the sign of realization. "That" which is, is. It is neither the individual (Jiva), nor God (Shiva). That duality does not appear there. We also cannot say that there is nothing. "That" is the indescribable Bliss. The speech, the word, is all illusory. The word conveys the meaning but it disappears as soon as the meaning is understood. The word ends. After giving the message, the word goes away. In Brahman, the word is false. Only its meaning should be taken. The word is different from what is seen, and what is beyond it, is Brahman, the Reality. "Pure Experience" is incapable of being pointed at. Self-experience is without the factor of giving any attention to it. To give attention to it is a quality. When you try to look at it, the "other" comes into being. The nature of attention is such that automatically, very naturally, there is some production by it. To be capable of producing is its specialty. It is its nature, its inherent quality, which cannot be destroyed by anything. Only by the "Knowledge of Reality" does it disappear. It is said that sky is filtered through a strainer and thus the core of the Life-Energy, Chaitanya, is obtained, but that is also imagination. The "rule of experience" is that it is not possible without duality. Experiencing means duality. The mother of experience is the daughter of a barren woman who is the original Illusion, or Maya, which is a concept of imagination. This "Illusion," this imagination, is a vehemently uttered bad word. This is known only by those who know their own Self. Where there is the phenomenon of experience, there is duality. Therefore, in the "True Existence of Reality," there is no place for experience. In the wake of Self-Realization, duality shies away.

The sun is the cause of day and night. Without the sun you cannot say, "This is day" or "This is night." Experience and reporting experience to others are only within the field of Illusion. Had it been the case that I am one thing, and Brahman is something other, then it would have been possible to tell somebody about the experience. See the wonder of this. He who was not born, was sleeping. In the dream, he saw another dream. In it, he achieved Knowledge by the blessings of the Guru, and then he disappeared. When there was nothing, what remained was his "Natural Essential Existence." He was awakened while he was discussing what "Knowledge" means. If you can catch the meaning of this, you will also have similar contentment. There is unity without the intervention of speech. The entity saw a dream within a dream, and he became awake by having arisen from sleep.

Since you have not grasped this explanation, I will tell you again. You are the one without birth. It is your delusion that you are born. It is your feeling. The dream within the dream is your thinking about what is Essential and what is non-essential, and when you realize that you are the Self, Atman, then you have this experience. You felt that the world is illusory. You felt that you are awake and that it is your waking state. You felt that you have obtained "experience," but still, your confusion, your illusion, is persisting as it was. You are yet talking about things in the dream. When there is true awakening, all the sense of "being" disappears. Even the sense that you are the Self, also dissolves. That is called "Knowledge Beyond Words." Now, have you understood what is beyond words? What remains? Only Brahman remains. The bondage that was false, is cut. The ocean of worldly life is proved to be a mirage.

Since childhood, when some awareness of this life dawned, the fear of death was imposingly menacing. As the vast experience of the universe was before our eyes, there was a constantly increasing hope to achieve and possess something very great, some kind of property. It was felt that I must have an extraordinary possession in the present, and also for the future. For future births also, it was thought correct to have some great possession. So, a very strong desire was harassing me relentlessly. There was a firm conviction that this world is real, and that the next world that I am going to enter is also real. Now, all that has proved to be futile, and I realized that this seemingly real world is only a mirage. Therefore, not a single thing is to be possessed and accumulated by me. The worldly existence seemed to be an ocean but it proved that there was not even a drop of water. Now it is all right. The Illusion is dissolved. The one who was without birth was liberated from birth and death. The man thought that he had become a tiger, but when he was shown a real tiger, his illusion of being a tiger was gone. He, who was not a family man, was being possessed by a ghost of family life. That ailment was removed and he was released. He was always non-dual, but the false duality was broken. He was engrossed in the world of people, and then he was brought to his own "Aloneness." He was awake, and then he was awakened. He was deathless, and was made deathless. The fear that he had harbored in his mind was removed.

He whose very nature is wisdom, and He, who is the Self, was made the Self. The "Nectar of Immortality" (Amrut) was given the quality of "Deathlessness." One who does not die is the "Deathless Self." One who cannot die is the Immortal Nectar. Even then, he was obsessed with the idea that he is mortal, but that obsession also was destroyed. He was made immortal. Now he will never die. One who is free was given freedom. There is no necessity of having hope that I will be free, because there is no trace of bondage. He was already united, but he was given unity. He was feeling that he was thrown out and therefore he was hanging, which made him afraid. In that place where he was banished to, he became convinced that he is not separated or estranged, that he is originally spread out everywhere, all-pervading, essentially One, alone.

After many days, he met himself. The division of the undivided was gone. All the spiritual practices bore fruit.

God whose real place is in the "Shrine Room," the inner sanctum of the temple, was properly placed there only. He was having a dream that he was wandering in a forest, but now he is convinced that he is properly in the Shrine Room where he belongs. That which he was running after, although it was always near him, he now has. He was sorrowful because of a very bad dream. Although he was a Brahmin, of the highest caste, he had become a so-called untouchable. That is now gone and he has regained his quality of being a Brahmin, a "Knower of Brahman." He is convinced that nothing has ever happened.

Evening, 28-9-1935

65. Formless Unqualified Brahman

In the Vedas, it is said that Consciousness, or Prajnana, is Brahman. That which is Consciousness is Brahman. The "me," the holder of the name "me," is Illusion. That which is there without any effort, is Brahman Consciousness, or "Prajnana Brahman." That experience of Being, without speaking about it, is Brahman. In it, if there is a concept that "I am somebody," it is an imagined ghost. Only that should be called "me," and should be dropped. When that is gone, the job is over. It is not necessary to set out to see what Brahman is. The awareness that "only It is," is sufficient. That is Brahman. However, in order to "know It," some other factor is created by the mind. In order to know, the intellect must create something separate. The intellect, in order to "know," imagines a duality, but, whatever is imagined, is not "That." The mind and intellect are like a continuous flow of a downward stream from That. When the stream comes out of That it cannot know the original reservoir from which it is oozing. This is why aspirants (sadhakas) try to contain the mind and intellect so that the leakage should be stopped. By example, there is a very large tank, that is full of water, and a small hole is there. Water is streaming through the hole. The flow of water coming down, cannot look back through the hole and know the content of the water in the tank. As soon as the flow starts, it forgets that it is part of the accumulated water in the tank. When it is out of the tank, everything about the tank is forgotten.

This is why you should control the mind and intellect. Do not allow it to flow. You should stop its nature of aimlessly flowing downward into Illusion. This is being emphatically told to you. The mind and intellect cannot understand this. When you drop all attachment, all is Brahman. You should leave aside the meaning of what the mind says. You should not follow what the mind says. Do not be attached to what the mind says. Mind is a thing that has fallen down. Mind interprets according to its whim, and suffers due to the mixture of happiness and suffering, while it flows. You should leave the mind and its interpretations. How do you leave it? People leave their homes, tear away their clothes, and try to be monks, but even after doing that, their attachments are not dropped. When one continues to possess that which one has decided to drop, how can one become a monk? He is not Brahman. One who realizes in one day has the straight path of the flight of the eagle (the birds way), and one who realizes after many days is on the slow path of an ant (the ant's way). When all attachment is dropped, what remains is Brahman.

What is our attachment that is to be dropped? This means that when you see only "Me," the sense of "my," and "mine" is to be dropped. "I" means the sense of "me." It is the sense of this separate "me" that is the state of the individual, the Jiva. When you say, "I don't exist," the individual is finished. When you have actually seen that you are not, there is no necessity of a means and an end. When the individual (Jiva) is gone, only God (Shiva) remains. The meaning of the end of the jiva, is the ending of "me." You have seen that you are not existent. There is a confirmed realization that from top to bottom in the whole body, that "you" are not there. Even after this conviction, there is still the experiencing of a body and of Consciousness. Now, this experience is of the nature of a gentle touch. It is but a slight touch for Pure Consciousness, Shiva. This means that Consciousness touches, or animates the covering that is the body. This is a simple sensation that is most natural. The quality of Pure Consciousness is what is called Shiva. That which is only an imagination without the base of actual experience or observation, is called Ignorance. The misunderstanding about that which is born as the body, as "me," is the essence of the state of the jiva, which is Ignorance. This is wrong knowledge. When the fact is one thing, and you think it to be something else, that is wrong knowledge. Ignorance means "not knowing." When you "know," when you understand, it is Knowledge. The gaining of Knowledge takes away the Ignorance, and "Supreme Knowledge," or Vijnana, takes away that Knowledge. After this, you do not have to study. You are simply Pure

Brahman. "That" is an open experience. Bread that is already baked need not be baked again, and you do not boil rice that has already been boiled.

The word Swayambhu becomes Shambhu (Shiva), by a slight change in pronunciation. That One who is Shambhu is Swayambhu, the self-existent One. Even if the body is cleansed by taking a bath, the Self is not cleansed by that process. Brahman is already pure. Why are you trying to bathe it? A tiger was advised that he should first take a bath and then kill animals. He followed the advice and began to die of hunger. A sage told him, "You did not follow your 'own religion' (natural behavior) and therefore you are going hungry." If this Brahman does many unnecessary and wrong things, everything goes wrong. So, do not do anything. It is told of how Shiva left his abode on Mount Kailasa and went to the cemetery where he attained Self-Realization. You are Paramatman, enjoy your own glory. Others are going to be pure by simply looking at you. You will find that things will happen as you say.

Remain where you are. Do not clean toilets when you are a king. Remain with yourself, fully aware of your Being. You are the unattached, self-existent Paramatman. It is for you to increase your power. The power of this Knowledge (Vidya) is such that one can create a new universe. This Knowledge was used by kings. The royal teachers in the past were not imparting this to others. Those teachers were appointed to the kings alone, and they were dependent on the kings. The real Saint does not care about this. This "Knowledge of Yoga" (Knowledge of oneness) is great. Lord Krishna enjoyed its glory. No doubt, it is a great thing to attain the state of Brahman, but it is still greater to enjoy it. But alas, nobody enjoys it. What is the necessity of the means when the goal is achieved? You are the primordial everlasting Brahman! Drop the idea of an imagined person. You exist without being imagined. Those who underwent tremendous trouble, and even faced death in the name of spiritual efforts did not die after dropping the "me." However, people die every day in vain doing much hard work in their life, but do not enjoy the glory and the majesty of Brahman.

One whose pride is gone, is automatically Brahman. This is samadhi without a ripple of thought. This is also called unbroken, unhindered samadhi. Either with qualities or without qualities, there is only Brahman. There is nothing else. The man was unnecessarily holding on to some false concept. Brahman is the same everywhere, for both the king and the pauper, to the woman or the man. It is not true that a brahmin's (priest's) Brahman is pure and a shudra's (laborer's) Brahman is impure. All of the sadhus, saints, sages, monks that have ever been, and even the Vedas, sing in praise to You only. The entire world worships only You. Mahadev (Shiva), Vishnu, and all of the other gods come to worship You, and are merged in You. They have no other place. For all, there is only one place of rest. To all, the resting-place is Paramatman, your Swaroopa (True Nature; literal translation of Swaroopa is "True Form"). Brahma, Vishnu, and all the gods praise only this God. The entirety of manifestation, Prakriti, is the servant of this God. She is trying hard to keep him in good mood. All glory is in God. The Almighty God is He. All the fame, all the greatness, and all the power vests in God. Therefore, the Vedas shout at the top of their voice that they are purified by having a glimpse of a Saint. All glory goes to God (Shiva), and poverty comes to the individual (Jiva).

There is only Oneness for the Guru and his disciple. There is no difference there. "There is only One, and no other" is the great statement of the Vedas. Unless you postulate the primary premise (discernment of the Essence and non-essential), the latter, final statement (only Brahman exists) is not evident. First, we have to recognize what is false, and from that, we have to find out what is true. For this purpose, the qualification or definitions of fourteen Brahmans have been told (this is explained in detail in the book **Dasbodh** of Samartha Ramdas). The essence of the five elements is called the "all-pervading Brahman." To be the witness, is a quality, only a facet of Brahman. It is all qualified Brahman. The statement from scriptures is, "That which is permanent is Brahman, that which is impermanent is Illusion (Maya)." The "All-Pervading Brahman" is impermanent. The "Witnessing Brahman" is also impermanent. Qualified Brahman is impermanent. The Life-Energy, or "Chaitanya Brahman" is also not permanent.

Whatever has a "name" has no base. It is false. All names are false. Various names are used to indicate the "Attributeless Brahman," (Nirguna Brahman). In Brahman, there is no bliss, therefore bliss is also false. Identification with Brahman is also a false name. "Indescribable" is a word used to indicate it, but that is also false. The rule is that we have not to speak about "It," at all. The word "unmana" (no-mind) is used to indicate That in which mind is not. Worry is merged and mind is dissolved. The entity that was saying "I," was the mind. When the structure (the mind) that is on the "thing itself" (Brahman) is gone, what remains is the "Natural State." He remains as He always is. The manifest Self (Atman), the Vedanta, and the formless Self (Shivatman) have remained One. Those who experience for themselves know this.

29-9-35

66. Seeing the Self-Reality

What is it that is called the Self, the Reality? That which is not perceived is Reality. That which knows all things is Brahman. That which functions with the help of intellect is the individual consciousness, the Jiva. He understands through intellect. Brahman, is indestructible. Truth is its Reality. On that, all other things appear. The "Realized One," the Jnani, looks upon Reality. Whatever is, appears on the Reality, and all that appears, disappears. Its nature is to disappear. The Jnani's existence is not an appearance. It does not appear, and therefore it does not deteriorate. It will not diminish. This is understood by one's own intuition. No effort is necessary to understand this. The Reality, your "True Nature" (Swaroopa), is natural. It is unbreakable and indestructible. The entire universe appears on "That." That is called Brahman. The Sun is sometimes called by the names Diwakar or Bhaskar. The Sun is also called SuryaNarayan. Brilliance, godliness, day-maker, and the "divine quality" (Light) are his nature. Light means that which enlightens all. Light means that intellect which knows.

Who is God? God is He who sees all. The Sun is greater than the material thing that is illumined, but because our eye knows the Sun, the eye is greater than the Sun, and the mind knows the eye. Who knows the mind? The intellect knows the mind, but He who knows the intellect is not known by anybody. He is self-luminous. The eye does not know itself. The Sun does not know itself. The Self is the Atman, that knows others and knows himself. That is why a person who is asleep wakes up by himself. Otherwise, who is going to awaken him? The Self is always awake. There is no necessity of another to awaken him. He is the self-luminous God, who lends "divinity" to God, and brilliance to the Sun. The Self is the one who properly places everyone in his right place, and gets the work done. He is not illuminated by any other. Everything is illuminated, or perceived, only by the Self. To know him once is enough. To try to know him again is sheer foolishness. It is not possible for the eye to know itself. Who else will venture to know that God? One who thinks that the apparent is real, insults Paramatman, and one who so insults Paramatman, becomes miserable as he thinks that what is apparent is God. He thinks that Paramatman is the darkness of Ignorance, and becomes a devotee of, and worships all that appears to, the senses.

To forget the Reality is the original sin. Thereafter, we function within the field of the apparent, the known, and show off. The mistake is forgetting Reality from the beginning. In this way, the individual respects that which appears and suffers many calamities. The Self is as He is, always brilliant. It is on Him that all appearances are recognized, and on Him that they are perceived. As it is He, who knows others, He is always existing, always there. He is beyond all appearances. He who knows all is the greatest. He is the controller of all objects that appear. That which is seen are objects, and being objects by nature, means that they are perishable. The objects of the senses are produced by the sense-objects themselves. This is the mischievous nature of these objects. One who accepts them as real becomes miserable. If you persist in following the objects of the senses, you will surely be miserable, because you will only see that which is "seen." If you see with the eye of "inner experience," He, the Self, is everywhere, inside and out.

Nobody has been able to show up to now just what "the observer" is. Just as the sky, or space, is in each and every thing, He is also all-pervading, permeating everything. It is only He, who is in everything in this world. All differences are due to ego. See what a strange thing has happened! God is sacrificed before the goat. In this, it is the ego that sees the difference. The difference means separateness is seen. Where only one exists, two are seen instead. To show that there are two, is the creation of difference, where one is made the owner and the other his slave. However, there was some trick in this. He by whose power experience takes place, the totality of the universe is experienced, and who is the essence of the experience of this cosmos, was made the slave, while the ego is actually not existing. It became an imagined entity and the "true experiencer" was threatened with the possibility that he will die. He was made to pay the penalty. Thus, he was made a scapegoat. The false entity had become "God," but his godhood was cut away by the advice of the Sadguru. This "God" was sacrificed before the goat (duality was dispelled) and the "True God" was restored to His godhood. He is the self-existent God. This was the wonder seen.

The demon is the buffalo bull on whom the God of Death, Yama, rides. All those who hold on to their physical body as "I," are the bull buffaloes. Yama rides on them. Yama means punishment, Yama means sorrow, Yama means death, and death means fear. There is definite fear and punishment for those who hold on to bodily egoism. Even the entity which says that "I am God, I am Brahman" is the same ego. When Paramatman says, "I am," or "I have experience," or "I have become

Reality," this is also all ego. The ego, the sense of "I," undergoes change of outer form. This energy is the desire to enjoy. It is so skillful at this, that it tries to deceive even God. It changes its form, its quality, very swiftly and very skillfully, but does not deviate from its desire, its lust, to enjoy. The ego very easily deceives even the so-called "Great Pious Sages." It enslaves even the various hosts of gods, by inspiring desires in them. It only becomes subservient to those who remain in their "True Being," ever alert against any distraction. This cannot be understood except by minute subtle observation. While the urge or energy of the ego is based on concept and imagination, the Reality has no aim before it. The imagination cannot measure the immensity of Reality. This means that the concept of "I," cannot know the nature of Reality. It cannot know what is its length, breadth, how much it is, where from and where are the states it pervades, etc. The sense of "I" is always incomplete, limited, and turned downward. So long as it is turned downwards, it goes on expanding, but when it turns upwards and ventures to grasp the immeasurable, it is dissolved automatically, and therefore cannot measure the end of the endless.

    The four stages of speech, Para, Pashyanti, Madhyama, and Vaikhari, are all destroyed in the Reality. Who should speak there? Who should tell anything there? If it is spoken about, then it is not Reality. To say that "I am Brahman" is not being Brahman. It is, as it is, without talking. It is, but it does not speak, which means it exists before the utterance of any speech. It is prior to any experience that takes shape, which means that it is there before awareness of the experiencing of the body and persists even in the awareness of the body. It started talking and utilizing other sense organs because there was experience of the body, but even then it is the same. When the body will be no more, and only some words may remain, and afterwards when even those words come to an end, it is still there, as it was. The body came and it is gone, but there is no addition or subtraction in the Reality. The ego sense, which experiences the limited body, is the only thing that seems to be wrong in the Reality. When this is understood, everything is made right. Reality is there even if I say it is not. It does not change. Even though many things may be said about it, it is as it is. It remains always as it is. The nature of Brahman does not change. The Reality, which is, does not change. It is always only "That," whatever you may say about it. If you use bad words, they are all only names of Lord Shiva.

    Peerless, without an equal, without a second, means only One. It is "That" which is spread out evenly everywhere. We are That, not anything other. If you kiss a dog, you kiss only Brahman. The dog is also Brahman. To remain like Shiva, as Shiva, is samadhi, and he who maintains Brahman-hood is truly wise. How can one call the toilet as Brahman? How can one call one's wife as Brahman? This question arises only through a kind of ego identity. If you see it by physical eyes, it is Illusion, which means the ignorance as to the "True Nature" of it. If you see with the "inner sight," it is Brahman. To pluck Tulsi leaves (A sacred basil plant in India) is considered a sin, but to offer Tulsi leaves is auspicious! Whatever the scriptures may say, to the truly wise it has no meaning. In short, one who does not know oneself is a great sinner. The Self is, naturally, as it is. The quality of "being the Self" is not the possession of the Self. This means that the sense of "Me" is not the Self. The sense of "this" and "I" as separate things is not correct. That there is One alone, is correct. There is not any other, therefore we should not use "me." "Pure Perception," or that which is experienced without any effort is correct, but to say so implies an "object" and "I" who experiences it. This is to be avoided.

That the Self is alone is the sign of detachment. Attachment means in company with something "other." Unattached means no company, no other. Company means "other." It implies duality. Companion means together. Unattached means it is not with "other." The Self is One, alone, and is unattached. This is the sign of experience. One who knows that he has known, or understood something, and knowingly remains as he is, is the one who has understood. One who has understood is satisfied, and becomes silent. One who has rightly understood is clear, he has no complaint now, and there is no further talk. When we have no complaint, what is the necessity to speak? He who has a complaint will surely talk. One whose complaint is gone, remains quiet. Absence of talk indicates "greatness." There is no reason left for talking. "I know it" is a wrong statement, as the need for words disappears. While describing Brahman, all adjectives are accompanied with "non" as a prefix.

The tongue of one who speaks is said to be split. It is obvious that no talk is possible with a tongue that is split. This saying is used to indicate that it is not really possible to utter any word to describe what is complete. It is said, "The tongue of the holy serpent on whom Lord Vishnu is reclining was split" because Reality cannot be described. Words cannot express Reality. The tongue remains useless. The Vedas have stopped trying to describe it by saying "Neti, Neti" (Not this, Not this). The word Shruti (Veda) means "Knowledge which is accepted after hearing." After listening, one decided "This is so," and accepted it as true.

But this is not the Knowledge born out of actual experience. A logical conclusion is not Self-Knowledge, nor "Direct Realization." That Knowledge which the Vedas postulate is believed to be so, and it is conjectured that it may be so, but to simply trust in this concept is not Self-Knowledge.

What is Self-Knowledge? To realize by our whole being, to actually feel it within us, as our Self, is the "Knowledge of the Self." "Not other" means that state that has no experience of "other." Self-Knowledge is not knowledge of anything "other." The state, the nature, the enjoyment of Reality, is the Self. That is the Reality of Self-Knowledge. What is the point in keeping up your adamant attitude when you have Realized? Samartha Ramdas says, "I am false. Everything mine is false. I have no place, no status." Everything is deceptive. Manifestation, Prakriti, speaks and that is deceptive. The Formless, Purusha, is also deceptive. He is also discarded in Reality. Prakriti and Purusha are artificial, false. They are futile. They are not real. Even their names are false. Where nothing remains, to say, "I have known" is false. You may be "knowing," there is nothing wrong in it, but do not say, "I am now having nothing remaining," because the "I" is still a remnant.

30-9-35

67. Eknathi Bhagwat

Videhi Janaka (Janaka was an ancient king; Videhi means he was without a body while having a body) asked, "What is this Maya which is so fearsome? Please tell how we can be free of this." At that time, the Sage Antariksha said, "Your question is futile, because you are asking about that which is not. That which is not, has made all the world mad. All this is Illusion. The entire world is merged in this Illusion. The time, sign of Zodiac, and name of the son of a barren woman is futile to ask about." Similarly, you are asking this. Illusion is like that. Is it possible to crush the head of your shadow? The daughter-in-law of a barren woman has delivered a son. The wife of Bheeshma (who never married) is having breast milk. The wind is being put into a mill and pulverized. The grandchildren of a eunuch went to hide in the house of the sun. Those who take these things to be true consider Illusion as real. Illusion means that whatever activities we do, whatever we experience, all active happenings, and even we ourselves, are meaningless. To prove that all experience in duality is false is the meaning of the word Maya.

What Maya is, is told by the Vedas and the Guru. It is up to you to accept or not to accept what is told. In short, Maya means, "That which is not existing." Maya, which says "I," is a very great Illusion. Not to understand is Maya. Maya simply means Ignorance, or misunderstanding. Misunderstanding leads to misleading results. You like to feed the body because you say that "I am the body." Accordingly, Maya appears to be real but is only Ignorance. What else is Maya? The individual, or jiva, who is a monkey, is not ready to drop his limited existence as jiva unless he is subjected to some great upheaval or change. Only after suffering great misery and calamity, does he feel that all is false. Then he knows that there is no happiness as such in worldly things. He then comes to know what Maya is. Maya herself says that she does not existent at any time. Maya means wrong knowledge.

The cause of Maya is delusion, and by the water of delusion, the tree of Maya grows. Foolishness is its branches, and sense-enjoyments are its fruits. Brahman and Bhrama have a very small difference in spelling. It is Bra or Bhra. Bhrama is Illusion. People say, "I realized the Self," or "I did not realize Brahman." It is only on the "Reality" of Brahman, that all of these innumerable offspring have been born. Objects of the senses are tied like rope by desire which has its youth in the sense of "I." Pearls from the waters of a mirage are taken to knit nets to ensnare. Maya has given birth to ego, her firstborn son. "Mine" and "attachment" are her other children. "Moha," or the identification with the body, is the son-in-law resident in her own home. The son-in-law is one who goes "waya," or useless.

What is the meaning in all of this, after all? It means that "all of this" is false. Maya wears the bangles of determination, and doubt. The ego, the jiva, is dancing to the tune of the jingling of the bangles. The son-in-law is given the mind as a dowry. She has expanded solely on the base of the three qualities (Gunas). This false Maya's nature is such that she affects the ignorant. How can we say that she is actually existing? With the "inner-vision" of Knowledge, she is not there at all. How can we say that she is? We cannot say that she is. In order to go beyond this Maya, many have let their hair grow, and undergone many austerities. They know the Panchakshari Mantra which shows that Maya is such that we should not ask any question about her. She is indescribable. We should not use words to describe her, as she is not even fit for that. She was not there in the past, nor will she be there afterwards. To think that this world is real, is Maya.

The Vedas were asked what is Maya? They remained silent. What can we tell about the beginning of the river in the mirage? Its beginning is in the Ignorance of the fools and her end is in Knowledge. She appears because we conceive of something. We hear our own footsteps, and look to see who is following us. Whatever a man thinks and imagines, is what is true for him. He is confused and he is afraid there. All of this is the play of the imagination. The original imagination is called the "Primal Illusion," or Moola-Maya. When man forgot Reality, the concept of Maya arose. Then man thought it to be true. Maya means "me." The wrong concept about ourselves here is the great error, nothing else. When a little piece of cotton is placed under a lens, and the sun's rays pass through the lens, the cotton burns. In "Pure Brahman," the "me" is not. In the chains of ego, the worldly life starts. This "me" is something of the neuter gender. The concept creates a ghost out of nothing and by concept only it disappears. We construct by our imagination, try to digest it, and when we cannot do so, we are afraid. There is no worldly life in the body, nor is it in the Self. Desire and body identification create the feeling that the world exists.

In a dream, the short period of five minutes may contain a prolonged period of life. When one is in deep sleep, neither the waking life, nor the dream life are present. There one enjoys a certain bliss. In that, there is the Self, but the body is not there, but the subtle ego is still there. Birth and death are also false. As soon as the Self is forgotten, the "me" comes into being, and that makes us see and experience birth and death. The entanglement in worldly life makes life extremely difficult and it has become very hard to go beyond it. One who becomes something is deceived by Maya. The lust for enjoyment of sense-objects becomes powerful in the individual, and by that, Maya's energy and strength are increased. They say that the image of Ganapati (Ganesha) should not be touched without first taking a bath. But who sees that the little son of the potter was passing urine in the clay before it was used for the making of the idol? In short, as soon as the jiva has limbs, arms and legs, they are bound to grow. However, when they are not there, or are broken from the beginning, how can one break them? How can there be any destruction?

Another example is there of a man who gives one paise (pai-se; a fraction of a rupee) in charity with a hope that he will get one hundred paise in the future. This is sheer ignorance. Maya is of this nature. To find it out and use some means to discard it is like an activity of a ghost. It is dissolved only by the teaching and advice of the Sadguru. Is the activity in the dream true or false? Will it ever be possible to find out how and when the dream took place? How can one enquire about that which is false? There was a town that was never built. To whom should one ask why the town was not built? It is senseless to make such enquiries. You must understand that Maya is only imagination. Everything that appears is false. All is dreamlike. It is very hard to go beyond this Maya for those who take her to be true. Many people say, "All this happened," or, "I said all this, and then I was awakened." While one utters "I am," repeatedly, they say that "I have done everything." While I was calling myself as either "happy" or "unhappy," I am now awake by the blessing of Sadguru. Say, "I am liberated, and it is by the grace of the Guru that this Knowledge arose." Otherwise one thinks that Maya is true and real, and becomes caught in the cycle of births and deaths.

To say, "I am my body" means birth through a womb, but to say that "I am Brahman," is to be without that process at all. One who says this is the "Son of the Guru." To have the sense of "I" in Brahman is to be the individual, a jiva. But, when "I" is nothing, then all is Brahman. We should see what is the structure of the "I." If "I" does not have any structure or shape, it is automatically proved to be false. When it does not have its own structure, how can we prove its existence? Therefore, any statement to be made should be made after we observe the structure of the "I." When "I" is gone, the whole world is gone, because the entire world together with the "I," is Illusion, it is false. Therefore, there is the saying, "When we die, the whole world is drowned into nothingness." One who has dropped the sense of "I" becomes the real "Knower of Brahman."

1-10-1935

68. Brahman is Attributeless and Maya has Attributes

Pure Brahman is experienced as Pure Consciousness. It is called Nirguna, or the "Attributeless Absolute." Illusion (Maya) is within it with attributes, and is visible. What should be called Maya and what should be called Brahman? I will tell you. It is only the mind that thinks about Brahman and Maya. Not to make any statement in the mind is Brahman, and to make a statement is Maya. To be identified with Brahman is a thought. To imagine anything "other" is also a thought. That which is natural, is attributeless. Even if you say, "I am not," it is a concept as the basis of your statement. Is it the case that it will be Brahman only if you declare it as such, and not otherwise? No! Even without any statement about it, it is there. It simply is, as it is. Whether you say so or not, it simply is, as it is.

To know that "This" is Brahman and "that" is Maya, is called the fourth body or "Turya State," which is also called the "all-seeing" state. Turya means to know all, but when "all" is non-existent, what is there to be known? Right thought is Brahman and Maya is false thought, imagination. The "Witness," the "Life-Force," the "Power," are all only impositions on Brahman. The quality of witnessing comes without any cause. Why? Because there is contradiction in duality, the quality of observer comes into being. The "Power of Chaitanya," the Life-Energy, is also a false imposition. The space within the pot, the space in the room, and the space outside, are names that are unnecessarily used. As Maya is felt to be real, all these innumerable shapes and names have come into use.

In deep sleep there is no time and no space. The waking state is but a long dream. As long as the Illusion appears real, the witnessing seems true. Mind is witness to all, but if it has nothing to say, it becomes "no-mind," or "beyond mind." Mind now has no complaint, and it has no desire for anything more. By realization of our own Being, desire becomes quiet. Only by this realization is the mind peaceful. That means, it has nothing to say. The desiring mind is no more. It is "no-mind," or unmani. These are all scientific terms. This world is Illusion. All the words and laws exist only in Illusion. When there is duality, everything is there. When duality goes, everything goes. All the laws, science, rules, everything, is gone. It is like a thing without any owner that is confiscated by the government, and is then owned by the government. The government is all-powerful. In this Illusion, you are your possessions. A moneylender lost ten thousand rupees. He became poorer by that much, as his wealth was lessened to that extent. The princess was married to a pauper, and she became a pauper. Had she been married to a prince, she would have become a queen. A piece of sandalwood was given to a cobbler and it was used daily to beat the hide of animals. One who keeps the company of the great becomes a great man himself. Then he is the owner of this entire world. When mind disappears the Knowledge contained at the level of the fourth body (I Am), the Turya State disappears, and the duality of the individual and God (Jiva and Shiva) also disappears. Duality and non-duality are both gone.

In short, it is but a matter of concept, or your attitude, that there is either duality or non-duality. Who is there to say that there is non-duality? This is where the problem of Illusion and Brahman is solved. When I say that "I am not," then the connection of Illusion to Brahman is broken. It is the mind that conceives of Illusion and Brahman. When mind is no more, everything is just Brahman. There is a saying that when a swan left for a journey, a crow became the Prime Minister. When the swan again became the Prime Minister, then all the religions were protected. Religion means natural function. Our own religion is beneficial, another's religion is fearsome. What exists devoid of any imagination is pure Brahman, which is experienced by the "Knowledgeable Ones," the Jnanis. When Brahman is understood there is no "other thing" remaining to be known. When one sets out to know Brahman, the Consciousness plunges into "nothingness." In the mind, one doubts "nothingness," because one cannot experience it. "How can experience take place without being there as the experiencer?" It is necessary to wipe out separateness before experiencing Brahman. Can the Sun ever meet himself? If there is separateness, Brahman cannot be experienced. With no separateness, then all is Brahman. If anyone experiences "all," how can he do so, except by becoming the experience?

Experience means the "other" enters Consciousness. The "other" means something else. We have to know what that other is. The imprint of that which is, excluding oneself, is to be fixed in Consciousness. When the "other" is understood, it implies that we also understand what we are. Realization is to understand. What else? To say that "I agree," that "I am convinced about realization," is Illusion. The very nature of the Self, is realization. Because He is there, there is realization. If He is not, there is no realization. If it is conceived that the experiencer is other than the Self, that concept should be immediately burnt, otherwise, it will decay and smell. You must understand Paramatman as not being the body, and that it is "That" which realizes. You have to merge in its unity, and see from there. That is the correct way of seeing. Those who say that they have known Him, are far from Him. That is the puzzle, for solving which, the Sadguru is necessary.

I tell you with decisive certainty that if you see as a separate observer, you will fall into nothingness, the darkness of Ignorance. If one considers that "void" to be Brahman, and then returns, take it from me that that void can never be Brahman. The void, or nothingness, is the quality of a particular state of Consciousness. Brahman is beyond that. Because the observer has not gained anything, the observer should be observed, and then experience Brahman as Brahman. So be That and stay as Self, which is "self-evident." The Saints say that you are the Self, so who is it that says you are the mind? By whose word did you understand? To have faith in the seer's advice is itself the experience. It is the natural urge of the mind that it should know Him, but in that effort the mind becomes blind, because the mind has no capacity to know Him. We are ourselves that thing which we have tried to have experience. How can the flowers enjoy their own fragrance? When identification with the body ceases, one is Brahman. One's self is actually always only Brahman. When this is understood, Knowledge has done its job. Thus, the portion of **Dasbodh** on Knowledge is completed.

2-10-1935

Master of Self-Realization
An Ultimate Understanding
Volume 2

Spiritual Discourses of His Holiness
Shri Sadguru Siddharameshwar Maharaj
Recorded by Shri Nisargadatta Maharaj

An English Translation of the Marathi Text
"Adhyatma Jnanacha Yogeshwar"
The Spiritual Science of Self-Knowledge

Preface to Master of Self-Realization - Volume 2

Written by Shri Nisargadatta Maharaj

This is the second part of the book Adhyatma Jnanacha Yogeshwar. The first part of this book was published earlier on the 4th of November, 1961 at Bagewadi. That which is written here in the second part, is Knowledge, but it is also called "Scientific Knowledge." The publisher and some other Guru-Brothers of mine were urging me to write a preface to this book. However, to venture to do so is difficult, because the subject of this book is extraordinary, deep, vast, and in a way, endless. When we call this Knowledge as "Spiritual Knowledge," or Vijnana, the words that we intend to use are better left unspoken. Ignorance means "no knowledge" or absence of Knowledge, while Knowledge implies that there is awareness of Ignorance. That which is "known" is Ignorance, and as it has no existence as such, it disappeared. The Knowledge which knows that "This is not That" has nothing more to be known, and has therefore, becomes mute. Lord Vitthala stands erect on this brick, and He stands very still. The capacity of knowing was not mentioned there. As speech did not get any object to be described by words, the speech was stopped. Here that speech made Vaikuntha its abode, which is the "Highest Heaven." Knowledge, together with speech became still. By the "Power of the Self," the Knowledge remained without any object, in the Self, only.

When we say that Knowledge must have something to be "known," it is Ignorance that is the "known," and therefore the term "Knowledge" became applicable to it. Now, as there is not any other object, it remained with itself without focus on any object. So, the function of knowing is gone. The sense that "I Am That" is also not functioning. He who saw that "Knowledge" has no place, actually lost his power of seeing, and then saw. Thus, the Life-Energy (Chaitanya), the "Spiritual Knowledge" has no status. The Vijnana is the "Power" which has perceived all of this. When Knowledge loses its quality of knowing because of "Spiritual Perception" that is Vijnana. It is pristine Life-Energy only, and it undergoes a natural transformation where it has no concept whatsoever, which makes for awareness of oneself as the five elements, or God, or Brahman. Now, that Vijnana is witness to the Knowledge that has lost its duality. It is also witness to egolessness and the appearance of forms, like waves on water. So, we define this as "Vijnana." In Vijnana, there is neither a doer, nor an enjoyer, nor a provocative agent for either. There is only natural Being, which is "Self-Knowabilty." It has no sense of being any "thing" that is a mixture of the five elements, or any form, any names, any shapes, or a devotee, or an Avatar, or any active principle. Only that Chaitanya, the "Power" which transcends all states, is Vijnana.

Blessed are those who were lucky enough to listen to the discourses which were like showers of nectar from the mouth of the Sadguru Shri Siddharameshwar Maharaj, who was the embodiment of this Supreme Knowledge, Vijnana. Equally blessed will be those who will read and listen to these discourses, and will become like the Immortal Nectar itself. They will never have fear of death, nor will they die. Those who devote themselves to the Sadguru, as if he is the most auspicious embodiment of the Absolute Brahman, may receive this sacred Knowledge, and realize that they are not the body, but that they are that Life-Energy which moves the body. Gradually, then again while being increasingly aware of this spiritual Self-Existence, there is the unnameable awareness of this Pure Awareness. When the understanding permeates the whole Conscious Existence, the spiritual aspect of life also loses its existence in the "Totality of Understanding." An example is not much warranted here, but it cannot remain unexpressed, and therefore, the example of a person who dines, is alluded to. When a person takes food and it is digested, the various articles of food are mingled in his system of the physical body, and he becomes satisfied and gets nutrition and strength. Similarly, the spiritual aspect of the Consciousness is mingled into the "Wholeness of Understanding," by giving peace, nourishment, and contentment. Therefore, that which is called the Science of Self-Knowledge, the Reality, which is Paramatman, the Absolute Parabrahman, remains unaffected as a permanent natural transcendent state, which has an endless "Compassionate Contentment."

Saint Dnyaneshwar said, "The ocean of all happiness is the husband of Rakhumadevi (Rakhumadevi is the wife of Vitthala), who is our father." Thus, even when the creative forces of the universe are taking place, this body of scientific understanding remains unaffected. Although it has multidimensional forces full of action, it remains beyond all qualities. It is inactive and unchanging, as a Reality complete with the very "Essence of Nature." It is a "Fullness of Bliss" beyond measure. By reading these discourses, full of Supreme Knowledge, those who are ignorant will have wisdom, and will reach the "Highest State" by deep devotion to the Sadguru. It is my humble prayer to all the people of the world who are themselves like Gods, that they will please read and learn this book.

Now, I will end my preface: Dear readers, unknowingly you are originally only Brahman. Therefore we request you, on our personal experience and conviction, that although you are Brahman today without being aware of it, you may knowingly be Brahman by having direct Knowledge through reading this book. My salutations!

Nisargadatta
Nisargadatta Ashram Vanmali Bhuvan,
Khetwadi, 10th Lane, Mumbai 4 Ashaddha Vadya 11 shake 1884

Friday, 27-7-1962.

69. Listen to the Signs of Knowledge

Self-Knowledge is "Real Knowledge." There are two types of Knowledge. One is True Knowledge (Vidya), which is of the Self, and the other is false knowledge, which is of the nature of Ignorance (Avidya). We should drop the false knowledge and recognize the True Knowledge. When the sense of "me" and "mine" both go completely, that is called True Knowledge. When the mind and intellect jump beyond the senses, logical thought becomes out of place. This is the mystery for which the mind and intellect are not required in order to understand. It is of the nature of Self-experience. The Self is self-evident. He knows other things, and of course, He knows himself.

What does it mean when we say He knows himself? It means He is already there. Only the one who is already there can know "other." How can one who is not existent, know any other thing? Just as when a man does not exist, how will he who is not there know whether anyone comes or leaves, or be able to tell about it? Who is there who says "I do not know?" This is the fact with the Self. We may well say that one is confused, but is it not true that he is there, and *only then* he can be confused? So, it is proved that before any confusion, the state of "non-confusion," or clarity was there. Actually, there is no existence to anything else except the Self. Those who are the "Sons of the Guru" (Guruputras) need dwell no further on this point.

There is the term "I Am" (Soham). "I Am" is continuously being repeated day and night. Without speaking a word, it is a constant awareness. The word "japa" in Sanskrit has one meaning as "repetition," but it has another meaning in Marathi, which is "to take care of," or to protect, or nurture. This is all automatic. In all the bodies of all creatures the repetition of the soundless sound "Soham," and "Hamsa," is continuous with the breathing. By understanding this a man is free of all bondage. In all creatures, the awareness of "I Am" is constant. The music of the term "I Am" is going on day and night. First it was the individual, or Jiva, and then it became Shiva. Then both disappeared, and the term "I Am" remained as "Am-ness." No one gets an experience that "I am not." To say that, "I am not" is to say "I Am." A student wrote a note to his teacher, "I am not present today." The teacher smiled when he read it. He thought "This student writes by his own hand that he is not present." A man said, "I have no mouth, I do not speak. I cannot speak." He was only able to say this by speaking. The experience of Being is beyond the origination of speech (Para speech) without needing mention. The world of Knowledge is the vision of "understanding." How can one know "I am dead"? The truth is "I will not die. I am not dead." At the time of death the dirt is gone, and what remains is pure. Let one think that the death of the dirt has happened. The body is dirt. The intellect attached to body is dirt. Have no attachment to the dirt. If one is detached, who died? How did he die?

To try to know is Ignorance. Eyes are there but they cannot see themselves. When the Self is conscious of himself by his own sense, it is Self-luminance. It is of the nature of Self-experience. One who tries to know is in Ignorance. The Self is not an object of knowledge, as it is He who knows all things. All things are objects of "His Knowledge." Whatever there is to be known, is known by Him. Whatever is known is called the object. That which cannot be known by any objects remains objectless. He is presiding over all. He is the first and primordial eye. He is that eye which sees all, which nobody or nothing in the world can shut. He is always awake. He does not forget. He is the Sun who knows all. The Sun is called Surya in Sanskrit, which also has the meaning that "He is endless, limitless, and all-pervading." Knowledge is there without thought. It is fully pervading everywhere whether thoughts are present or not. It knows the emergence of thought, and if thought is not there, Knowledge remains.

It is foolish to try to see the Sun with the light from a torch (flashlight). It is similarly foolish to try to see the "Sun of Knowledge" with the torch of the mind and intellect. That Knowledge is "Pure Spotless Knowledge." The Knowledge that witnesses the world is called "mundane knowledge." But that is not "True Knowledge," it is not Reality. It is thought, or the focus of attention (Vrutti.) All people say that one day we will have to die, but nobody knows what "dying" is. You should die once in such a way that you will not have to die again. The Knowledge that is the fourth body, the "Turya State" (SatChitAnanda), is not "Pure Knowledge." It means that "you" remain. The Turya State is aware that "you" and Brahman are two separate things. Turya indicates duality. Turya ends, it is not permanent, but Brahman does not end. Turya is Time, and Time implies ending. To end, is the nature of Time. Brahman has no end. Brahman alone is real. This is the "Pure Knowledge." The Mahavakya is the "Great Statement," the "Ultimate Statement." It has a good meaning and it is truly great in itself. The great statement "Aham Brahmasmi" means "I Am Brahman." Its utterance itself is very high, but you have to pursue its meaning, its experience. Mere repetition of "I Am Brahman" does not break the spell of Illusion. The meaning of the statement is not grasped by any other means except through the teaching of the Sadguru.

One who does not think at all is but a beast. He does not care to become acquainted with and understand the life that he is living, so he is the fool. It is useless if a man performs great feats of bravery in the world but does not know himself. It is just like a blind man going for a tour around the world. When one knows first hand his own life and gets experience in it, only then has he fruitfully used his life. To meditate on the great spiritual statement "I Am Brahman" is an indication of wisdom. To gain Oneself, by Oneself, is like deducting one from one. What remains in the equation "one minus one" is the Supreme Self, Paramatman, who is without name and form. We have to die completely and yet remain, without dying. This is a rare state of wisdom. It is "Real Knowledge" when one meets "One's Self." All ties (bondages) are broken suddenly. Finally, when we think very keenly about it, it is revealed that this experience comes into being of its own accord. In Vedanta to know that the root of all the moving and unmoving creation is One, is called "Absolute Knowledge." There, all the various arguments are gone.

When we search into ourselves there is omniscience. We meet ourselves through fine perceptive thinking. Once you have gained real insight everything is only Brahman even though you may call it by any other name. Then you may call a snake as a snake, and a scorpion as a scorpion, but you know that it is only Brahman. When the observer gets "True Experience," the job is over. When both the "field of knowledge," and "the knower of the field" are gone, only the Supreme Reality, the "Parama Purusha," remains. It is experiencing without the experiencer or the observer. You may perceive that the outward focus is turning back into itself. The evident meaning and the hidden meaning are both gone. Even the slight notion of saying, "I am someone," or "something" is also gone. A lamp in a painting does not dispel the darkness. For that, a real lamp must be lit. When the notion that "I Am" is gone, the complete withdrawal into "Oneself" is what remains. The notion that "I am a limited being," is a concept, a limited notion. It is but the narrow conceptual focus of Consciousness. "I Am" is a conceptual state. When it is dropped, only Brahman, the "Absolute," remains.

Evening, 3/10/35

70. In Praise of the Guru who is Shiva

Exposition from *"Eknathi Bhagwat"*

With palms pressed together, the disciple bows before the Master who is the form of Shiva. After so bowing, he says to the Guru, "You bestow upon the one who bows to you, the status of Shiva." That status which you give is "Your Own Being." You do not allow the separate entity as an individual (jiva) to remain, so how can the identification with the physical body remain? You do not disturb one's life, but you accept one's service to you. This means that the disciple is apparently just like others in the physical body. The living moving principle in the disciple is as normal as that of everyone, but you change the "Inner Consciousness" into the vastness of Shiva. You give your devotee the high state of the Self that is beyond the body, yet somehow the physical body still serves you.

The great demon of doubt is that which thinks that one is an individual although one is truly Brahman. By killing this demon of doubt you carry this dead body. When the wrong notion that one is the jiva goes out, you carry his body, and you give the status of Brahman to that body. Then, as Vishnu, the all-permeating God, holds together the body, and operates through it, you reside in the body as Janardana. Now, Eknath has run away. There is no one who is the owner, named Eknath who is in this body. There is only the Guru, the Master, who is Janardan. The sound of the conch is evident because of the one who blows it. When this body is able to speak, it is because you make it do so. This body is moving and doing its activities because of you. All actions are possible because of you, and whatever was "mine" has gone along with "me."

Now, all actions are done by you. The sense of ego which was in the body has gone and is now replaced by you. Now the "Kingdom of the Jiva" is gone, and you, Shiva, are the ruler. It is by your prana, that the body's prana works. The eyes that see out, are your eyes, and it is your nose that takes in the fragrance. You are the perceiver of the nose and the eyes. The ears listen as you want to listen. The tongue takes the taste, by your will, and the intellect understands by your Power. Whatever the mind says, is by your Power. Without you, the mind is unable to say anything. Discrimination and "selective knowledge" (sifting the Essence from the non-essential) are possible by your will. Speech is your adornment. Understanding is possible because of you. Being awake, or having dreams, happen by your Power. Even deep sleep is experienced because of you. Whatever things are enjoyed are because of you. You are here, calling yourself "me." By your grace, people recognize this body as Eknath. That name is yours now. Instead of calling you Janardan, they call you Eknath, but it is only you who acts, not Eknath. By taking up the name Eknath, you have become the director.

It is you who gives life to everything in this world. You are "The Life of the World." You make possible all actions. You are such a great Sadguru, Janardan. Salutations to you, with your own Power! Arati lamps are offered to the Sun, but the light of the lamp is given by the Sun. To worship Shiva is to become Shiva. That is His worship. In this way, it is you who directs the body. When the house burns, all the pieces of wood and dung-cakes become fire along with it. Similarly, by the fire of Knowledge, the "me" with a body has become Knowledge. That means "I" became non-existing, and now, only you remain as Knowledge. By your Power, you are continuing the book of life. Sleeping, eating, taking meals, everything, is possible only because of you. Your purity is never blemished. Auspicious and inauspicious are all one in you, Lord Rama. Who is it that says, you are the doer of all? What name should be given to you? It is you, who says so, it is you who is aware of "Awareness." You are "Yourself."

Shri Siddharameshwar Maharaj's commentary:

When your belief is that you are other than the Self, duality comes into existence, you have to be careful about attentiveness and inattentiveness. When actually only "Pure Experience" is there, making unnecessary efforts in the mind bring into being the trinity of the observer, the observed, and the act of observation. When you have eaten a sweet, why make the distinction and say "He" has eaten? You must be very clear to say "I am Brahman" and "I enjoy all pleasures." This means that Brahman enjoys Brahman. After having known the world, and after experiencing, "you" are still there, but you are a nonentity. To feel this is essential. It is the Guru alone who resides in the body.

4-10-35

71. Be Alert Within

However scholarly or learned you may be in the world, it is all an outward show. Your Consciousness should be unwavering from within. A man who has earned great fame in the world is wasting his life if he is not free and awake inside. One who has missed the "One God," has thrown away his life. What is the use of being famous in public life? When one has no Self-Knowledge one is ignorant of the Self. If you are a devotee of God, the place where you are now, and after death, is "God's World." If you are only keen on worldly things you will come back to the world. When you are devoted to the Self, you remain in the Self, one with Him. The purpose of telling all of this is that you have to burn off all unnecessary garbage, and be one with the "Wholeness of the Absolute." If you have dissolved the desires of the body, and the elements making up the body are merged into the vast elements of the universe, then you are free while still having your outer body (Jivanmukta). That is itself "Freedom." A man who constantly thinks about women takes the next birth as a woman. As you think and meditate, you become that thing. One whose attention is always for the worldly things has to come again and again into this world.

In other creatures, this "Knowledge" is absent. Only human beings have this Knowledge, and therefore it is only easy in human life to do such meditation. It is not true that by complete saturation in multiple pleasures that you eventually become desireless. No! The desires will never die this way, they only increase. The desires of one who has no chance of enjoyment, are already very much increased. All will occasionally say that they are disgusted with life, but this is because they cannot find the solution to their problems. That is frustration, not real "desirelessness." You cannot get the dream how you want it. The dream experience is caused by some continuous craving. A brahmin had to take birth in a cobbler's home because of his desire. As you put your energy into any particular feeling, you get it. If you concentrate on Brahman which is attributeless (Nirguna), you will experience that. There, the attributes or qualities (Gunas) end. It is when the gunas (and desires) constantly repeat themselves and became multiplied, that they take the form the of universe. This is the "Original Illusion," MoolaMaya, the "Illusion Producing Consciousness."

By meditation on "That which is without Attributes" (Nirguna Brahman), we achieve the dissolution of attributes (Gunas). In this way, you can become singularly One. It is a rule that a renunciate (Sanyasi) has to remove his hair and shave his head. This means that the pride of attributes should be removed. It symbolizes that any overgrowth should be removed from the Self. What was there originally seems to have become something other. The "other" must be removed and that "Original Being" should remain. The "Original State" had no qualities such as Sattva, Rajas, or Tamas. Then, one of these gunas appeared. The nature of that guna is the power of imagination. Embracing that guna, the Self mistook it to be his own nature, and forgot his "Original Nature." That is where confusion took over. The Self has to be very alert there. He must realize that the power of imagination is not his "True Nature," and that He is without duality. He has no qualities. He is "Completely Free Being."

The final fruit of all of this is only to recognize the "One God." To recognize God is to think about what you are. Thinking is only within the field of Illusion, so what is the meaning of this? It means to think that "I am nothing," and the Self prevails. This at least, should be understood. To know the Truth, is called Right Knowledge. To know Truth is Knowledge. When the firm conviction that "I Am That" (Soham) is fixed, we know that we are nothing. Whatever is, is only Brahman. Now why fight over logic? The Self is in its "right place." Without the Self, can anyone even say his own name? Does the child say that a certain name should be given to him? You may give any name to that which cannot be described. What was to happen has already happened, it has come into being and then the name was given through imagination. The name was given from whatever the mind chose. It was only for social convenience that the name was given by using a certain word. The name Wadhi is given to a girl who comes to serve food. Wadhi means one who serves food. Similarly, the name Shende means last, and that name is given to one who is the last. The names are simply coming out of imagination. Sometimes they were adequately denoting the qualities of the person, and sometimes these names were not sufficient, so surnames (lastnames) were given. They are added because the first names were not adequate.

The Self is where it is. There is no sense of the body to it. The five elements are in their places. The body is not there. We are not there. The body is a bogus form. No one has ever really had a real body. Brahman also has no real body. None can get a real body. Nobody is real because of the body. Whatever the form, the body is false. Everything is really without form. Everyone should look at oneself and achieve what is to be achieved. One who says that the body is real is a great sinner. He is like a murderer of a Brahmin (a knower of Brahman). God is formless. Now, no further conjectures please. The Self in itself, is already accomplished. What further spiritual practice (Sadhana) does he need? Once the head is completely shaved, how can it be shaved again? Should the head itself be cut? How can the one who is free have bondage? Spiritual practice has for its purpose for us to find our Self. When it is found, what is the use of the sadhana? If a potter becomes king, would he still take care of donkeys? Why should he bother to prepare the clay? All the various types of effort and spiritual practices are the results of our own aptitudes. When one is beyond these, why should he bother about them?

One who is a sinner, should do good deeds. If you think something evil is done, do some good deeds. This is a mental attitude. For the one who has renounced, why should he fall back into moods of the mind? What is there to be achieved through various practices? What fruit is to be gained by observing rules of conduct? When one has oneself become That which was the aim of sadhana, and That is experienced within and deeply imbibed, then you may remain a devotee of the Guru because of your love for him. However, that devotion should be without desire. You are already one with Brahman. In order to keep in memory what the Guru has done for you, sing in praise of him. We are "That." The body belongs to the five elements. The individual is really only Brahman. Think deeply over just who you are, and where you really are. Without intentional thinking, what do you feel that you are? When you think, you come to see that you are nothing. What is, is the Self. The verb "is" denotes natural Being. If you say you are an individual, or jiva, you experience jiva. The Self is really God, Laxmi-Narayana. Permeating everyone, or "Narayana," is its nature, and "Great Fortune," or "Laxmi" is its quality. He is Radha-Krishna. The Self is whatever you may call it. If you say Illusion, it is Illusion.

The "Wholeness of the Self" is "All," and the one who is really a wise person searches to find out who he is. Man examines everything but cannot recognize himself. One who cannot recognize himself, cannot have realization. When the intention to say "I Am" is dropped, then there is "no thing." What remains is Brahman, which is truly what you are. To be convinced of this is very deep, and is called the "Realization of Spirituality," and the "Science of Spirituality." It is not the case that we are separate from the body and from God. The fruit is not separate, and we are not separate. We are the fruit. The aim is the Final Reality, which is one with us. One became the fruit while he was trying to get it. A man while worrying about his poverty has became king, so why should he now worry any more about poverty? We are already That which the seeker and the Master were so busy doing sadhana to achieve.

It is to meet "Oneself" that all the paths are laid down. Now, we are That. This is proved. This is realized. Now, there is no question of doing something or not doing anything. Those who were afraid of the orders of the king, have themselves become kings. Fear has disappeared along with poverty. What study of the Vedas should the Vedas do? How can a place of pilgrimage go to itself? What "God" should be met by God? What "Nectar or Immortality" should the nectar drink? Which "immeasurable" should be worshipped by the immeasurable? What "qualitylessness" should be the object of devotion for the qualityless? Which "Reality" should enjoy Reality? How can "Pure Untainted Brahman" experience itself? How can the "object of meditation" meditate upon itself? When you realize yourself, everything is beyond words. The indescribable "plunging into Brahman," is now proved.

5-10-35

72. The Doubting Thomas

The "Sadhu" has become the Reality. Who should we call a Sadhu (a Saint)? Only He, who has become Reality. There are statements to the effect that "One has become Reality," that "We are Brahman," that "All is Brahman," etc. To say or conceive that one has become somebody, and that someone is transforming somebody else, is nothing but the ego's game. Our being "good" or being "bad" is a kind of bondage that compels us to remain in the body. Actually, there is nothing but Brahman. As it is completely impossible for a rabbit to have horns, it is also not possible for anything other than Brahman to exist. Therefore, it can rightly be said that doubt has been banished beyond the universe. The doubt is itself the nature of the individual, the jiva. That jiva is gone, and with it, doubt is gone. The main doubt pertains to "Who am I?" or "Who should I be?" When I am convinced of who I am, and how I am, then the doubt disappears. It goes beyond the universe.

In Reality, doubt is non-existent. This doubt is in a way, King Dhrutarashtra and his sons (from the Hindu epic Mahabharata), the

Kauravas (the family who was fighting against Arjuna's family, the Pandavas). This Dhrutarashtra (doubt) is an image formed by mental projection. In the Puranas, it is also called Mayasur. One who understands that this Mayasur, or doubt, is a non-entity, is a Saint. He is Paramatman. The Vedas have been telling the same thing all along. One who realizes this fact becomes a Siddha (an "Accomplished One"). The example used is that the Saint is like sugar. It does not matter how it is kept, either vertically, horizontally or upright. Whatever its position may be, it is still only sugar. Similarly, a Saint may be in any situation, but he is still a Saint. He is neither fresh nor stale, neither pure nor impure. That which is pure, cannot become impure. The Saint is that "Pure Reality." The quality of the tongue or stomach is not changed by whatever taste the food may have, or whether it may be stale or already tasted by others. Similarly, when the entirety of existence is looked upon by a Saint, he does not discriminate as to whether anything is auspicious or not. People think that it is auspicious for the bride to put her right foot first while entering the home. Such concepts are superstitious, and only breed doubt. The doubt of the Saint, is totally vanished from the universe. One whose decision is steadfast, is a Siddha, a Master. A ghost is not there in the darkness, but if a foolish person believes it there, what can be done?

The guruputras who have attained Knowledge are accustomed to getting experience according to their determination or faith. To reach conviction about anything is possible in two ways. One is total devotion to the Guru, and the other is through intense austerities or ascetic practices. These austere practices must be firmly fixed in purpose. This is clearly stated in the Vedanta. If even once the understanding is imparted by the Guru, one's Consciousness is transformed, it is Brahman. The Saint is one with the Absolute. One whose doubt is gone is the Saint. There must be faith in the teaching of the Guru. When one has no Self-Knowledge, and does not know who one is, one must try to concentrate the mind with all of one's determination. When we think that the Guru's teaching is not true, it is by that doubt that we remain as a jiva. What is there finally if it is not Brahman? Somebody should prove it. Do not raise doubt without some base. In the beginning, there is naturally a certain attitude of doubt in the seeker's mind, but gradually it disappears. A Saint has no doubt. One who knows that he is Brahman, whose conviction is unshakable, is truly the Saint.

The path of rituals and actions (path of karma) is full of all kinds of doubts. Suppose a brahmin (someone of the priest caste) bathes in a river and then proceeds towards his home. If someone says that an untouchable has touched the water, immediately that bath is useless! Many people insist that a mantra must be in Sanskrit. They say that if it is not in Sanskrit, it is not true, or not proper. All of this is because of the tendency to doubt. Houseflies sit on dirty things, and then they fly towards good food and sit on that. Doubt makes the food useless. It is only a doubt, but the overly careful ritualist throws away the food. It is very difficult to perform any ritual wherein there is no fault, because there are so many who will create misgivings in your mind. It is almost impossible to escape from it.

There must be renunciation of karma. One must realize that he is not the doer, the actor. This is very necessary. The sense that is created in our mind, that actions create results, and that we have to suffer those results, is a very powerful poison. Actually, we are not the doers. The seeds of rebirth are there in the results of action. That fruit, which has no seed, is not a fruit. Where action (doership) is, the fruit is, and fruit invariably contains the seed. This chain is going on unbroken. Therefore, with great attentiveness you must renounce the concept of being the doer of actions. There should not be even an iota of the sense that "I am the doer," "I have done," "I do," etc.

In the wake of action, the concept of doership arises, and in the wake of that, doubt arises. Without devotion to the Sadguru, renunciation of action will not be understood. Without that understanding, you will not be able to drop action (karma) altogether. The story of the disciple who left the ground and sat in a tree to try to escape the dirt, has already been told. The path of action and ritualistic performances is full of the pitfalls of doubt. Knowledge however, is without doubt. A Saint was once sitting in the vicinity of shit. People laughed at him. He said, "All right then, keep me in a place where there is no shit. The shit is also in the intestines. Where then, is there a place for me?" There is nothing sacred except Knowledge. Knowledge is pure and sacred. Others want to compel you to give something in charity, or to do sacrifices in the fire for the fruit that you may receive some comfort. All of this is only for a sense of purification of mind. Through the false, gradually the True is discovered.

To have Self-Knowledge is the highest achievement of all. All of the difficult labors of selfishness then drop away. In other countries, they do not even know what the real fulfillment of having human birth is. All that they aim for is to be born like any other animal and do hard work continuously until the time of death. It is true that the advice is given to people to perform religious rituals and ceremonies, because through these the real path to freedom is gradually discovered. The ocean is vast but it is also full of internal disturbances that are continuous day and night. The Saint has no doubt. That knowledge where doubt is lurking is false knowledge. Desirelessness or asceticism with a doubtful mind, is of very poor quality. Devotion with doubt in the mind is false. Where you are one with Brahman and continue to sing devotional songs, that is real. One with Brahman means to be without doubt. There is no doubt about what one is, and what one's nature is. That devotion where there is a devotee who is existing separately is duality. There is no unity in that type of devotion.

Brahman is One, therefore when you are Brahman you are doubtless, and that devotion is real. If there is some doubt about God, that God is false, because you yourself are God. If doubt prevails, then you have not become God. When there is doubt, it is like this. The feeling of doubt makes everything futile. Great is the caliber of total conviction. Blessed is he who has complete faith. Blessed is he who thinks that there is a God, and who has total trust in that God. There is a great difference between a faithful devotee of God and another person. The life of another person and the life of a devotee are not similar. The intelligence of a devotee and the talent of an ordinary person are not the same. The life of a devotee of God is completely dependent on God's will, and whatever his destiny may be the devotee is content with it. Really, the family life of a devotee is just a namesake. Everything is already settled after the devotee and God have a perfect mutual understanding. It does not matter at all whether the life of a devotee is ideal or disturbed according to earthly standards. A person who denies that his family life should be comparable with the lives of other people is not yet worthy of the trust in God.

"Divine Trust" is very different from petty cunning, so a devotee of God should have total faith in God. Blessed is this kind of faith. The habit of doubting everything is useless. Without decisive faith, spiritual life has no meaning. The most important thing is that you must have faith in yourself. I asked the mind, "Why are you not leaving?" The mind said, "When was I there? It is your mind, that is against you. The difficulty of the problem is within you. Practically, it is like a castle that has to be conquered. I ask you, were you born? When? When did you lose your chastity? Did these things really happen? That which has no birth, when and how was he born, and when and how was he spoiled? This commentary has the sole purpose to change your earthly attitude. Your book learning is of no use here. Keep faith. Be Brahman, and experience It. Do not get lost in doubt once you are convinced. Do not destroy yourself. Not to doubt after being convinced is called simple belief. Confirm what you experience, and keep firm faith. Really, blind faith is nothing other than this strong conviction.

Everyone should have trust in a Saint who has realized Brahman and get their own emancipation. The individual, who is a non-entity, is always imagining things that are not existing. We cannot even be certain about our parents, as to whether they are really our parents, or if someone else is. The man who has slain the demon of doubt has gained the entire wisdom of the Vedas. To "Know" is the "Vedic Religion."

6/10/1935

73. The State of Victory

Any completed work is not worth its name if you are not sure of yourself. The entire world is swept away by the current of doubt. Sureness, or conviction, means to sure about being the Self. One must be sure of what one is. Otherwise, everything is useless. We are the Self, but without being definite about it what is the use of talking about it? We must be sure in our mind and then we may do whatever we want. If the disciple's heart is very pure with respect to one's Master, only then will further study be useful. It is that confidence in the Guru that is going to give one the fruit of spiritual efforts. All other talk is nonsense. Of course we feel that without being certain everything is a travesty. But what is the point in speaking about it? There will be no benefit in such talk. Where there is Knowledge without any doubt, there is true contentment. This "contentment" is not dependent on anything. This contentment is not the product of any rituals or actions that one has done. Contentment that is dependent on such things is not real contentment. Independent contentment is possible only by Self-Realization. When you are convinced about being Brahman, that itself is contentment. Contentment is an indication of the achievement of Reality. The absence of doubt should be known as the indication of contentment.

The listener asks to be told what is the sign of conviction, and the Guru tells him to find out who is the one "Absolute Almighty," and to be sure about it. God is that Power by which this world has come into being. You have now in you that by which the whole world moves, and you are using it now. By that only, you are experiencing yourself, and the world. See what you have! The world "is" because of it. By that Power this world is fed and nourished. By that the sun, the moon, the stars, and the five elements (Earth, Water, Fire, Wind, and Sky) are made. All of this is happening without any trouble, and without a lot of hard work to construct or destroy. Such "Power" (Chaitanya) is within you. It is by this Power that you are getting the experience of the world. However, as long as you are not convinced about it, your mind is not at rest. The gods made of copper and brass are not gods. What do the various incarnations of gods (Avatars) in the mythological books, such as Brahma, Vishnu, and Mahadev (Shiva) mean? What is the extent of their godliness? Only so long as the Power enlivens them, are they gods.

What is the sign of a devotee (a bhakta)? He has to recognize God. He must realize who God is. What are we? We are nothing. By leaving the attachment to the body, you should remain only "That," Brahman. Where the "me" is, there is bondage. When "me" disappears, bondage goes away. Whom should we call a devotee? One who is searching himself and is finding out himself, is the devotee. We inwardly search our Self, and by its speech, we meditate on God. We are engrossed in our self-search, and by spoken words, we are busy meditating on God. When we find the Self, we eliminate everything else, and select that which we are. We become convinced about our Self, and we are sure. Sure about what? About Reality. Here complete certainty was possible because of the spoken word. Thus, the grand moment of "God-Realization" has come! The ocean is as it is. Only the wave arises and disappears. What is freedom? To know one's Self is freedom (liberation). The elements are born through the elements, but they are also born from the Life-Energy, Chaitanya.

Both the persuasion and the discrimination approaches are contained within this Life-Energy. The primary approach contains the discrimination and elimination method (sifting the unessential from the Essence). This is stated in order to prove that all that has an appearance, is false. In the "Siddhanta," the final statement, or final conclusion it is said, "All is Brahman." The four basic states of consciousness (manas, buddhi, chitta, and aham), the three states (waking, dreaming, and deep sleep), the three qualities (Rajas, Tamas, Sattva), and ten organs of the senses (and the various things and the various ways in which the things are enjoyed or experienced) all taken together, are nothing but the Chaitanya, which is Jnana, or Knowledge. That same "One Knowledge" is experienced as the entire world at the time of "knowing." The Knowledge is experienced, and beyond this you cannot experience or renounce it, nor can you arrange to artificially nullify it. At the time of knowing, that experience is possible only because of the self-existent Chaitanya. By very keen minute observation there is certainty and definite conviction. This is called Siddhanta, or "Final Truth." Then very serenely, there is certainty about God. There is the realization that there is only One, and nothing else. However, by the insistent attachment to the physical body, that peace and contentment is destroyed. For this you should say, "Tell me who I am!" The demon of doubt should be asked, "Tell me who I am!" However, then he keeps quiet, because how can he show anything other than Brahman?

We should not deviate from the confidence about our "True Nature." The "body-consciousness" brings in something else. It only increases doubt and misgivings, and it tries to bring you down. Do not fall. The gods and various deities are all Illusion. They are our own imagination. Don't harbor false ideas, or false doubts. The story of King Nala of the city of Nishadha tells us that he did not wash his feet after answering nature's call of urination. He entered his house and because of this fault, evil, or Kali, entered his body and mind. In this story, "the feet," mean the base, or the root that should be cleansed. One must examine what is at the root of all things. Observe it. If you see clearly to the root and wipe out doubt, then there is only basic purity, fundamental clarity. That which is basically clean is strong. Then there is surety, certainty, and no place for doubt. As long as the fundamental cleanliness is not there, evil, or doubt, will surely enter. Everything is full of doubt, and it is the tendency of the mind to turn towards body-consciousness. Therefore, it is said that the aspirants should not deviate from the Self.

The body has a particular shape according to its state (childhood, youth, old age, etc.). It cannot hold on to its shape of its own accord. It has the shape because of the miraculous power of the Life-Energy, Chaitanya. Consciousness, although it is in the body, has no particular form or shape. Consciousness has as its natural quality to make us feel or sense something. That quality is called "Chaitanya as Knowledge." That Life-Energy as Knowledge assumes that it is this or that body, and functions accordingly at the time of identifying with some form. Without thinking of its being the Self, the Consciousness considers as true whatever is seen, or whatever appears as existing, and functions with that confusion. Actually, whether it wields a body or not, it is "Life" without bounds, or any particular form. It is flawless, but it assumes that it has a form, or rather, that it is itself the form of the body, which is a foolish blunder. With the concept of being a body held very strongly, it demands outer property and possessions that it thinks to be suitable for it. Thus, because it becomes ignorant of its Reality it becomes enamored with the body that is perishable. It gives the body extraordinary importance and unnecessarily suffers lots of sorrow.

The body form is not our Original Existence. It is but a momentary unwanted state. If you very carefully look at it, you can burn the net of desires and longings without fire. The Saints tell you, "Do not be enticed by body-consciousness. You do not need anything." Therefore, the aspirant should not deviate from being the Self. You should never allow your contentment to be disturbed. Your Self-confidence should be that strong. What day or time is auspicious or otherwise, for "That" which is Brahman? The Self is the power that is above time. What is a bad time for It? It is the "merit" in the "meritorious time" itself. Anything called "bad time" has nothing to do with it. The Self is the "God of Gods," who gives the "Best" to all. Body-consciousness makes you forget the discernment of pure reason. Therefore, you must be very alert. Even when you sleep on your bed, you must think that you are Brahman, the God of the Gods, and have peace. Never forget the brilliant truth that you are formless, clean, pure, and stainless. You must be steady in that contentment which remains unmoved by anything. Does the God Vitthala lose being Brahman because Rukmini (This refers to the unification of the male and female principles, the formless and manifestation) is near him? Both of them are pure, formless, sacred, Life-Energy only, through and through. Remain as Vitthala. Keep up the concept that you are the Self, Atman. Here the word Atman means "Formless Consciousness," Chaitanya. The constant conviction that you are this Supreme Self, is liberation, or freedom. Freedom is always existing, and does not need to be cultivated. Being the Self is being free.

You should never forget that you are the Self. I tell you this, but this will not be imprinted on your mind except if you keep the company of Saints. Surrender yourself to the Saints. If you are outwardly agreeing and being alert but secretly are having doubt, what good will all your agreement bring? Listen now to one great principle: One who has absolutely no doubt, is the Siddha, the Master. There is the story of Visoba Khechara who slept with his feet on the stone Shiva-Lingam. When asked about it, he said, "Is there any place where Shiva is not? All this earth is a Shiva-Lingam. My feet are also Shiva. They are not anything else. This entire world is Shiva." This must never be forgotten. This determination should not falter.

In the stage of Siddha, it was not the one formerly named "Namya," who became Saint Namdev that visited the Sage Visoba and was enlightened about the all-pervading God. There is no "other" there. There is nothing like the "second," or another. The second is not there. The "other" is not relevant there. One who has understood this is the Siddha. One who has doubt is still a seeker, an aspirant. There is no shortage of sin and merit in the world. Once you identify with the body, the ocean of sin and merit is filled. All of these things are told in the Vedas. The Vedas teach us how to perform actions while we think we are a physical body. When man's intelligence surpasses the limit of the body, the Vedas cannot give any instructions to the one who is a bhakta, a devotee. When one is beyond his physical body, beyond the perceptible, what can be said about him? What are his signs? Signs are only facets, or qualities. The Self is devoid of any shape. When we realize that we are the Self, how can we describe its qualities or lack of qualities?

One who understands himself as the Self, is beyond sin or merit, and has transcended the boundaries of visible forms. He is "Victorious." That is his victory-day (Vijaya-Dashamee). That day is the "Golden Day." It is the day of drinking Immortal Nectar. Birth and death are gone. The state of being an individual, a "Jiva," is gone. The Vedas themselves have put their own boundary. When you have crossed, then you are without doubt the Self and not the body. The "me" who was in the body, has become Shiva. He is victorious. He is now the Master, with the "Absolute Power of Brahman," the Power of the Self, the Reality of Himself. The Supreme Self, Rama, has resumed "His Kingdom." That attainment is the state of "Victory."

7-10-35

74. Non-Dual Brahman Explained

Non-dual Brahman is not something other than oneself. There is nothing "other." There is no need to imagine. We "are" without imagining. Everyone experiences oneself without imagining anything. That which is and that which appears, is all only Brahman. The listeners have said that by this teaching they are satisfied. Yet, the listener still raises a question. "By this explanation I have become one with the Absolute. Now I will remain in that Brahman. I feel that any thought about family and worldly life should not enter my mind. I become Brahman while I am listening. However, again I remember things about my home and it so happens that the jiva becomes aware of the family. Thus, there is confusion and the mind wanders. Please tell me what I should do. I feel that we should have no memory of those things, or rather, that we should not have this body. So long as I remember myself having a body, I cannot agree that I have become Brahman. How can one who is Brahman come back into family life? Either there should be Brahman or one should lead the family life. Please tell me how to reconcile this. Even desire and anger still prevail. What should be done?"

This listener contends that he should lie down leisurely when Brahman is realized. The Guru asks, "When those who have realized become still like a stone, have the other Saints like Vyasa or Shuka gone to waste? You say that Shuka and Wamadeva are liberated, but others have failed. How can you say only two are free? Then the Guru of Shuka should also be considered not to have destroyed Illusion. If only two have crossed beyond, then why are the Vedas and scriptures still there to be followed? So, all of this is not the case. Many Rishis, such as Vyasa, Yadnyavalkya, etc., all were emancipated. One who says that only two have become free, is stupid." When knowingly someone says foolish things, he is a wise fool. For example, your neighbor may be wise, but does it follow that all others are stupid? The truly wise person will not agree to it. Now, if you say that only two are liberated, then where is the power of the Vedas? Is it false what the Sage has said about the Vedas, that even if only one word of the Veda is understood, that man is a meritorious one? If any other third aspirant will not be free, who will respect the Vedas? You think that only one who becomes hard like wood, is liberated, and even if we agree with your opinion, how is it that the Sage Shuka has not become still like a log of wood or a stone? He gave instructions to King Parikshit. If he has taught Parikshit, how can you say that Shuka became like a stone? Had he become a stone, he could not have explained the Vedas.

If one falls like a log of wood as soon as he realizes Brahman, who would be there afterwards to show the way to liberation? Who would impart Knowledge to others, and who could have even taught that man in the first place? If he lies like a wooden log, who would teach others? All Knowledge would have been lost. While explaining, one has to talk about all things, either permanent or perishable. Therefore, it would not do, being sanely aware one moment, and being motionless the next. That man would also be in bondage. That is why, without falling like a log of wood in samadhi, we should have the "Knowledge of Brahman" while we are awake and active in speaking etc. Brahman is self-existent, without imagining. However then, if everything is Brahman, your imagination is also Brahman, and worldly life is Brahman. Where did this so-called "worldly life" meet you? Where is it and when is it? All is Brahman. You are also not outside of Brahman. Where is separate existence of the mundane life as such? The very nature of the realization of Brahman is like this.

How can one set out to find out the darkness by taking a lighted torch in hand? Extinguish the torch, then the darkness is near you. The one who searches, is himself Brahman. If without knowing oneself, one wanders all over the earth, one will not meet Brahman even after eons of time. On the other hand, if the seeker knows that he himself is Brahman, then it is the nearest thing to him, and wherever he may go, he is alone. Brahman is filling every space. He will experience that there is nothing except Brahman everywhere. The torch, means the sight that sees. If it is itself Brahman, whatever it looks at, is automatically only Brahman. Moreover, if that sight, the power of seeing, is ignorant, then whatever it sees, is Ignorance, the Illusion, that is seen. Everything is already without any entanglement. A man may lie down after awakening from his sleep, yet he is still by all considerations awake. Once you realize Brahman, even if you try to forget it, you will not forget it. On the contrary, you will be deeply aware of it in unity.

There is a story in which a man gave the mantra of Shiva to an aspirant to repeat, and warned him that while repeating that mantra, he should not think of a "monkey." Then what happened? That man always thought of a monkey while repeating that mantra of Shiva. Not only this, but even in dream, he saw the monkey. He got into an illusion and saw a monkey in everything, his wife, his children, other people, and even his house. Therefore it can be said that what is prohibited comes foremost in the mind. What is expected to be forgotten, is twice remembered. To forget is very difficult. So long as you have the body, there is involvement. How can you avoid it? You collect things for enjoying. You have accumulated things by your own desires, and now you feel it awkward. You are destroying your contentment. Please remember a simple fact. As a rule, no one does anything for anybody for no reason. In short, do not hope to get rid of your involvements in the future, and to be free afterwards. This will not happen. Everything including the family life is Brahman. How can you say that there is Brahman in deep sleep, and there is no Brahman in your waking state? The life led with the concept that you are your body, that you are an individual, is dangerously destructive. However, when you are Brahman, in each and every active moment, then life itself is Brahman and there is only Bliss. Only if you live with the identification with the physical body, is it harmful.

8-10-35

75. Narayana Plays in All Forms

Everything is Life-Energy, and nothing but Life-Energy. When the Life-Energy, Chaitanya, expresses itself, it becomes "Wind" (Vayu). We say salutations to the Wind God, salutations to the Fire God, salutations to the Water God, or salutations to the Earth God. When Chaitanya expresses itself, we give it many names. That which is the outcome of something, is essentially of the nature of that thing. That which is manifestation of Life-Energy, is only Life-Energy. Wife and children are all only the Life-Energy, but we call them Illusion, or Maya. It is conceptual, and therefore it is called Maya. It is also called the individual, or Jiva. This means that all of this Illusion is false. Within that false, there is some good and some bad. People even say that a golden ornament is good or bad. This habit of calling things as good or bad becomes applicable even to the "Basic Thing." The Life-Energy is the basic thing, so it is called by various names. One woman is called daughter, wife, wife of the brother-in-law, sister of husband, wife of brother, sister, aunt, maternal aunt, paternal aunt, grandmother, great grandmother, etc., etc... So what is all of this? Only one thing called by many names.

God takes many forms and the one who knows this fact is called an aspirant. Golden images of God Khandoba and a golden image of a pig are equal when the gold is considered, as their price per gram is the same. The price is related to the basic metal, and the value is given to the basic metal. The real worth is related to the original thing. That thing is made to assume various forms and the whole game is going on. It is a fun. It is an amusement. It is a play of imagination indulged in, in idle time. It is playful attitude, an idea of fun. There is no consideration whether there is profit or loss, good or undesirable. It is just merriment of Consciousness. There is no need to feel sorry or happy about it. It is just a joyful mood of Consciousness. However, one who takes this seriously as true, falls into an ocean of sorrows. The things and the numbers are symbolic emotional concepts. Any particular thing, person, or scene has no reality, but the one who takes it to be real is a fool. Really, he is totally mad. Such madness is destroyed by being in the company of Saints. Then one fully enjoys Brahman. What does this mean? It means that one remains in the state that is at the base of all experience, yet is without change.

The goldsmith was interested in the price of gold. He was not interested whether the image was of a god or a pig. This is the point of view of a wise man. Illusion means the changing of the form of things. One who sees the singular Consciousness in every being is a Saint. This is the Illusion of Ghatotkach. Ghat means shape, and utkat means the best, or true. When a thing that appears, is taken as true or real, that is Illusion. Here Ghat is our body. The thinking that "We are our body, it is my own being. I am as I appear bodily" is our illusion. That is Maya. The usefulness of my body, the salient features of my body, and the concept that this body is useful to me, is Illusion. The concept that "In the future I am going to be benefited by this body, and for that future I am going to do hard work, and I want to enjoy all the pleasures," and the one who does everything with this idea, is entangled in the Ghatotkacha Maya (the Illusion of the body as being true). All of this Illusion has arisen from Ghata, our body.

In the ancient stories, Lord Krishna said to his devotees, "Do not take anything new. The old things that you have are true." Here old means that which is the first, or original thing which is the One abiding in all. That is Brahman. Stay with "That." Ghatototkach told the people to take new clothes, and new ornaments, and give him their old clothes and old ornaments. People took beautiful new clothes and ornaments with greediness, and gave him all their old clothes and ornaments. Afterwards, it so happened that miraculously those who took new things, suffered in various ways. Their hands and feet were painfully constricted, many became mad, and many lost their memory. In some cases, the clothes around their bodies became invisible, and they became naked. Head dressings disappeared, some lost their upper garments, half the ornaments disappeared, and some, being naked, began to hide themselves and run here and there seeking cover. Thus, all those people were shamed. When those people were exchanging their clothes for new ones, Lord Krishna was giving a warning from some distance, himself being invisible, that "The people should not accept the new clothes that are all the jugglery of Ghatotkacha." He warned them that they should not give away their own things, and that Ghatotkacha was deceiving them, putting his evil spell over them. However, the people did not listen to his advice, and were thus ridiculed.

Really, the "oldest thing" is our own Being which is the Self, that is prior to any new experience. That is the gold that should not be given up. Either old or new, everything is no doubt only the Life-Energy, but do not be deceived by the new because of its newness. That which is formed is perishable. Lord Shiva told the demon Bhasmasura to bring to him some ashes daily. The meaning of this is that Shiva likes everything when it is burnt and turned into sacred Life-Energy. The entire world that is seen goes into the "Great God" Mahadev (Shiva) in the end. Now modern science believes that Air is the origin of all life. They have not searched beyond that. There is Brahman beyond, but science cannot approach further through chemistry. When two come together, some third thing is formed. When a carpenter and the wood come together, a chair is made. Now this power of man is called Bajigari, the power of creating new things. The creative power that the demons practice is called Wodumbari, and the power of God to create this world is called the "Creative Power." One who defeats all of the three is called a "Knower of Brahman."

All of the power to construct or create new things is in a way the power of mesmerism. It is an art to create delusion before people's eyes. The one who takes these created forms as real and permanent is a fool. He is bound to be born and to die, again and again. One who does not get enchanted by all the three types of creation is just like "Almighty God." One who knows the three processes of creation, goes beyond them, and sits on the throne of Paramatman. Bha'va means an ocean which has been created, and you are fish in that ocean. By avoiding the bait, you should go beyond the ocean. If the fish thinks that he is ocean, then he is ocean. He is made of water. One who knows that everything that is seen has come into existence from Paramatman, is free of this Illusion. To know and to understand this is "Right Knowledge." When King Janaka understood this Right Knowledge he was joyful.

When one meets a wise man, one should ask him the right questions and learn. Then, that one is a clever person because he gets his own welfare by asking the right questions. King Janaka asked, "Please explain to me what is Brahman, who is called Brahman, Vasudeva, Paramatman, Narayana, etc." That from which all this has been created, is called Brahman. The word Padartha in Sanskrit has a special meaning. Pada means the term, or the word, and Artha means the meaning, the significance of the term. All of these that Janaka was asking about relate to Brahman. That is the Artha, the meaning of the term. As there was not a single word giving us the meaning of the "Primordial Thing," it was called Brahman, and man was content with this one word "Brahman" which completes whatever was intended to be told. The terms Krishna, Bhagavan, Vishnu, etc. are all the names of this "One Thing."

Now listen to the nature of this "One Thing." That which is completely filling everything in the universe as the base of all, is called Narayana. The Rishis (Sages) who are well versed in the Vedas called it Narayana. The Sage Pippalayan says, "Oh King, the primordial cause of this universe is Narayana. When He is non-existent, the universe dissolves, and He who exists, moves and is full of joy within the body is Narayana. He who creates the body, and remains in it without being affected by it, is Narayana." How was this world created? I will tell you. He who sleeps, He who dreams, He who sees things in the dream, and knows the world that is seen, is Narayana. As soon as Narayana became space, there He was awake, and the world came into existence. Whether it be for a short duration, or for a prolonged time, Narayana is the experience of the waking state. That experience does not happen because it is wished for, or because it is not wished for. It does not disappear because it is not wanted, and it does not happen in any way depending on the desire of the experiencer. The world comes into being and disappears as a natural phenomenon. Know that the experiencer of all of this is Narayana. The one who says that the dream is false, is Narayana. The one who says that the dream is fictitious, the one who knows the awareness in the waking state, and the one who is fully aware of the bliss of deep sleep, is only Narayana.

That which recognizes all states and all experiences is also called the Supreme Self, Paramatman. He is the "Highest Brilliance of Consciousness," the "Supreme Formless Beingness" (Parama-Purusha), all-pervading Narayana. Now listen to the easy way of realizing the state of Brahman. See That which is total, That which is whole. That Paramatman, is in the "Om" sound, which is in you. That by whose power the mind and the intellect work, is Paramatman. This Narayana is shining like a star within you. Narayana is the Life in all beings. He is the mover of all beings. He is awake in deep sleep, as well as in samadhi. He is called the "Lord of the World" (Jagadeeshwar, or Jagadisha). He who sees this world, is the "Lord of the World." He is the Primordial Lord (Adhi-Isha). If He did not exist, the vacant space in the nose would not be able to smell any fragrance. He, by whose power you say, "I Am" is Narayana. He who protects us is God Narayana. Narayana is the doer of all actions.

9/10/35

76. The World as Knowledge

The world is threefold, meaning three planes of worlds, or three worlds. They are the waking state, the dream state, and the deep sleep state. The deep sleep state is called Paataal. Narayana is He who dwells within everything. There is nothing at first in the dream state. How many people are there? The one who dreams, and the one who knows the dream are one. The dream, which comes into existence, disappears, and deep sleep also comes and goes, but the one who dreams and sleeps does not disappear. He is the ruler of the three worlds. He is witness to all. He is Paramatman, the Supreme Self. He who knows all of the three states of the body, is that Paramatman. He by whose power the mind, the intellect, the pranas, and the sense organs function is Narayana. If you say that He is dependent on the sense organs, it is not true. He is King. He is God, who is not dependent on the sense organs. If you try to know Him, you will be deceived. He is there without being known by anybody. If you assume that you are a certain being, a particular entity, and try to know him, you will not be able to do so. Do not try to know him. He is "The Knower."

Without trying to know him, He is there. That is how Oneness is actual. That Oneness was already there. It is only re-established. The "Man of Knowledge" (the Jnani) cannot be "a knower," or "an observer," and try to know or observe him. Knowledge is known by Knowledge itself. It is to be silently understood. It is by itself. It is like one's Self looking at one's Self in a mirror. Reality is to be seen in the mirror of Knowledge. The capacity of the tongue to taste happens only by tasting. The "Book of Knowledge" is like a mirror. Consciousness is only One. How can the One Consciousness know anything "other"? We have to understand it by learning it through the Guru's personal teaching to us. In our heart, the One who knows everything and everyone is Paramatman. That which is, without assuming any state, is Brahman. To assume any state is to introduce a "second" or "other".

Water in a pond rises in the fountain in a gush towards the sky and it sees the sky, but when it falls down, it is again thoroughly mixed with water in the pond. There is truth when the water knows that it is only water in the pond. That should be realized. The "Son of the Guru," the Guruputra, knows this. Others sit only wondering. If you try to know it, you will lose your faculty of knowing. You cannot meet the Reality through the process of objective sensory knowledge. Only confusion is created by those who insist on trying to know it by experiencing. Leave this approach. Leave your efforts to bring Reality to the level of experiencing. Leave knowing, and not knowing. Both are just concepts, your attitudes. When both are left off, only "Existence," which is the pure state of Being, remains. Only then does understanding arise. "That" is our Self. How can That be known? You are coming daily and asking me to tell you how you can catch yourselves, and I have agreed to do so. I know that you are not lost. I know it very clearly and therefore will supply you with your own address. The Self's nature is to "Be." You may not want him, but He is. He will definitely Be, even if you do not want him. He is the Supreme Self, Paramatman.

It is the mind that imagines the "Abode of God" (Vaikuntha). The mind imagines "I am Vishnu." However, the mind cannot imagine anything about the Self. That mind, which imagines the three worlds cannot imagine the Self. If it tries to imagine about the Self, it ends. The eyes cannot see themselves. They can only see others. The pot, which measures one liter or two liters can measure hundreds of kiloliters, but it cannot measure itself. Similarly, the mind cannot measure the Self. How can the speech understand that which is not knowable by the mind and intellect? The Self cannot be known by wearing a loincloth and sitting in meditation for thousands of years. It is He, the Self, who knows the loincloth. We should know the way to understand Him. The "True Master," the Sadguru, knows the way. If you try to tie the sky up in a piece of cloth, all the four corners of the cloth will remain empty. The body functions because of the power of the vital energies (or breaths), the Prana. That Prana also cannot know Him. Speech cannot know Him. He is the mind of the mind, the intellect of the intellect, the knowledge of the knowledge. He is the eye of the eyes of all.

Consciousness is itself of the nature of Knowledge. It is in itself the body of the Universe. It is the Life in all living beings. It is the Life of all. Physical bodies are like leather dolls or puppets. It is He who lives in them, and plays all of the games. The eyes are blamed in vain for seeing things. It is only He who sees everything. The sense organs are in vain called the organs of perception. It is He who knows. The imagined individual, the jiva, in vain says that he exists. The individual is eating the remnants of food which is really being eaten by the Self. The true owner eats, but the jiva says that he is eating. The individual is thus eating secondhand food. This jiva, who is a dog of doubt, barks in vain.

Is anyone's body a burden to one's self? Similarly, the Saint who has Self-Knowledge has become one with the world. The universe is his body. He is "unity" by his very nature. What burden will He feel? Because the entire universe is one unit, one complete whole, the "Totality of Knowledge," the universe and the nature of Knowledge are one. The universe without Knowledge, and Knowledge without the universe, is not possible. The universe is Knowledge, through and through. The entire universe is contained within Knowledge. Knowledge means Brahman, and appearance means "the universe." Therefore we say "Brahman is true and the world is Illusion."

10-10-35

77. Evict "Me" from the House

That which gives light to all of the sense organs, that which gives life to them, that which enjoys the senses conveyed by them, and to whom all the sense organs and their objects are subservient, is the Self. Although He receives the impressions from the sense organs, He remains aloof from them. Smell is the object of the nose, but the nose is not controlled by the smell, smell is controlled by nose. Similarly, the Self is the controller of all the sense organs. Objects have less value, while the Self has more value, and is the owner. "Owner" is a word that denotes "to be of more value." He is superior to all objects. He is superior to all experiences that take place. That superiority is indicated by the word "owner." To say that "All things are of lesser value than the owner," means that all the material and all the property involved in that which is experienced is owned by Him. He is the enjoyer of all the property. He has power over all the objects of senses. All the material is in His possession. He does not become knowable to the senses. He is the director of the senses. He is superior to them.

The objects and the sense organs cannot know the Self. Objects are the things to be experienced. The experiencer is the enjoyer of these. He knows the objects. The objects do not know him. How can the mind reach where the intellect cannot reach? How can any of the sense organs know Him? The four speeches do not know Him. The vital breaths, or "life energies" (Pranas), do not know Him. When the sense organs cannot know Him, how can organs of action such as hands and feet know Him? The magnifying glass does not contain the Sun in it, but when the Sun's rays pass through the glass, a very hot spot is created that can burn any article that is there on the other side. The waves do not contain the whole ocean, the ocean contains the waves. Similarly, it is not possible to know Brahman with the help of senses. The sense organs do not know Brahman, it is Brahman that experiences the senses. It may so happen that a banana tree will be created from a banana fruit, or that salt will produce an ocean (these things are impossible), but the sense organs will not know Brahman.

If the sense organs cannot know Brahman, it is natural to think that ignorant simple-minded people will not know Brahman. This is not so. If you think so, I have something more to tell you. In order to teach the so-called "simple-minded" about Spiritual Knowledge, the sacred word Om (AUM) has come forward. This word indicates Brahman and then disappears. Otherwise, people will not know Brahman. The word is heard and the action of hearing is done by the ears. The word, which is heard by the ears, reaches inside where the living "Om" is vibrant. That living word, is "knowing," the art of recognizing. Knowledge is the action of knowing. It is its natural quality. The senses have perception about any outer thing, and this art of knowing is the inherent quality of Consciousness. The explanation of Brahman is the description of the Self, which is the Knowledge of our own Self, our nature, and the function of Consciousness in life. The sense organs do not know it. That capacity to know uses the sense organs to know outer things. Its main quality is "to know." That is why it is called "Brahman with Attributes," or Saguna Brahman. When that knowing quality is not there, it is naturally "Brahman without Attributes" or Nirguna Brahman. No special action is required for that. Thus, the Saints are teaching us that the Self cannot be understood by the sense organs. The Self is God who knows the sense organs and controls them. He provides the Power that gives them the ability to perceive the sense objects. The Saint is therefore called the one who has conquered the sense organs (Jitendriya).

A man sees another man sitting nearby. He does not know that man by name, but he correctly points to that man with his finger. When that man is pointed out by the word "that" the word vanishes because its function is over. Similarly, the word tells us that this and this and this is not Brahman. Brahman is beyond any appearance or object that has a name. This is just like a man who wanted to tell about a wristwatch, but could not remember its name, so he said, "That round thing that is tied to the wrist." So, by describing it by using some skillful means of explanation, the word then vanishes. That is why the Masters have made a statement that if you understand one word, you will become God. By the Guru's advice in a certain few words, we can come to understand God. It logically follows that words make the meeting with God possible. The word is itself very great. It is by word that we know the past and the present. It is by the word that Rama and Krishna and other great Masters are known to us. It is in certain words that Lord Krishna taught his disciple Arjuna.

The life as a human being is worth its name because we understand the word. By the word, human birth has become great. Words make one God. Knowledge of the Vedas is conveyed by words. We can have a dialogue with Shuka and Vyasa. The author of a book actually talks with us. Talk is possible by words. The books contain only written words. We can say that the "word" has undertaken the job of imparting Knowledge. The word discards as Illusion many things, and lastly makes itself useless and mute. The "me" and the word both disappear. Here "me" means the ego, or pride. The word reaches that place from where it arose, and then it is mute. It is the word, that has taken an oath to teach us Reality, Brahman. The fly dies in the food and makes the man vomit the food. Similarly, but quite in a good way, the Vedas keep only one reserved word and discard everything else. They say that Brahman is not whatever you say about it (Neti; Not this). What remains is Brahman. So saying, the Vedas have also become silent.

The scientists of metaphysics say that Brahman is that which cannot be directly described. One who understands the premise by skillful explanation is the "Son of the Guru" (Guruputra). He is the son of the Master. When "you" disappear, That which remains is Brahman. Like a cobra that sits on a heap of gold coins, so is the "I" sitting on Brahman. Only when the cobra is killed can you take the money. Similarly, as soon as you kill the "me," Brahman is there. The man who knows "That" which cannot be described by words, is himself Brahman. "That" which remains after discarding everything, is "ever-present." When Bhasmasur put his hand on his own head, he was turned to ashes. What then remained was only One, who is Mahadev (Shiva). He who was not, died. A house was not occupied by any tenant and a notice was affixed to the door to vacate the place within three days. There was actually no one occupying the house. The house was vacant. Similar is the stupidity in the case of this "I." When the existence of the "me" is denied by the word, what remains is Brahman. In words, the deities like to be hidden. We give them godhood by our word. All of creation is the business of words. The whole world is created by word. The word, the sound, is the quality of the sky, and the world is annihilated by the word.

He whom the speech cannot compel to speak, makes the speech speak out, He by whose power the eyes see, but whom the eyes cannot see, and He who knows all, but who cannot be known by all, has no second to know Him. That which is Self-knowing has no "other" to know him. There exists nobody except Him. There is the smell, and the act of smelling, but by removing the middle factor, the smeller ("I"), what remains is Paramatman. If the three factors of the observer, the observed, and the action of observation are formed, He cannot be understood. If one is naturally silent, it is He. Without Him, everything else is futile. The organs of action and the organs of senses are all functioning, but without Him, they are dead. "That" without whom they are dead, is God. Do not "know," or perceive any other "thing." Leave aside your knowing it. Then what is? Only He is. One who exists without recognizing any "thing" objective (or other) is Himself, in his own Majesty, his own Glory. He does everything, and He no doubt exists, but the "me" should vacate the place.

When the individual, the Jiva dies, one remains as Shiva only. In Marathi "Aaji" means one who is today, and "Maaji" means who is and has been from the past, one who is Self-existing. If you insist to call the jiva as only jiva, it is your own wish. However, one thing is sure, it is because you exist that you can experience anything that you are doing. Experience is possible because of Consciousness. Therefore "you" means Consciousness, and Consciousness is Knowledge. This means that you are in essence, "Knowledge." Knowledge is called Brahman. You are "That," you are Brahman.

Evening, 11-10-35

78. The Appearance of the World

Words give the "Knowledge of Brahman," but it is only when everything that is to be told is finished, that the Knowledge of Brahman takes place. After the word ends, realization happens, and the word remains silent. The Veda is the king of all scriptures, and even He has remained mute. When the Veda said about Brahman, "Not this, Not this," (Neti, Neti) other sciences were at a loss for what to say. They could not find any sign or indication of what Brahman is. The sciences, or scriptures (Shastras), are the product of the Vedas, and as the Vedas become silent in contact with Brahman, other scriptures cannot give a glimpse of Brahman. Other scriptures are intended only to describe, while the Vedas tried to show it directly. One who is set on marrying, intends only to marry. He is one-pointed about it. That is the main aim for him in life. Sugar is sweet, and only if you eat it do you know the sweetness. There is no need of employing the scriptures to describe sweetness. This entire world is One. It is filled by only "One Thing," and nothing else. To understand this, to get its experience, is the most important thing to be achieved. There is no other appearance of anything but the One, everywhere. With this experience, the knot of the ego is loosened, the hidden bondage to the body is slackened, and all spiritual powers are one.

The fruit or merit of worshipping the image of Lord Ganapati is the same even though the image may be small or big. What is the significance of a bigger image? It is only more quantity of earth. The earth is the image of Ganapati, and the image is nothing but earth. The difference is in the sentiment, or one's feeling about it. It is for mental satisfaction that we impose the image of God on a particular shape and color of earth. We want to derive the joy from the image. The whole thing is only mental imagery. The earth does not become Ganapati and Ganapati does not become the earth. The worship is the product of the sentiment of our mind as it is a projection of the mind, and is not permanent. The Saints think about what is permanent and therefore they do not fall for any emotional involvement. They are convinced about the Absolute, the "Imperishable." Intending to convey the truth that all of manifestation is Brahman, the Sage Pippalayan says, "One who understands that he and Brahman are one, functions like others, but all of his actions, his feelings, and behavior is nothing but Brahman. Like Shuka or Brahmadev, his sleep is samadhi, it is called Brahman Samadhi."

There was a false conceptual man who did not exist but was only imagined. He was working, and then he was nullified, being proved to be unreal, a non-entity. The whole life of one who has realized the falseness of "I," becomes Brahman. His uncleanness is clean water sprinkled on Lord Shiva according to the Vedas. The knower of Brahman, is Brahman himself. He whose pride is gone and who has the understanding of Brahman is the Greatest God, Mahadeva. It is a great sin to give trouble to a devotee of the Guru. One should not harass a devotee of the Guru. Who else other than Shiva is he whose ego has gone, and who has achieved the vision of all-pervading Brahman? All of the actions of a "Man of Self-Knowledge," the Jnani, are the very life of God. His body, and his family life, is the house of Shiva. His speech is of great value, the great mantra. His wife is Uma (Paravati) and his son is Ganapati (Ganesha the god of meditation and remover of obstacles), the Son of the Guru. To worship him is more meritorious than doing puja to thousands of images of Ganapati. Good and bad are not different in Brahman. To him, hell and the portal of heaven, are the same. To him, Shiva is omnipresent in the lingam symbol and in an insect in mud. His glance, full of compassion, is the direct blessing of Shiva.

Illusion, Maya, is non-existent but she has created actions (karma) for all the world. She conceived Paramatman as having a body, and Shiva was thus ridiculed by her. She created both Knowledge and Ignorance and expanded the activities of the world. She created man and woman and introduced the chain of births after births. She created the forgetfulness in Shiva's consciousness and made him a donkey or a pig. She created a multitude of forms for the formless. Just as there are only threads in all the clothes like pants, a shirt, a cap, and so on, but many forms and shapes are created from that thread, such is the strange game of Maya. People have a concept that a woman who is standing in a lotus flower is the Goddess of Wealth, "Laxmi" and a woman standing under a tree is the opposite, an evil spirit. She has thus introduced various imaginary beings and the world at large is so formed. On the day of Diwali (Diwali is a Hindu holiday where people light lamps for Laxmi), people prepare images of Lord Krishna, gopis, etc, out of cowdung and actually worship them with flowers. See how this Maya makes the individual, the jiva, to bow before even the cowdung. In Krishna's image made of dung, what else is there except dung? It is all make-believe, all false. The truth is that all is Brahman, but fools make this falsehood of Maya appear to be true. The individual sings the same song that was once sung when putting the child in the cradle and doing the naming ceremony. The jiva is caught in the chain of birth and death by holding tight to the name and the form, and says "I, I," every moment. This has caused the chain of unending births and deaths.

In the one Brahman many shapes and forms have been created and it is being said, "This is like this," and "That is something different. That belongs to the other, etc." In the game of chess, the Queen, the Knight, the King, etc., are all made of wood. All are simply wood. Yet, even in the game there is unnecessary argument. The more clever that people are, the more they fight. Similarly, there has been a false appearance of many in the One that is Brahman. This is Illusion. This is mesmerism. This Illusion is a game of hide and seek. It is a play, a cunning game of emotional imagination. One who knows her, will discard her immediately. If the game of chess or any other game will be proved true, then the world will also be proved true. The world is not true. It is an appearance in Consciousness of illusory things that are going to disappear. The entire apparent world phenomenon is not real.

Evening, 12-10-35

79. Be Quiet Like God

Brahman is the Self, the Atman, and "Atman" means our Self, alone. The ten experiences of the ten sense organs are not ten different individuals. They are all the single action of the one Self. There is a story of the various organs going on strike, not willing to do their work. The Self is the King, and it is for him that all organs work. He alone is the greatest. Body-identification is the nature of the individual, the jiva. Even the sense that "I am Brahman" is also dissolved in the case of one who has become Brahman. "That" is the state where there is no "I" and there is no "you." It is neither existing nor not existing. It is something beyond both. The pride that "I am the Self" is also not in the Self. There is no such thing as "is" and "is not." The wave of seawater is only sea, but instead of being separate, it simply has to be quiet. The explanation of "it is not a thing" is that all that has an appearance, is not it. All differences are perceived in relation to Illusion. In relation to Truth, there are no degrees like bad, best, medium, inferior etc. A Jnani, was asked, "Who are you?" That man kept quiet because Reality cannot be described. He only said, "We are told by the Vedas to be silent." The Sage Pippalayan said, "I will describe what Maya is. She is not, and that is what I will describe. I will tell how many ships were drowned in the water of the mirage."

There is something in us that gives response to a call by saying "O." That is "Om." The three syllables A + U + M make up that OM. Sattva, Rajas and Tamas are respectively related to these three syllables. Om is the power of "knowing," which is Consciousness, the "Mahat" principle. It is also called the "Power of Action" and the "Power of Matter." To say, "I Am" is Brahman, but if you mean "I am the body," then you are not Brahman, you are but an individual, a jiva. The treasure which is within us, is beyond any value. It is Brahman. It is "godliness" itself. If it takes pride in the physical body then its perfection is diminished, and it suffers great sorrow. However, if it drops the petty pride of the body, it is God. We never forget that we are, but we never say, "I Am." The experience of our being in existence is there without saying anything about it. It is, just as it is, and that is Brahman. While coming into this world, the jiva comes crying. All come crying, and only for crying. The only aim of being born is to cry. Crying is the destiny of one who takes the birth. Everyone is going forward crying. Nobody looks back. If one would look back (to one's source), there would not be any cause for crying. That which is very natural, is Brahman. What study are you doing? All study is nothing but crying. Let everything that is, be as it is. Do not say anything and it is so. The Shruti (the Vedas) says that you are nothing. Then why are you forcefully calling yourself as somebody?

We must be silent, just like a dead man. To be silent like God is to be God. Brahman is silence. Our concepts are our enemies. However great and rich your achievements may be, in the end, you will be insignificant. All of your achievements are of no use in the end as you will die with a concept that you are a petty individual. You cannot gain real greatness as an individual. Whatever you have gained is going to be destroyed either in front of you, or afterwards, and you will die as a petty jiva. Therefore, you actually get nothing. Even though a jiva is really a part of God, even a god dies as an insignificant jiva, repaying the debts of his actions every moment with fear in his heart, and without the realization of his godliness. All of his riches prove to be useless. Whatever happens is Illusion, and what is as it is without becoming anything, is Brahman. Again and again people fall prey to the great Illusion, trying to do something, or become somebody. Whatever you may become, it is becoming something "other," and other is always petty. Silence is the quality of the great men. Whatever you give a name to means a coming down from the Reality, so do not try to become anybody.

There is no higher authority than Brahman. Do not touch anything "other." As soon as you touch (take it to be true), it is spoiled and you are stained. Because you utter a word saying that "Yes, I am such and such," Brahman is called an individual. Whatever you call yourself, it is that name you will be called by by the people. You may call yourself anybody, but to do so is to fall down, to come down. It is only gold, which is called by the name of a bracelet. By giving emphasis on the name, you have forgotten the original thing. Gold has never become an ornament. It is always only gold. By the name, the original thing goes behind a curtain. It is covered with the label. The original thing becomes invisible. The name is used and the original thing becomes eclipsed. It is as if it were out of sight, and somewhere else. By pride of the name, it becomes important, and its empire spreads. The original thing remains covered. The Illusion is like this. There is no hair on the tongue. To say that there is hair on the tongue is Illusion. The objects of the senses give the fruits that are pain and pleasure. The individual thinks that objects are real and thus suffers pain and pleasure. Though he is the Self, by the force of lust and desires, he becomes a small individual.

The power of "Knowledge," of "Action," and of "Matter," are one in the wholeness of Brahman. This means that they were only Brahman from the beginning. The five elements are all only Brahman. All together, there is only One, alone. In this body also, it is only He who is there. Everything is He. Brahman is the only One. If a jackfruit is made of sugar, all of its parts like the skin, the pieces of the fruit, and the bean, are all simply sugar. Similarly, that which is called "this world," in its numerous forms, is only Brahman. The form of the body grows by the power of Brahman. It is only Brahman. Like a doll that is made of cloth is completely only cloth, similarly, the body is all only the self-powerful Brahman. It is in all of manifestation, and it is natural. It is not disturbed at all by any appearances, and never has it been corrupted. Ghee (clarified butter), when it is both solid and liquid, is always only ghee. Ignorant people think them to be different. To the wise, ghee is the same, be it either solid or liquid. To understand one's uncorrupted existence like this, is to know Brahman. Brahman remains pure and unpolluted by any thing. If there is a currency note of one thousand rupees, and if there are one thousand coins of one rupee each, its value does not change. The shape and form is a distortion of the underlying value. To be solid is a distortion of the ghee. The solid form is a cumulative result, a process of storage.

The "Basic Existence" is Brahman only. The man who says that Brahman has undergone some change is stupid. Brahman has no parents, it cannot be exhausted, and it cannot increase. "Atheism" and "Theism" have no place in it. It is, always as it is. Only what is created has growth, and modification. Brahman has no growth, no modification. If you take a bath in the water of the river, the river does not lose any thing. Its water returns back into the same river. The states of childhood, youth, and old-age are only experienced by the body. Brahman does not become a child, a youth, or grow old. One is neither man nor woman. Although in the body, one's Existence is different from the states of the body. Know that you are Paramatman. But remember well that it is He who is there, not "you." When this is confirmed, then the goal is reached.

Evening, 13-10-35

80. Brahman is Always Awake

The Self is always of the nature of Bliss in which there is never any sickness. The Self is always safe, never breaking, and nothing can go away from it. All material things are likely to be damaged or increased. When you experience any material thing being damaged you think that you have sustained this damage. The individual imagines that he himself is somehow damaged. The Self has no things in it. There is nothing in it that can be damaged or will decay. It is without any dirt. This means that there are no material articles in it. That is why it is called clean, and as there is no dirt, it is indestructible. To decay is the quality of dirt. It is bound to decay and be destroyed, and to return back to the earth. However, the stainless Self is indestructible. Although He is in the body and the sense organs, He is not affected by them. The Self has neither birth nor death. Death can only be spoken about in relation to the body. The Self is never corrupted, and is without parts. It is not put together with various parts, or the sum of any parts. If you want to know who He is, this Self is He who lives in your body, and who knows the body.

When we say that knowledge is temporary, we mean that the knowledge in the mind is temporary. The speech ends but Consciousness remains. Had a man not been aware of himself, he would not have returned home when he had gone out for some work. The desires pertaining to the sense organs eventually die, but the essential nature of Knowledge, Consciousness, remains. Childhood, youth, old age, etc. are the states of the body. These are natural phases for every material thing. By the medium of the vital energy, or Prana, these states are understood when they come. However, the Prana itself does not become young or old. Its quality of energy remains the same. When Prana has no change in its state, how can the Self who is the "Prana of the Prana," the "Life-Energy of the vital energy," have these states?

Eggs, the combination of heat and moisture, live birth, and seeds, are the four sources of creation of all beings. In all beings, Prana functions only by the "Power of the Self." The states like childhood, etc., do not have any effect on the Prana, so then how can they affect the Self? The individual, by his own wrong concept, binds himself. In desire, there is bondage. I will explain. Whatever you want is at a certain place. If you want it, you have to go there where it is located. You have to wait there until you get what you want, and sometimes, the desire is fulfilled. Then, when you get what you want and it cannot be carried away from that location you have to remain there. Only there, can you enjoy that object or use it. When it cannot come with us where we go, we have to live near that object because we are needy. This is the bondage because of desire. If you do not wish to be bound, you have to give up your desire. Only then can you leave it. Where there is desire, there is detention, which means having residence living there (in the world). Desire entails being in the vicinity of the object. When desire dies, detention departs. By giving up desire, "Liberation" is certain. However, to harbor desire is itself bondage. When all the desires are dropped forever one becomes the Reality, while the individual, with all its desires holding him tight, goes downward towards destruction.

The Self is untouched by all qualities or modifications. It is said by some that in the waking state, the Self is limited by the limits of that state. However, if this were the case, He would not have the knowledge of the dream state, and would stay tied to one state only. He would have continued to eat only either sweet or only bitter things, but He is not like that. This means He is unaffected although in the body. In the dream state, He functions only by mind without the help of a physical body or sense organs. When He goes beyond the dream, in deep sleep, He remains alone without any sheath or body. There is no ripple of any kind. You may say, "Where is the Self? There is nothing there," but this is not really the case. Who is it that can say that he was happily asleep? Who is it that answers to the call given to him by the name which is given to the body? This would not be possible without the Self. The deep sleep and waking states are of the physical body only, and not of the Self. He, being a witness of all the three states cannot be "nothing." He is the Supreme Self, Paramatman. You may ask how is it that when He awakes from sleep, how does he remember again all the environments of the waking state. Listen closely to the explanation. Environmental circumstances are in relation to the intellect, or brain, and not the Self. If the intellect is transformed, the worldly life becomes unreal. Then there is no bondage of, or freedom from anything.

Worldly life exists because you say so. You conceive it as so. It is real only because of your concepts. If you say, "I have dropped it," then the worldly life and any bondage is gone, totally destroyed. If you increase it, it increases, and if you destroy it, it is destroyed. Mind is the source of worldly life as well as spiritual life. While going to sleep, you remove your outer garments, and when you wake up, you again put them on. In deep sleep, you are not aware of the body covering on the Self. When you wake up, you see, and by your attention, you remember everything. To one whose ignorance and egoism is gone, it is all only Brahman, even the waking state. The individual gets dissolved and becomes Paramatman. Then there is no desire of any sort. There is no simile to be used. The meaning of simile in this case, is something that is used in order to show that the Knowledge of the nature of "Truth" is like something else. There is nothing equal to it or anything similar to it that can be shown. Nor is there any word that can be used to describe That state, or its meaning fully and adequately. There is no form, object, or words, which can compare to That state. Therefore, That state is called beyond simile, or it is said that no simile is available to explain it. For "It," there are no other things. The entire world is only Parabrahman, or Paramatman.

When Self-Knowledge is evident, there is only happiness itself, happy to be. Bliss itself revels in bliss. One who will be a selfless devotee will have this experience when Illusion is discarded. This is why devotion should be continuous. One should never forget to devote oneself. There should be no forgetfulness. When some other object or achievement becomes attractive to the individual and he thinks about that object, he forgets his devotion to God. Therefore Saints insist on incessant devotion. When the devotee discards desire for money, children, material riches, and fame in society, and indulges totally in the devotion to God, the dirt on Consciousness is cleaned, and it becomes one with God, abiding in its True Nature (Swaroopa). When the love and devotion for God increases, the sayings of the Vedas are subservient to the devotee. That which the Vedas have declared to be the "Highest Truth," is uttered by him very naturally. It is then that Existence is experienced as "One Total Whole." This is the devotion of the highest degree. This devotion liberates everyone including women, men, the lowly, and priests (brahmins) without any discrimination. However, if the mind is not clear, there will be no light of the Self. One who has unbiased devotion reaches Reality. The veil over his eyes disappears. The Sun *and* the multitude of things are seen all at once. When one drops all pride, and the mind becomes free of doubt, everything is seen as Brahman.

King Janaka asked, "How, is one to carry out one's duties after realization, and how is the bondage of action, or karma, broken? How does one remain free from any stains, even while doing one's duty? By what remedy are the ties of karma broken, or loosened? How can one achieve the state of inaction, although performing actions, and how can one meet the Supreme Being, God? Please tell, why is it that the Sage Sanaka and others did not give answers to the questions of children?"

These questions are difficult to answer. The Sage Awirhotra Narayana said at that time; "The problem of action, wrong action, and non-action is not an ordinary one. The lawmakers who thought about these matters were tired, and great sages were at a loss how to explain these things. Millions of seers have exhausted their brains, and in the end quarreled amongst themselves out of pride. It was not easy even for Brahma the Creator, and others, to give proper divisions, and analysis of actions. Action is at the root of the Veda, and the Veda is Narayana only." It is at this point that the Vedas keep quiet. Action, non-action, and wrong action, are in a way, all the same. Like in the case of sugar, where you have a soft, a white, and a brown sugar, "sugar" is the same. Similarly, action is one, yet the one who is attached to action finds various differences. In action, non-action is inherent. In wrong action, again inherent are action and non-action. If any action is started, it is called action, or karma. To differentiate between good and bad is vikarma, which means wrong action. The disappearance of action is non-action or akarma, which means that the action is as if it had not taken place. The one who knows that the non-doer is the true doer, has become a sage. He has attained "actionlessness." Oh King, if you come to realize that the actor and the one who causes action, is only one in this body, only then you will be actionless. The doer, who exists at the beginning of action, is himself the receiver of its results. Only by the blessing of the Sadguru is the state of freedom from action achieved. There are many actions arising out of one action, and they are called right or wrong actions. However, by the teachings of the Sadguru, all actions (karmas) are cut off. The song of action is like this.

This question is very big. That is why the Sage Sanaka and others did not impart this knowledge to children who were not mature. These differences of action and non-action should not be told to those who are not mature enough to understand. Paramatman is, at all times without any disturbances and without any impediments. It is permanently indestructible and perfectly clean. Be certain that you are "That."

Evening, 14-10-35

81. Give Up Doubt and Discrimination

Discrimination means differentiation, or separateness. This means the absence of equality. In equality there is no sense of high and low, and no distinctions such as dirty or clean. Equality is that feeling where there is no enquiry as to how "another" is. By removing the doubt of inequality we must know that Brahman is One in all things. Even in respecting all as Brahman, we should prostrate before them. By completely disregarding the social etiquette, we should do this. Lord Krishna has clearly told about this spiritual practice (sadhana). We should view everyone, including our own body, as Brahman. We should cultivate this attitude up to the time that it is imprinted firmly on our heart. Whatever appears to our eyes, and whatever one feels is there without actually seeing it, including the mentally imagined concepts, are all only Brahman without making any effort. This should be the conviction of our "Inner-Being." Everything is the Life-Energy, Consciousness, which is of the nature of Knowledge. What the mind sees, and what the eyes see, is all only Brahman. Our sadhana should go to this extent. We should be convinced that the imagined and the unimaginable are only Brahman. That is the last check as to whether we have understood properly or not. When you are sure that what is imagined by the mind and what is beyond the scope of the mind, is all Brahman, our own Self, that is the culmination of the "Vedic Karma" (the actions taught in the Vedas), and all of the actions of our daily life.

The sadhana of the one who is convinced that all is Brahman, has been completed. Sadhana must be done so long as Brahman is not proved to oneself. To one who is convinced that whatever is experienced in waking consciousness, in dream, or in deep sleep, is all only ones own Self, there is no further need for sadhana. You should feel that the person whom you were despising up to this point is also only your Self, Paramatman. If you still feel enmity towards him, you can be sure that your sadhana is not yet complete. One who does not feel separateness is truly perfected. All of the activities that you do are the activities of Paramatman. There is nothing else in the world. You should have devotion in such a way that you feel that your Self is in every being. The Lord says, "You will not have My vision, My experience, by any other methods, even if you try for eons." Knowing this, you should meditate that only Paramatman is everywhere. Leave your clever logic and all other types of mental acrobatics. The one who very easily and naturally sees Brahman everywhere, is on the right path of devotion. I have told you here the very essence of the key to attaining the state of Brahman. By this, truly you will realize your Self, which is the real wisdom. This should be done wholeheartedly with body, speech, and mind.

The mind is very cunning, but the mind cannot touch Paramatman. It cannot really even create bondage for Him. Paramatman is always undisturbed and without any blemish. It is spotless, meaning that it does not contain any matter. Matter is prone to deterioration and destruction. Matter can never touch Paramatman. You should not try to do anything with the mind such as supposing Paramatman to be junior or senior. All activity belongs only to the mind. You should not misuse your speech in uttering malicious thoughts, and it is even worse to be jealously fermenting inside. Everyone has some vice, but nobody wants to reveal their bad side. They try to conceal it. This is all a matter of misunderstanding. At least try not to browbeat others. Why should you expect that everyone should obey you? Everyone should have freedom. In short, why should they act according to your wish? Why should there be such a tyranny? So, do not be like that. Consider all of your actions as expressions of Paramatman. If one feels that one is in body, speech, and mind only Paramatman, their experience will be according to that sentiment. Even the concept that "I am alone, looking at all beings as if they are Paramatman," should also go, because what "other" is there for "me" to see? Is this entire world Paramatman only because "I" think so? Even if you do not think so, the whole world is already only Paramatman from the beginning. One need not assert it. The fact that "I am Paramatman" should be very clearly and firmly understood. Only then is the mind in "That State" which is without any cause. Brahman is always existing without any cause.

One whose Consciousness is fixed on the Self immediately understands what is said here. However, for others we have to tell it again and again in various ways. So, we should prostrate ourselves in humility to all beings, respecting them as Paramatman. By humility we can have a place in everyone's heart. By humility, one is always unassuming and remains pure and blemish free. In this way, our unselfish life can permeate all beings. Humility is a great virtue. There lies great strength in being humble. It requires great bravery to remain humble. In humility, all is Brahman, and even the thought that "I am Brahman" also disappears. What else is there, except Brahman? Where the sense of yours, others, and mine have been swallowed up, all similes and comparisons disappear into one "Unity." Then, one is fed up with trying to even talk about Brahman. That is a state where God and his devotee do not remain separate. Both God and devotee are gone.

God created Illusion and for some time the devotee abided in it. Afterwards, God and the devotee were both gone. Originally both were not really existing at all, and accordingly they have disappeared. The "One Thing" without duality, is as it is, always. A Saint is often criticized. "What kind of Saint is he? He is not a Saint." Even he himself says, "What Saint? All is only Illusion." He is fully aware of the futility of giving any name to the Reality. The aspirant should be very alert and careful. Emotions and passions will arise unbridled and will run after the enjoyment of sense objects. We must recognize the very subtle desire that is residual in our Consciousness. Desire, or the lust for sense enjoyments, should be as lifeless as flowers once offered to a deity which have become wilted, and are then disposed of. This should not remain only a verbal assertion. It should be an actuality in our Consciousness. If there is not a speck or drop of desire in our being, desire itself dies. When the desire dies, "desirelessness" becomes the expression of the mind, and contentment is its essence, the very nature of the Self. There is no urge arising to enjoy anything, because there is nothing "other" as such that is attracting us. It is only when we speak the word "other," that the thought of having something, or enjoying something arises. Something other means something outside of us, or objective to us, and "Oneself" means contentment in the Self, alone.

In the Self, the duality of one thing enjoying the other does not remain. After all, as the feeling of enjoyment is but an attitude of mind, its dissolution is possible by the opposite attitude of the mind. The Self is One, self-existent, without any relationship of a dual nature. It is true that by the disappearance of the sense of worldly life, all is Brahman. However, this is always true even before the sense of any disappearance of a worldly life (belief in objectivity). Whose Illusion is it, yours, or someone else's? It is only you who is misunderstanding. This Illusion harasses the one who holds on to it. This worldly life is there only so long as you treat it as true. It ends when you are sure of its falsehood.

Evening, 15-10-1935

82. Take Care in Spiritual Life

When the concept that the rope is a snake is gone, the rope is as it is. When the illusion of "snake" is gone, the rope is clearly only the rope without being anything else. Similarly, the cause of involvement in worldly life is ignorance, which is ego. When that ego goes, Brahman is already fully there. Similarly, although the world is mistaken to be true, one must see it as only Paramatman. Spiritual study should be like this. You may listen well to the words of Knowledge, but it is your emotions and desires that will bring in their effects in Consciousness. For example, a king is no doubt Brahman in the spiritual sense, but when he works as a king he must be very alert in his duty and act as a king. In all appearances, there is nothing else except Brahman, so you should make efforts to maintain the conviction that "All this is only Brahman."

The "Son of the Guru" (Guruputra) can achieve easily and naturally that which many other great people could not. He becomes "That" which he intends to recognize. That immensity, which is attained after billions of incarnations, is realized as one's own nature. We must never look for bad or good qualities in others. We must drop all such frivolous activity. The individual (jiva) generally thinks, "All others are bad, and I alone am good." The jiva has a habit to find fault with everyone and everything. However, in spiritual practice, this quality does not lead one to a higher state. Close your ears when criticism of others is going on. The one who magnifies the small virtues of others, is truly great. It is better still if you are appreciating and praising the man who is against you while not harboring any enmity. It appears to be good to listen to criticism about others. What else is sweeter than nectar to the individual than bad gossip about others? On the other hand, to one who is wise, not to hear gossip about others is sweeter than nectar. Care must be taken by the seeker on the spiritual path not to indulge in gossip. You should never harbor malice for others in your heart. If you are not this pure you will not experience "The Almighty" in all beings.

In order to be of the consciousness that "All is Brahman," there should never be any trace of criticism or malice towards anybody. If you make the distinction that someone belongs to you, and somebody else is not yours, you will never be a Saint. Therefore, one who is wise should always feel that all beings are one's own Self, that they are not different.

The world is always keenly observing to find out whether the sage is looking at the good and bad points in others. People will purposefully trouble him because they are testing him. If you have the feeling that everyone, including even these troublemakers, is Paramatman, then everything is all right. When "you" are not there, who is blaming whom? If you know this, all riddles are solved. The seekers who wish to have Self-Knowledge should not read newspapers, etc., because they definitely disturb one's spiritual study. In order to reach the highest fulfillment of life it is necessary that our Consciousness should be pure and one-pointed. Only when it is one-pointed can it merge into Reality. While approaching Reality there should not be anything other to attract the attention of our Consciousness. Therefore, one should leave aside the newspapers and all of the other spectacle about the world's affairs. The aspirant should always be churning over and over the teaching of the Guru, and meditating on the Supreme Self, Paramatman. Where our own mind's agitation is not wanted by us, why should we think of inviting more disturbance from the affairs of the world?

While meditating on the Self, the aspirant must be steadily and definitely avoiding the indulgence in the sense organs' demands, and instead, turn one's focus in the other direction, towards Paramatman. In short, it is futile to bother about the mundane affairs of the world. You will not get any real benefit out of that. Devotion and singing (bhajans and kirtan) in praise of God, is above all, the best activity that one can do to realize God. Lord Krishna says that He himself has become God because of this sadhana. "I have become God of all because I have been united with the realization that only the One Self, Brahman, is residing in all beings. My state of godliness is based on this unity with all things. On the strength of Oneness, I have remained non-affected, a non-doer. Even though doing everything for billions of years, I have remained a non-doer. As a sculptor who makes many earthen images of Lord Ganesha inwardly knows that all of the images are merely clay, I also see Brahman in all created forms." The aspirant who knows that all things are great, that "All are Brahman," becomes Paramatman. To have the realization of one's own Being, the Self, means to always remain in that state.

Lord Brahma has come to me to take refuge in me, because he decided to emancipate billions of human beings through such all-permeating Consciousness. However, the understanding of my True Nature is not possible by merely reciting the verses of the Vedas. The only way to achieve success is that one should be lucky enough to meet My devotee. By being in the vicinity both physically and mentally of My devotee, the seeker will know Me. Someone may say that he will of his own wish perform a very strenuous sadhana and realize Paramatman. However, he will not be successful. Why is this so? This is the most sacred secret. Ultimate success will be attained only through keeping the company of the Saints. Otherwise, the seeker will miss the mark and think that his imagination is Brahman.

Evening, 16-10-35

83. Atman and Paramatman

We should not feel sad when something happens which is not liked by us. If all is God, then where and what is the difference? We should know this fully. To know that "All is God" is the real devotion with the mind. A man may belong to a low caste, the so-called "untouchable class," or be very evil in his behavior, but in his "Original State," he is still God. There is only God in him. God means that we ourselves are only the Supreme Self, Paramatman. We are that foundation on which all experience takes place. Paramatman does not get dissolved. All experiences have a beginning and ending. That Consciousness which is the subtle awareness of the beginning and ending of experiences, is called the Self, or Atman, and that background on which all experience takes place is called Paramatman. That which remains after experience is over is the Supreme Self, Paramatman, which exists before the experience begins, and after the experience has ended. That "root of all" is not destructible.

The serpent and scorpion are the same. Even in them, our very own existence pulsates. When we have this feeling, it is called "God Consciousness." One who knows that all creatures are God will never use harsh words to others. Nobody insults anyone whom they love but they will quickly speak harsh words to others. This is the habit of the ego that believes itself to be the individual, the jiva. When we understand that all things, all beings, are Paramatman, we should not say anything about anybody. "What do I care about him? I don't care!" All is the Self, Paramatman, only. Even at the cost of our life, we should never speak about defects of others, or hurt anybody by word or deed. We should act in such a manner as will be helpful to others. If we have money or any other asset, we should give so that it provides happiness to others. We should behave in such a way that others will be satisfied. This is called "physical devotion," or devotion with one's body.

We should even be kind to one who does wrong deeds to us, just as the Sage Vasishtha forgave the Sage Vishwamitra. Those who are still aspirants get angry. An aspirant or someone studying some system of yoga may not yet have a proper sense of self-control, and therefore desire and anger may still harass such people. They may sometimes curse others and put them to a lot of trouble, just as sons of rich people doing sadhana have no self-control. We should be able to see God Almighty, the Supreme Being, even in our enemies, because that is the sign of selflessness. One whose ego has gone is the real Sadhu (Saint). The nature of people is to find faults with others, but the nature of a Saint is not to look at the bad points, or what is lacking in others. How can one who is concerned about good and bad qualities in others can be a Saint? The Saint is different from those people. If he behaves in a different way than the people of the world, only then is he a Saint. The nature of a bad man is not to see anything good in others. The Saint, or saintly person is without any particular qualities or signs. The man who is truly great sees the good in others, and he knows that that good is the very "Light of God" that is shining within himself.

Be kind to all and take pity on all, and you will feel no need for anything. Pity for all beings, or compassion, is the best means to destroy the net of Illusion. There is no other sin that is greater than evil gossip. Speak well, but never speak evil about others. One who blames others will never get good food to eat. If you want to get good food, you should speak good words. One who talks trash, eats trash. The tongue that does not speak sweetly does not get sweet food. The scriptures say that the evil-tongued people get the birth of a pig that eats shit. The man who says good and true things has the "Power of Speech" that is always true.

Lord Krishna says, "I have so ordained that the path of devotion is very pure. There is no difficulty in devotion, and the devotee becomes successful. Even though there are many religious and sacred books, the path of devotion is greater than all of them. The seeker is helped by all, and calamities therefore never show their faces to him. He knows that he and all of the beings all over the world, and Paramatman, are one. Just as a serpent is afraid of the eagle, and a man is afraid of death, likewise, calamities are afraid of the devotee. Dear Uddhava, this is my path of devotion which I have not told even to my mother, but now I have told it to you."

Evening, 17-10-1935

84. Offer Everything to God

If you conceive that everywhere there is only God, you get the experience of Brahman everywhere. "That" is such a thing that it is beyond "is" and "is not." Once you are certain that you are man, there is no necessity to repeat "I am man." Similar should be your concept that "I am Brahman." Only then does the seeker become Paramatman. When he understands that all is Brahman, then desireless devotion automatically remains. To be without anxiety is the highest sadhana. You should know that whatever happens is beneficial, and you should not worry. Not to fall back from conviction, is the state of Brahman. The actions (karma) may be done with a desire for fruit, or may be without such a desire, but know that all activities are done by Atman only. With this knowledge, all actions are naturally surrendered to God, Lord Krishna. "That devotee who is one with Me, is really the true devotee." Even if our efforts in everyday life are not successful, that should also be offered to God. When we play Holi (Holi is the Hindu festival of colors where people playfully put colored dyes on each other) and make fun, we should also offer that to God. A man hid himself in a jungle to avoid a robber and luckily he found some gold there. Similarly, perhaps if by someone's actions we get some benefit, we also should offer that to God.

"One who believes that all actions are done by Paramatman becomes one with Me" (Krishna). If a husband slaps the wife, or if the wife slaps the husband, let it be offered to God. If you put on a coat, let that action be offered to God. If you put on your shoes, offer that action to God. You must be all the time thinking about God. All deeds are done by God in the form of Consciousness, so you should do all things as if you are God. Suppose the milk pot is toppled over by someone. You should think that it is done by God and let it be offered to Krishna. The aspirant should know definitely that everything is done by Consciousness. The porridge of bitter gourd (which has a very bitter taste) should also be offered with all sincerity to Him. He will like it. If some flour is wasted, offer it to God. In short, anything that may happen should not cause you any sorrow. Something may be good or may be bad, but you must never dwell on it. You may gain some profit or suffer some loss, yet your mind should be content and not sorrowful. Be without anxiety at all times. The food that is eaten by a person playing the role of a tiger is not eaten by a real tiger, but only by the man who is acting.

What is the meaning that something is offered to God (Lord Krishna)? It means that everything is restored to the "Basic Existence." Even though something may fall on the ground, or become spoiled, nothing is wasted. All goes to the "Original Reality." Where else can it go? Where is there any other place? In all the bodies, the only doer is "Consciousness," Rama. This is all only the doing of Paramatman itself. To know this is the real "intelligence," or wisdom. That intelligence in particular should be offered to God. It is not good to show unselfish devotion in the outer world, and still keep hidden desire burning inside. Do you think that the Life-Energy, or Chaitanya is only for you and that it is not in others as well?

Some people are very well-read and knowledgeable, but because of their pride in their knowledge, they become separated from others. For example, salt can be separated from water, but it can be again mixed back into the water. However, the pearl which is considered valuable goes away from water, is put in the nose-ring of a woman, and is fastened there thereby becoming bound. Many intelligent people study hard some system of yoga and increase their karma as "do's" and "don'ts" are impediments in their way, and they are caught in actions. They are over-anxious not to commit any wrong action, and in that, they become very proud. Krishna says that his devotional path has no bondage. Those who drop the pride of doing actions (karma) and remain free, are his real devotees. All others, by the strength of "ego (pride) of knowledge." fall short of realization.

We should discriminate between what is sacred and what is not. All actions have the aim of attaining Self-Knowledge. There are no duties and no actions after you attain Self-Knowledge. When "That" which is the fruit of all fruits is attained, then all other activities are not necessary. In the case of the Siddha, the actions that are being done are the actions of the all-pervading Chaitanya, and are one with the "Universal Life-Energy," the Universal Consciousness. When action is being done by such an "Accomplished One," it does not remain as individual action with particular name and form. What is the meaning when we say that now you should not do any individual action (karma)? This means that the source and substance of action is only Universal Consciousness. Then there is no compulsion of doing it, or not doing it. Action creates bondage only so long as the concept that "I am an individual" is prevailing in the mind. When you attain Self-Knowledge, the action becomes the natural expression of the Universal Life-Energy, and with this conviction the sense of separateness of the person disappears. Therefore the name given to such actions in freedom is Brahma-karma, the "Action of Brahman," or Nish-karma." Be "Nish-karma," which means that you are no longer bound by any actions.

If a person who has passed the examination of Barrister (Lawyer) returns to primary school he would be a fool. Likewise, when there is "Realization of the Self," who will go with ritualistic pots and spoons to perform puja to an image of God? If he will wash his own feet, that will be enough. That is a better puja. How can one worship a stone image when he has understood the "True God"? The wife of Uddhava gave some bananas to her house servant to place them as an offering in front of the image of God in the house. The servant went in the shrine room, and ate the bananas instead of offering them to God. At the time of puja, Uddhava enquired about the bananas. His wife called the maid and asked, "Where are the bananas which I gave you?" She replied, "I fed him the bananas, and He ate them." When asked by which mouth did God eat the bananas, the servant said "By my mouth." Uddhava intervened and said to his wife "Please do not say anything against her. By constant listening to what we speak about God, she has understood and become one with Krishna." In short, we must understand that one who constantly meditates on God, becomes God. Then, what other God can one worship?

Most people harbor pride in their mind about their past achievements. However, it is that one whose doubt has gone, who is really performing "sandhya" (morning and evening prayer to God). To sip the holy water from our open palm is really drinking the whole ocean of worldly life. "Aachaman" is a Sanskrit word meaning "the One who gulps everything," and is happily enjoying the bliss of the "Garden of Happiness." The "Realized One" is the one who really knows what Aachaman means. Those people who have great pride about the devotional activities that they have done in the past, and which they continue to do, are prey to the Illusion and only suffer loss. Those who are blessed, become my "true devotees." I become the direct perception of Truth in their intelligence, and I bring them into Me. I give My devotee that intelligence. He no longer has anything to do with east or west! Why? Because he is beyond the eight directions, and is not concerned with any particular time. All concepts of sin and merit are destroyed in My devotee. He has understood what is required to be understood. Now he is resting in Me. For him, all is of the nature of

Brahman. Is not his speech, whatever he says also Brahman? His harsh language, seemingly meaningless babble, and all his good deeds, are all the speech of Brahman.

Lord Krishna says, "All actions are surrendered to me." Do not harbor doubt. Nobody should harbor any doubt. The highest intelligence is to see all as Krishna and that no other thing exists. That intellect knows that it is the highest intellect, and only loyal devotees of the Sadguru can have this. All others are caught in the net of doubt. Those who think that they are their bodies are not able to realize Paramatman, and they perish with the end of the body.

Evening, 18-10-35

85. Meditate on the Divine Tree

All beings, all that we see, and all that we feel, is only Brahman in its completeness. One who knows this, realizes that "All is Brahman." Just as the banana tree is full of water, similarly, all of the five elements including the earth, are only Life-Energy (Chaitanya). All of the winds are that Chaitanya, and that Chaitanya is God. The houses are earth, and people are earth. They eat earth and return back into earth in the end. Similarly, all of this Illusion is in the form of Life-Energy. We may paint many pictures but there is nothing but paint. Knowledge (Jnana) means "Right Knowledge." What is Right Knowledge? To know that which is the "Original Thing," is Right Knowledge. The creations born out of the five elements are all a myth. With the dissolution of the elements, what remains is only Life-Energy, Chaitanya. The wise man should know what is at the root of everything. That which functions within all is Chaitanya. One who knows this is in all the elements everywhere and in all beings, and he is truly God.

In all beings, it is Me who lives, and that "Me" is God. This is the one "Single Quality." It is natural "Self Being," the True Religion, the Natural State. When this quality disappears, what remains is beyond qualities or attributes (Nirguna). This One Quality, or Existence, is nothing other than the Supreme Self, Parabrahman. It is the Great God of all beings, all of their activities and functions, and their Glory. "That" is "One Alone" without any facets or attributes. It is original, permeating everywhere, whole, self-created, self-luminous, Paramatman. It is the

Supreme Self. Of all that is moving, it is the Essential Life. It is not possible to describe such a one who has realized it, and has become the Reality. To conceive of this state is the highest achievement of our intelligence. That Knowledge which is cognizant of Brahman, which is All, is the Supreme Knowledge. Nothing further remains to be learned. The aspirants who study in such a way become Brahman. They attain this Knowledge that is the pinnacle of intelligence, and the highest wisdom of the wisest person. They experience that there is nothing else but that one "Singular Existence."

To conceive and insist that all of this appearance is a multiplicity and real, is the greatest stupidity. Brahman exists even before you became cognizant about any appearances. Everything is of the nature of Brahman, but people started to think that the "I" is something separate and started acting with the illusory concept that this world is real. What has happened? The mouse is riding upon Lord Ganapati. When you bow before the Lord, Ganapati says, "You are doing the right thing but please see this little mistake and correct it." Then it will be all right, and that is the end of Illusion. The sin of many lives is wiped out. Ganapati here is the Primordial Male Principle, the Original Formless Existence (Adhi-Purusha), and in your misunderstanding, instead of God riding over the mouse, the mouse is riding over him. It is this mouse that is dictating to you one thing or another. All the sciences and the Vedas are advising good things to this mouse (the ego) but it is not listening. Then the Sadguru said to his disciple, "My dear, there is not any mouse. The thought that there is a mouse is false. This ego is false. What is true is this Original Formless Existence, Adhi-Purusha. Drop this illusion of ego."

When you take a vow of renunciation (sanyasa) you get your head shaved by a barber, but that is only an initiation by the barber. That will lead you nowhere. Action should be taken so that the roots of the hair will never grow again. Brahman is not caught in the hair on your head. The hair will grow back again and again. Doing things of an outward nature to your body will not enable you to realize Brahman. What is necessary is the company of a great Guru. By the light that he kindles in your heart by bestowing upon you the sacred mantra, your very initiation in the cycle of birth and death should vanish together with its evil effects. By nipping in the bud your initiation in the birth and death cycle, you can arrive at the basic state of your Inner-Self. Let the hair on your head remain. The hair of the tendencies (samskaras) inside you that lead you into the world should be cut off with the Knowledge given by the Sadguru. The renunciation of the six vices (Greed, Anger, Hatred, Desire,

Craving, and Pride) should take place. What is the need of getting your head shaved by a barber?

The meaning of the "Key of Knowledge" is that when the "I" is dropped, the nuisance is also gone. The house should be vacated. That is the only thing to be done. Only one thing should happen. That is that the state of having no "I" should be adopted. The all-pervading, omnipresent Brahman is as it is, only "I" am not. I am not, and in that egoless state everything is unqualified Brahman. "I" means ego, the sense of being a separate entity. The pride of that separate existence should be renounced. This is the height of true wisdom. This shape of the body is going to perish one day. However, it is only due to, and with help of this body, that one can become the eternal Brahman with the realization of the state of "Self-Consciousness."

There is no doubt that Illusion is unreal, but this body which is so useful is created because of Illusion. Those, who with the help of this body constantly devote themselves to Me, reach Brahman. See how great the gain can be with proper use of the human body. Those who spend their energy for worthless things and lose this greatest benefit go to hell for a very long duration of time. We should not be enticed by worthless gain thereby losing the complete fulfillment of our life. Who would be such a fool to indulge in those actions by which rebirth is destined to be our lot? If by doing but one insignificant action one could attain Brahman, then why would the wise not do that action? Who will not gain the "Wish-fulfilling Tree," the Divine Tree, by giving up the "'rag" of imaginary concepts? (Note - In rural areas of India, villagers hang old clothes on the wish-fulfilling tree, Kalpataru, in hopes of having their wishes granted) He who would not do this would be a fool. Who would give up the great benefit of realizing one's unity with God by not doing the simple act of offering all actions to Him? This advice of spiritual life was given by Krishna to Uddhava. (The word Uddhava means "the conviction becoming firm.") This is the pinnacle of all devotion. He said, "This Knowledge of Brahman is given by Me like a sweet morsel, with all the love of a mother. This Knowledge is unattainable to those who go into the complications of the Shastras (sciences). The Sage Gautam, by just walking around (doing Pradakshina, or circumambulation) a cow got Ahilya as his wife. All of the others, and the gods are still going around the earth. Vishnu and Brahman went to search for the feet and the crown of Mahadev (Shiva). However, Vishnu could not reach the feet of Mahadeva, nor could Brahma reach his crown. Such Knowledge (of Shiva's greatness), Oh Uddhava, is given by Me to you."

Those who follow the Vedas and other scriptures are only entangled in them. They quarrel in vain without knowing the "Real Thing," the Absolute. Many great people fight over the nuances of meanings and interpretations of various scriptures (Shastras), but even by dissecting them to pieces they have not arrived at God. They did not attain the "Knowledge of Brahman," because it is not possible to describe Brahman in words. The Vedas have declared "This is not Brahman" (Neti, Neti). How then can one man describe it? Those who describe it have never visited that town. How can they describe the town that they have not seen? Only those who have not realized indulge in profuse descriptions and endless talks. Vedanta scholars expound many arguments about Brahman, but they have not enjoyed the bliss of "That." This is the main thing that is lacking in their case. I have given you that Knowledge which has nothing to do with the Vedas and Shastras. Only the True Guru (Sadguru) gives this Knowledge to worthy disciples by use of various tricks and examples. I have given it to you without your going to any trouble.

By attaining this Knowledge all doubts are burned and the devotee becomes the Absolute Brahman. This is called the "King of Knowledge" which I have told you. One who listens to it, and reads about it, is truly the fortunate one. It is only the fortunate who listen and think over what is being told here, and gain this Knowledge. It is no wonder that the wise will be liberated by learning this Knowledge, but even the simple-minded will be emancipated. People get the milk from the cow, which is truly for the calf. Similarly, by the devotion of Uddhava, others are benefited. "I gave out to you openly what was hidden in My heart. You have gone to such a land in which even the name of Death is not known. Even the Immortal Nectar may perhaps have an end, but you have attained such a state where people have no birth or death because they have drunk at the fountain of this nectar-like Knowledge."

Eknath wrote the epic Sanskrit book "Bhagwat" in the Marathi language and the brahmin priests began to harass him. They made him an outcast and then that book was sent to Varanasi where some other brahmins praised this book tremendously. Then those critical brahmins became silent. This book, the **Eknathi Bhagwat** is called "The Question and Answer System." When we have taken birth in this world, the only aim before us is to be unconditionally free. However, very few who are truly lucky and blessed have this aim fulfilled. One who cherishes in his heart this understanding, this Knowledge, becomes Brahman himself. The listener and the teacher become one.

Once you gain this Knowledge it never perishes. "I become the servant of those who teach this Knowledge to My devotees." The result of giving out this Knowledge to others is told by Lord Krishna himself. "This Knowledge should be given to those who have surrendered themselves to Me with body, speech and mind. This Knowledge should not be taught to one who is not a devotee. This secret should only be told to the devotees who have love for Me. I myself become the servant to that devotee who is excellent in Devotion (Bhakti) and in Knowledge (Jnana)."

19-10-35

86. The Power Where "No Karma" Remains

Those who have surrendered to God's feet with the physical body, the speech, and the mind have become like God, and are the Gurus and "Sons of Gurus" (Guruputras). They utilize that which is dear to them by offering their body and their speech. It is very natural that one who loves the Saints becomes endowed with the virtues of the Saint. This is the result of keeping the company of Saints. When one places one's faith, body, speech, and mind surrendered at the Guru's feet one attains the goal that is desired. For the mind to be attracted to spirituality, and be engrossed in it, is itself honorable. The attitude that is opposite to this, is worldliness. Many who came into contact with Lord Krishna became free, for whatever reason the contact might have taken place. Even in his lifetime, some were against him. They were after pleasure obtained through sense objects and were selfish. The man who is obsessed with sense objects desires those pleasures only. He keeps company of similar people who only indulge in sensual pleasures. Such a person does not like to turn to the "Formless State," and hates those who like to devote themselves to being "objectless." This hatred has some reason. Such a man who is born and conditioned in circumstances full of objects, fears that he would die if all things are taken away from him, and therefore he continues to be attached to the sense objects. He is afraid to be without his preoccupation with objects, and thus he starts opposing and criticizing those whose interest lies in the nameless and formless Existence.

If the husband turns to the path of devotion, his wife hates him. This is because there comes in her life a lack of indulgence in sensual pleasures. Because of this subconscious opposite attitude, a person obsessed with the enjoyment of objects thinks that the enjoyment experienced through sense organs is the best sweet dish that one can have. One who believes that happiness can be found in sensual pleasure does not turn towards spirituality by giving up this joy. Desirelessness is the only food that helps us turn towards the Reality and attain Self-Realization. It is natural that one who becomes desireless is hated by his friends and family who are simply worldly focused. Those who have sought Knowledge have become wise. Those, who for the sake of reaching "Me," give up all wealth, the home, and everything collected, together with body, speech, and mind become one with Me. Only those who do not like anything except Self-Knowledge can attain it. Those who are My devotees to this degree see only Brahman wherever their eyes turn. When they think, even their thinking is Brahman. When they see themselves, they see Brahman.

Saint Ramdas told his mother, "That ghost who is called Brahman has possessed me." This is the most mature state of spiritual understanding. When a person does not like anything else, that is called "Right Knowledge," Complete Knowledge. One who gives the teaching to My devotees to such perfection that nothing more remains to be taught, are so dear to Me that I am indebted to them. Although I am the Supreme Self, Paramatman, I am under their obligation. I cannot be free of that obligation. Such authority, such highest status is only for the Saints. They are Sadgurus. Even the gods Brahma, Vishnu, and Shiva, cannot bestow this high position. The poet Waman Pandit requested Vishnu to liberate him from the chain of birth and death but God said, "That is not within my power. I will give you huge wealth and high intellect, but I have no freedom. For freedom, you must go the Saints. They will be able to help you, and you will become accomplished, a Siddha. It is the business of the gods to put all creatures on the treadmill and revolve them. To stop that treadmill and to give liberation is only within the power of the Saints. It is their capacity. Only they will give you Self-Knowledge." It is not possible to repay the great obligation of what the Saints do, because nothing is equal in value to that Self-Knowledge. There is neither any capital nor any valuable thing to give as payment for it. God says, "I give 'My Own Form' and 'My Being' to the Saints. Even this is not correct, as I do not really give it to him, as the Saint himself attains the state of Brahman. I am in his possession! Abiding by the words uttered by a Saint, and obeying them, I give 'My Own State of

Consciousness,' 'My Own Status,' to men, to women, and even untouchables."

The word "Karma" means to start action, and the word "Vikarma" means the ending of Karma. For this, it is necessary to know the stage of "Nishkarma" that is between the two. One should know how one can perform action but remain a non-doer of action. Truly, one does not act, has not acted, and will not act. To know this and to experience this is inaction, or Nishkarma. This means that there is no doer of the action. In this state, one remains a non-doer. To realize this is Nishkarma Siddhi. Actions prove to be impediments in the life of the aspirant, therefore by listening to the teachings of the Sadguru we should experience the state of "non-doer" by attaining Self-Knowledge. When all of the things pertaining to the body disappear, something remains that is imperishable. It remains as the non-doer although a great number of activities are done. How can Brahman imagine anything about itself, and how can it perform any rituals? One who knows how this is taking place has finished his sadhana, and abides as Brahman. One who teaches this is the "True Master," the Sadguru.

The One who takes care of all, is really the non-doer. Whom does Illusion affect? Only one who holds on to it. She puts the individual in bondage by giving the food of sensory gratification. When the person who is accused admits his crime, only then is he proved guilty. Maya puts the jiva who admits his crime into bondage and subjects him to endless births. What crime is it that these fools admit? They admit their slavery to sense objects. What is this slavery? Even though one may have already enjoyed many pleasures, the desire to enjoy them again and again persists. The jiva thinks that the objects of the senses are real, and although he may have some understanding, he thinks that he will derive pleasure from the sense objects. Even though such people may have Knowledge, they worry and ask, "What more can I do? How can I behave now?" You harbor such useless doubts and become slaves to Illusion. Actually, there is no question of how to behave, or what to do. Action and non-action are both irrelevant. When the whole life is One, why ask how to behave? That question is finished.

Lord Krishna says "I am his servant who realizes this Nishkarma." He also says, "I have also been taught by the Sadguru, who has realized Brahman. The question is why and how does this necessity arise? I am Paramatman, the one Complete Bliss, the only Reality. There is no sense of anything being separate from Me. My 'Life' is one all-pervading totality spread out everywhere, Oneness. That is why it was necessary even for

Me to go to the Sadguru to understand the Self. Such is the great secret of the Self. I am the body of such a 'Realized One.' He is My Self, My Atman. The Self of all the Realized Ones, is One, and that is My Self. The Self of the Sadguru, and Myself, are One. There is no doubt about this. The physical actions of the Saint are my own physical actions. I am called Avatar. Why? Because I know Brahman. Otherwise, there were and are many children of cowherds (Gopis). I am called Avatar (an incarnation of God who comes down from Brahman) because of My 'Knowledge of Brahman.' Similarly, the Saint also, is actually 'My Own Self.' He is another incarnation of mine. His knowledge has also increased in addition, and therefore the Jnani is greater than I, just as the coach driver is definitely superior to a man who is only riding a horse. As the various sciences in this world develop further, Spiritual Knowledge also progresses. Thus, those Realized Ones who have appeared in this world are very great and you should know them as one with Myself. I cannot repay the debt to the one who teaches others about the Knowledge of Brahman. How can I repay Him? I am constantly attending to them. I become a household servant at their home. It is I, who am living in their houses. I am the servant of that man in whose body and speech Spiritual Knowledge finds an expression."

Krishna said, "This dialogue of ours is called Pure Spiritual Knowledge. The one who makes wicks of the ten senses and the mind, and in that light reads this Book of Knowledge attains wisdom." Illusion treats Self-Knowledge as an infectious disease, because if one attains this Knowledge he gathers many others to give them Knowledge. Illusion gets very angry with the Sadguru and Saints, but it is ineffective in their case. The one who holds dear the feet of Saints has emancipated many of his ancestors. Likewise, in the family, if a person has no devotion to me, the ancestors are angry, they curse him, and bring difficulties in his life. Even gods like Brahma and others bow to the feet of the man who is in the company of a Self-Realized Saint, as He attains such a high position. One who examines Illusion, is King Parikshiti. He is the one who observes and judges properly. If anybody gives even a pot of water to such a Saint, that man is sure to be released from bondage. Not only this, but even the bullocks who are yoked to their cart are ultimately destined for liberation, because they were physically useful for the work of the Saints. Just as the light of one moon is equal to that of millions of stars, the one who is learned and becomes Realized liberates the entire world.

In the case of one who listens but does not think over what has been heard, his listening is non-productive. Thinking and meditating is necessary after listening. The story may be over, but the meditation should be continued. Aspirants should constantly attend to their meditation. Together with meditation, the singing of bhajans (singing in praise of God and Guru) is increased, and devotion of a very high degree is evident in one's life. This is called Parabhakti, which means "Supreme Devotion." The devotees of the Sadguru attain this Supreme Devotion.

20-10-35

87. The Seed of Karma

I am Para-Bhakti, the Supreme Devotion. What does this mean? Devotion is of two kinds. The lower and the higher. The higher devotion means to see oneself as one is. By the higher devotion the devotee can see Me (God). Those who are My devotees have no bondage of any kind. Not a single action can bind My devotees. This is a great secret. This talk is private and secret. This is the heart to heart talk between Paramatman and his devotee. Only the great devotee and Paramatman will understand this and nobody else. The Knowledge that leads to liberation comes of its own accord to one who really wishes to be free. One who desires something gains strength and bravery in that work, and becomes perfect in it. In human birth, many people have many kinds of desires, but it is very rare to have this good desire for liberation. One who has great faith, and becomes steadfast in devotion may even try to discard this Knowledge of attaining freedom, but it does not leave him. This Knowledge is the "resting place" for the one who really wants to listen.

This Para-Bhakti or Supreme Devotion is so great that by only listening, devotees realize Me. Have you not gained Knowledge by listening to this higher devotion? If you are given sugar, or any sweet, it is but natural that others will also find it sweet. I have told you this Secret Knowledge in its pure form. This is the Best Knowledge of all the types of Knowledge. This Knowledge is the Essence. It is the core of Knowledge. It is by this Knowledge that the Vedas are considered important. Only the intelligent Brahmins (the "Knowers of Brahman") can have authority for this Knowledge. I have given this Knowledge which is not given by Vedic scholars nor the Vedas to others. By this Knowledge, ignorance of all kinds will go, and the individual (Jiva) and

God (Shiva) will get rest. I have given you this wisdom which is beyond the mind and intellect. I have bestowed all of "My Wealth" upon you.

What I have told you is now fully present in your Consciousness. Are you convinced that all is Brahman, as I have told you? Is there any doubt still in your mind? If you have not followed, I will tell you again. All of this world appearance is only Life-Energy, Chaitanya. Everything, including your body, is Brahman. One who is convinced of this should never have duality in his mind such as "I" and "you." Really, this duality does not exist. When "I" is gone, that which remains is the state of Brahman. There is no duality of "me" and "you" from the beginning. Whatever you see with your eyes is a form. It is seen by you, and that is not your Self. When it is experienced that something is not your form, then you become formless. Naturally, the notion of "you" will disappear along with the sense of "I." This sense of "I" is the ego, but as your form is nullified, that ego also disappears. Unless there is some form, the ego does not have any base. Without a form, there is no place for it. Now you have become formless as you were originally. There is nothing that can be tied to the formless, nor is there any way to bind it. The formless always remains free from bondage. It has no bondage. That is why it is called unattached, and egoless. Now, the meditation, the meditator, and the object of meditation are all gone. If the meditator is not in existence, who is there to be meditated upon? When one knows this, he has no karmic bondage.

Action is the activity of Illusion and it belongs to the individual, the jiva. It is the jiva's concern to think, "I will get benefit out of this action," or "I will get some auspicious things." Good and bad are all part of the Illusion. For a man of Self-Knowledge there is neither good nor bad. Who will do the work when no benefit is desired? Action is meant for getting some benefit. Who is the entity that receives the benefit? That which was the jiva has gone, and he has become Brahman. The customer has gone. The owner has remained. He is whole, total, complete. There is nothing wanting in him. As long as one is proud of one's actions, he must be considered to not be certain about the Self. He still has doubt. Knowledge with doubt is false. Since you are not certain that you are yourself God I have told you this. When all of the Illusion is basically false, what harm is there if there is a multitude of false things in it? When everything is false or untrue, where is the truth in it? And what is wrong in the Illusion, if the "I" is proved false? Both heaven and hell are false. It is all nothing but imagination.

Nothing can be equal to Self-conviction. When this Self-conviction is truly established, that is Paramatman. Self-conviction should not waver at all, it should be unmoved. That is the Almighty God. Unwavering conviction is God. By conviction, further conviction is developed, and finally tremendous power is achieved. Self-conviction should increase. If it is wavering it is of no use. While there is no steady Self-conviction a huge meteoric catastrophe is going on, which is our own imagination. Do not be deterred even if many such meteors fall. Whatever happens, let it happen. Always keep on strengthening your Self-conviction. Is trying to prove the unreal Illusion to be real, a vow of truth? By trying to do so, you build it up, and go astray from your own "True Nature" (Swaroopa). There must not be any intention to prove true, that which is not true. The conviction that you are the Self should be made stronger. The fall from the Self is the worst fall of all. It is necessary that you should have very strong conviction that you are the Self.

A great Brahmin once said, "Until the Sun accepts my offering, he will not set." The story goes like this: It was evening. A Brahman who was well versed in the Vedas and was a great ascetic, was asleep. As it was evening and his wife tried to awaken him saying, "The sun is about to set, the right time of performing sandhya (prayers) will be missed." He said, "Let me sleep for some more time. The sun will not set so long as I do not get up." This was his actual experience. The body is but our shadow. You should not be proud of the body. That is why a man who has realized Brahman has not one iota of respect for rituals. All rituals are performed because of fear. Only those who are afraid perform various rituals. Loss is the father and the mother of fear. The fear is that one will suffer a loss. If one is having no fear why should he perform any actions? Fear is the reason for all actions. One who is fearless has neither fear nor karma. The fearless man is beyond the body. He is formless.

Karma is born out of doubt. Doubt is the seed of karma. To be doubtless means to be seedless. If roasted rice is sown, it does not grow. Similarly, karma does not give any gain or loss to one who is wise. When the Self is realized as formless and bodiless, God is known to be formless. Such a Realized One, is himself formless. Formless is his town and formless is his house. He is his own food and maintenance. Everything is the Self. This is the achievement of Reality that is imperishable.

Evening, 20-10-35

88. Those Who Are Worthy of Spiritual Knowledge

What is the sign of the "Realization of Brahman"? The identity that "I was such and such a person" must totally disappear. Then, we are as we are, and not "somebody." Then, there is no sorrow. Sorrow is the fate of a man who is identified with the body. To one who has the sense of being somebody, there are surely desires and sorrow. When Brahman is realized you do not remember what you are. When this advice of Lord Krishna was heard by Uddhava his identification as "Uddhava" was gone and he was one with the Bliss of Reality. His speaking faculty was no more. As he realized himself, his "I" was dissolved. The identification with the body was gone. The sense that "I Am Everything" was also gone. There was neither "I," nor "you." The indescribable state appeared. There, who would answer the questions asked by Krishna? He himself became the questioner, and Krishna and Uddhava were merged. Fullness remained. Speech ended. When Krishna saw the condition of Uddhava he knew that Uddhava was completely merged in Brahman.

When the disciple becomes one with Brahman, the Guru is very joyful. Just as a mother is happy if her son becomes very rich, the "True Master," the Sadguru, is very happy when the disciple realizes Brahman. Only the Guru can know what a great happiness he feels when his disciple experiences Brahman. Lord Krishna is the "Completeness of Happiness." The highest joy for the Sadguru is that a disciple should enjoy the "Bliss of Brahman." Had this not been the case, the whole tradition in which Gurus give spiritual instruction to disciples might have not continued. If there is no understanding, how can there be any experience? With the disciple having the experience, the Sadguru is happy. He was happy with the fact that "My Uddhava has become doubtless." Although Uddhava had realized Brahman, Krishna told him, "Do not teach this to those who are not my devotees, those who are lazy and those who always blame the Guru. This Knowledge should not be given even in dream to those who like popularity, who are attached to worldly activities, or who have no faith in the Vedas, Scriptures (Shastras), and the Guru. Even the wasted particles of the husk of this Knowledge should not be allowed to be seen by heretics. Giving them the grain is out of question. Non-devotees should not be allowed to touch this Knowledge, because it only increases their evil thoughts and evil deeds. Those who outwardly show that they are good but have no respect in their heart are called rogues. This Knowledge should not be given to one who hates the Guru by deed, speech, or thought, nor to one who is proud of his own family, or one who boasts of his own cleverness. This Knowledge should not be given to one who does not serve the Guru, nor to one who is ready to give money but does not do anything as service to the Guru. Nor should it given to one who has pride about his fame and tries to enhance his own snobbishness.

Some people consider it undesirable to do ordinary small jobs for the Guru and think that to be in the high mood of unity with Brahman is sufficient. Those who are deceivers of the Guru in humble service never gain anything although they may listen or read about this Knowledge of Brahman. One who does not do any service to the Guru and instead says that he will send some servant, or who promises money and gives false hope of some donation, should not be accepted as a disciple. One who says that he will get the Knowledge of Brahman by giving some fees should not be accepted as disciple. One who does not serve the Guru when such occasion arises, should be discarded. One who does not believe that he will attain freedom through devotion to the Guru, should not be given this teaching. One who does not believe that the Guru is the embodiment of Brahman, or is Brahman itself should not be taught. He will not understand it anyway. This teaching should not be given to non-devotees, nor to the one who disobeys the good advice given by the Guru. One who thinks that he is purer than the Guru, or more sacred than the Guru should not even be treated equal to a non-devotee. He is of a lesser level of inner life than a simple person who is not a devotee of the Guru. No Knowledge should be given to such people. One who has no love for me, Lord Krishna, who is giving this Knowledge, should not be taught this Knowledge. Those who have faith in the Guru have interest in the Knowledge of Brahman, but those who are arrogant should not be given this teaching. This should not be taught to one who abuses My devotees. My devotees are my very life, and one who blames them should not be given this Knowledge. Even the servant of My devotee is respectable.

One who abuses another person and then goes to see the Saints and bows before them, is not worthy to receive this Knowledge. After hearing this, you might say, "Then I will not find any worthy disciple." The disciple should be acutely desireless. That desirelessness should not be like that of a mad man. Such a man who abhors objects of senses for some four or five days, and then suddenly indulges headlong in sense-pleasures, is not the deserving person. Someone who loses his attitude of desirelessness starts finding faults with others because he becomes proud of his own knowledge, and even indulges in criticizing a respectable man. When intensity of one's desirelessness becomes less, the pride of knowledge increases. There are two states of mind in this world. One is desirelessness, and other is attachment to objects. When there is no thoughtfulness, there is no freedom from desires, and where the desirelessness is diminished, the lust for pleasures increases. One must be extremely aloof from material desires so long as one has not attained the Knowledge of Brahman. One who is such an ascetic is fully worthy of the teaching. Simple believers and faithful souls have many good virtues. One who is detached in mind has no cause for competing with anyone. He is really the King among yogis.

Evening, 23-10-35

89. The Superiority of the Path of Devotion

There are two states of mind in this world. One is desirelessness and the other is attachment to the objects of the senses. Attachment implies giving more value, or having more of a liking for sense objects, than in the spiritual life. The one who places greater value on the spiritual life has no liking for sense objects. The desire is not there. One should choose whether to indulge in sensual pleasures or to follow the spiritual path. One who is keen upon spirituality makes any effort that is necessary to achieve his goal and becomes united with it. One's life can go in one of two directions, that of desirelessness, or that of attachment to sense objects. When you know the sense objects to be unreal, then naturally desirelessness increases. Where desire increases, the pride of the physical body and sense objects becomes more important. In this way, one becomes more deluded.

Sometimes one will even create hurdles in the path of Self-Realization by putting forward the argument, "Can anyone be free in one life time?" So saying, he teaches the same to others also. His desirelessness is gone and he falls. He turns away from the ascending path towards the downward path. However, the one who is fully averse to sense enjoyments is already fully surrendered to the Guru. He remains faithful. He is a gem of a man, worthy of receiving Spiritual Knowledge and Authority. The desireless man becomes completely one with his goal.

Many disqualifications were described yesterday. One who is free of them is a worthy disciple.

The mind has a tendency to be attracted to things that it likes and that are similar to it. This is why a man launches friendship with people of similar nature. The actor likes actors, the rogue likes another rouge, and the Saint likes another Saint. He has friendship with them. Those who are knowledgeable and spiritually enlightened are the only real Brahmins, the "Knowers of Brahman." They have love for each other. One who has surrendered himself to the Guru looks with equality at all beings knowing that they are essentially Brahman. For such a person devotion and the state of having no desire for sense objects are joined. Devotion means love. Desirelessness means he does not want anything. In short, one who is straight minded finds everything simple and straight, and the one who is crooked, finds everything crooked.

The Guru will love the disciple, but as long as the disciple is not wholeheartedly faithful he will not realize Brahman. Only one who is of a loving nature and devotional attains that Knowledge. One who gives more value to money, wife, and children than doing service to the Guru, does not find freedom quickly. One who thinks that his home and wife are but transient and false is practically as good as liberated. The Guru, "Lord Krishna," is the fruit that he gets. He is truly great who thinks it an honor to be called the servant of the Guru, who does all sorts of odd jobs. One who does not give so much regard to the gods like the creator (Brahma), as he gives it to his Guru is the truly great disciple. The disciple is also really the Saint. The "Knowledge of Brahman" is gained only by such a devotee who ardently aspires to it, leaving all worry of what people will think of him and never fearing public opinion. Those who are discarded by the Vedas, who do not follow the edicts of devotion given in Vedas, are not worthy disciples. There are really the low caste people. Yet, those who aspire to be free of birth and death and go to learn at the feet of the Guru, attain the Knowledge of Brahman.

The strong desire for the Knowledge of Brahman is in itself another name for desirelessness. Those with this strong desire attain the quality of desirelessness. One may belong to any caste, even a lowly caste, but if he is faithful in following the teaching given by the Guru as the only way, and studies accordingly, he should be given spiritual instruction. Those having an eye for earning money and who teach only the upper class people should not be considered as Gurus. They do not have such a status at all, and the teaching given by them is fruitless. However, those who might teach even the lowly stationed people, only with the desire to emancipate them, should not be considered blameworthy. It is said that women should not be given spiritual teaching because normally their interest is not toward ascetic life, but see those great Saints who have given such high teaching to women! The sage Kaplila gave this Knowledge to his mother Devahooti. Lord Shankar (Shiva) gave this Knowledge to Paravati. Narada gave this teaching to the mother of Pralhad, and Lord Krishna gave this teaching to the wives of Brahmins who were doing Yadnya rituals near Vrindavan. Only those great Gurus who have such a state of mind which sees only Brahman everywhere, and to whom all are equal including women and children, and who sees Paramatman pervading all beings alike may give this teaching to women.

These instructions may be given to such women who have no desires for mundane sense objects, whose faith is increased, who have great interest in gaining Spiritual Knowledge, and who are keen on devotion to God. The desire for this Knowledge should be important. One may belong to any caste or may be a man or woman. This teaching should be given where real thirst for Spiritual Knowledge is found. If the teacher is lacking, what will be the plight of the one who receives his teaching? The teaching should not be given to an unworthy person. If the teacher has doubt as to whether teaching should be given or not, he should not give the teaching. Doubt is a fault. Fault is with you and non-fault is also with you. Only where there is no "objective thing" is everything faultless. As there is no matter, there is no shape, and as there is no shape or form, there are no good or bad qualities, and because there are no qualities, there is no scope for any fault. The Reality has no fault or even a blemish. It has no relationship with the doubt as to what should be done or what should not be done. As long as the teacher's doubts about the properness or rightness of giving advice are not gone he should not give advice.

The question as to whether the realized sage should teach others or not, is a foolish question. Unless one is completely blind about the Self and Reality one would not ask this question. The problems of sinners and the ignorant are never solved and will never be solved. Those who are unworthy do not put into practice the Knowledge imparted to them. When there is understanding, the purpose of this Knowledge is over and the Knowledge itself disappears. When the worldly life is totally dropped, why bother about whether something is proper or not? For the "Liberated One," there is no duty as such remaining to be done. There is no question of blame or no blame. Uddhava asked, "When there are various paths to achieve the four aims, Religion, Financial and other achievements, Fulfillment of Desires, and Liberation (Dharma, Artha, Kama, and Moksha), why do you advise only one path?" Upon hearing this, the Lord said, "The path of flight for a bird depends upon where he flies. Similarly, Knowledge is the only way to snap the chain of births and deaths." There are four traditional methods of approach to conquer the individual. They are to appeal to reason, makes some kind of sacrifice, physical punishment, and the cessation of all relationships (Sama, Dana, Danda, and Bheda).

For those who are not on the devotional path, there are various paths of yoga, and rituals. These are activities that are done with the desire to attain worldly position, power, better conditions, higher entitlement, desire to rise higher step by step, and to surpass others. These activities are full of ego and greed and are associated with the pride of having achieved certain goals, and the desire to achieve further goals. All of this is rooted in the false ego sense. By merely achieving all of these goals real peace is never gained and will never be fully attained, as the ego does not drop its fervor, its wanton nature. Being prideful, one tries hard to attain many illusory achievements which are not actually real. This is the very nature of the root of Illusion. One who recognizes this is the highest man who has no need for these imagined achievements. A man of wisdom has no need for the previously mentioned four aims. In other paths of seeking, many faults are rampant and the result is spoiled. Only through devotion to Me, are all four of life's aims, the Purusharthas, automatically realized.

24-10-1935

90. Brahman Is Reality

"I fulfill all the desires of those who take total refuge in me. The four goals (religion, financial achievements, fulfillment of desires, and liberation) are such that tremendous efforts are necessary to attain them, but still they are not attained. Even a shadow of liberation cannot be seen. Liberation is the conviction in saying that "I have gone beyond all karma, I have no need of anything. I have complete peace in myself." However, My devotees, those who have the understanding that they are Brahman themselves gain all of the four goals, and the hosts of gods come to obey them. The hosts of gods are in a way the highest virtue and good qualities of human beings which are imbibed with the spiritual powers in them. They are themselves the embodiments of gods. This is achieved only by one who surrenders to Me.

One surrenders to that which he likes. Some are slaves to worldly life, and some come to Me. "I am the fulfillment of desire, the liberation, the money, in fact everything, to those who surrender themselves to Me. Those who are not My devotees have attachment to pleasures and sense objects, and get rebirth. However, for My devotees, I give them liberation even though they enjoy the things in the world. I give My devotee whatever is his wish and also free him from bondage. Dear Uddhava, all of the four aims of your life are not separate. I am all of those for you." So saying Krishna forgot his identify as Krishna, and Uddhava forgot that he was Uddhava. It was quite a different kind of embrace. Both became Chaitanya, the Life-Energy itself, and the objective in their mind, to teach and to learn disappeared. God and the devotee became One. The sense of duality as the teacher and disciple was gone and all sense of duties and performance of actions were lost. The sense of both separateness and non-separation were gone. Understanding has gone upon gaining conviction.

It is Illusion to feel that "I have become Brahman, Paramatman." When was there such a time when you were not Parabrahman? So why do you say, "Now I remain in That state?" It is not a new state achieved by you. The fact is that you are already Brahman. You may say, "By your teaching the Illusion is gone, but how to remain in the state of Brahman?" You cannot cleverly think of some measures to be taken in order to remain or continue in That state. You are naturally "That." You have nothing to do to be constantly there. There is no becoming, or not becoming. "It" is to be as you are. There is neither becoming nor non-becoming. What is there to become? How are you to become? There is no becoming Truth. If you become, then it is not true. Therefore, it is not that you have to become Brahman, it is already so. When the state of the Self was already with us, some delusion affected us. What "happened" was only Illusion and even if anything does happen or you experience that you became something, it is only Illusion. If there is a certain notion that you have direct "Realization of Brahman," it is only the delusion of a confused mind. This confusion is only the enhancement of the Illusion that is already there. It is the spectacle, the festival of Illusion. Every so-called "Realization of Brahman" is Illusion. Brahman does not come into existence and does not end. It is always as it is, in its Pristine Being. It is

"That" which is not possible to be experienced separately, and it cannot be avoided. It is always in the present, as Reality.

Having left all other efforts, the one who surrenders to Me without any desire for anything has what is called "total surrender." The one who is undivided in his faith, has what is called "undivided devotion." Only such a one is the faithful devotee. I give him unity with Me. I fulfill all of his four aims, of religion, money, desire, and liberation. That "liberation" is not relative freedom, but total freedom. Such a one is a non-doer although he may be performing his ordained duties in the social structure. I make him desireless in this way. I give him such understanding from the inside, and I give him my six-fold riches. All of the "Four Kinds of Liberation" are at his feet. One who knows that he is the Self has planted the "Tree of Freedom" in his courtyard. Lucky is he who plants such a tree.

Lord Krishna fulfills the desires of his devotee and gives them the state of "Selfhood." Lord Krishna says, "One who leaves all efforts aside and surrenders himself to Me, is given all that he aspires for, and I liberate him." The day a man takes refuge at the feet of the Guru, that is the day that his downward fall stops. I cannot tolerate even a little suffering of My devotee. Therefore, I give myself over to him completely. I am the protector of My devotee. His suffering is tantamount to My suffering. He is not separate from Me. Let My devotee look at any person with blissful thoughts, and I emancipate that person as well. How can My own devotee suffer any fall? I cannot tolerate even the words that "My devotee has suffered." As I am his protector, I see that he has no wants. He never fails to see Me, in "My Own State." Whatever may be the state of My devotee, I emancipate him. Those who are devoted to me by leaving aside the objects of pleasure of the body, speech, and mind in the material world are well cared for by Me. What does it mean to leave aside the body, the speech, and the mind? It means that even if nothing good or pleasing happens to the mind, the devotee has only one desire. And, that if all of the things that are happening are opposite to his liking, his faith in the Almighty is not disturbed. I consider only one such as this to have given up his body, speech, and mind to Me. Such is the greatness of "undivided devotion."

24-10-35

91. The Greatness of Dasbodh

The word "Shri" denotes riches and plenty. It precedes all. The one who desires to regain their original grandeur receives the blessings of the Goddess Saraswati. Saraswati means intellect, the intellect of the Self. One who gets this "intelligence" is one whom Saraswati is pleased with. However, for this the Guru is necessary. One who desires to have the blessings of Saraswati should go to a "True Guru" (Sadguru) and serve him. When the Guru's blessings are received, Saraswati dances on the tip of the tongue. Such are the blessings of the Sadguru. All of this is the prayer and praise of Ganapati and is itself the form of Ganapati, his "Real Being." It is both with a beginning and without a beginning. Knowledge is not merely information. It is discretion also. Only one on whom the Sadguru's blessings are bestowed can speak on the subject of Self-Realization. Only the very lucky are able to receive this Power, by the "Grace of the Guru." These things may be taught by the Guruputras. Others have no authority or power to speak of them because these are things worthy of the "lion-hearted." Why is this so? It is because others are thinking that their identification with the body and this worldly life are all very real.

The identification of the "Son of a Guru" with the physical body and the bodily life are taken to be real by common standards, but spiritually speaking, they are unreal, which is a proven fact. That is why the individual, who is without the blessings of the Guru becomes depressed and dejected. Even with a minor loss, he will suffer. However, the Son of the Guru has already turned the body and all its activities to ashes, including its natural functioning and activity. He has no fear as to whether he will suffer a loss or get some benefit. He has burned everything that can be burnt with the "Fire of Wisdom" that he has received from the Guru, and he has become free and pure. Therefore, the power and the authority that the Son of the Guru has attained, and the power obtained by ordinary people are not same. That is how a real Saint is different from the rascal who deceives others. It is not possible to give out anything without the express order given by the Sadguru. Rats have no power to tell tall stories of lions, nor have they the capacity. To say that "I am the Self" is like the roaring of a lion.

There are secret things that are safely kept with the Sadguru. It is at the feet of the Guru that you can learn what true Knowledge (Jnana) and

Devotion (Bhakti) are. It is from the Sadguru that one can learn the way of devotion. Only by the Grace of the Guru, by the teaching that he gives, is it possible to know what the "Nine Types of Devotion" are, and how to practice them. The book Dasbodh was written with the sole purpose that devotees should realize God Almighty. In the dialogue of the Guru and disciple, the most essential teaching is given there. Dasbodh gives us the knowledge of what we are, and what our real nature is. It explains the state of detachment, and who the only real God is. It tells what the Jiva, or the individual is, and what Shiva, or God, is. It shows the way to Brahman, and finally to one's own "True Nature" (Swaroopa). The book also contains instructions on how a fool can become wise, as well as tells the nature of Illusion and how it arises. The original beginning of Maya is told there, and it is explained that Maya is our imagination. All doubts on the path are cleared in that great book. If you really wish to know what is taught there in that book, it is better to go through the text yourself.

The word "Dashak" (Chapter) is the name of the larger chapters in the book. There are twenty Dashakas in Dasbodh, and each of them contains ten sub-chapters, which are called "Samasas" (Sub-chapters). The word Dashaka indicates the ten sense organs and organs of action. In the Marathi language, we can twist the word Dashaka to "Dahashat" which means fear. "Dhasti" means fear or "Daha-Asti" which means a very hot sensation that is felt because of this worldly life. That fear, that heat, should go. One must drop it. Ignorance should go. We should throw it off. That is called Dashaka. The preface, or preamble, is called Upoddhat, which means, "To create some interest to know what is given." It creates the intention to know. It is said in Dasbodh that the Dashakas are broken into sub-chapters (Samas) in order to explain the "Path of Freedom." Self-Realization is taught in this book. The things described there can easily be tested and verified in one's life. It is said that one who out of jealousy and a warped view says that there is no truth in this book is like a man who says that he has no nose even though he does. One who says that the book contains foolish statements is like a man who calls his forefathers fools. One's forefathers are great beings such as Brahma, Vishnu, Shiva, Guru Dattatreya, Lord Krishna, Shri Rama, and all the Saints who have appeared in this world up to now. As they were born in the past, they are called ancestors or forefathers. Those who were born in the past have now reappeared. It is not that some new Saints have come. Those who were already existing are continuously existing. We have to search that "Original Existence," the origin of all things. We have to see "That" again. As they are from the past, they are called our ancestors.

Dasbodh contains the Knowledge told in all the Gitas (Great spiritual texts; Gita means song) like the Bhagvadgita, Hansgita, Shivagita, etc. These are the words of God himself. One who says that what is contained in Dasbodh is false, is already doomed, a fallen person. The God who prevails in the world in the form of wisdom is Ganapati, the Supreme Self, Paramatman. The one who has this wisdom is called Bodha, which is Consciousness. This is Knowledge, or "understanding." One who realizes that he himself is "That," has already finished with all bondage in one sweep. All of the spiritual powers come to him simultaneously. "Dasbodh" is such a great book that it is called the "King of Spiritual Books" (Grantha Raja).

Morning, 25-10-35

92. The Company of the Saint

What has happened out of Ignorance is gone. Now, since there is understanding, you should gain benefit from it. When you are aware of what is right, you should seek the company of the Saint. You should serve him and gradually learn the wisdom that he has. You should learn from the Saint his purpose in life and his enlightenment. You should do good things for the Saint, and you should come to know his way of thinking. Meet him frequently, ask your questions, and clear away your doubts. You should take all necessary troubles for this. Use discretion in your own life as he does, and if at all you yearn for company, you should seek the company of the Saint and work as hard as he works.

There are two important things gained in the company of the Saint. They are the description of the Self, and the surrendering of one's self. The description of the Self is to come to know what the nature of the Self is. Surrendering one's self means to behave as the Saints behave, to speak as the Saints speak, and to conduct your life as the Saints do. Listen to the words of wisdom and put into practice what you have grasped. Know what his strategies are. You should learn as he teaches and understand his nature, which means that you understand your own nature. Learn about his inner thought and his logic. Learn his speech and his objectives, his shrewdness, and his way of telling things. Learn his words, their sweetness, kindness, and the various nuances of the words he chooses. Learn how charitable the Saints are, and follow their example. You should learn how the Saint utilizes his time, and learn about true renunciation. Learn about how to meditate, how he is unattached to anything, and how he is beyond body-consciousness.

The Inner-Self is "the knower." Nobody can see the limit of his capacities. Dialogue with one's Self should be constant. This will bring about tremendous Joy. The more thoughtful that one is, the more content he will be. The Almighty Supreme Self, Paramatman, creates the whole world, yet He is not visible. He can be known by thinking deeply and by being compassionate. He meets you through constant meditation. You get something only when you become very determined about it. One who removes worldly thoughts and thinks only about the Self with strong determination will realize and attain That state. By constant contact only with the false, you get only the false. One sees or feels only that which the mind is always thinking about. Therefore, you should always think about God, and talk only about Him. The one who is determined about realizing Him is the true devotee. If determination is not there, one is not a true devotee. The pinnacle of all worship is when God is the devotee and the devotee is God.

This human life is very valuable and rare to have, so do not waste it. Get the best out of it. For the one who does not do so, it is as if they were committing suicide, as if they are throwing away their life. Do not waste the human body and human life that are so rare to gain. When death comes, you will not be able to breathe even one more breath. Do not waste your breath. It is helpful to you. Do not waste your time in useless loose talk. Devote yourself and surrender yourself in this way. Think deeply and patiently, and behave with great discretion. One who does not think properly wastes his life and destroys himself by thoughtlessness. Many have perished through evil company. They have taken a fall. By frivolous foolishness the blow of destruction fell, and that man was destroyed. What can we say about one who does not benefit himself by this human incarnation? One who does not know the importance of anything, whose mind is not interested in Self-study, and who does not study, is a foolish person indeed. He is one who blames others, and has no consistency in his speech and thought. He has no good future in the hereafter. You should concentrate your mind with all effort, and do spiritual practice (sadhana), forcing yourself if need be. Ask the Saint where you are mistaken. Drop all vices, and develop virtues.

It is through the test of actual life that one learns and becomes wise. You should speak with careful discretion. It is no good saying whatever you feel without cautious discrimination. Your whole life is wasted if you spend it only in talking about worldly things. Think well about how you want to use your life. Really, nobody is essentially evil. All enmity is due to "mis-understanding." All quarrel is nothing but misunderstanding. It is best not to talk about anybody. If you talk at all, get your doubts and misunderstanding cleared. You are endowed with speech, mind, and intellect, so use discretion in your speech. Be very careful about what you say about others. Your tongue is like a spade! You should not hit anybody with it. Remove all your bias, and all distortion from your mind. Only then will you be free. As one makes the effort, one gets the result accordingly. The fruit of effort is certain. Upasana is effort, or the constant practice of any action, the holding in mind a certain goal. The result is of the same nature as the effort. Recognize what correct effort is. In whatever way that you think about others, you will get the result accordingly. Never think evil things about others.

The knowledge of a musical combination of tunes, a Raga, is like what is in your mind. Knowledge of the beat is your actual behavior. To come to the frequent placement of your singing is the Dhrupad, and is equal to constantly coming back to your original intention. When that is achieved, the seeker enjoys the fulfillment of Bliss. You should realize the unworldliness of your Self. Be aware of it by "Self-observation."

Evening, 25-10-35

93. Parabrahman is Non-Perceptible

Parabrahman is not perceptible by the senses, but it exists. "That" which is not perceptible, is Parabrahman. That is Real which exists, but is not visible. If one says that it does not exist, even that person who says so is himself only Parabrahman. If there is a form, its body or shape is knowable, and it can be known, perceived, and understood. However, the shape or form of the Self, which is He himself, has no shape or form at all, and is not perceptible. One ends the enquiry by saying that it is unknowable, but it is always one with you. The tragedy is that you do not admit to its existence, and that it exists as your own Self. The understanding that "I am the understanding, I am Shiva, I am Shiva"

(Shivoham, Shivoham) is perceived by the eye of the "inner-vision of understanding," which is Shiva. Understanding is perception. The Earth is giving support to all creatures. It is called the ground or "Bhoomi." Just as all things appearing to our senses are on the ground and of this earth, likewise, everything that is visible is perceived on the invisible existence of Parabrahman. It is because of "That," that everything begins and ends. We cannot go anywhere else outside of it. There is no leaving That. Everything ends, it all gets destroyed, however That which does not end, remains, and what remains is "That." It is the same in every situation.

That which is indescribable, unimaginable, and which cannot be grasped by logic and conjecture is "That." It does exist. If anyone will try to say "It is like this," or "It is like that," his statements are false. It is not possible to talk about "That." Let anyone put a proposition about it in any manner, yet it is not caught in that proposition. So, whatever one may say, even though he may be full of wisdom, "That" cannot be described. Therefore, you should approach this problem very subtly, with determination. You have to nullify the belief in the reality of the bodily existence, and the seeming reality of the apparent existence of the universe. Only then will you understand "That."

Brahman is said to be "all-pervading," but when the "All," is not real, how can Brahman be pervading it? What we see is not real, so how can Brahman permeate it? In deep sleep, there is nothing that is perceived, or permeated. When you are awake and you are present, what you see is the seen, the form. Form is what is seen. To say that it is seen, is to say that it is known, or perceived. Only then is it said that, "I see it." However, whatever is seen is really seen by the sense organs, and the sense organs are known by the intellect, as well as by Knowledge. Now, please pay careful attention. Who sees the Knowledge? The state of "knowing," the "Knowledge," is itself seen, but That which sees it cannot be described. The "seer" cannot be described, yet, reference is being made to it. So, "to see," means "to know," "to perceive," and that which is so perceived, is perceived by, and permeated by, Brahman. Only that which is so permeated, is known or perceived. So long as that which is known is in the state of being seen, it is permeated. However, when the apparent thing disappears, what is there to be permeated? To be permeated by Brahman is only to be seen, or known. When "knowing" ends, there is nothing left to be permeated.

The milk and cream are together in milk. When the cream is separated, it appears separate to our senses. It is the important ingredient of milk. It becomes separate if we separate it, otherwise it is one with the milk. The empty expanse, and the quality of permeating are false terms. The One who remains after the imagination disappears, is the Self. He is not within the realm of imagination. When the concepts, imagination, capacity to move, the movement, understanding, consciousness, etc. are seen, only then do we become aware of the male and female (Purusha and Prakriti) principles. Inherent in this, are the three Gunas, the five elements, the states of consciousness, and various circumstances and numerous properties of matter. "That" which is aware of all this is called "The Nature of Existence, The Main Goal, The Power Beyond, The Power of Knowing, The Glimpse of Totality, Cosmic Being, The Glimpse of the Immensity of Brahman, The Primordial God," etc., etc... That understanding which comes out of this name and form is the simple and the most natural experience of "Being" which the "Primordial Beingness," Purashottama, itself feels, yet, it is a kind of direct perception which imagination cannot grasp.

The purest and simplest spiritual effort is listening (Shravana), then comes "thinking" (Manana) which is superior to it. When there is no "knower," either as a being, or as the quality of understanding, the mind is merged into its higher state. Where the state of effort or sadhana ends, there is "Spiritual Knowledge," or Vijnana. One's life is fulfilled when spiritual effort is culminated in the "Final Achievement." That which is beyond the qualities (Gunas) is permanent, non-moving, not disturbed by anything. It cannot be destroyed, it is the most impenetrable solid, it is never-ending, and never disappearing. You are That. This understanding ensures that "That" never ends. Then the problem of Illusion is solved, as it is not seen at all. Gone is the Illusion. For example in the dream a man sees that he is married and has a wife and children, but when he is awakened, where are they? Where will he search for them? Where will they meet him? When the man is awake, the dream is proved false. The perception of other things, was happening due to Ignorance, and that Ignorance was the dream. The dream was that Ignorance, and that was the worldly life. The vast sky was being seen, and the vast earth was there, and many men were living on the face of that earth and they appeared to be happy. Many families were living happily, and my own little family was among them. However, that family, a small dot, was not there from the perspective of Consciousness, or Awareness. All of that scenery was shown by Ignorance. The family is generally not understood in its "Reality" by anybody. The one who knows the Reality is very rare, as the "knower" is Paramatman. "Knowing" the Reality, you are awakened. The dream is over. What does this mean? What is awakening?

It means that there is now the "Knowledge of Reality." Awakening is Knowledge, and Knowledge means you are awakened.

To experience worldly life is itself the experiencing of Ignorance. The man may be enjoying a very happy luxurious life, but he is merged in Ignorance. On the other hand, he may be leading a life full of troubles, and hard work, but then also, what he enjoys is Ignorance. The worldly life may be of any grade. It is only Ignorance that one is enjoying. Ignorance has itself appeared. What is evident is Ignorance. Then, there comes a change. Knowledge appears, and with that, awakening comes. The man awakens and says, "Oh what a worldly life it was. Now all of that is proved false." When one awakens, he still sees, but all is indescribable, unutterable. This is to be softly and subtly felt by discrimination (Viveka; the discrimination between the Real and the unreal). The experience of awakening must recognize its own signs, its own nature. The book "Dasbodh" was completed by "The Word of the Self." The one who meditates on Paramatman, knows this "Book of Life."

Sakal, 26-10-35

94. The Importance of the Grace of the Guru

Having heard about the greatness of the "Path of Devotion" from Lord Krishna, Uddhava was very happy. His separate identity as Uddhava was gone. Uddhava was truly blessed. The Sage Shuka, a veritable "Sea of Bliss," said to the King Parikshit, "You are lucky to get this Knowledge by listening. Listening itself is a great good luck. Now you are aware of God Almighty. There are very few who get the good opportunity to listen to this." When King Parikshit came to know about his unavoidable death, he found out the way to Total Freedom. Blessed is the King Parikshit, who obtained the most valuable gem, which is Liberation.

There is a story of a King, in the book "Vicharasagar," that relates to this. Nothing can equal the "Joy" of Spiritual Life. The Eight-fold Manifestation (sky, wind, fire, water, earth, mind, intellect, thinking, and the sense of "I") are the eight ministers of this King. The King should not act according to their dictates. They only give wrong advice. One whose fame is described by Yogis continuously, and the very dust particles of whose feet are worshipped by all the hosts of gods, has

Himself promised this devotion. That "Great Lord" has said that there is nothing more beneficial than devotion. It is called the "Yoga of Bhakti." The path of Bhakti Yoga is the path of Pure Love. When there are doubts in your mind about Pure Love, this path will not be understood. When Uddhava listened to these words, he was overwhelmed with the ecstasy of Love. His breathing became slow, his eyes became half-closed (they were neither completely open nor closed). Uddhava was on the verge of total annihilation, but Lord Krishna controlled his ecstasy. Uddhava said, "My life is fulfilled. I have got the very essence of all the spiritual riches." He began to think as to how he could repay the Lord for His benediction. I cannot repay the Guru by giving him wealth. If I think of giving my body to him, it is only perishable. By giving the perishable body, and in turn obtaining God, how can one possibly be able to repay what has been gained? If the individual is to be surrendered to the Guru, the individual is only conceptual. It is not a fact, it is false, and it is not possible to repay the Guru, even by surrendering the body, the speech, the mind, the money, and the life itself. As the disciple was not able to be thankful through all of these, he quietly prostrated before the Guru.

Uddhava placed on his own head the particles of earth below the feet of Lord Krishna and praised God in many ways saying, "You are the greatest of all the wise people who know Brahman. You are the support of the world, the guardian of the world, and the dissolver of the world. I was dumped in the dark night of Ignorance, and your nectar-like teaching destroyed my sorrow and desires, and saved me by lifting me out of the quagmire of the world. This was not possible without your power. How can the desires and ego trouble me now? The cold of Ignorance was dissipated by the Fire of Knowledge." When the "True Master," the Sadguru, and the disciple meet, the disciple experiences that all of his earthly desires are no more. Yet, when he goes home, the Illusion again confuses him. The Illusion is destroyed only in the case of a disciple who understands the teachings of the Guru. Only the pious disciples know this fact. These things will never be known to those whose vision is blinded by Illusion, and who have become arrogant about their achievements.

The significance of the company of Saints is known only by devotees who have Pure Love for God. Uddhava said, "Oh Lord, you have saved numberless devotees through your teaching which was seemingly meant for me. However, the teaching requires the faith of the listener. Only then can he pluck the auspicious fruit of the teaching. Therefore, the disciple should be intelligent. The greater the faith, the deeper the knowledge that a disciple gets. Faith is like a good lamp. The two wicks of this lamp are discrimination (between the Essential and unessential; Viveka) and desirelessness (Vairagya). By these two wicks, the flame of Knowledge is kindled. However, the ghost of hope (the desire for worldly happiness) extinguishes the lamp. The ghost of hope should not be allowed to come near. Only then does the great "Light of Chaitanya" dazzle the entire universe. The greatest devotee, Uddhava, had now become One with the Cosmos.

Evening, 26-6-35

95. Freedom and Devotion

There is no other useful way to Freedom, than to be in the "Company of Saints" (Santasangha) When one sees any form, any object, there arises some sentiment towards that form. Likewise, when you look at your mother and father, you have the appropriate emotion befitting that relation. However, when you see the Guru (to have his glimpse, or Darshan), the heart is overflowing with a feeling of reverence. In this way, Saintly Company is the greatest. With respect to the Saintly Company, being near the Sadguru is the most purifying. Illusion has no place near Him. Illusion does not remain in the proximity of the Sadguru. Most people live their lives in vain, and give importance to useless worldly benefits, only to become miserable and anxious. The individual foolishly gives importance to objective things, which are not important at all, and remains ensnared by Illusion. But when one is in the vicinity of the Sadguru such useless attraction automatically disappears.

Uddhava said to Lord Krishna; "You have given advice to dispel the darkness of the so-called knowledge of the poor ignorant people. The wick of the lamp of 'Real Knowledge' is kindled by the ghee of Discrimination (Viveka) and Desirelessness (Vairagya), while the adamant hope for sensual gratification is like a moth that tries to extinguish the lamp by jumping on the flame (trying to satisfy desires). When the devotee concentrates on your 'Divine Presence,' desire is destroyed. Only the Sadguru, who remains as 'Understanding' in the heart of the devotee, can attain unity with your 'Real Being.' Now I am convinced that you have bestowed upon me 'Total Identity with You.' As You are the innermost dweller of all, your form is already very naturally abiding in me always, but that form was veiled. By the Yoga of Devotion (Bhakti Yoga) that I followed, You are fully pleased with me. You have given me the inner wisdom to understand you, in your True Form. Now, that is my own Original Being. You have convinced me of this fact. The Saints and Sages call this miracle 'going back,' or the 'right return.' While doing this, You have enhanced the intensity of my devotion to you. You gave me that Knowledge which was already my own Self-Knowledge. Now the Illusion and doubts will never be able to cover me again. You are so benevolent, and especially gentle to your servants who have become wise, and have devoted themselves to singing your praises (Bhajans)."

Singing bhajans does not mean simply the beating of cymbals or playing of musical instruments. People say that those who are beating the cymbals and playing instruments repeatedly are devotional, however this "Bhajan," this devotional song, is not of that type. It is very deep. Whatever the worldly people constantly meditate upon, that is their devotion, their way of worship. Whatever dwells in the mind, is the object of one's worship. When one thinks about worldly objects, with the purpose of experiencing the joy derived from them, it is a kind of worship. The concentration on that object is their meditation. If there is obsession for any sense object, that obsession is a constant contemplation. Listening, contemplation, meditation, obsession, and the comfort felt in obtaining objects, is not the contentment of the Self or real "inner contentment." On the contrary, the desire for more sensual pleasures only increases, and the hunger for indulgence is not satisfied. Desire breeds desire, and as long as this is so, the Self will not get Self-satisfaction or contentment.

Therefore, "true worship" is the meditation and contemplation, or in other words, the constant preoccupation, with Self-satisfaction, which is called the inward urge. It is the feeling of anguish, or the emptiness that is raging inside the devotee when he feels that he is without this Self-satisfaction. There is no path of return from that state of longing. That is called a man who is longing for the experience of the "Inner Reality." When this urge is there, there is the certainty of the "Contentment of the Self with Itself." That contentment is called Inner Peace. When achieving this state of Inner Peace, one no longer suffers from the cravings for objective things. When those cravings no longer arise, the desires are fully quieted. This is the real nature of inner worship, and this is the way of it. Those who go astray from this essential worship and devote themselves to obtaining gratification from objective things, are simply wasting their human birth.

Uddhava said; "Oh Lord, Those who babble about useless things without worshipping you, are only two legged beasts in the human form. They are not only ordinary beasts, but asses of the first rank. Only the time utilized in worship of Lord Hari (Vishnu) is properly fulfilled. All other time is gulped up by Illusion, which the Illusion in turn uses to give one rebirth. Only that time which is spent in the cause of Self-Realization is truly worthwhile. All other time is gone, wasted. Even all of the effort that has been done to protect the body is also futile. However, that which has been done in devotion to Hari, is true merit. The human life is very valuable. If it is utilized for good deeds and devotion, it is worthwhile. Those who know the signs of God's blessings in their mind, speech, and in their physical body, are truly blessed. In this manner the bondage of worldly life has been cut away from me.

Previously, there was the attraction of wife and children, which only expanded the physical world entanglements. I have also had a notion that I am born in my family and was brought up in their midst, and I was thinking that they belonged to me. However, as soon as my mind was engrossed in meditation on your Being, I came to realize that all of these things are illusory. This attraction to Illusion makes it appear to be true and nobody else is there who can show the real nature of this phenomenon. You are the Power that expands this universe and you are the "Power of Knowledge" that withdraws all of this into yourself. You have removed the cover of attachment from my mind. I had a fondness for you from my childhood. Now, I will cut the bondage of all other people, with the "Sword of Knowledge" that you have given to me. I have now fulfilled my life, but there is a small wish. Please grant this to me very kindly. Only You are able to make possible what is impossible. You are also the Great Maya who weds together the living and the dead (Formless Consciousness and matter). You control that Maya who has deceived even Lord Shankar (Shiva) and the like. You have destroyed the three factors of the knower, knowing, and the known. Gone is the separation of 'I' and 'You,' the sense of separation of 'God and the devotee.' I have remained full of the Bliss of Self-Knowledge, but to say so in words again becomes part of Illusion. Now, all the four types of speech and the four Vedas are mute. All is the void, and the cause and effect are gone.

Now with that love which a mother has for her child, may you please do what I pray for? Now, this is my last request. I was having such great Illusion. Liberation, or the state of Jivanmukta is not a happy state, although you may say so. Therefore, give me 'Devotion to You.' I do not want Liberation, which is dry, and tasteless. Liberation is possible by the Blessing of the Sadguru, and it is necessary to have the understanding of Reality. But, please, give me 'Devotion to You.' Give me the worship of You, which is superior to the 'Sayujya Liberation.' In the past, you bestowed upon many only Liberation, but you did not give them this 'Devotion to You.' Actually, You have deceived them by giving them only Liberation. Please, with me, this deception won't do. May you please bless them with your devotion, those who have attained Real Knowledge. Those who neglect the 'Devotion to the Guru' and declare that they have attained Liberation are deluded. Please, give us the Devotion to the Guru. Do not tell me that Devotion to the Guru is not necessary. You are able to make possible that which is impossible, and make impossible that which is possible. You have given Liberation even to animals in the forest who eat only leaves, and you have given Liberation even to the cow-maids (Gopis) who became so sacred that even the creator Brahma worshipped them. The monkeys and others did not know that You are Paramatman. Unfathomable is the greatness of 'Your Devotion.' He who becomes One with You holds all of 'Your Glory.' Devotion contains within itself Liberation. By devotion, the Liberation becomes sanctified. Even if I will gain Liberation, I desire only to be Your devotee."

So speaking, Uddhava held the feet of Lord Krishna with all reverence. He would not let go. Then God blessed him. "When the state of the Totality of Brahman is attained, one thinks that devotion with its inherent duality is no longer needed. One should not suffer from the pride of having achieved any such state. When one says that when Liberation is attained devotion does not remain, this is the pride of Knowledge. Please, may you give me 'Devotion to You.' You may ask me, why are you requesting devotion, when I have given you Liberation, which is attainable only after millions of births?' and I will say that for me to be deprived of devotion to the Guru is the greatest hindrance. So, please give me that devotion which is beyond Liberation."

Evening, 27-10-35

96. Devotion After Liberation – Blessed is Uddhava

Uddhava said: "Oh Lord, Lord Krishna, I request that you keep my state of Liberation permanently, yet give me 'Devotion to You' without any selfish aim. There should not be any selfish objective, or motivation, yet devotion must be continued. You may say, 'I have given you Permanent Freedom, Total Liberation, so why do you still have the request for devotion?' To that I respond that I was already having Liberation. It is not true to say that you have given it. You have given me that which was already with me. So, do not make the claim of being the giver. If you give me 'Devotion to You' above the state of Liberation, then I shall call you the truly benevolent God. I request this 'Devotion to You,' but you do not seem to be interested in it. You are not so happy about it. Regarding this, your miserliness seems evident. If by being liberated as Jivanmukta, I am going to be deprived of devotion to the Guru, I do not want that Liberation of yours! Freedom is an Illusion. When there is no bondage, from where did you bring in this 'Freedom'? I do not want any type of Liberation, either permanent, or bodiless. You have deceived those to whom you have given it. Now, please give me Devotion to the Guru." So saying, Uddhava held reverently the Feet of Lord Krishna and very wisely requested for devotion to the Guru after Liberation. This gave great joy to Lord Krishna. He said, "My Uddhava, you have learned good things. You have requested rightly. You are truly blessed." Lord Krishna then gave Uddhava "Devotion to the Guru." Devotion beyond Liberation is the essence of Lord Krishna. The teaching of the Sadguru consists of the maxim that "The Guru and his devotee are indivisible."

"Devotion after Liberation" is the right gift for the deserving disciple. Devotees who came earlier only wanted Liberation, which was given to them, but Uddhava surpassed all of them. Uddhava requested for the impossible state and Lord Krishna gave it to him and then said that "Devotion after Liberation is my own power to incarnate." If one becomes lazy with the notion that he is liberated, that is wrong. Instead, the state of devotion where the disciple feels that all the things in the world are nothing but his Guru is higher. That is Brahman without any distinctions, which is the same as the Sadguru. Devotion after Liberation is itself the very status of Sadguru. To "become" something is a downfall. That is the function of the individual, the jiva. The sense of "I" is already there. But, in this state, the "I" is not there. To whom are you giving Liberation? If there is one owner and the second man is a servant, then one of the two can be given Liberation. Devotion after Liberation means that everything is only one single unity. This devotion is My "Power of Incarnating." I Myself take birth, and I do things to give happiness to people. That being who acts in this way is called the Avatar, or "Incarnation of God." He is called My incarnation, but he is independent. He is not somebody's incarnation. All things including the body are only Brahman, the One Almighty God. We call it as "God with qualities" (Saguna), meaning with form, but really there is nothing that can be said about him. He is not an incarnation of somebody else. The "Incarnation of God" is only God. With this understanding that one's Self is Brahman, one should remain naturally as one is. However, in this case, it is neither existence, nor non-existence. There is no "other." The duality of knowing and the knower, as well as the brilliance of the form, are only One.

No Date Given

97. Devotion and the Blessing of the Sadguru

Uddhava did a great feat and earned renown. He requested for "Devotion after Liberation." He asked for something that cannot be gained, and Lord Krishna gave it to him. Many sages have tried very hard to attain various states, from the "Knowledge of Brahman," to the "State of Liberation." By describing them as the only desirable states to live in, that meant that they were proud of those states. The pride that one is attached to does not dissolve, so therefore those sages, with their particular pride, remained separate from Brahman. You may look at their long hair and flowing beard and take them to be great ascetics, but this is not correct, so do not think like that. The "Knowledge of Brahman" (Brahmavidya) is neither old nor new. The Brahmavidya was not different for them from what it is today. Knowledge means to know, and "Yoga" means union, or to join. Whatever a man agrees with, he attains with relative ease.

The one who has understood the key, knows easily what Brahman is. One who has wisdom correctly recognizes God. Those sages who were undergoing particular practices such as exercises and postures of the various forms of Yoga (the Yogis), and those performing austerities such as vows of silence (the Munis) were attached mentally to their bodies. They valued the body, which is but an instrument. The Self and the body are separate, but those yogis became sidetracked because they became proud of the body. It so happened that Krishna respectfully worshipped those sages but asked them to leave and go into the forest, to build huts and live there. Thus, He himself enjoyed his "Aloneness." Krishna saw that the sages were taking up various rigorous ascetic practices like living only by breathing air, etc. and he told them to be devotees of Paramatman, which was He himself. Krishna told them that only He and Lord Mahadeva (Shiva), were "Knowers of the Truth," and that nobody else had attained "Complete Knowledge."

One who attains this "Devotion after Liberation" is of the high rank of an Incarnation of God. Krishna says, "This is My 'Power of Incarnation,' and it is by this Strength, this Power, this Principle, that I do everything, yet remain a non-doer. I enjoy all comforts or pleasures, yet remain unaffected, a non-enjoyer. I am the Creator, the Sustainer, and the Destroyer of this world, and yet remain unrelated to any of this activity. One who does not have any understanding of this Divine Yoga has only wasted his efforts and suffered in vain." Lord Krishna says, "This Yoga was not available in any books or in the Vedas, and only Myself, and Lord Mahadev know it. I hold this 'Yoga of Unhindered Continuity.' This yoga is never broken, never stopped, and therefore I am called Yogendra, or the King of Yogis."

This Yoga of "Devotion after Liberation" was secret and hidden, but I have revealed it today. This is the immortal blessing of the Sadguru. I am the same cowherd boy, and I am also the Yogendra of today. "Bodh Avatar" means that I have revealed this "Secret Knowledge of Divine Yoga." Those who only give importance to the ritualistic aspect of worship and merely perform ceremonies, do not reach up to the attainment of Supreme Knowledge (Vijnana). Brahmavidya, the "Knowledge of Brahman" is the most sacred, complete, indestructible, Highest Knowledge, that never ends. It is not only indestructible, it is never lessened. It is always complete, faultless, immovable, perpetually existing, dazzling, radiant Life. It does not need feeding. It is total happiness. It is the dearest relative, the highest Self that looks with equanimity upon all the beings in the visible and subtle worlds, and endears itself to them. In "It" there is no less or more intimacy for anyone. This means that it is equal for all. In "It" there is not anything such as more or less for anybody. To be always in a state of equilibrium is its very nature, its very quality. It is the nearest relative to all beings.

It is not possible for a person who is proud of his ritualistic activities to meditate upon the "Totality of Brahman," it's Reality, to get a glimpse of it, or to attain it. A person who performs rituals holds a concept in his mind. He holds a biased concept regarding a particular image of God with particular qualities, and he receives the fruit of his actions according to this concept. The form or image that is worshipped is formed in a subtle world. A form means that which is seen. In the seen, the main object is the cosmos or universal field, and in this field, the individual has a body as desired by him in order to have the enjoyments which are desired by him. He perceives all of this according to his strong desire. He has a fixed concept that he enjoys all of this world and accordingly gets the fruit of his practice. However, that form and those qualities which are the product of imagination, are bound to eventually disappear, and then the concern about gain and loss increases. Then again imagination, concepts, the strong desire which he calls "determination," and such repetitions by the individual who is attached to actions (karma), go on and on without end. He does not give up his attachment to passion, which gives but fleeting pleasure. If by giving up the pursuit of fulfilling of passions he would meditate on the Reality, he could easily gain the benefit of "Total Life." However, generally no individual is ready to give up attachment to desires. As one does not give up one's desire and habits, the pride of actions also cannot be dropped. As the pride of action does not drop away, the heavy results of shortness of life is also not dropped.

Alternatively, it is very different, as well as easy to have the complete fulfillment of one's life. If the one drops desire and habits, one becomes the owner of a complete, fulfilled life. Then one easily gets the experience that the play of Consciousness, or lack of it, is played out on the substratum of one's own Being. All types of pride can be let go of, but the pride for Knowledge is very difficult to be dropped. This spiritual science was kept well hidden. Now it will definitely spread because the same sages and seers have come again by taking birth, and as they will be coming, they are going to have this Knowledge. This Knowledge cannot be attained by many sacrifices in fire (Yadnyas). All of the sages have explained what this Knowledge is, but they themselves remained deprived of it. Only Lord Krishna bravely declared that he is God, and He actually lived like a God. The sages have no capacity to be so bold. Only Lord Krishna had the Real Knowledge that is without any doubt.

Shiva is the second who has this Knowledge. Lord Krishna told Uddhava that the knowledge of others is not comparable to His Knowledge. Uddhava was convinced about this, and therefore reached Complete Happiness. Lord Krishna gave Uddhava the status of "Incarnation." Because of this honor, all say that he is an incarnation. This is a kind of ornament. Lord Krishna gave that Knowledge to Uddhava that is not known by any man of spiritual science, or even by the one who wrote the Vedas. Uddhava requested and got the "Complete Power of Lord Krishna," the Power of Willful Incarnation.

I have imparted this "Knowledge of Brahman" to you that was secret up to now. One who will spread this will be the uplifter of the Vedas. Devotion to the Guru is the only tonic that gives this Knowledge. Faith in the Sadguru should be very deep. This Knowledge will be beneficial only to one who has complete trust and faith in the Sadguru. Even a lump of clay will be turned into gold if the Son of the Guru will hold it. One who will not serve the Guru, being proud of the body and proud of knowledge, will not get the benefit from this. Today on the auspicious day of Diwali, I have given you this "Power of Taking Incarnation," which is the devotion to the Guru. He who will take care of this Knowledge will be famous as an "Incarnation" in the world. Not only this, he will be honored as Lord Krishna, Paramatman, and people will get the experience of "That." Therefore, all of you should let go of your sense of ego, and have devotion to the Guru with one pointed attention. One who will abide by my teaching is given by me my "Power of Devotion to the Guru," as well as Myself, and my Power of Incarnation. Let this be fruitful in you by the Grace of Sadguru Bhausaheb, and by my blessing. Victory will be sung of him who will understand the nature of *this* Devotion and abide by the words of the Guru.

Evening, 28-10-35

98. The Nature of Avatar

How and what is the Power invested in an Avatar? Avatar means the "coming down," or "Incarnation of God," on earth. Who is called the "Incarnation of God"? Only God, who is already existent will take an incarnation. Who else can do so? The one who has fully realized

Brahman walks in his life in an unspecified transcendent state although he is physically living. Why should we not call him an "Incarnation"? He is surely an incarnation. To say "I am not the Self" is ignorance. You may not say so, but, He is what He is. The One who understands his own eternal nature, without doing anything to be in that state, is the self-evident Brahman. Whether eating, drinking, or enjoying objects, all is Brahman. This definite certainty itself is the Power of Incarnation. Incarnation, or God "coming down," is an idea conceived of by the mind. All of this is a matter of emotional concept. So long as there is a sense of something being amiss, or when some doubts still trouble the mind, there is the concept that there is something still wrong. One whose mind is not disturbed at all, no matter what may happen, is the one who is free from even the subtle body. One who does not feel shaken, even if any disaster may fall, is really Brahman. He has realized Brahman.

As long as there is a doer, he will surely do something. If there is no doer, who will act? Whatever is done should be examined by asking the following questions: When was it done? When did it happen? How did it come into being from before it was known, and from where did it come? What was "I," at that place from where action appeared? What was my name there? What was my form there? Were you in it, or did it happen in you? When the doer does act, you should know the shape, the form, etc. of the doer at the stage where the feeling of action or karma arises. The doer is not existing. How can that which is formless and qualityless, ever be affected by actions? He is beyond joy and sorrow. He is not concerned whether a particular means is necessary, or no means are necessary. You are He at any time. He is King at all times. One should become Shiva and then be a devotee of Shiva. To live as Shiva means to lead the "Life of Devotion after attaining Liberation." To live as God is called the Incarnation of God.

Devotion means "Unity." The name of the devotee may be any name. What is important is that he has become the Sacred Self, and is God, whatever his name may be. There are many that live in a conceptual state of being the Self, but really there should be no concepts of any kind. To attain Brahman, and to live in That state, are also wrong notions. There is no becoming Brahman. You are already Brahman. There is no question of becoming or not becoming. You should not make any statement. To be like that, without saying anything, to actually live, and behave like that, is called "Devotion beyond Liberation." When the appearance of the snake on the rope is gone, then the thought about the snake and the illusion of it is also gone. Gold cannot "become" gold.

Shambhu (Shiva) is, as He is. He has not become. Whatever He may be doing, He is Shambhu. While eating, sleeping, walking, He is Shambhu only, not more or less. To say that a "Sadhu" (a liberated wandering ascetic) should follow the law of the land, is the talk of ignorant people. There is no law or rule for a sadhu. It is only important what he feels about himself. There is no question of how he appears to others. He is what he is. He has removed all his clothes, and has also psychologically thrown off the cover that is his body. The outer garment, as well as the inward garment of conceptual identification, all cloth, all covers, are removed by him. There is no question of how he should behave in life. He is Brahman, He is Shambhu, He is Vishnu, He is All.

God has no law, rule, sin, or merit that is conceived of by human beings. The king makes his own law, and abides by it. Brahman is neither static nor moving. The sadhu is Brahman, and Brahman is not different from the sadhu. How can it have a state, movement, or bondage? When you have sold your ox, how can you use it again for your yoke? Sold is sold. How can it come back? Similarly, when the ego is gone, He who remains is only God. He is outside of all rules. What are rules to Him? He has no duties to perform. People may say anything, the sadhus never get disturbed. What are people? Human beings are called people, but the sadhu is not a man. He is God! One who is God, behaves like God, and is always in His Own Glory, wherever He may be. He who is God, is in His Own Power. The word Samartha means the "One who knows His Own Significance" in the highest sense. One behaves according to one's understanding of one's Self. The sadhu correctly knows his value, the significance of "His Own Life." He knows that he is of a particular nature, and actually is "That," and will be so at all times. He will never change, even at the end of the world. He has become "That" which is final. He is now complete. His state is fixed. It does not change or break.

As his state is unbreakable, his conviction about himself is fixed. The sadhu does not break. When correct understanding is there, he lives in His Own Power. He is not concerned with what people say about him. He is not affected. When an old man is eating with difficulty because he has no teeth, people laugh, but he being old, is as he is, how can he become young? The old man will act as he is. Similarly, when a sadhu is Brahman, he will act as Brahman. He will function with all of the "Power of Brahman." The rules of this world are not applicable to Him. One, who being a sadhu, thinks about what is "right behavior," is not a realized sadhu, he is not Brahman. One who is "Free" is Brahman, and what that

Brahman is, naturally functions, as it is. That sadhu and Brahman are One.

Evening, 29-10-35

99. The Fearless State

God says, "Devotion after liberation is 'My Power of taking Divine Incarnation.'" Devotion after liberation is the 'Power of Brahman.' The 'Power of Brahman' and Devotion are not two things. When there is realization of one's Self as Brahman, the state of being an individual, or Jiva, vanishes. Paramatman is the only Existence. To remain in the state of Paramatman is this 'Devotion after Liberation.' The Jiva is full of fear. It is afraid. However, God, Shiva, does not fear anything. Be fearless. The tiger and the mouse do not think alike. The mouse is afraid because when he is confronted by anybody it means death to him, but the tiger is always on the hunt for any animal. Whatever confronts the tiger is potentially the tiger's meal. Only the one who is not afraid of any being is the "Man of Knowledge," the Jnani. He does not have fear of anything. Fear is only a psychological thing. When a man is asleep, he does not feel fear even if a snake were to go across his body. However, if he were to see a snake from afar while he is awake, he feels fear. Fear is the mind. When you are all things, what are you afraid of? The greatest fear is about sin and merit. Because that fear is about God. But when you yourself are God, what is the cause for fear? As soon as you were born, fear came into existence. You were ignorant when you were in the womb, and then when you saw the world you were afraid, and that fear has remained. The child is given honey and milk to pacify it, but the fear persists. It does not disappear. It is only dispelled by the teaching given by the Sadguru. Knowledge is given to make you understand, to give you the correct illumination. Thus, Knowledge makes you fearless. Pralhad prayed to God to make him free of fear. Self-Knowledge is "fearlessness."

A man may be very rich, but if he is one hour late to get up in the morning, he is afraid, with a feeling that, "Today I am late. There will be some monetary loss." Everyone is afraid in this manner. When going to sleep, he tells his wife to waken him early. Why is he afraid? He is afraid because he fears that his daily work will not be done. Some wake up of their own accord. They wind their inner clock, and are awakened by their own awareness. This fear is all pervading. You are afraid while dining and you are afraid while working, and because of fear there is a lot of confusion. Fear itself is the cause of the confusion. Be fearless. Sleep happily, eat happily, do everything happily and peacefully. Do not be worried about what will happen in the future. Do not be anxious in vain. Be quiet and peaceful. It is not easy to be adaptable and peaceful, but try to be at peace with yourself. The mind gets confused and disturbed, but what is the trouble? When you ask it why it is afraid, it becomes silent. When you ask it "What are you doing?" it remains quiet. Nobody can answer or explain what all the agitation or worry is about. Sometimes, when a visitor is asked what the purpose of his coming here is, he replies, "Nothing in particular. I have just casually dropped in." This is the habit of replying, but this is not a true reply. After some time, he opens his mind, tells his need, and expresses his anxiety.

The tiger always roars, which indicates that he is not afraid of anybody. He is always fearless. To be unafraid is Liberation and to enjoy that state is Devotion. Fearlessness means not being afraid of anybody or anything. That is the real state of "godhood," in which you always live. You always live in the state of Paramatman. This is called "Devotion after Liberation." This means to live in our own Glory. Those who are real incarnations of God know *this* Devotion, and they are devoted to God after attaining Freedom. How can those who call themselves liberated and yet are still afraid of some physical injury or consequences of ordinary worldly affairs be "liberated" in the true sense? One who is "Free," must really be Free. One who is free should never think that there is purity if he performs certain rituals and impurity if he does not perform such things. Once there is Self-Realization and you become liberated while living, the state of living in that "Glory of God" afterwards, is itself the "Devotion after Liberation." That is the "Power of taking Divine Incarnation" which is called Avatar. You should live as God. God has no fear. If you feel fear, then you are the jiva and there is some misunderstanding remaining.

Desires and emotions are the cause of the results from which you suffer. If one still behaves in the same manner as before after the attainment of Self-Realization, what is the use of that "knowledge"? One who acts according to his understanding is the truly illumined one. He is God. Lord Krishna says, "I have become God of all beings because of their concept of creation, existence and destruction." God creates hundreds of worlds and destroys them, but does he commit any sin or earn merit because of that? Who will punish him? There is no other. Then who is there that will make him afraid? He is beyond all concepts.

He is formless, invisible, and at the same time, He is everything. Nothing is existing anywhere without Him. You are here because of Him. Without Him, you would not exist. "I am the entire universe. I enjoy all, I eat all, I destroy all. I am my own playfulness." If you lick your own tongue, it is not contaminated, yet we consider the spit of others dirty for us. The One who has all of the tongues that are licking, who is everywhere, alone, yet in all things, is completely fearless, and therefore lives as an "Incarnation of God."

Evening, 30-10-35

100. The Supreme State

I am here telling you about "Devotion after Liberation." To be Brahman *is* Liberation. Brahman is our birth name, and Devotion means "to sing in praise of God and Guru" (Bhajan). The one whom we were calling by the name of "Mr. So-and-so" is himself now Brahman, and his spouse is Laxmi. Now, all of his actions including his breathing are those of God. Action cannot take place without Him. When you know that you are Brahman, all actions are of the nature of Brahman. Some people are professing the propriety of active life after Self-Knowledge and go about in society obviously mistaken in their understanding. They say that it is necessary to behave like an ignorant foolish person in order to teach people, but this is not right. A "Man of Self-Knowledge" must behave as he is. If he goes around acting like an ignorant person, how can he be a wise man? How did the great men of wisdom like Lord Rama, Lord Krishna, and King Janaka lead their lives, and why did they do so? How did the other great Masters behave? Whose behavior was truly proper and whose behavior was useful to all? The one with Self-Knowledge should think about this. Behave as God, with the qualities of God.

For example, in order to make his spiritual state known to others, a man could cut his arm, but in doing so there is the pride that "I have cut my arm." This is not the way of surrendering the ego. The way of surrendering the ego is the very understanding that "I am nobody." When you know this, the ego is gone. Some people arrange for a car to drive over their body in order to show that they are nobody, and that they are renunciates, but that is also ego. When you purposely behave like an eccentric, it is still ego. There is the ego that you have done something extraordinary. One who does not act in a peculiar way but acts very naturally, is the "Man of True Knowledge." However, this path is only known through the instructions given by the Sadguru. The ego cannot be cut away with a weapon. No matter how hard one tries, it cannot be cut away. It is only through understanding that it goes. The ego is a myth. When you know its nature, the ego disappears. That is the way of the ego.

Everything belongs to God. There is nothing of "mine," or even any "I" there. Is it right to behave like a mad man in order to guide others, professing that you are functioning in society after attaining Self-Knowledge? No, this is never appropriate! Should elder children, while teaching younger ones, themselves become younger children? Why would one leave wisdom and become ignorant? It is true that God alone does everything. The concept that the work that God does, and the work that we do, are different, is a wrong concept. It is also unwise to think that we should worship God, and thereby God takes pity on us. Really, everything is only God, and He acts of his own accord and provokes action. It is He who makes all things happen. God cannot tolerate the sense of duality, or that we are separate from Him. The one who is wise alone knows the True Religion. People say many things such as, "We have bathed God. We have fed God. We must not to eat anything before we have done this," or that "We are not to touch anybody, or anything." Is there any thing, or any article, that is not touched by God? Who is it that the impurity of touching something affects? There is no "other" except God. Everything is done by God himself. It is only He who eats, and dines. Who else eats?

If someone bows down at the feet of a Saint, people ask him, "Why do you allow this prostration?" The answer is, "You see, I am only God. These people will be liberated if they bow to me. That is not an obligation on me. Their sins are washed away, and they are emancipated." Who is it that makes the people bow down? Only God can do it. Nobody gives salutations to anybody without reason. He is not God only because you bow down to Him. He is God, and it is He that eats and drinks. If He is given a Vida (a betel leaf; also known as "pan"), it is not given to a man. To know that it is given to God, is the Devotion after Liberation. When you become God, you act as God. Should you act like a ghost? One who behaves like God, is God. One whose actions are like a sage, is a sage. One who behaves like the great people of old, is called an incarnation of that particular person. If he acts like God, he is the incarnation of God. If he acts like a certain person from the past, he is his incarnation. If he acts like Tukaram, he is Tukaram's incarnation. If one acts like God after liberation, he is God. Those who called themselves as incarnations have acted like Me. One who is truthful, tells his true name. As Krishna was sure that He is God, He constantly said that "He" is God. Even from his childhood, he started saying that He was God. Now, you have to be told, but you are ashamed to call yourself God. One should behave the way that he is. One should live in the light of this understanding. This ensures that the doer is absent.

You are not the doer of any actions. Having enjoyed all pleasures, I am free of the sense of being the enjoyer. I remain free even after creation, sustenance and dissolution of the worlds. One who does not know this "Yoga," (unity; union) suffers sorrow. This is the "Unending Yoga." This Yoga is never lost. One who knows this Yoga is the happy man. Lord Shiva and Myself, only the two of us know this Yoga. Others also say that they have understood Yoga, but theirs is not *this* Yoga. This state of Consciousness was fully imbibed by Uddhava. He said, "I have come upon this mysterious secret path that only a True Guru can show." Both he and Lord Krishna were of one heart, one mind. He got the great gift of Devotion, the "Great Key." What Lord Krishna already knew in his heart, Uddhava came to know. He understood the proper state of the Self. He understood that the True Nature of the Self, the very Being of the Self, is Pure. There is nothing mixed with it. It is "He" who attains the highest realization of His Own Self, His Primordial Being. That is called the Supreme Self, Paramatman, Atmaram. Uddhava attained That.

31-10-35

101. Raja Yoga – The Power of God

What is being presented here is called the Royal Yoga, the "King of Yogas," or Rajayoga. Rajayoga means "The Natural State." Brahman is "Natural Existence." There is no devotion to anything "other" in that Existence. The Highest State, the original Natural State, is called Rajayoga by men of wisdom. When there is awareness of Absolute Totality, this is called "Unhindered Yoga." There is no question of doing anything, leaving anything, or giving up anything. That which has been done, has been done sincerely, and has been made "Free." Now, whatever more is done, is already in the state of Freedom. Therefore, it has no meaning, nor is it meaningless. Moreover, whatever activities are carried out, are totally unselfish and desireless. Therefore, it is called Sahaja Samadhi, or the "All-pervading Samadhi." There are many names for this "state" that are known by people from various books, but they do not really know what it is. Only two of us know it, Myself, and Lord Shiva. There is no question of doing anything in this Yoga. One who tries to do something does not have confidence about himself. The one who is confident does not set out to do anything. He only looks at whatever is happening in the natural course of things. He looks on, as there is nothing else to be done. The "looking" takes place. That is the only thing that He does, and it is enough for him.

Whatever you plan is going to be successful, but the determination should be firm in purpose and full of bravery. Whatever one decides with one's full determination becomes possible. Even if you do not say anything, whatever is going to happen is surely going to happen. Everything emanates from Paramatman, so whatever is happening, and is going to happen in the future, is definitely going to take place. There is nothing to do, or to hold onto. When the thing to happen is thus naturally powerfully effective, there is no question of deciding or not deciding to do anything. To decide to do only creates a sense of carrying a burden, so let that also be dropped. One who thinks that without his active part everything should naturally happen, should be quiet. There is a story told to illustrate this. There was a man who thought that he would take food if God gives it, otherwise he would just sit quietly. People used to advise him to do something, but his faith in himself was different. He did not accept people's suggestions. He thought that whatever would be naturally available was enough for him. To sit silent was his way. One day he went into the forest and his foot was placed upon a stone where he sat and this caused an unusual sound. He called out for some other people to come to him, and when the stone was removed there was a sizable treasure underneath that stone. He gave all the money to the people who had come. He never felt any want for anything. The confidence in Oneself should be total. One who knows himself as he really is, never feels any want.

Saint Tukaram has said, "The power of determination is its own fruit." If you feel that success is not possible without doing something, surely do it. If you do not feel that way, do not do. If you have faith that God does everything, He is surely doing it. If you feel that you are doing, you are definitely doing. Whatever is your faith, is true. It depends upon what you propose, and what you decide. Either you act as you really feel sure, or if you have trust in the word of the Guru, then follow only his advice and do not do anything contrary to the instructions of the Guru. That will spoil both. You should not be confused and suffer by mixing the issues. Determination, or "perfect decision," is supreme. Having realized Brahman, you may do what you want. After realization, this question of choice does not remain. Whether the King should fix a code of conduct for himself is totally his affair. Therefore, whatever you do will take place. You should think of what you want and do not want. You should not have any pride of doing good for others. That also you have to decide. Only you decide whether you want to remain free or in bondage. "Only Lord Shiva and Myself know *this* Yoga." This secret was taught by Lord Krishna to Uddhava.

Self-Knowledge is "Supreme Knowledge." Enjoy the bliss when you attain "That." Now all sorrow has been relieved. It is a tragedy when you bury your money and go through a painful struggle. When you have realized Brahman, you may worry or not worry, the realization does not tell you anything. When the king is on the throne, his command is automatically felt in his kingdom. A man who has no discretion will suffer from sorrow even though he is enlightened. If one wants to live as a jiva, he will. What can the spiritual realization do if one chooses foolishly? You see, we are the "Power" of the Universe. Then how can whatever you decide to do be a failure,? One who knows this really benefits from it. Whatever you decide, must happen. Why should it not happen? In principle, you are God. What you decide must happen. The only necessity is that you must be determined.

The one who realizes that he is God, and speaks only the Truth, will get the power to create another universe. Devotion to the Guru has this one purpose. You must be doubtless in your mind. When this devotion is complete, why will not all that you say be successful? However, to be very sure about this, Devotion to the Guru must be very deep. Your mind is like a nagging wife. Don't listen to your mind. You must decide for yourself. Your mind should not have any inward hesitation. It should not prick you. When the mind is full of courage, then that is all that is required. The mind should not be uncertain. In short, everything depends upon your concept. Your mind, your determination, will decide the fruit you get. The mind must have courage. The one who is confused, his results will also be confused. God is as you feel about him. You are God. You will say so if you are convinced. If you say so, it is so, if you say no, it is not so. Will your merit be decreased, or will sin be committed by taking something or giving something? No, that is not the case. The creation and destruction of the world depends upon you. What are you going to lose if you give your blessings to anybody?

Evening, 1-11-35

102. The Joy of Inner Realization

This Yoga that has been described is called Raja Yoga. "This Yoga is known only to Me, and to Lord Shiva." Krishna revealed this secret Yoga to Uddhava, and Uddhava fully understood it. Both Krishna and Uddhava had the same Self-Realization. Self-Realization means to realize that one's Self is Brahman. Brahman is the Creator of this universe, and "I am Brahman." So, there was the realization that "I am the Creator, the Sustainer, and the Destroyer of this universe." Now Uddhava had become Krishna. Once a cowherd becomes King, his function as a cowherd ceases. What is the meaning of the statement that Uddhava became Krishna? Iron had become gold. The seeker became Brahman. All of the "Power of Brahman" was now being held by him. The seeker had become Brahman. The whole universe is He himself. He became the Water pervading the entire world. He became the Light in the universe. He is the Wind animating the entire universe. He became the all-pervading Space that holds within itself so many vast universes. He is the "Consciousness of Perception," the Power of Knowledge, the quality of "knowing," the Life-Energy itself. He has become all of these. He is that "Aloneness" which remains as peaceful Existence after the disappearance of the world of the five elements, which became tired after its multi-faceted internal play in all. He holds all of the "Power of Brahman." Thus, the seeker has become Brahman.

By mixing together and uniting all of the activities of the universe, He has alone been doing all the functions of the universe, and now He is alone, doing bhajan to himself. The proof of devotion is known, the benefit of spirituality is known, and also fully known are its fruits. When one is truly free, Devotion after Liberation is the behavior of such a liberated one. To live as a devotee is to live in unity with God. Uddhava understood this fact. He was overjoyed. His bliss of the "Jiva" being Shiva knew no limits. There was the Supreme Joy of being united with Brahman. He had become Brahman, and he wielded the "Power of Brahman." He became the "All-Powerful Paramatman." Lord Krishna gave him the ornament of being an incarnation of God, just as a mother adorns her child with various ornaments, or just as a King is crowned and is given royal ornaments as well as power. It is not that this boon is not attainable by all, but it depends upon the faith of each person. If one's faith is that he is Brahman, then one will get the power as if he is the ruler of all, the creator of the whole world. One will get the fruit according to one's concept, and if one decides that a particular direction is east, it will be so. To stay in bondage after attaining Freedom is a mistaken concept.

Lord Krishna had complete faith, and knew that he is Brahman. He is the creator of and enjoyer of, "That State." Only then could He wield "That Power," and only then, could He give "The Power of Incarnation." This Siddhi that Uddhava attained, is really the most mysterious state, which cannot be understood by the mind, and cannot be appreciated by the intellect. Everybody interprets and accepts the meaning according to their concept. Even though one attains the "Knowledge of Brahman," and even though the Guru has given that Knowledge, the original defect remains. How can one leave the original defect even if one has realized Brahman? Everyone wants to do this and that, and they thereby get confused and suffer a loss. Instead of being in the "State" and "Power" of Brahman, they are struck with the sense of being a limited individual, a jiva. Remain in "That State," in which you naturally are. When you attain the "State of Brahman," remain in that state, Do not accept the sense of being a jiva. Many have realized, and many have the experience, but everyone experiences according to their concept. The state of incarnation however, is not known by all. The pundits who are well versed in the Vedas have not known it. Lord Krishna gave that Knowledge to Uddhava. You should also know it, and get the benefit of it.

Someone has asked "When Brahman is realized how are we to enjoy it?" The answer to that question is, Devotion after Liberation is the "Power of Incarnation" of God. All is Brahman. All of the actions in this world are only Brahman. Formerly there was a person, the "me" who was imagined. Now, by listening to the teachings of Vedanta, that imaginary person is gone. He was only a product of imagination, yet he was being harassed too much. That jiva, who called himself as "I," disappeared by the instructions of the Guru. "I" and "you" have both vanished. All of this, everything, without any doubt, is only Brahman. All actions, whatever they may be, are only Brahman. If the one from the one million is removed, what figure remains? Nothing, the counting stops. Only Zero remains. How many should we count? If one is counted, many will have to be counted. Who is proud of that which is nothing? "That" which is nothing, is Shiva. He may get up, he may walk, he may do anything, still, He is Shiva. There is no name that applies to "Inner-Realization." Originally, it has no name, but in order to tell about inner-realization, we put some name to it. It is necessary to give hundreds of thousands of names to express it, but that "Inner Joy," is as it is, unaffected. The enjoyment, the object of enjoyment, and the one who enjoys, are all only Shiva. This is the "State of Incarnation." Understand how this is.

There is a story of a devotee who was accepting the common way of spiritual practice and rituals by going to a temple every day and offering the full meal offerings to the image of Shiva (the Shiva Lingam) that is in the temple. He then distributed that sacred food to the men and the various pet animals that are near the temple, then took some of it to be distributed to his relatives, and finally took some for himself. In this way, he worshipped daily and offered food to the Great God (Mahadeva; Shiva). Once when he went to the temple, he saw a stranger sitting by the side of the "Lingam" of Shiva. He was wearing saffron robes, had a long beard, an overgrowth of hair on his head, and he had a stick in his hand. He prostrated before this person and said some prayers according to his knowledge. The devotee was sure that the person must have been pleased with the praise and further he was convinced that the person who was so pleased by the prayer must be Mahadeva himself. Therefore, he requested for that person to accept the meals offered to God. That person agreed and took the food as per request of the devotee. As the devotee had faith that the person was Shiva, he did not find it awkward that he was eating so near the Lingam and some particles of food were falling outside the dish. When the person had finished dining, he asked the devotee to collect the remnants. Without thinking that the food had already been tasted, he picked it up. The person blessed the devotee saying "All your wishes will be fulfilled. Now, you should go away from here, without any further delay." Accordingly, the devotee went home, distributing the small amounts of food to others on his way. Afterwards, that person in the temple also went away. Now, what is the difference between this devotee and God? That God was a human being, and the devotee was also a human being, and both were male. But, there is great difference between the two. The inner difference is much farther than the distance between the sky and the netherworld. If you see ordinarily, both are human beings. However, the Self-confidence in the man in the temple is full and total, while the Self-confidence in the devotee is incomplete. The Self-confidence in one is as complete as in the other it is incomplete. The original roots, the birth, the development, and the state of both of them are the same. However, as there is a lack of Self-confidence, the devotee is identified with his body and skin while the man in the temple is fully imbibed with spirituality, intelligence, and the great wealth of Self-Realization. Identification, or pride, means that one takes on the physical consciousness, the "body-consciousness." Though their True Nature is the same, there is a great difference. One is the mortal jiva of temporary experience and the other is always the complete indestructible, "Total Joy." This is the effect of the Knowledge that is possible through the Sadguru's teaching.

Even though "That State" is attained, people are shy to say, "I am God." There are many sages, who although fully realized, have remained in the idea that they are seekers only. Only Lord Krishna said, "I am the God of Gods." What was the actual difference between those sages and Lord Krishna? Lord Rama was sitting with his wife Sita seated on his lap, and nobody found fault with him. Lord Rama (Shri Ram) had also passed beyond the state of a seeker and became a Siddha. He reached the state where Consciousness loses its separateness and there is the conviction that the whole world is permeated by God, and that everything is of the nature of the Self. That is why he performed all of his actions most naturally and easily. So, why is this renunciation of actions (karma) as well as full performance of actions not possible to be attained by men who have the attitude of only being seekers? The lack of "Total Joy," and the lack of complete Self-conviction about Reality is the cause. They are not able to decide what to take, or what to reject, and that is why the pride of actions remains.

Shri Rama's identification with karma was of the nature of Brahman, and therefore he sat with Sita in his lap in front of all people. Others are not of that caliber. Shri Rama had won over Illusion (Maya). He said, "I am God. Everything takes place according to My will. So, whom should I fear?" The Illusion overpowers those who are afraid. The Illusion was controlled by Shri Rama. He had shifted her from his head, to his lap. He realized that "This Maya is My servant. All are My devotees. All worship Me. I am the 'Lord of All.' I do not rise or set. I am always complete, and imperishable." Self-conviction should be there with such strength as this.

2-11-1935

103. Transform Clay Into Gold

Lord Krishna's disciple Uddhava attained Devotion after Liberation, which is the power of Brahman to incarnate. The Illusion, Maya, holds the power to control the jiva, but Uddhava possessed the Illusion. He controlled Maya. This means for example, that if we have some idea of something new, it is possible for that to happen. You have the power to call Illusion a myth, and determine that it is false. Maya has created something, and after Liberation, if you desire to create something, it is possible because of this creative power. As the world is imagined it is possible to modify it by our own power of imagination. In the dream, the imaginations that arise are immediately experienced. For one who is totally convinced that he is Brahman, there is the Power to do anything in this world. This is called "The Power to Control Maya."

There is no need to do anything to bring completeness in Brahman. Whatever effort you will do to gain something will be nothing but Ignorance, or Avidya. After Liberation, what is remaining is flawless Brahman. Now what exists is not in the realm of experience, because without our going out to meet it, it is as it is, without trying to remember it. It is not something objective that can be remembered. Memory disappears together with forgetfulness. It is beyond truth and untruth. It is not truth, and it is not untruth. "That" which is, is. What "That" is, cannot be told. Mind and intellect do not reach there. Words cannot express it. Its "color" or "lack of color," its "letter" or "lack of letter" (Varna), cannot be uttered in words. It is not possible. If one tries to utter anything, the word becomes indecipherable. Where the word has run away, who can describe it? The meaning of "word" here, is known only as Knowledge. When you expect that Consciousness should give it expression, Consciousness itself disappears. There is nothing near "That." Nothing is there, which means that there is nothing near, there is only "Wordless Non-Existence," stillness. Where there are two, there can be experience. Where there is only one, who can have experience, and of what? Without the any factor of experience, He is the "Greatness of Experience." He is one who gives the experience of all things. He is the "Great Experience," himself. He knows everyone, yet nobody knows him. All that appears to be knowable and available by word is temporary. All things come into being and disappear. He is not supported by, or dependent upon Time. It cannot even be said that time knows him, as time has no entry there. Time has no power to live its life together with him. Time ends, it sets. How can that which is described by word, know That? Its "Existence" is there all the time.

He is the "Great Experiencer" (Maha-anubhaava), but a "thing" that is in existence, which means that it has form, cannot know him because that thing is false. The tongue cannot taste itself. The experience in the dream has disappeared but the "Great Experiencer" remains. The experience in the waking state, *and* the "experiencer," is Maha-anubhaava. The experiencer of the dream is real, but the dream experience is false. Maha-anubhaava is what He has always been, and He is complete. He is originally there, but the sense of "me" being somebody separate, some "other being" is now gone. The five elements, and the sixth, the sense of "me" were all imposed on the Self. The "five" were recognized to be false, and the "me," the sixth, was butchered like a goat. Now who remains to be united with Brahman? That which identifies, is himself false. This was actually experienced. Now who will study? The one who studied is dead. It was experienced that he is dead. Just as yesterday is gone, similar is that experience. The sense of ego is gone.

There is a story of Namdev and Lord Vitthala. Namdev had a friendly relationship with Vitthal. When many sages and Namdev were together, it was found that Namdev was not so perfect as is expected of a Saint, and he was told that he was not ripe. So, Namdev went crying to see Vitthal. Vitthal said, "That is true, but I cannot make you perfect. You must go and see the Sage Khechara." When Namdev went and saw Khechara, the sage gave him the true "understanding," and thus he became perfect. Afterwards, Namdev ceased to go and see Lord Vitthal in the temple. The Lord asked Namdev, "My dear Namdev, why are you not coming to the temple these days?" Namdev said, "One should take care of one's Self, and he will see only That. Should I now recite my own Abhangas (singing verses in praise of himself)? Now, if I sing devotional songs for you, are both of us really two? Are the house and the temple now two? Now all the world is a temple." Vitthal was very happy when he heard this answer. So long as the "me" as a jiva is separate, all the sciences, the Vedas, reciting of devotional songs, etc. have some place in life. When that "me" is gone, all of that is finished. What remains is faultless Brahman. Who is to pray, or to offer devotion, and to whom? After the form of the ornament is gone, only the gold remains.

The visible qualitative Supreme Self with the "Universal-Body" is Brahman. He is called "Saguna (with form), or Sakshat-Parabrahman, Sakshat-Paramatman" (Supreme Witnessing Reality). If there is only one without a second, how is the body (or the Universal-Body) separate?

When the "me" is gone, "you" is also gone. Either "I" and "you" remain, or neither "I" nor "you" remain. When the "I" is not, the "you" is not. Uddhava realized this state. To imagine anything on the "One True Brahman," is Maya. Anybody can imagine anything! That imagination which you indulge in will come into existence. What is good in this world? That which we will imagine is good. As this world is itself an imagination, whatever you conceive will be successful. This is the "Controlling Power," the "Power of Incarnation," that was understood by Uddhava. He completely realized that Maya is false. He knew all to be false, and accordingly he was desireless. With this desirelessness arose the "Devotion to the Guru." Then, why shouldn't everything that the devotee conceives, take place? When there is complete Devotion to the Guru, total desirelessness in us, and our conviction is total, realization is easy and natural. One who understands that the Guru is his own Self, Paramatman, becomes as happy as if he had met the "Four-Armed God" himself.

Only the devotee of the Guru is the one who is so happy as this. He has no desire for anything else. He who considers money and dirt as the same, gets this Power. Someone may not be able to relinquish anything because he thinks that everything belongs to the Guru. He is also the devotee of Guru. He thinks that the Guru's Power is everywhere. He has given even his body to his Guru. Whatever he eats, when he dines, everything that he does, is all for his Guru. He has faith that all is happening by the Grace of the Guru. If necessary, he is ready to give up everything for his Guru. This is called Devotion to the Guru. Who can control the Illusion, the Maya? Only the one who has no regard for Maya can control Maya. Such a one places the same value on gold as he does on dirt. Only he can turn earth into gold. One who is convinced that it is all a concept to call one as "gold" and one as "clay" is truly powerful. To create Maya and destroy Maya is the "Power to control Maya," and to provoke Maya and withhold Maya. This "Power to control Maya" was given by Krishna to Uddhava.

Only the one who worships the Guru can know and recognize from where all of this that is visible comes into being. Only he knows why and how all of this Illusion comes into being and how is it wiped out. Only he who has already worshipped the Guru, or is able to worship him knows that which is our True Place, our True Status, and True Time. Only such a devotee knows what he exists before the beginning of time and after the end of time. Only He is the controller of Maya.

Evening, 3-11-35

104. The Game of Chess

Illusion, or Maya, means "that which is not existing." It is not anything. All is Brahman. Maya is only imagination. Maya is what is not existing. In the ocean, there are bubbles and waves, but all of that is only water. All manifest phenomenon is created by ideas. To spread it or to contain it is all nothing but conception. Many pictures on the wall are in essence only various colors. To name it as a picture is stimulation of Illusion, and is only an idea. Pictures are drawn or painted only by imagination. To stimulate, or to contain, is the sign of control over Maya." Krishna gave this "Knowledge" to his disciple Uddhava. The word Uddhava means "making a conviction become firm." He got everything and thereafter he was free of anxiety. Once one becomes convinced, he does not deviate. When one is firm in the mind, one becomes the very state of Self-conviction. One is no longer disturbed. Uddhava had ended, which means that Uddhava, being quiet in his conviction, became Lord Krishna.

In the game of chess, there is no residual past karma. There is the basic material of wood out of which the various pieces are formed. However, they are in fact, all only wood. There is no inherent enmity in any of them, but the game of chess is virtually a war. The players call out, "The Knight is dead. The Rook is dead," etc. But, by just saying so, does it mean that the Knight really dies? If a Knight overpowers the King, does he get any real kingdom? There is no life in the pieces, but the players say, "The Knight is dead." One wins and the other is defeated, but is there really any death or victory? No, there is nothing like that. The one who plays does everything in the game. All is his concept. If any piece is killed in the game, what is his sin? Similarly, to be in bondage or to be free is all simply a product of imagination. One who conducts his affairs in worldly life with this wise attitude has neither bondage nor liberation. For him all this is only a dream. By thinking that the dream in the night is what is actually occurring in the day, a man acts like an ignorant fool, and cries and laments in vain. The dream in the night cannot be the reality of the day even though some ignorant people may think so. It is the dream in the night, and when the night ends it becomes daytime and there will not be any sign of the dream.

In the waking state, the husband, the wife, the king and queen, are all as false as in a dream. The one who understands this well is the incarnation of God. He is God himself. The scriptures, the Vedas, you, I, all are only a myth. This world is a dream. One who awakens from this dream is truly awakened. In this world appearance we really own nothing. We say that we should not die and we have to be careful accordingly. That is not how it is in the game of chess. In chess, the man who is defeated is not hanged, nor does the one who wins gets any real kingdom. This Illusion is like a game of chess. When a game of chess is over, the players go away with only what they brought with them to the game. What kingdom or spoils can they take away? In short, this world is a game of chess. What is visible is Brahman, but I ask you, what is beyond this appearance? It is Parabrahman. I ask you, "What and how is it?" "That" is Shiva. "That" is Brahman, which is the Truth. There is no horse, house, or man. There is only One, nothing else. However, "That" has no name or shape. It is, that's all. There is no asking what it is, or how it is. The dictates of the Vedas are all like a dream. Bondage and freedom are false. One who understands this and lives a natural life has no insistence that some thing should be done or should not be done. To do, or not to do, is the thought belonging to the body-consciousness (mis-identification with the body). Many were able to be completely and perpetually free by withdrawing from the worldly life, but they also kept the sense that they were "somebody" even when they attained victory. To be immovable or movable are factors belonging to the body. Such a one values himself, or conceives of himself, only in relation to the body. Such conceptual delusion should not be there. Really we are nothing and at the same time, we are all things. Not one, not two, not even zero. Elephant, dog, horse, we are all these. We are everything.

Gold was asked, "What are you?" It said, "I am not a certain number of rupees, and all of the various ornaments such as bangles, and bracelets do not exist. I am all. The ornaments and rupees are not. I am only gold." Like in the example of gold, we are all, but we are not any particular thing. I am in all. There is no thing in me. Even the "I" is not here. The Guru was asked, "How did you enter into everything?" He said, "When the I in me vanished, I entered into all." The "all" has become all-pervasive. Where could it be found as any particular thing? When some became liberated by renouncing the world, they were asked, "Who became free?" and they replied "I." This is proof that this "I" has not really gone. Whatever remains after the dropping of "I" is beyond the grasp of logic. This "state" that is unimaginable, this "Devotion after Liberation" is not understood by anybody. Only the one who has realized that there is only One without a second, has attained this Devotion after

Liberation. Everybody says, "Death is certain." However, you should be able to die once to such an extent that there will be no need for taking another birth. "I" as such, does not exist at all. Whatever is, is only Brahman, nothing else. One who has understood this, has the Devotion after Liberation. He says to all, "If you think that there is anything else other than Brahman, search, find it, and bring it here." He understands the "Oneness of Brahman," but he also has devotion.

Some say that "qualified" Brahman, or Brahman with qualities (Saguna Brahman), is only Illusion, and what is beyond, is really Brahman. Really, there is only one single Existence. The world is like frozen water in the form of ice, and Paramatman is only water without any other attributes. This is the only difference between the "Qualified Brahman" (Saguna Brahman) and the "Formless Brahman" (Nirguna Brahman), nothing more. To differentiate between the two is duality, and to realize it as only One, is non-duality. Namdev said, "The Saguna, and the Nirguna, are only one God. So, to whom should one bow down?" God says, "Dear Namya, now you have really understood. Truly blessed you are!" When one is free, one remains as he is. All of our actions are only "Brahman Consciousness." All activities, such as eating, or dining, are only the Supreme Self, Paramatman, acting. This should be very deeply realized. The one who is able to understand this, attains the Devotion after Liberation. The individual is always ready to say that he is an individual, even after attaining the state of Absolute Brahman. He is always ready to tell lies. He has this habit only. The individual resists, being too shy to say "Brahman." This shyness must go. Brahman is never bashful. It is the only Truth.

Evening, 4-11-35

105. Know That You Are Paramatman

It was explained earlier that you yourself are Paramatman. No doubt you are a tiger, but what is the mark of identification of the tiger? Similarly, what is your understanding of being Paramatman? The first sign is that there is neither birth nor death. The word Jiva is a combination of the two words "Ja" plus "Iva" which means that he is "as if born," but not actually born. The sign of Paramatman is that He neither takes birth nor dies. The experience that Paramatman is birthless and deathless should actually be felt. The word "akasha" means "void" or "empty space." The empty space is in a pot, in a house, and in Consciousness. Even if a pot is broken, or a house collapses, the sky or space which it is contained in, is not affected. Similar to the space (akasha), the Self also does not come or go anywhere. The Self is prior to all attributes, so, He has no coming or going. Before there was either Sky or Water, at that time, the Supreme Self, Atmaram, was there. You count time, the years, by the Sun rising and setting, but at that time there was no Sun, there was no Earth. Atmaram is so ancient, it was there before any elements came into being. Days and years are all fictitious. Even though great spiritual powers or miracles may become evident, they are all a dream. This world is not really even of one moment, but it appears as if it is millions of years old. All of it is false. Think about the fifteen minutes of a dream. There you can experience births and deaths by the hundreds. Listen now, the "Glory" is to know that all appearances are illusory, all are false, and there is neither coming nor going, and He who has this Glory, is Paramatman.

Now, since you have gained Knowledge, you may not be giving much value to it. But, when you were ignorant, what was the situation then? He who knows that there is neither bondage nor freedom is Paramatman, and is beyond all qualities and forms. The One who knows this by experience is Paramatman with "complete realization." Just think about what Glory this is! This is not ordinary glory. This is *very rare* Knowledge. The awareness that the Illusion and its bondage is cut away is useful for the "Original State of Existence." Money and worldly riches are not useful there. This is the wealth of Knowledge that belongs to Paramatman. If you ask what property is there in the home of Paramatman, the answer is that this property is "Knowledge." Lord Shiva was asked, "What property have you got?" He said, "I am alone, complete, Shiva. There is nothing else here." In the house of the jiva, there is lamentation that is poverty and sorrow. He who really knows this is Paramatman, and the one who thinks that he is the body of three and a half arms length (the length of the gross body), is the jiva. Just as an old man of a large rich family says, "This is all my property," even though he may not have anything valuable on his body, is very happy, likewise is this ancient Paramatman happy, who says, "I am all of this world." The One who realizes this, is the Glorious Paramatman, full of happiness. Nobody knows this Paramatman, or what its nature is. Nobody can know its farthest limits. The only One who knows this, is the all-pervading, only One, Paramatman, that is everywhere.

Evening, 5-11-1935

106. The Eternal Home (Sayujya Sadan)

You are Paramatman. This is your "True Nature." You have no birth, no death, and no coming or going. The things that have form are not what you are. Water has no form, and the wind and fire also have no form. We are also that which has no form. "Nirguna" means having no qualities. The word "Ananta" means "That which never ends." Paramatman is eternally existing, without a break. The one who knows that we are like this at any place and at any time, is Paramatman. When one knows the real qualities of Paramatman, one has these qualities in oneself. They are imbibed in "Him" and they must be consciously imbibed in oneself. As Paramatman is all-pervading, He is called "all-pervading," or Vyapak. In all of the various things, there is only One that exists, just as in all ornaments there is only gold. Many names are used in order to facilitate the gaining of understanding but Paramatman is beyond description. These qualities attributed to Him are simply His property. All of this world appearance is the wealth of Paramatman, it is His real estate. The One who has the adornment of these qualities, is Paramatman. Through devotion, "His State" is attained. The nine types of Devotion, or the "Nine-fold Devotion" (Navavidha Bhakti), is that devotion by which many have become purified. Among these nine kinds of devotion, the ninth, is "self-surrender," which is called Atma-Nivedana. We should meditate on this ninth type of devotion through our own inner experience. This is described as the "State of Power," the state of being "The Witness," and the state of "Chaitanya." We should examine our own experience according to this.

We offer our head (by bowing down) to God or the Guru after we complete our worship (Puja). This means that we have to let go of our attachment to every possession. Among devotees there are very few who meditate on the nature of the Self and think about what their actual "Being" is. There are very few who enquire, "What am I?" The nature of this way of devotion is that we should observe who we are. When it is known that we are nobody, then who is? Someone is! That someone is Paramatman. Flawless and qualityless is that Supreme Self. He is all objects, all qualities, the ego, everything. Only "you" are not there. Everything is Paramatman but when you become a petty little ego, you are an individual, a jiva. Worry and sorrow are your lot in life. You become powerless. Because of the acceptance of the state of jiva you become a prisoner. With the dissolution of the state of jiva, what remains is Shiva. All of the servants of this "Great Beingness" are also great. Vishnu is His mind. The sun and moon are His eyes. Shiva is His ego. Brahmadev is His intellect. The earth is His skin and hair. All of this is the "Glorious Power of the Lord." In this, nothing is insignificant. When the sense of being a jiva goes only Shiva remains, and He is Paramatman. At that time, all of the sense organs are raised in that "Glory," and they are given the names of the various deities. When the house is owned by the owner, naturally the doors and windows are also owned by him.

The discovery of the devotee and God is self-surrender (Atma-Nivedana), or the finding of one's own Reality. The devotee himself is the "Ancient God." The devotee himself is the Primary God, the Original God. To call him a devotee is false. You yourself are God. The devotee tried to identify God and he became God himself. God and the devotee are not separate. The devotee is God. Because he is not in bondage, he is free, and that freedom is the "Original One." By the standards laid down in the scriptures and by his own convincing experience, he is only God. Before recognizing this, they are two. When recognition takes place, there is only One. Whether called Toop or Ghruta, the names are two, but the thing is only ghee. The thing, Existence, is only One, the difference is only of the name and the shape. God is called devotee, and the devotee is called God. Only if you examine this by your own experience, will you be convinced. When doubt is gone, the difference of the two names is also gone. Then there is the true experience of the one and only Paramatman. The devotee who was thinking that he was only the body started to worship God, and as soon as he recognized his true Self, he vanished as a separate entity. The threefold phenomenon of Existence, Consciousness and Bliss (SatChitAnanda) all became One. The "men of wisdom" (Jnanis) experience the final end, the dissolution of the world, in the immediate moment, and even though they are living in the body, they become formless and of the nature of Brahman.

When the ninth type of devotion, "self-surrender," is achieved, there is unity with God and there is total freedom or the "Sayujya" state. The "Salokata" state of freedom means to be in the company of free men, and to be again born after Liberation, as a free man. The "Sameepata" state of freedom is to know oneself, and the fourth state of freedom is "Sayujyata," which is the surrendering of self which results in true "Self-Realization." If you have really followed what I have told you up to now, then that is Self-Knowledge. You have understood your own Being. We then see clearly as we are, without any prejudice. The "Totality" which is not dependent on anything is our full, complete, Existence. There is understanding of this. That one who surrenders the self, becomes unconditionally "Free." The "Eternal Home" (Sayujya Sadan) means "All-Oneness," or Aloneness. This "Undivided Devotion" is indestructible. The devotee surrendered himself to the Saints and he gained Self-Knowledge. He is unified. Now, he cannot be separated. If one has not surrendered oneself totally, the God of Death (Yama) gives him another birth, and he is again subject to Illusion. When one forgot his true nature as being Shiva, Paramatman, he said he was a jiva. If "Devotion to the Guru" is abandoned, there is Illusion again. Therefore, one should take refuge at the feet of the Saints.

A rich man was asleep, and in that dream he was deluded and people said that he had gone mad, that he had become insane. He got up and began to live as a beggar. But, by the blessings of a Saint his illusion disappeared. He again enjoyed his wealth and his delusion was gone. We should have faith. Our father has given us an estate, why should we not remember his name and enjoy the property? What is the good of eating our food while criticizing him? You have received and you should enjoy, but remember His name, and then eat. If you wish to enjoy the freedom and the glory of Paramatman, you should serve the Guru. Have great respect for Him, and enjoy His Glory. Only one who has such faith, will gain Self-Knowledge. One who has doubt in this Knowledge will be haunted by doubts all the time, everywhere. The Saints and Sages have advised us to treat even small ants and insects as God. One who blames the Saints will surely suffer great sorrow. His intellect gets confused and Knowledge leaves him. As you are Brahman, you should not blame others. One whose pride is gone is the real "Sage." One who is proud cannot be Brahman.

Knowledge is like a mango, which when it is ripe, you judge it to be so by its appearance and other signs, and you feel like plucking it immediately. If you pluck it at that time, then it is surely sweet. It tastes sweet. The signs of Knowledge are that one loves all of the Saints and Sages. Such a one has a feeling of Oneness, and is affectionate to everyone. One who has Self-Knowledge respects all of the Saints and Sages, and has no pride about anything. One looks upon co-disciples as equal to the Guru. One thinks that the entire world is only God. Such a one is like a mango that is ready to be plucked. He is worthy of real contentment. So, the devotee with Self-Knowledge should not be proud of anything. One who does not like a lowly type of work is not a Saint. If the devotee of the Guru is only God, then it is one's duty to look after the welfare of all people. There is no possibility that you could hate anybody. God is the all-pervading Self of all, and the devotee of the Guru is like God. One who sincerely respects the Saints, will as a matter of course, respect all people. Therefore, one who serves the Saints gets the "Eternal State," the Sayujya State.

Evening, 6-11-1935

107. Self-Surrender

When we know who we are, we know that we are nothing, and that there is only the Self, witnessing all. That is "self-surrender" or Atma-Nivedana. The word Bhooma means support. The Self is this Bhooma, which is of the nature of experience. We are thinking that we are individuals but that is not correct. The Illusion has to be removed. The rope was from the beginning only rope, but there was an illusion of a snake on it. Knowledge destroys Ignorance. The knowledge of "rope" has destroyed the ignorance of "snake." Knowledge has not done anything, it has only removed the ignorance. There is a story of ten people who were traveling. Along the way, one of them counted how many they were, but forgot to count himself. The others also counted in the same way, and over and over again each one forgot to count himself. It so happened that a wise man came along and showed them their error by counting all ten. Similarly, there is the illusion of calling oneself as an individual although one is really the Self. Knowledge is understanding what is the "true fact." Knowledge is necessary only for disillusionment. After one's illusion is no more, the Upanishads, the five-fold classification of nature's principles (the five elements), and all other knowledge are no longer necessary. When the war is over, the armor, the sword, the shields, everything, is given up, and then the victory is celebrated. Similar is the case of Knowledge. When the goal is achieved, the instrument is no longer necessary. For those who do not understand by one letter, large volumes are required to be written. As soon as the Guru meets you, he instructs by one statement or phrase, which is, "Tat Tvam Asi" (You Are That), however that was not understood by you, so doubt has to be removed by offering more explanations.

What is the use of various sciences or scriptures to one who has realized Brahman? One who has realized "Pure Knowledge" by the grace of the Guru needs nothing. Vijnana or "Supreme Knowledge" is pure mystery. Some of the people advise that the flow of attention should be like a thin stream of oil being poured. But, will it be ever possible for any such an attitude to realize Brahman? How can Brahman, which cannot be captured by study, and cannot be grasped by intellect, be found by any attitude? Only one whose ego-centered thinking has disappeared can realize this. When self-surrender has taken place, that state is called "Total Liberation" (Sayujya Mukti). That annihilation or dissolution of Illusion through the utilization of "discrimination" is called Viveka-Pralaya. When this happens, then the one and only God remains. One who surrenders oneself to the Saints, attains "unity" through the teaching given by them. Then one remains convinced that all is only One, and there is no second. To one who looks at the world as Brahman, it is Brahman, and to the one who looks at it as the world, it is the world. It is not that the world is, or that it is not. To the ignorant, it appears as world, to the intelligent, it appears as Brahman. There is never a time when the one who is the individual is not existing, nor is there any time when the individual is existing. Blessed is the one who understands this. Wise is the one who has this wealth, as this is the wealth of Paramatman. To be really cultured is to see everything as one Paramatman. When there is the realization that "all is myself," one cannot be made separate even if one tries.

In short, how can one who is "one with the world" be separated from it? Can someone be the all-pervading God (Vishwambhara) by simply calling him by that name? Moreover, if he is actually that Vishwambhara, will he cease to be so, even if no one calls him by that name? The One who is all-pervading will always be so. Nobody can separate Him from his "wholeness." He will not be separate even if you say so. Suppose a man has gone to the city of Benares and comes back. Will this fact be nullified by anyone saying that he has not gone there? Similarly, one who has become united with Brahman will not degrade oneself to the state of an individual. The net of Illusion will not affect him again. For example, a lamp that is painted in a picture is not extinguished by the wind. Brahman is neither existing nor non-existent. It is not Illusion, the individual, Shiva, or Brahma. Whatever it is, it is, but it is not qualified in any way. Both the terms "You" and "That" are gone and still, there "Is" something, which is known by the term "Are" in the statement, "You Are That." One who has reached that state of Existence will not be "nothing."

There are two states in the world, "is" and "is not." Which of these was first to come into being? How did the state of "is not," come to be? First, there has to be one thing that "is," and thereby "is not" can come into existence. One man is present he can therefore say that someone is absent. If nobody is present, who will be there to say that the other is absent? Only the one present can say something, and therefore the word "is" becomes valid. Only one who "exists" can say "is not," and thereby the existence of the man present is proved to be a fact. The man who says that he has died is a liar. Gold may say that it is iron but its value as gold is not diminished. It's value remains fixed. One who has "realized," may very well come back into the world. It is not wrong to be busy leading the worldly life after one has attained the "Complete Knowledge of the Self." However, he should act properly, without mistake. One again becomes as one was before realization. He has now come back after becoming what he already was. Now he is at liberty to act in the world. There is no objection to a man who has been "There" (Reality) and has freely come back. It is not correct to say that one who is realized does not use the term "I." However, such a one is fully aware that the "I" is false. He has been "There" and has now come back. There is no such written law that a man, after the attainment of "Pure Knowledge" should talk a different language. Some people purposely behave like insane stupid people, even after attainment of Self-Knowledge. They have a concept that they are different from others. What comments can be made about such people who purposely live shabbily? The only thing that can be said about them is that it is their own bad karma that they are suffering from. Whatever is a good or a bad object seen is pure in itself. There is no cause for doing eccentric things, but they do. This is nothing but the destruction of wisdom. They will repeat whatever their Guru has taught, but they have no real understanding of their own experience.

The only thing indicating the true "Understanding of Brahman," is that the "I" is gone. The "I" is removed. One who has this Pure Knowledge has no Illusion. Once he becomes God, he is God. What does it matter if he is called by any other name? The false appearance on the Reality is gone. It is known how the phenomenon of false appearance has taken place, and what Reality is. Reality does not disappear and the illusory appearance does not last. The nature of what is, is known, as it is. Now, the karma is completed, and self-surrender has taken place.

7-11-1935

108. The State of the Perfected Man

One who surrenders oneself to the Saints is illumined with the "Knowledge of the Self." One who understands that the entire world is only our own Original Nature cannot become separate even if such effort were to be made. Such a one has no fear. The fact is, that once it is known what the Truth is, one's understanding cannot be changed. Even if one tries, one cannot be made separate. For such a one, all visible objects, are only Brahman. Iron that has been turned into gold by the touch of the "touch stone," will not turn back into iron. When one has the understanding that, "Not only am I Brahman, but everything is Brahman," never again becomes separate, or estranged. He is a devotee, but he becomes God. He has understood by his own experience that primarily he is only Brahman. Even to use the word "became" is a wrong statement. He was already God. One whom the Saints declared as a free man and have called as their own relative has become a perfected man. The individual is Brahman, nothing else. Saints have taken him into their fold and given him a place of rest. He is convinced that God is the devotee, and the devotee is God. Now all need for further talk has ended. God should be seen in the devotee. The true seeing, is to see oneself as God.

That which we were calling a monkey (the mind), has now become Maruti (Hanuman). He is now God. He has become Paramatman, as He is. In name and form he became God. Laxman, the devotee of Rama, is also without birth and death, invisible, formless, and without color or shape. These are the attributes of God, and this Glory has been absorbed in him. This is the real Glory, real Wealth. All other scenery and any other glory are all fictitious. The essential quality of a scorpion is to sting. An inherent quality of water is to drown anybody who may fall into the river. This quality is inherent in water. Just as sweetness is the quality and glory in sugar that never leaves it, similarly, the "Glory of Brahman" is its own. The eight spiritual powers are its inseparable qualities. One can perceive very minute things. This capacity is called the "Anima Siddhi." Such spiritual powers (Siddhis) are all inherent in Brahman. When you think of a cow, her tail and horns never leave her. Similarly, the siddhis, or the Glory of God never leaves Him. Your real power and strength is complete omni-presence. Therefore, you should not pay any heed to the siddhis (powers). Do not repeatedly test whether the power is in you or not. It is not proper to check with your fingers whether a mango is ripe. When it is ripe, it is definitely going to give a good flavor. It will taste good because the fruit is ripe.

God should remain quietly in the temple, and when worshippers are there they will definitely worship. When the son comes of age, he is sure to have a mustache. If you are sure about Brahman, you are sure to attain "His Power" through Knowledge. You should not be devoid of faith by being depressed if your strength is found to be limited. The "Man of Knowledge" (Jnani) should always be sure that bad omens or defeat will never turn their face towards him. In short, one's confidence should not waver. One should never forget one's position. Our true nature of Being, which is the same as the Sadguru should never cease seeing only Paramatman. We should have the continuous unhindered darshan of Paramatman. God says, "The one who takes my name will be successful." Then who will hinder or show any bad omen and how? Your own Power, your own Strength is always with you, filling you inside and out. The God who is neither good nor bad, resides only in you. He is the highly benevolent God. All of the spiritual powers are only at His feet. Do not look at them. Your real Glory is your own Existence, Reality, and not the eight spiritual powers. All that exists is only Paramatman, which is the essence of all these powers. It is by His Power, that the siddhis have the inner motivation of the spirit and by His Power, that they are powerful. If this "God Self" (Atmaram) is not having the power of the Self, or the strength of the Self, then from where are these spiritual powers going to draw their strength and wealth?

All of the powers which create and maintain the numerous worlds, draw their strength from the "Supreme Self," Paramatman, only. Thus, the only thing that is necessary is Self-Realization, and then the job is finished. When a devotee who has attained spiritual powers through various spiritual practices wishes that a particular work should be done, only that much work is accomplished. For that, he has to expend his own energy, but the Jnani is Self-sufficient. For him, all things have become pure, so therefore there is neither good nor bad. He is himself the embodiment of goodness, so who can create any difficulty for him. How can His Power, who is "All-Powerful" and complete, be diminished? All siddhis get their power and strength from Him only. Shiva is the embodiment of goodness. So, never think of bad things. All glory is in your own Being. Do not harbor weakness in your mind. All is well, and auspicious. In the individual, the jiva, all types of evils and unwanted things are there, but in Shiva, all is "Glorious Fullness," all is auspicious.

There you get the ownership of the "Divine Kingdom," and all of its grandeur. God is the Primordial One, having no beginning, and His devotee gets all of His Power. Now the devotee is God, right before our eyes. How can His Power leave him? It is not possible. It is said that when a black cat crosses our path, it is a bad omen. But, what effect can this have on His devotee? I am the essence of Time. I am the auspiciousness in the auspicious moment. I have created Time. Time cannot cross my path. The fact that you are the "Ruler of All" must be steadily fixed in your mind. People eagerly wait for the death of a rich man. So, good and bad are of this world, they are not essential in our true Being. When the Saint imagines something, that power depends upon the imagination, but what is wanting in Paramatman, who is complete with all powers? Paramatman contains all the riches, all the wealth. Why bother to know what is going on in another's mind? What are you going to know except his anxiety of "what will happen?" and "how will it happen"? When you are God, why should you wish to hoard gold in your home? If you have such a desire, how are you Paramatman? There is no happiness gained from the powers that one expects to get. It is only a way of passing time.

Your True Nature is "Eternal Happiness." It is surprising that you are imagining some other kind of happiness. You yourself *are* the Glory, you *are* the Happiness. You are the Supreme Happiness in all happiness. It is your duty to see to the welfare of all friends as well as enemies. The Saint never thinks badly about the person who troubles him. One who has come to Me, has seen Me as God, and has only come as God comes, to enquire. Let someone worship you and pray for your blessing, or let someone throw abuse at you, you should give him only blessings. Do not feel elated by some good effect or sorry because of the lack of some desired effect. One who has faith will get happiness from you. Only those will meet you who are to be benefited. They will not meet you until that time. That which is to happen is already fixed in the invisible world. Your prophesy is just an indication, but it is true that it is necessary. Your benediction should be there. That the work will be accomplished is the extent to which it is already fixed. The doctor gives medicine in order to restore one to health, but some patients might die. What blame is there on the doctor? Is it not enough that the doctor should have a real desire for the patients recovery.

You become a Saint not for other people but only for yourself. If anybody gets the benefit from this, let him have it, but you should not think about what you will get, nor should you worry about your power.

Never deviate from the faith in your own state of the Self. Think about whether you have become Brahman for its own sake, or just to satisfy the Illusion. The status is very high. Do not become removed from the throne that is rightfully yours. It is said that the Sage Narada had attained Brahman, but when he saw some man, the man died. So, do not be afraid that even someone may die by your sight. Do not let your faith hesitate. Are you not Brahman, no matter what happens? If the faith is fixed in Brahman, then Power is increased through the Path of Knowledge. However, see to it that your "aloneness" is not disturbed. Once and for all, be certain who you are, where you are, and how you are. One who is Paramatman can never not be Paramatman.

8-11-1935

109. God and Devotee are One

There is nothing but God. You are only God. Whatever is seen is all God. One who has been convinced about this is the greatest among Saints, and the greatest among liberators. The effect of seeing God is such that when you are sure that you are God, you get His Glory. Just as one knows who one is and what kind of person one is, in the same manner, one knows what one needs and what one does not need. All of this is very naturally understood. One also naturally knows what things he should possess, and how far he should go in controlling things. However, all actions are suggested and all activities are done only in accordance with one's own concepts about his status, his appearance, and various qualities. In accordance with that one enjoys one's own Glory. For example, there is a story of a small child, a prince, who by a strange turn of events became estranged from his parents and was wandering in unknown parts of the world. Seeing the plight of the small boy, people had pity on him. As there were no clues to be able to recognize him as a prince, nobody knew his real status, and they were nurturing him only according to their own capacity. During his travels, he was met by a rich shepherd who had no son. The shepherd made an arrangement that this boy should live with him as his own, and that he should be the enjoyer of the ownership of thousands of sheep and goats, as well as a vast hilly land. However, the shepherd's food was not liked by the boy because he was eating only milk, curds, roots, and fruit. As the boy was always aware of his royal ancestry, and as he was a prince, he did not think that he would like the ownership of the shepherd's property. Therefore, after some time, by various ways and means, he re-established his royal heritage and became a king. Similarly, according to the divine Spiritual Power within, and the continuous remembrance of one's Self, one gradually achieves Divine Glory, the Knowledge of Reality, one's "True Origin," which is one's Essential Nature. One attains the status that is the original status of one's True Self. One who lives in identification with the body suffers the pains of the body. One who suffers bodily pains in the present has to suffer them again in the future, and one who is even now beyond the limited body-consciousness will continue to be so, even afterwards the body's dissolution.

The student, who without study asks questions while the teacher is speaking, is not wise. The student asks, "How can I be beyond the body? In addition, tell me how I will attain that Glory." The Master says, "The kind teacher again started giving him the teaching." It is the individual, the jiva, who says "I am the body." That which is beyond the body is not objective. It is the "Original Thing," the subjective. That which is emotional, imagination, and conception is all objective. As is the concept, or imagination, so is the world. It is all conceptual. The individual, the jiva, is false. One's "Existence" in itself is bodiless. The person who is called by some name, is the embodied, but That, the "Inner-Existence," is bodiless, and you are That. If you ask as to when you are beyond the body-consciousness, the answer is, when you are sound asleep. You are actually beyond even the state of Deep Sleep. In that state there is no world and no pain. This is why deep sleep is restful and gives contentment. The happiness of Existence is much more transcendent than the comfort of sleep. That is your True Self. Who sleeps? You are That which is beyond the body. Because of That, deep sleep is comfortable. This is similar to a warm piece of food that is kept in ice. It soon becomes cool and preserved. In this example, the food has become cool by the quality of the ice. Similarly, by the virtue of your Existence, deep sleep is felt as an experience of happiness.

"You Are That." You are of the nature of "That." Therefore, you should not say that you are a body. It is wrong to say so. To say "I am a body" is totally false. To be only a body, and to function within that limit is what is called "sin." The One who has understood this is Paramatman. He is free, beyond qualities, beyond form, indestructible, and invisible. He is the One who is honored by the Vedas. The Vedas and other scriptures are the adornments, the congratulations of such a one. Even then, the Vedas still have not been able to describe Him. He is that Paramatman for whom description is always inadequate. What is Glory? All sciences, prayers, and mantras sing in praise only of Him, Paramatman. Mohammedans say "Khuda" or "Allah," for Him only. Christians worship Him only. He is the God to whom all religions pray. When you leave the identification with the body, it is you who enjoys this "Glory." If a man who is truly a king behaves like a peasant, that is his bad luck, what can anybody do about it? We are the complete wholeness of "goodness" itself. This bodiless Paramatman is such that success, fame, power, indeed everything, is His Glory. When your faith in being Paramatman is totally firm, then that is "God with Full Conviction."

Where one has no idea of Paramatman, there are all varieties of evils which are the snakes and scorpions in life. Where there is no devotee of God (Vishnu), that is where there is no idea of Paramatman. There, all calamities come to stay. To say that the world is conceptual, or psychologically imagined, is to speak in terms of Illusion, or Maya. The husband of Maya is Paramatman. She first feeds Paramatman with good food, then she gives perishable things to others. Where Krishna dwells there dwells success, fame, and power. Your own home is heaven, and your wife is Radha herself (Krishna's wife). What you eat is the offering to the Great God, Mahadeva (Shiva). When you are sure that you are Paramatman, the water flowing at the time of your bath is itself the Ganges. A particle of food left out when a Jnani dines is equal to the merit earned by feeding hundreds of thousands of Brahmins. In Hindu mythology, it is told that at the Raja-sooya ceremony, the Sage Shuka ate some remnants of food by taking the form of a parrot, and at that time, for every particle eaten by him, there was the sound of bells in heaven. It is said that if you are Self-Realized, even an ant which eats a particle of food left over from your plate, will attain Liberation. When you loudly proclaim the name of God once, it remains resounding throughout the universe for the whole day.

There is a story of a disciple of Saint Kabir. who once went into the village where he visited a very sick man who was in a near death condition. The person was overjoyed to see the great disciple of Kabir in his house. Other people also begged of the disciple his blessings for the well being of the sufferer. Accordingly, the disciple kindly consoled and assured the person and told him to utter the name of Rama three times. As soon as the person did as told, his ailment disappeared and he was completely cured. Then after some time, this disciple of Kabir returned home, and narrated this episode to Kabir. Kabir however got very angry with him and said, "Had you only once uttered the name of Rama, that person would have been cured. Then why did you tell him to take the name of Rama three times?" The disciple was ashamed. In short, the meaning of this story is that the "Realized One" must be completely sure about his "Power" and his "Capacity." Only then does he become "Glorious." He should live in his "Own Status."

There is a story of a sage who was really a perfected Mahatma (Self-Realized being), who lived with his wife. One afternoon, he was taking a nap. When he did not awake even though the Sun was about to set, his wife, thinking that if the Sun were to set without her husband offering water to it, would be a sinner, she awakened him. He asked her, "Why did you disturb me? If I do not get up, the Sun will not set!" So saying he again slept, and the Sun waited. This was because the Mahatma was very sure about his Power. The fact is that you are so powerful that the world would not function without your wish. However, first you must have faith as to who you really are. You get that Glory only if you drop the idea that you are only a body. You must see for yourself that you yourself are Happiness. If you can see the already existing Happiness that is your True Nature, you need not go into all the troubles of imaginary things. It is by the completeness of your Joy, your "Inner Happiness," that the happiness in the outer world is conceived.

Evening, 9-11-35

110. Enjoy Glory by Dropping Body-Consciousness

By leaving the identification with the body, you attain Glory. This means that you attain the state of Brahman. In this way one becomes great, but by holding on to the body one becomes very petty. When the mind has the hope to get money and many other things, one becomes still smaller. By being Brahman in one's concept, one becomes very great. When the mind starts becoming narrower, it becomes very small, and when it starts becoming larger and larger, it becomes Brahman. The attachment to the body makes you small, and being one with the Self makes you great. At the door of God's home, the king is the bigger beggar and the poor man is the smaller beggar, because as soon as one drops the body-identification there is the state of Brahman. By identifying oneself with the body, one goes down the wrong path. You should firmly believe in the advice given by the Saint.

The questioner asks, "What is the advice of the Saint, and, how and what is the belief in his advice. Please tell me." The Guru says, "The Saint always knows that you are the Highest Joy, that you are the Self." You have no birth, and you should have no fear about anything. Parents and other relatives only try to reinforce your body-consciousness, and you are forced to have fear because of that. However, by listening to the advice of the Saint you become fearless. Therefore, listen to the advice given by the Saint. The "Great Statement" (Mahavakya) of the Vedas is "You Are That." That statement says that you are only Brahman. One who does not forget this is God. The meaning of that statement is that "You are Paramatman," you are of the nature of Brahman itself. This is the meaning of the Great Statement, which is supported by all evidence. The fact that you are Brahman is self-evident. You were always only Brahman even though you thought you were an individual, you just were not aware of it.

Some say that you will attain Brahman only after death. However, when you do not attain it while living, how can you attain it after death What is the proof of experience that that is the case? Who can give that proof? One fool says, "How can we be free now at this moment? When the world comes to an end, then Liberation is there automatically." These fools do not realize that when one world ends, another is bound to come into being. It is stupid to say that attaining Brahman will be there as a matter of course when the Illusion vanishes, or when the body dies. Only one who is beyond the body while actually in it, and who does not perceive the Illusion has achieved "The Happiness of the State of Brahman." This must be attained while we are living in the body. When one really understands, he enjoys the body-consciousness as well as the world. He never loses his equilibrium, or equanimity. Once a man saw a long root in the road that he thought to be a snake. When he verified what it was, he knew that it was only a root. Then there was no need to kill the root. On the contrary, it was good for firewood. In this way, the illusion of the snake was gone. Similarly this world appearance was experienced at first, and now it has become false. The anxious thought of "what to do now?" has vanished. All of this is only a false, illusory appearance. Why should we do any effort now? There is neither drowning nor floating. There is an actual experience of being the owner of the world. One's Self is the owner. "I am always non-active. Even with the mind, I do not project and conceive of any activity. Everything comes and goes of its own accord. Now the concept of bondage and freedom is uprooted and gone. The one who was asking for soup, got the 'Nectar of Immortality.'"

Vedanta philosophy is so charitable that it offers the "Bliss of Brahman." However, the person who offers it must be a "True Guru," a Sadguru, who has realized Brahman. Without him, the Vedanta is unable to give you anything. The Vedas are but like a pauper without a Sadguru. If you enquire of the Vedas, the Vedas will say that if you want to know our Glory, you must go to the Sadguru, otherwise you will not understand. In the dream you experience that a tiger is attacking you. How can you escape it? What is the remedy? The remedy is that you must awaken. Learn to pinch yourself for "That." This means that you must make the conviction that "I am Brahman," very firm. Then, all suffering is alleviated. To be an individual is the work of Illusion. The one who conceives that he is an individual perceives the world, and the world harasses him. As soon as you hold the conviction "I am Brahman," the world disappears. Its falseness is revealed, it is proven unreal, and the Self is "Self-evident."

Evening, 10-11-35

111. The Ghost of Worry

So, up to this point you have had the delusion of being an individual, a Jiva. As soon as the concept of being a Jiva is gone, the concept of God, Shiva, its counterpart, is also gone. The Illusion, Maya, has appeared to be very fearsome, but it is really nonexistent. It is only an illusion. The result of Self-Knowledge is complete fearlessness. Self-Knowledge means that there is no fear of any beings. That life which has no fear of any beings is a formless life, and it is beyond even the transparent. It is not a material form that is perceivable by our senses. It cannot be destroyed by any experiments involving the five elements (the dissolution of the five elements). It is not even touched by the sense of having Knowledge. When the Illusion is unreal, why should we harbor any fear of what will happen, or how things will happen? In a dream, one may be afraid, but upon awakening, the fear is gone. Similarly, when one is awakened to one's True Nature, all fear is gone. Many ignorant people consult an astrologer to get their dreams interpreted. Similarly, although this world is proven to be false, as soon as you worry, it shows that you are not using proper discrimination (Viveka). Whenever there is worry, there is no "Bliss of Self-Knowledge." The only one who gets the enjoyment of this Bliss is the one who is sure about his True Nature.

One whose mind is depressed is never free of anxiety as he is suffering from the false notion of being an individual. One whose mind does not utilize discrimination never asks why he should not worry. All people are taking on the veil of anxiety and dying of worry, but they never think about why they should not even worry at all. You allow the dog of worry to enter and reach the "Shrine Room," the inner sanctum of your own home. Worry is not helpful for anything. The question is "What should the formless Self worry about?" In every living being there is strife going on day and night. Even the judge or the king is not free of anxiety because they do not give the proper justice to anxiety, or even go to bed without anxiety. As soon as he puts his back to the bed his worrying starts. Why, I ask? At least, he should sleep peacefully. The next day when he gets up, there is going to be some benefit from taking a rest from the worry, which he gets during deep sleep. However, this man still never stops worrying. Even if there is some benefit or profit that has been gained, he still continues to worry. To awaken to the Self is itself what is truly beneficial. So, I ask you, why should you be anxious? Whatever you want to do, you should do without anxiety. Because of worry, knowledge becomes impossible to gain, and Spiritual Knowledge is not grasped. What is destined to happen happens, so why then should there be anxiety? Even the Lord, Shri Rama, had to go to live in the forest one fine morning instead of sitting upon his throne. Thus, only what is destined to happen, happens. So why worry for anything? The "Bliss of Brahman" is very delicate, very subtle. However, that great Bliss is not possible because of worry. Those who are doing spiritual practice (sadhana) with a desire to enjoy that Bliss should never worry. Only then can that Bliss be attained. When the illusion of being a jiva is gone, the Self is fully realized.

Why should you have any anxiety? Illusion is only visible to the imagination. If you have no imagination, the Illusion does not do anything. There is a story about a moneylender who was always worrying about what will happen if this, or another thing were to take place. He was a very rich man with a large family, and he had a large number of cows, buffaloes, and horses. He had many servants, and his house was always full of grains. Once during the days of Diwali festival, after having a rich dinner with family members and children, he was comfortably reclining in his hall. At that time, he remembered that some years back there was a drought where many cattle in his town and other villages in the vicinity had died and many other people were on the verge of death due to hunger. As he sat there in his comfortable surroundings he remembered those past events, and he was overwhelmed with sorrow. Tears came to his eyes as he sat there in that depressed state. After a short time his wife came and saw this. She was curious, and asked what has happened, what was wrong. He said, "My dear, if that situation comes again, what will happen?" and he started openly crying. His wife got up, went to where he was sitting, and also started crying. Seeing them there, some other women asked her, "What happened, why are you crying?" She said, "Nothing very serious, but if that situation comes again, what will happen?" It is often the case with rich sophisticated people that it happens that whatever they are feeling, all the others around them also feel. So, all the other people began to follow the lead of the man and his wife, and started crying as well. All the servants and relatives also began to cry. Gradually, this news spread through the town and as he was a famous rich man, the other nearby villages were also affected. Everybody was asking each other, "If that situation occurs again what will happen?" Then, as the crying was everywhere, wise people began to enquire as to what was the fact behind all of this fuss. Respectable people went to the house of the rich man and asked him, "What is really the matter after all?" He then proceeded to tell the whole story of the drought in the past. Listening to this, they all became very surprised! This is the case with the whole world. Everything gets distorted by imagination.

Do not think that this is only the story of that moneylender. This is your story. If the Self foolishly starts to worry without cause, everything gets twisted, and all the sense-organs and bodily functions also get confused, worried, and unhappy. All beings are constantly worrying about what will happen, and how it will happen. This pathetic story about worry for the future is found everywhere. Man was born crying and will go on crying until the time of death. What is it that makes a corpse look good? It only looks good because of the sorrow of other people. If nobody cries the corpse is not honored, and does not really look so good. There is a saying, "Is there anybody who will lament upon your death?" And, if someone doesn't lament they say that he has no feeling. So, you should think, "Why to cry? Why to worry?" It's alright, be worried, but it should be true care, true worry. Why do you worry in vain? Be confident and certain. Only that which is destined to happen is going to happen.

The tiger is definitely going to kill you and eat you, no matter what name you may give it. Then why should you not kill the anxiety that is needlessly created by the name? Destiny is going to play out as it will. Why worry about what will happen in the future? In short, Bliss comes near where there is happiness, similar to how some culture has to be added to milk in order to get yogurt out of it. In order to attain the state of highest Bliss, you have to enjoy without worry. If a rich man worries more than the beggar, the rich man is worse than the beggar. Worry is such that it does not go without your dropping it. Even if you are given great prosperity, still you go on worrying. What can God do about it? What can God do for you if you do not let go of all worry? As you have lost the quality of discrimination, worry is always troubling you. The individual thinks that it is he who does everything, and suffers accordingly. It is said that "over-wise is otherwise." The individual thinks in vain, "Nobody ever does their work properly. Only I can do the work nicely. No good job can be done without me." In vain, he always worries like this.

You will not have peace if you continue to hold on to all of this worry. So, let go of all worry. Come what may, you must be without anxiety. The Illusion creates fear only for the one who is constantly worrying about what will happen, and how it will happen. Those who worry are going to die anyway. As soon as you project an image of what will happen, worry starts. You start worrying about a thing that is not even existing. Why do you let yourself become unhappy by being anxious about future things? Because you have lost the power of discrimination you are worried. A madman imagines about happiness. In his imagination, the madman may even give a kick to the God Indra. He is happy in this imagination and also very courageous. You should be happy and content with whatever humble bread you get. One who worries even after getting the Nectar of Immortality is surely the enemy of God. You see that another person is happy and you become unhappy. Why do you become unhappy by seeing someone else's happiness? It is because you think, "I do not have what he has." How strange and surprising is the nature of the jiva! This is not a desirable condition. The reason for this criticism is that those who are indiscreet are unhappy. A beggar is free of any worry. In a way, he kicks the anxiety. He eats his bread and chutney with royal majesty. Just see how he enjoys such a simple meal! All things are possible without feeling the need to worry. Never bother yourself unless circumstances really demand. Whatever may be, let it be, undisturbed.

Only one who releases oneself from the clutches of anxiety is fit to possess this "Knowledge of Brahman." It is only he, who can gain this Knowledge. To the one who is joyful, Bliss comes of its own accord. He enjoys Bliss at all times. Grief joins grief, and sorrow joins sorrow. One who completely lets go of worry is the brave man who rides the tiger. Lord Vishnu is reclining on the body of the most venomous serpent, the Shesha, and he is not afraid or worried about the extreme poison. The poisonous hissing of that serpent is not troublesome to him. On the contrary, it gives him joy. The one who is Self-contented is enjoying the "Bliss of the Self." That is why he is the spouse of Goddess Laxmi, the deity of wealth and riches. As he is in his own "Inner-Bliss," the Goddess Laxmi is massaging his feet. However, there you (the individual) are, at the feet of the perishable thing that is worry, and she is burning you without any reason.

Let go of anxiety and be happy. Anxiety is poison. Why have that bitter taste in your mouth? A blind man does not have a fly in his soup because he does not worry. The snake does not bite small children. Our own imagination becomes our enemy. You imagine that there is a ghost, and it is demanding something from you, and then the worry becomes a daily affair. It possesses you, and then it controls you totally. You must let go of Illusion. Never imagine about sorrow. The anxiety has snuck into your mind. Discard it by quiet discrimination, recognizing that it is unnecessary and unessential. Then you are surely happy.

11-11-35

112. Illusion is Only Visible to the Imagination

Illusion, or Maya is only a concept, and concept is the individual, the jiva. That concept which takes the form of the jiva, is Maya. From the beginning of understanding in childhood we have various emotions arising in us. That is Maya. The very nature of the jiva is to be aware, to begin to perceive, and to sense something. The jiva means Maya. However, this is not realized unless one becomes very subtle, very quiet and peaceful, and remains steady in this peace. Only if you remain quietly unmoved, before any urge arises in your mind, does this become evident. Illusion is only visible to the imagination. Gold is only gold to the one who sells it, but it is an ornament to the one who is wearing it. The merchant sold it at the price of gold, and took the money for the gold. Just as gold is only gold for the goldsmith who sells it, similarly is Brahman for the wise man. Brahman as male, and Maya as female, are false names. They are like a magician's illusion.

Gold in the form of "ornaments" is like Illusion appearing as "forms" or manifestation. The ornament is the form, or the visible object that is made only of gold. Thus, ornaments are like Illusion. Gold without its form of being an "ornament," is like Brahman without any manifestation of Illusion. The name and shape of the object appears separate from other forms, and it is because of this belief in separateness that there is some liking or attraction to that object. Where there is a separate form of gold as an ornament that is taken to be true or is liked, this is the attachment to "form" in the Illusion. The ornament is itself enticement. Enticement, or attraction, is for the form, which is visible. The form is taken to be true, and therefore we are attracted to it. This attraction to the form has confused the Self. This confusion is ego, and that ego takes the role of the "Protector of the Illusion." This should be clearly understood. Form is like the ornaments. Although we know definitely that we are not the ornament, we are still attracted to it. This is the "Great Illusion." We are not individuals having a body, we are Brahman beyond all forms and bodies. When the body seems to be real, then you are the individual, the jiva, otherwise you are only Brahman.

It is said, "Brahman should be as Brahman." The king behaves with the awareness that he is the king, and the soldier behaves like a soldier. In the same way, Brahman, or one who has realized Brahman, should behave as Brahman. It is obvious that as a rule, everybody should live according to their status. This is natural. A person earning three hundred rupees lives in his own style and behaves accordingly, while someone who earns only twenty rupees lives according to his status. Self-Knowledge is similar to this. One surely behaves according to one's understanding, but the question is, does he understand properly? Everything is God. God is beyond every form, and that God is our Self. This world belongs to Him, and He is the enjoyer of this world. Therefore, He must remain with his "Full Awareness." He should never forget that He is God in any lifestyle or occupation. It is not simply by some attitude that one can be Brahman. It is not by some particular mood or attitude that Brahman is attained. It is as it is, naturally. One should live in its "Royal Glory," with full recognition, remembering one's own Grandeur. One should behave by remembering what one is. Then all becomes very easy, but only for the one who realize this.

There is a story of a woman who used to always contradict her husband. As a rule, she did not do what her husband said. The poor husband was fed up. He was then met by a sage. The sage advised him that he should say exactly opposite to what he really wanted. When he followed this advice, he became very happy. The point of this is that if your thinking is good, you will get the experience. You are naturally Brahman (the man in the story) but your thinking goes astray (the contradictory wife) and leads you into Illusion. This is what happens. However, by simply maintaining a certain attitude or one-sided thinking, one does not become Brahman. An attitude, or thinking, cannot sustain the state of Brahman. All of the teaching is only addressed to the thinking, for gaining a grooved attitude. However, Brahman itself cannot really be advised at all. Brahman is in its own Being. It is Brahman, alone, and attitude or thoughts do not come near it. There is nothing more or less in Brahman. A fool is happy at the time of death because he was very secure with a great sum of money. The fool is very easily satisfied. Is there any way out of death? Absolutely not. Is all of that money useful to him in any way in the future? No. He had not used proper discrimination in his life at all. Happiness and sorrow belong to the attitude, and not to Brahman. The attitude is dependent upon the concept of the jiva. Brahman is beyond Illusion while the jiva is entangled in Illusion. This entire visible world is false.

Our True Nature is that we are the Supreme Lord of this world. This world appears because of us. We are the support of the world. Had we not been here, on what background would the world have appeared? Those who meditate in this way are truly blessed. One should wake up with the memory that one is Brahman and eat, drink, work, etc., only with that awareness. The Illusion appears only to an illusory awareness, or "Purusha." Illusion is conceptual, just as Purusha is also a concept. It is only an idea and therefore it is false. Our nature is Brahman beyond all concepts. To the man who has no ideas or concepts, the world is also not an idea or concept because he has not imagined anything. One should conduct oneself with the full awareness that he is beyond everything. For example, if a man has one million rupees, he knows it, but he cannot take a bite of that money. He does not, and will not eat it. He only constantly lives with that memory, that awareness that it is there. The contentment that one experiences after a full meal cannot be experienced unless the dinner is finished. Please see the difference between the enjoyment of eating, and the full contentment that is experienced after meals are taken. Self-Knowledge is one such "Full Contentment," or Bliss. To remain in the state of ecstasy of the Self is called the "Maintenance and the Glory of Brahman."

There is a saying that "As one thinks at the moment of death, so is his progress in the higher world." When we die to ourselves, when the "I" is gone, then there is the direct experiencing of being Brahman. With the death of the "I," we witness our own death. When the four bodies (gross, subtle, causal, and great-causal or Turya), and the five sheaths, or coverings on Consciousness (Annamaya, Pranamaya, Manomaya, Buddhimaya, Anandamaya) are gone, all limitations are also gone. You are the Self which is independent of the four bodies. You are independent of any progress, qualities, or degrees. What can anybody say about that where the Vedas have become mute, where their power of description is nullified? When there is Self-Realization there is full verification of what the scriptures say, what the Guru says, and what one's own experience is. This is called the triple verification. The Self-Realized One who verifies the truth of all three is the real "knower." This is the sign of the Self. This is called "True Knowledge."

There was the illusion of being only a jiva, which is now gone. Other people had also deceived us. All of our close relatives had gathered and by conspiracy they decided on the twelfth day after our birth (this is a Hindu custom) what we should be called, and fixed our name. That person who was born by the desire of others, in vain, throughout his lifetime lived all puffed up, thinking of himself proudly by that name. He was thus framed by the other people's conditioning. Then by great fortune, he was helped by the Sadguru, and was lifted up. He was saved by the Guru, and was reminded of his True Nature. Only then did he understand that it is He himself, the Self, the beginningless primordial Brahman, who all the world is hoping to find, to pay homage, to do spiritual practice for, and to constantly repeat His name. Thus, he became Brahman confidently by his own experience and in Reality. He left his identification with his occupation in the world, and became an outsider to society. He realized the he is himself Self-sufficient, and beyond all objective things. Gradually climbing to higher and higher states of awareness, he reached Himself. The King, who is the father, gives his kingdom to his son. Similarly, the Sadguru has enthroned you on his elevated state. Enjoy "That."

Evening, 12-11-35

113. The City of Brahman

The state of the individual, the Jiva, is Illusion. It is Ignorance, the original sin. Illusion means that which is not true. The state of Jiva is "not true." The word Jiva is comprised of "Ja" plus "Iva" which means that it is as if born, but not actually born. It is Illusion. If this individual is not true, then what is true? The truth is that "I am that which is not born." It is not true that "I am born" and am called by some name such as Tom, Dick, or Harry. There is a story about a lion that was under the illusion that he was a man. He went to a shepherd to be his servant. For some time the shepherd was feeding him with milk, and later he started giving him dung. Naturally, soon the lion was starving. Then his Guru met him. The Guru of the lion said to him, "You are a Lion, who kills and eats any animal it chooses. Why are you eating dung?" When the lion came to know his capacity he went to the forest and began to hunt and feed himself adequately. Similarly, the individual is actually Paramatman but has taken himself to be a Jiva and has become unhappy. Stop being a human being, and drop the habit of eating the dung that is the sense objects. To eat the dung means to take the results of action (karma). The result of whatever action the individual does is the dung, which the sheep that is the Illusion has given out. When you are certain that you are Shiva, these results of karma that are like dung are avoided. For Shiva, no karma is binding. The Self is Brahman. The imaginary body acts along with all the sense organs. With Self-Knowledge the inheritor of the result of karma is discarded and there is no entity to receive any result. Thus, there is no one to be "convicted."

When the Illusion of the Jiva is gone, all actions are also gone. He is free of all karma, the mountains of sins are burned to ashes, and a mountain of merit is erected. Merit here means the Truth, Reality. One who has realized the Self has become God. Self-Knowledge is itself the mountain of merit. There is no limit to the merit of one who has Self-Knowledge, while one who does not have it earns mountains of sin. Sin means thinking that you are the individual. When the Jiva is not existent, sin also is not present. As soon as the illusion of being a Jiva is there, one raises mountains of sins. With the understanding of our own "True Nature" as Brahman, the mountains of sins collapse. A man who was a brahmin priest thought himself to be a man of low caste, and ate the meat of a buffalo. That concept of being of a low caste was accompanied by the commitment of what was a sin for the brahmin. If a slave is given a blessing that he may live forever, that means he will remain a slave eternally. Misidentification is the creation of sin. Great is the gain on the day that we come to know that we are not a Jiva, but that we are Brahman. Then, the slavery is gone, and the illusion of being a Jiva is gone. On that day, the mountains of sins are drowned to the bottom of the sea. The "Sun of Knowledge" rises, and one again reaches that place from where he has originally come. He reaches his root, and the four bodies vanish.

To turn to the objects of the senses is going downward. To be turned towards the Self is to go upwards. When one realizes the Self, one is totally free. This is called Sayujya Mukti. The total annihilation of everything is this Sayujya Mukti. When there is no "I," and there is no "you," who is there that wants liberation? Blessed is the one who by dissolution of the "I" has realized Brahman. He is the owner of that liberation, and can bestow that state to others. It is the Jnani who has understood that whatever is visible is false. Things are seen, no doubt, but it is only Brahman, and there is nothing separate. In this vast city of Mumbai, if you pick up a handful of earth, is it earth, or is it Mumbai? People give the name of Mumbai to the earth and function accordingly. Really, it is only earth. There is no Mumbai. Without this earth, Mumbai has no existence. Similarly, without the Life-Energy, Chaitanya, the world has no existence. After all, you cannot find anything except for this Life-Energy. There is only this Chaitanya. If you look carefully, and see properly, there is no visible world. If you see in this way, and perform all actions knowing fully well that all of them are false, and you behave with only that attitude, then this is "Liberation while having the physical body" (Jivanmukti). One who remembers the advice given by the Guru, and puts it into practice is entitled to this Liberation.

Is it necessary to learn by heart the whole alphabet in order to know what the word sin means? What is the need of all the scriptures and sciences when you have realized that you are the Self? There is a saying that "Through suffering does the path to Bliss go." The Sadguru says that this is true, but it means that this body should be given up. This is the price you must pay. We should not live life as a physical body, but as pure Life-Energy, as Chaitanya. Liberation is very near and easily available when you go to the Guru. However, Illusion holds a very powerful weapon to be used against the disciple. That weapon is the lack of faith in Guru. We should serve the Guru, and work with devotion to him until we get the fruit. The devotee should wait patiently and faithfully until the fruit ripens.

Those who declare, "I am Brahman," but do not have realization, become demons after death. A mango tastes sour if eaten before it is ripe and you do not enjoy the good taste. You cannot get the real benefit from the fruit if it is not fully ripe. The Sadguru has given us the third eye that is the "Inner Sight of the Direct Perception of Truth." This is the third eye of the "Fire of Knowledge of Lord Shiva." This is not a physical eye. It is the "Eye of Knowledge." We have our two physical eyes, and the Guru has given us this new eye which is the "Sun of Knowledge." The Lord of the whole world, the Formless Existence (Purusha) pervading all, is this eye. When you see with this eye, the whole world disappears. It is destroyed, and we see only Brahman. This visible world is the bondage of Illusion, and this new eye given by the Sadguru destroys this Illusion.

The devotee of the Guru enjoys the "Bliss of Aloneness" while in the body. When Lord Shiva has Self-Knowledge, he says, "I am experiencing this dream of My Own Self. Now I have known this dream as Myself." The dream is the Self, it is "Existence" as one's Self. The experience is ours, and it is so only because of our Existence, therefore it is called "Self-Experience." Because of the Self, and by taking the support that I give, this flame of intelligence is kindled. When we observe all with this flame of intelligence, we see that all is born only of the Self. There is no "other" in this. As this is the experience of the Self, by the Self, it is called "Self-Experience."

All of the terms, Oneself, Brahman, "Self-Experience," mean only one thing, that all of this is the dream (swapna) of the Self. The "Self-Experience" (Atma-Anubhava) is Self-Realization. It is said that the world is a playhouse of adult people. This means that the "adults" are people of Knowledge. They have Self-Knowledge, and they are great. For them, this entire world is a toy, a thing to play with. In this game, they have no sorrow or elation, loss or gain, grief, death, etc. To those who see this world as "Self-Experience" it as a natural game of joy. Ignorant people take the world as real. For them sorrow, grief, worry, and fear are their lot in life. The wise however, know that the world is unreal and happily live in their own "House of Contentment."

A wise man says, "We live in that country where nobody can go." We should remain in our own town. "Our town" is that place from where nobody comes back. One who has realized Brahman talks about things in that town, and enquires only about that town. That town will only talk about itself. Rich people will talk about their own rich life, and those with Self-Knowledge will speak about Brahman only. If anybody meets another man, it is known by his speech and behavior what his caste is, what his religion is, what his occupation is, etc. The behavior, speech, and actions of a Jnani are always full of wisdom. The wise person will always live as a wise person.

No Date Given

114. The Root of Birth

When one is illumined by the teaching given by the Sadguru, all of the four bodies (the physical, the subtle, the causal, and the great-causal body) are dissolved. Then, everything becomes false. In fact, it is already false. Only one state calls everything false. After leaving aside all things, the mind becomes engrossed in "Oneness." Then one becomes that which was the aim to be achieved. One becomes that final home of "Total Freedom" (Sayujya Mukti). One becomes the owner of that "Freedom."

That which remains after abandoning what is visible, is Brahman. In Ignorance, the observed and the observer are two things. When that which is observed is dissolved, the observer remains alone (without any object of observation). "That" is Brahman. In deep sleep, the ignorant one enjoys that objectless state unknowingly when he leaves behind the visible world. One cannot live without enjoying that Bliss. The one who does not get proper sleep, is sure to leave the body, which is the final rest of death. The state of deep sleep is a need that is shared equally by the poor as well as the rich. The happiness of deep sleep is common to all creatures. A man may owe a million rupees or may be expecting a million rupees from someone else, but both are equal in deep sleep. The great sinner and the yogi are equal in deep sleep.

"That" which is beyond the visible is the Self. If we discern properly, this universe is not what it appears to be. Ignorance is that which is false, and to treat it as Truth is also Ignorance. To know the false as false, to recognize that it is unreal, is Knowledge. To know the Reality, is Supreme Knowledge, but to take the unreal to be real is Ignorance. The wise see the false as false and they experience accordingly. A hill is really only a heap of earth, not a hill. When you look at the city of Mumbai, the earth that is the essence, the reality beneath, is not seen. If you see it as earth, then Mumbai as a city disappears from your view.

Liberation is to recognize what is "True" and what is false. To treat the false as true is bondage. The one who leaves this world, knowing it to be false, will not return. The one who is convinced that the world is false, has no desire to return. However, desire will not leave the one who thinks that the world is true. The desire of those who have no further need of the world, dies away. Nobody else compels one to take birth. One takes birth, or is born, according to one's desire. One makes the preparations for their next birth today. For one who is ignorant there is the hope that perhaps they will at least get some happiness in the next birth. The ignorant person says "What else am I to do, if I am not to take birth?" There are many who give in charity because of their belief that another birth is unavoidable. Those who are wise know that this world appearance is false, and accordingly become desireless and free.

Meditate on the teaching given by the Sadguru and hold it very near to your heart. Do not forget that you are the "One Self." Listen to the Guru and meditate on his words with extreme respect. One who does not do this surely kills himself. One who has to live in this world should not extinguish the "Lamp of Knowledge." The one who abides by the great statement that "I Am Brahman" is the one who is entitled to Liberation. Afterwards, this concept, the observance of ritual, and the great statement itself, all disappear. Then there is neither seeing, nor the unseeable. The "Natural State" is attained. Meditation and holding any object in the mind both end. Imagination is dissolved. It merges into the non-conceptual. Then, the one that is named as "Mr. So-and-so" is Brahman, and only Consciousness remains. This is called "Subtle Brahman." This itself is the Natural State. The dream ends, and along with it all of the people in the dream also disappear. "He" alone remains. The prolonged dream is gone and Brahman remains alone. Then the Subtle Brahman, which is Pure Consciousness, alone remains. The bondage of the world, as well as sin and merit, are all finished. The appearances end, and only the observer remains. The One who has no birth, is Liberated. The Illusion had him entangled in the sorrowful cycle of birth and death, but now all of that is dissolved. The Sadguru, like the "Brilliant Sun of Freedom," met him, and he was given his own "Original Nature." He is convinced about Brahman without coming or going anywhere.

No Date Given

115. The Tragedy of Family Life

The mirage that is this ocean of worldly life is now dried up. We generally feel proud of some particular thing, and accordingly, we put upon ourselves the bondage of the completion that particular work. The feeling that we must finish a particular job is pride. It is pride when we wish to live our family life happily. However, the family life will never be a happy life. A clay wall will never be clean, no matter how constantly you may wash and clean it. Even the family life of Lord Vishnu was never happy. Family life is like a dog's tail. It will never be straight. We wish to do something, and it is nothing but our own pride, our ego. Only the life of the Masters, the "Accomplished Beings" (Siddha Purushas), is properly lived. They have dropped all pride. Let the world be drowned, a Saint is not bothered about it. The child of pride does not see the real butter, the essence of happy life. It cannot see it. Lord Krishna only saw the essence, the butter, and ate that, so he is called the "robber of the butter," (Makhanchor).

The one who is full of pride suffers only pain and sorrow. People desire that many things should happen, but what is real in all of that? The individual, the jiva, is always full of doubt. The jiva never says "enough." God came to give a boon to a devotee, but after six months elapsed, the devotee still could not complete the list of things that he wanted. He was always saying that he wanted something more. In the mean time, God disappeared. Happy is the one who has no pride. For him, the ocean of worldly life is dried up. The Illusion does exactly opposite to what you set out to do, so the man who has no pride is happy. He has no desire to do anything. Actually, happiness is happy because of him, and all sorrows are abandoned. They are ended. In short, where there is pride, there is Illusion, and where there is no pride there is the highest state of happiness. A man who has no ego is never defeated while a man who has ego can never be free of worldly life.

When does the mirage of worldly life get dried up? Only when one is devoid of pride. Through the egotistical decision that I will complete some certain work, three kinds of troubles arise. They are bodily ailments, accidents by outer things or beings, and calamities coming from natural causes. It is easy to see whether the family life of a selfless man, an egoless man, is being lived properly or not. Even though you have killed your ego, the cosmic order, or destiny is very much there. It is doing its work continuously. However, human nature is such that in the mind there is a challenge to verify how God makes things easy for a prideless man. As you are getting your humble bread, you should live on as God wills for you. You ask, "If God is doing everything, why is he not giving me an elephant to ride?" In this way, man in vain strengthens his hope and becomes unhappy.

To draw paintings on a wall is the nature of worldly life. People paint pictures on walls and give them various captions. A man with desire to get applause from all drowns himself in fictitious pictures, which is the ocean of worldly life. Rama lost Sita, the embodiment of peace, by running after the deer. Such is the power of this mirage. Illusion is the axe of death, the noose of the God of Death. The entanglement in Maya is the noose of death. One who is free from pride snaps this noose of the Death God (Yama). He is not subjected to the punishment, the rod of Yama. To be beaten with Yama's rod is to suffer from sorrow, and pride is its cause. When pride is gone all fear and sorrow is gone. Then, everywhere there is only "Contentment."

No Date Given

116. Drinking the Nectar of Immortality

The mirage of the world is dried up. It is called "Bhava" which means "that which has come into existence." The Self is non-worldly. There is no outer or inner existence of anything. The existence of the world appears due to the different attributes (Gunas). Attribute means only Ignorance. Kama means desire, and because of that desire, the virgin goddess Sharada came into existence. It is called the "virgin desire" or Iccha-Kumari. It is that which created the ability of the perception of Truth in man. The One who has no pride was shown the world as Illusion, which is called Maya. The Saints are always desireless, while Maya creates fear for the one who desires something. It is Maya who considers even the gods Hari (Vishnu) and Hara (Shiva) as beggars. The ordinary beggar has small demands, but such great beggars like Hari and Hara have tremendous needs.

There is a story of a king and a sage. The king worshipped the sage and offered him a good seat with all due respect and honor. However, in the inner "Shrine Room" of the temple, the king prayed to God to give him a great many things. The sage, who was sitting in the outer hall, heard this and began to leave. The king asked the sage why he was leaving. To this the sage said, "You are a beggar. You are demanding many things from the god in the shrine room, and then you will give me some meals. I do not want all of that. Everyone is a beggar just like you. The difference is only of degree." Everyone in the world is a beggar. The one who does not demand anything is rich. Such rich people like Saint Tukaram are the real Saints. They enjoy Bliss and say, "Let Maya take away whatever she wants. Whatever is the maximum that Maya can take away, let her take it away."

When Shiva willed it, only then, did the Jiva, or the individual, come into existence. This is called the virgin desire. Desire is the world. Desire is the ocean of worldly life. For the one who realizes that what he desires is his own Self, the mirage of this worldly life gets dried up. It is as if he has sipped this ocean of worldly life once and for all. One who demands anything of this world is but a beggar, and one who does not have any demands is a Seer, a Sage. He who has withdrawn his desire becomes the "Totality." What does one who is in the grip of a bear gain by kissing the bear? The bear does not kill quickly. It tantalizes, tickles, and kills slowly. It plays pranks on its victim. One who understands this does not consider anything in this world to be valuable. The Jiva takes a false vow, prepares himself for activity by means of the ego, and creates a fictitious bondage. But, this bondage is broken when this entire phenomenal world is seen as only Brahman.

Thus the one who is truly without birth, becomes free of birth and death. He was afflicted by pleasure and pain but now understands that the enjoyer is himself God, and finds that this visible mirage has disappeared. The ailment in the form of attachment was affecting the one who is in reality without any attachment. It was He who is beyond the body who seemed to have been caught in body-consciousness. Although he is unworldly, he was caught in the attachments of worldliness. Now, all of that is dissolved. In the totality of Being that is primordial and without a beginning, there entered a sense of "I," which created the duality of "me" and "you," but now it has again become "Unity." Aloneness had become divided into two, but has returned to Aloneness. The suffering has ended. It simply ran away. The one who was and is endless, has returned to "That" which has no end. He has understood that he is Wholeness itself, without any disturbance, forever. Through the advice of the Sadguru, he has realized that he is never going to end. He became convinced of this, and remains in his "Original State."

Ignorant people try to free the sun at the time of a solar eclipse by giving some articles in charity. There is a great distance between the sun and the moon, but in ancient times, it was believed that the sun was swallowed by the moon when there was an eclipse. The moon has no power to go near the sun. It would be burnt up as soon as it would go anywhere near the sun. It is not that scientists did not know this, but it was declared in the scriptures that the sun was swallowed by the moon with the intention to encourage ignorant people to give something in charity. Similarly, it was written that by giving one rupee in charity today, one will get many more rupees in the next birth. The scribes had the intention to encourage people to be charitable one way or another. However, the Guru says that you are Brahman, and that Maya cannot touch you. You are the "Sun of Intelligence." The Guru has awakened the one who was asleep. He has awakened the one who was already awake. To Knowledge itself, the Guru revealed that your nature is Knowledge. When the illusion of the "I" disappears, you are free. You are he who came into the womb of the mother where there was previously no fetus, and you are he who remains after the body is dead. Before going to the Guru you were as if dead. You were accepting death, and you were eating dirt. To you, the one who clung to death, the elixir, the "Nectar of Immortality" (Amrut) was given. To him who was enjoying this earthly body, the Guru gave the "Nectar of Deathlessness."

In Hindu mythology, the drinking of wine is called Surrapaan. That wine was given to the demons (Asuras) to drink. That wine or sura, means the objects of the five senses. The "Nectar of Knowledge" was taken by the gods. Lord Vishnu is the "Great God" who drinks that nectar. The jar of nectar that was the outcome of the churning of the ocean, was this Nectar of Knowledge. The Sadguru gave nectar to the gods, and the wine of sense pleasures was created for the demons that are attached to the physical body. Those who drink the Nectar of Knowledge become deathless, and those who go to the city of "Deathlessness" never come back. Yama, the "God of Death" tears away from his book the page with their name on it. This worldly life is like a kind of contagious disease. If there is anybody's account in this bank of worldliness, others will also surely be affected. However, you will not find the name of the devotee of the Sadguru in the book of Yama. Only by the Grace of the Guru can one receive this nectar to drink. He is "God Incarnate" who has received this nectar to drink, because he has no sense of anything "other."

No Date Given

117. Curing the Disease of Maya

The Illusion is so strange that the "unattached" was caught in attachment, the "deathless" was given death, and the Supreme Self, Paramatman, was given the state of the individual (Jiva) and subjected to untold sufferings. This Illusion, this Maya, is difficult to cross. By the Power of the Sadguru the Illusion becomes ashamed and disappears. However numerous the ways and means of spiritual practice that you may invent, all of them only serve to strengthen the Illusion. These efforts are like using petrol to extinguish a fire when the house is burning. The fireman himself gets burned in such an effort. Whatever effort one may invent by imagination to surpass the Illusion only helps Maya to appear even stronger. If we try to destroy Maya by using imagination it is only more strongly cultivated and will never be reduced. It is only through the instructions given by the Sadguru, and not by any other means, that it is possible to have contentment without using any concepts or imagination. There should be complete negation of the sense of "I" in one's sadhana. That is the only way to destroy the Illusion. If this subtle point is not understood Illusion only becomes stronger. It is only with the "Master Key of Self-Knowledge" that is given by the Sadguru, that the Self can be understood and realized. All other means only strengthen the sense of being a separate individual.

There is a saying that when a man dies he becomes God. This means that when the separateness of the individual dies, what remains is only Brahman. When the sense of "I," the ego, disappears, there is only Pure Brahman. When the delusion of "I" goes, only Shiva exists. He is without any attachment. The ignorant one was playing hide and seek by closing his eyes, and he won victory when he opened his eyes. By force of habit in daily behavior there was the illusion of "I," and in its wake, the sufferings of hell and heaven are inescapable. The greatest of all diseases is the concept of the separateness of "I." Some call it the disease of worldliness. All creatures are suffering from this disease. The diseases of being a snake, a scorpion, an ass, a horse, etc. are due only to this ego of being a separate entity. This Illusion is the mother of all diseases. She is called the evil goddess "Mari," in front of whom the goat (who cries "me, me,") and the buffalo, who are symbols of Ignorance, should be slain. Mari desires this offering. The bleating of goats and the bellowing of buffaloes are her feast. This is similar to the chattering or meaningless babble of the human being. Time is always eager to devour all things including the sun and moon, but "That" which is the Supreme Death of death, even swallows Illusion. Time is afraid of the one who has Self-Knowledge. Time says that "This hunter hunts me without error, but no other can escape my clutches."

Death strikes everyone at their particular appointed hour and minute. Before birth, Time was there. Time, Duration, Death, etc. are its names. Brahman is prior to Time. The Saints have reached "That" which is beyond Time. The Saints used Time as a stepping stone to go beyond the river of worldly life. Time is death, and just as people build a bridge by putting stone upon stone, the Saint built a bridge of death itself. The individual was transformed into Lord Narayana by virtue of the teaching given by the Sadguru. Lord Rama who accepts and goes through life in a forest, does so by the strength of the teaching of the Guru, and kills Ravana who is the ego. You are that Raghuveer, Lord Rama. To avoid the suffering of forest life you should be the devotee of the Sadguru. What is the meaning of undertaking any vow or doing rituals? It means that you are not, and only Narayana exists. That is called "Navas" in Marathi language which means, "You are not." You are only Brahman, the one Narayana. There is no other such miracle. This disease of Illusion is very strange. No other disease is as incurable as the notion of being an individual. A doctor cannot cure this disease because the one who cures this disease must be before the appearance of Illusion. He must be the "Knower of Illusion," knowing the whole truth of "That which is prior to Illusion." For this disease, no medicines are useful except the "Nectar of Immortality," which is a dose of the realization that "I Am Brahman." Only the Sadguru can dispense the medicine of "You Are That."

When you follow the instructions given by the Sadguru, and when you do service to Him, the disease of Illusion is gradually cured. You must have the "divine medicine" ("I Am That") that kills the root cause of the disease that is the sense of "I," the ego. When the medicine is finished, the disease is cured. Actually, the disease was false, and the medicine was also false. There was a flood in the mirage that was created by concepts and imagination. When the imagination is destroyed, the water in the mirage dries up along with the imagination. Then the story ends. There is no need to do spiritual practice for the one who has understood this. Pride, or the ego, was having a thousand arms before the disciple went to the Guru. The Guru, as Lord Krishna removed all the other arms and kept only two. The mantra that means, "I Am That," was given to the disciple making him unattached.

There is a story about a king who was once imprisoned because while he was making a nightly tour as a disguised person he was arrested by the night guard, to whom he said that he was just an ordinary man roaming in the streets. He was immediately nabbed and put behind bars. He forgot to tell the guard that he was the king. Soon, he was reminded by the Self who is the real teacher, that he was the king. As soon as he revealed his true identity as the king, he was released from prison. Similarly, the Self identifies himself with the container of body in which he enters, and says that he is that container. It is really always only the Supreme Self, Paramatman who takes all of the various forms and appearances. To know this is the real medicine. Paramatman is the "Lord of the World." Such a tiny life as a body is not benefiting of His Greatness. It is foolish to say so. The Illusion is so stupid that it is like saying that a bug was married to a camel, and their children were lice. When the jiva came to know his own reality, he was ashamed. How will Paramatman say that he is just an ignorant jiva? To consider oneself to merely be an individual is Ignorance, it is nonsense. One who is awakened by Knowledge becomes free from worldliness.

No Date Given

118. The Duality Broken

The One who is alone conceived that this world is dual in nature, and was deluded by the confusion of Ignorance. It is like the example of a man who saw the firefly giving a tiny light after the sun had set, and started performing some rituals to possess that light. Duality was seen by "He who was Alone," and by the teaching given by the Sadguru, he again was One. He who was always in seclusion, had become the multitude. He who was always awake, had the illusion that he was asleep. Whatever is perceived or seen by us, what appears to us, what is understood by us, and all that which we recognize, is experience. This experience is the arising of duality out of "unity," and is only a dream. This experience is like the time in a dream. When experience is even of a minute nature, it is the "Time of Ignorance" which is the nature of time itself. The perception of Time and the experiencing of the outer world is the slumber of the True Being. The state of ordinary knowledge is duality and Illusion. Unity is not Illusion and therefore there is no witnessing of "other." Therefore, it is only He who has awakened himself. Being only the Self, in reality we never go to sleep. The sense organs take rest, and that is what is called sleep. The Self is unattached to the sense objects. If the Self were to sleep, then the sense organs would not awaken at all. There would be no movement. But He is awake. He is not asleep. There was only an illusion, which was removed. He who is awake has awakened himself. One who is always of the nature of the illuminator, who is of the nature of the "Original Observer," was given Self-Knowledge. This is the description of the one whose ego is no more. This is not a description of the individual, it is pointing to Paramatman.

This is the teaching about Brahman. The tiger was apprehensive about being a goat, but then he was made aware of the fact that he was a tiger. He who is self-created was reminded of his "Original Nature." Even though a man may be ignorant, it is a proven fact that he is deathless. Because of Ignorance one has to take birth again, while by gaining Knowledge he becomes "One with Reality." That is the only difference. For one who dies while identified being with the body, the idea that he is a petty jiva persists. When attachment to the body is dropped by gaining Knowledge, one becomes vast, and is one with the all-pervading Being. The realization that "I am everywhere" is the death of the limited knower. If you want to test this, see what happens when you are asleep. When you know that there is no birth, you are also sure that there is no death. A man forgot where he lived and was wandering. Then he was taken back to his house. Similarly, the "One beyond qualities" was made to realize himself through the teaching of the Sadguru. The One who is the "Life-Energy" was again made into that Life-Energy, that Power. He was shown his "True Nature," his "True Form" (Swaroopa). He whose nature is Bliss was shown that he is only Bliss. When the "Great God" Shiva (Mahadev) became the bull Nandi he started to pull the yoke. But when he was reminded that he was Mahadev, he was freed from the yoke. The individual will definitely experience suffering and sorrow if he is born again.

An owner of slaves had the power to bring dead slaves back to life. He used to arouse the dead slaves and employ them again into slavery. His power was taken away, and the slaves got freedom. God was pleased with a poor man and granted him a gift, a boon of whatever he desired. Upon demand God gave the man a lot of money. When he received the money, thieves beat him and robbed him. He got this gift of money hundreds of times, but all of these gifts were wasted because he was also beaten and robbed hundreds of times. Then a Saint met him, and took him securely to his own abode with all his money. That abode is the state of the Self. He buried that man's four bodies, the physical body, the mental body, the causal body, and the great-causal body, and thus he became deathless. If a servant is given the boon of deathlessness he is destined to eternally remain a servant. What is the use of such deathlessness, as it is not a desirable thing to remain deathless in this way. Be that "Deathlessness," which is beyond the four bodies, and then "Freedom" is given Freedom.

The yogi is always united with Shiva. However, when the worship of Shiva is performed with a notion that one is a jiva who is doing the worshiping, and if there is a feeling of separation in the mind, this worship is not real worship of Shiva. The jiva, with a notion that he is the doer becomes involved, but does not know what he is. As soon as he realizes what he is, he is beyond both sin and merit. They say that "Chitragupta" writes, and Chitragupta sees. (Chitragupta is said to be the one who keeps all accounts of all the good and bad things that one does in life). Is there any crime that has been committed that we ourselves do not know? Is there any sin or merit that the mind is not aware of? All of this is told in order so one should discard fear. However, do not think that whatever you may do will be condoned. Only the one who is desireless becomes free of the fruits of his actions. It is the sense that "I am the enjoyer," or "I am the sufferer" that must go.

No Date Given

119. The Golden Day

The attributeless Paramatman takes on attributes and becomes unhappy. He then gets taken back to His Own State. The king was freed from bondage and was again crowned "King." The sadhana that was undertaken was completed. All the sciences, the guidelines for daily actions, are written in order to help us know Paramatman, and these all are fulfilled on this day. It was proven by experience that when one properly uses the human life he becomes God, Narayana. This is the day that Saint Tukaram has called the "Golden Day." Dnyaneshwar has said about this day that he has drunk the nectar from the golden pot. Today this history of endless days was thoroughly known, for I have met my Self after many, many, days. Up until now, I was doing so many actions and serving others thinking the individual to be "me," but today is the final fulfillment, or elimination, of actions (karma) as God rests in himself. The rider on a donkey was by Illusion thinking that he was himself the donkey. He was under the delusion that this body is a donkey and that this donkey was "me." The body is called a donkey without a tail. Saint Eknath has described this at length. A barber was called to cut the hair of a donkey, but he thought that he himself was a donkey. Such foolish barbers are spread all over the world. We suffer all of life's sorrows by identifying ourselves as donkeys. This is to be thought about deeply in this human life. All the people of any race or society take objection to a man who tries to drop this foolishness and thus he remains caught in it. The man who identifies as belonging to his community remains the donkey. The ignorant individual is like something that is dead. The jiva does hard work for the sake of the body, and serves the body, which amounts to serving the five elements. He serves the body from birth to death, and in the end the body is burnt like a heap of grass. All of the hard work done in the entire life becomes nullified. The jiva just goes on cleaning this lump of five elements, which is only burnt in the end, for the whole life. We must know who we are and whom we are serving.

Like a man who becomes drunk by drinking the liquor of the Shindi tree respectfully adorns that tree with his own hat and becomes very pleased, similarly, the jiva decorates the body, which is actually only a dead thing. This is all nothing but the intoxication of the ego-sense, the misidentification of oneself with the body. Rukmini said to Vithoba, "My dear, why have you put your hands on both hips?" God said, "I am fed up with teaching these foolish people." Then the Goddess said, "Why do you keep the eyes open? Close them! Why witness what they are doing?" The Sadguru says, "Only one who has realized the Self, gets the final fruit of spiritual practice." Only then is all action (karma) fulfilled. Only then are your dead ancestors satisfied, and they are celebrating in the other world, saying "We are blessed, because in our family is born one who has emancipated us, and our purpose is served well." The parents are happy with the birth of a son, but they utter curses when their son goes to see a film at the cinema with his wife. When one goes to serve a Sadguru who has realized Brahman, and attains Self-Realization, all of his ancestors are emancipated because he now knows himself. That which is called "the fulfillment of life in this world" is now achieved.

We can say that this earth is rotating with the sole purpose of creating faith in Brahman. It rains in order to help one achieve this goal.

By this Self-Knowledge, the burden of the divine serpent Shesha who bears the Earth on his hood is lessened to some extent, and he feels happy. The man who plants "The Tree of The Knowledge of Brahman" in this world enjoys perpetual fame, and he is endowed with eternity, the "Deathless State." The Sadguru has turned the jiva into the deathless Life-Energy, guided him to the Eternal Self, and made him "One with It." Let whatever may happen, happen, and let everything go. You may beg or sit on a throne, wherever you may be, you are happy, as you are of the nature of Bliss. This Self-Knowledge is like a valuable diamond that is lustrous at all times. Wherever it may be, its brilliance does not wane.

There is a story of the barber named Sena. God substituted himself for this barber and went to another barber named Badshah for a haircut. Badshah saw in the mirror the face of God with four arms. In short, God says that his devotee will not remain hidden by anyone's action. The Self-Knowledge that is evident in this body will not remain unexpressed, as it is illuminating everything. Wherever My devotee will go, he will be applauded. There is a saying that "One moon is worth more than a million stars, and one man of Self-Knowledge is worth more than the world." The "Knowledgeable One" (the Jnani) is himself Total Victory. The devotee of the Sadguru, whose faith in the Guru is complete, is always Brahman in its "Totality."

Evening, 19-11-35

120. The Fulfillment of Fulfillment

We have attained that which is not easy to be understood with the help of the Vedas and the sciences (Shastras). Many in the past have undertaken very difficult spiritual practices, but still nobody honored them as sages because they did not have the "Knowledge of Brahman." However, even the parents of the one who has attained this Self-Knowledge are to be praised. Those who performed the great sacrifice called Rajasuya, and gave great lands in charity, attained the status of Indra, the "King of the Gods," but they did not attain the state of Brahman. However, blessed is the father, blessed is the womb of the mother, and blessed is that uterus like a cushion of nectar where that one took birth who then went on to attain the "Knowledge of Brahman" through the grace of the Sadguru. One may be very educated and become a barrister, but that is only to fill the belly, what else? Even dogs fill their belly without doing service anywhere. They simply roam about in their own dignity. In a nutshell, all the fourteen sciences and the sixty-four arts should be considered as dirt. Blessed is the one who has attained Brahman. All others are like rats that have wasted their lives by only filling their bellies. While going through innumerable births as dogs, cats, etc., we have arrived in the human life by chance that has only been possible after millions of years.

Lord Krishna and Arjuna are embodied in the "One Being." When the "Divine Vision" was opened, only then was this vastness recognized. "Behold my existence, which has innumerable eyes, infinite arms and infinite faces." I have now understood the "Nature of Brahman," which means that "I am alone in everything." The vision of the intellect does not mean seeing with the physical eyes. Seeing only One in everything is the "vision of the intellect." Before, I was seeing many gods, many religions, many castes, but with this vision, I came to know that everything is "One Single Being." Such vision of understanding is called the vision of the intellect, the "Third Eye," or "The Vision of Fire." But it is not a normal fire. The eye that sees with Knowledge, the inner eye, is the vision that is the direct perception of the Self. You are Allah, and whatever is seen or felt is only your Self. You are All.

A man once asked Saint Kabir, "How do the animals attain freedom? He said, "You see, it is the hide of the animal that makes the sound in the shoe while one walks, and that gives out the sound of the beat of the drum. If the gut is prepared and used in a stringed instrument, it becomes capable of giving out a musical note. It makes the sound Tuhee, Tuhee. (This means, "Oh God, you are real, the jiva is not real.") When a man comes into contact with the Saint, he also starts saying Tuhee, Tuhee." This is the Knowledge that Krishna gave to Arjuna. I have been telling only this, for the last twelve years, but people say that this is just the meaningless babbling of words because this Knowledge is free. I freely give this Knowledge at no cost. Lord Krishna gave it in a very short time. At that time, a man was giving gold for free, but he was only giving it out very slowly. One man said to him, "Please give it quickly." The man said, "Alright, but it will cost 20 Rupees per ounce." (Gold was sold at that price in those days.) Then the other man said "All right, you can give it at your leisure. I will wait." That is called patience.

There is a story about patience regarding a disciple who served his Guru for 24 years. After the disciple had faithfully served his Guru for twelve years, one day when the disciple had gone out, the Guru had the thought of leaving his body. Before leaving his body, he wrote a mantra intended for his disciple on a sheet of paper and kept it by his side. After some time, a woman came there and saw the sheet of paper lying next to the corpse of the Guru. She picked it up, and secretly kept it for herself. The disciple returned and saw that his Guru had left his body and searched everywhere to see whether the Guru had left anything for him but he did not find anything. When the disciple was sitting quietly in mourning after the final rites for the dead body were over, the woman told him, "I have found a piece of paper left by your Guru, but I will not give it to you just yet. I will give it to you if you will work hard at my house for twelve years." He readily agreed and did the work of a shepherd at her house for twelve years. He did the service because the sheet of paper that was written on by his Guru was in her possession. One day while hunting, a king entered the same forest where this man was herding the sheep, and by some chance it happened that the king met him. The disciple then told his whole story to the king. The king gave out a call to the woman who brought the paper and gave it to the disciple. That paper contained on it only one sentence, which was "TatTvamAsi" or "You Are That." As soon as the disciple meditated on this sentence, he immediately realized Brahman.

Blessed is the devotee who receives *this* Knowledge. You are receiving this teaching at your home, but you are too lazy to listen to it. This "Science of Brahman" was taught by Lord Krishna to Arjuna, by Mahadev to Parvati, and it has come to us by great succession from ancient days and is eternally sacred. It is very difficult to get this Knowledge. The one who gets this Knowledge goes back to the place of his origin for eternal peace. The Sadguru has now given you the passport. He has given you the permit, saying "You may go anywhere you wish. You are free, totally free." This "inner-vision" is given by the Guru. When all is seen as Knowledge, there is no division of any kind, nor is there any sin nor merit. By our own saliva our mouth does not become contaminated, and our tongue is not called a contaminated tongue because the mouth that the saliva is from is our own. We feel that whatever is ours is good and pure. Similarly, this entire universe is ours, and therefore there is no sin or merit, or heaven or hell in it. It is all only Brahman. The veil of attributes is torn away. The one who discerns this has no fear of any blemish. The five elements were haunting like ghosts and were not leaving throughout innumerable lives, but the Sadguru has freed us from them by making them our servants. They have become "gods." The influence of the elements that was like that of ghosts has gone, the spiritual practice was has born fruit, and there is now the fulfillment of fulfillment.

No Date Given

121. The Third Eye

After many days, I met myself. I am not limited with qualities. I am beyond qualities. After many days, this meeting of myself by myself took place. Previously there was feeling of only being a jiva, and there was happiness in that ignorance, but now He has recognized himself. Just as the potter was obsessed with the idea that he was a donkey, likewise, this jiva was indulging in a similar illusion. People give everything to the body only, but they say, "I have eaten, I have done this." In a way, the jiva was envying and desiring something that was someone else's. This is a kind of debauchery, or excessive indulgence in that which is not ours. To say that another's money is our money, another's religion is our religion, and to act accordingly is the debauchery. The one who says that another's things are his, is basically a sinner. The one who was doing like this, and undertaking another's duties (the bodies, or ultimately God's), met Himself after many, many, days. The one who has so far been saying "I," was proved to be a false claimant.

When the true nature of the Self is known, it is experienced that all the happiness of the world is our own happiness. As soon as the veil of duality is removed, all of the pronouns of grammar such as I, you, they, she, etc. are finished. The duality that creates these differences is totally finished. Then everything has become that vastness. The "Great Reservoir of Knowledge" has been opened. The one who is the servant at the feet of the Sadguru finds that this whole world is filled with his own Self, or "I am He" (Soham). While for the man who is not a devotee of the Guru, this world appears as "Who am I?" A man was asked, "How is this town?" He said, "This town is as your tongue is." What is the actual taste of the tongue itself? To one who is Brahman, the entire world is only Brahman. If you are good, this world is good. In other words, the world appears according to your viewpoint, your concept. Only the one who sees that this world is Brahman is himself Brahman. It is the "Man of Knowledge," the Jnani, who sees himself as he actually is. This world reveals its "Reality" only to the Jnani, while it shows all of its various forms to the ignorant. This world seems full of variety to those who are not devotees, and it is "One" to the devotee of the Sadguru. In fact, the person who is ignorant has two eyes so they show duality. This world is called Duniya, which means two. One who is ignorant will see only duality. Ignorance is born of "two."

The son of the Guru was given one eye, and both of the former eyes, the eyes that see duality, were taken away. This is because what they show is false. As the dual eyes are false, the world that is seen by these eyes is also false. The disciple of the Sadguru was given one eye, and as it is only one eye, it sees only One without a second. The veil of duality was removed. The veil of Illusion was torn, the sense of unity arose, and all division was gone. Before, you were deceived. Now, that deception is finished along with the sense of separateness. Unity is proved. The five elements are gone, the planets are gone, and the preachers of delusion are stripped of their preaching. A single planetary combination is in the destiny of all (Oneness). That constellation does not change, and its owner does not change. All of the planets, along with their influences are now finished, and the three qualities (Raja, Tamas, Sattva) are gone, along with the six enemies (anger, lust, greed, desire, craving, and pride). The gods Vishnu, Brahma, and Shiva all went to their own places, and only the one Paramatman remains. Gone is the obsession with the five elements. The transit of Saturn and the phase of seven and half years of misfortune that was associated with it, is also gone. The jiva, who was harassed by the five ghosts of the elements, is dissolved. Only the Eternal God, who did not change, remains. Originally, He was pure and stainless, and by discrimination, He regained his "Purity." Being among men, God thought himself to be a human being, and in Illusion, He was calling himself as "I."

Hanuman was thinking himself to be a monkey before meeting Rama. When he met the Sadguru, Rama, he became one with Rama both inside and out. He broke a garland of jewels to see whether Rama was inside, and then he tore open his chest to prove to Sita that Rama dwelt inside. At that time Rama said, "My dear, why did you tear your chest, and are not those jewels also one with Rama?" What thing is there which is without Rama? When both of the eyes are given to the Guru who is Rama, we get the "one eye" that is the "Eye of Knowledge." Rama, who is pervading in all things, is visible only to this third eye. The one who was missing "his own true thing," regained it. We are kings and we are the subjects. We are God and we are the worshipers. We are the Earth and we are the stream. He becomes everything himself, and then He gets what was his. His birth and death are dissolved. Rama told Hanuman, "You are Eternal."

Now, the Guru who is Rama says, "All of you monkeys, you are Hanuman, so be Hanuman." This means that you should slay the ego. The word "Hana" means slay, or sacrifice, and the word "Maan" means pride, or the ego. When the ego is slain, only then does the man become Hanuman. I am telling all of you to be Brahman. Gone is the birth and death of the one who sees Himself.

Evening, 21-11-1935

122. The Line of Demarcation

A brahmin (someone born into the priest caste) once had a bad dream. In that dream, he felt that he was an untouchable. Because of that dream he began mixing with laborers and started doing all sorts of work befitting that caste. After suffering many hardships, he became fed up so he went to a Sadguru, and the Sadguru awakened him. Then he said "What a miracle! I slept, and in the dream I suffered. Then the Sadguru awakened me!" He was suffering only because of Illusion. The jiva takes this dream world to be true and suffers, and then the Sadguru awakens him. You are not the mind, intellect, or sense organs. The word "my" which you use, in order to say that objects are yours, is only a verbal utterance. You are the witness of all. All that is seen is transient, ephemeral, and destructible. It is all destructible, the mind, the intellect, everything. The mind and intellect are seen by you, and they are going to end. The "you" who says "this is mine, this is mine," is separate from all that is seen. Who are you? You are Pure Knowledge, Pure Consciousness without any stain or blemish. You are the Self who is conscious of the dream, deep sleep, and the waking state. You are "That" which says "I" in the body. The great statement "Tatvamasi" means "You Are That." You are "That" which is different from all that is visible. When all names and words disappear, then "That" which remains is He. "That" is what you are. "That" which says "I," when all experiences are left behind, is final. You are "That" which remains. Then "That" says, "There is no thing," and remains quiet. Then, even that quietness also is left behind. Even the experience of quietness goes, and renunciation comes into existence without saying so. Let go of even the recognition that you are not conscious of anything. Even the one who says, "I should do something," or "I do not understand," or "I do not know" is only God. That God is called Brahman.

There is a story that is told about Saint Muktabai. One day, the cowdung cakes that were prepared by her, were stolen. (In parts of rural India, the village people use cakes made from cowdung mixed with straw as fuel for their fires) Muktabai said, "I will be able to identify the dung cakes prepared by me." She selected and picked up the cakes that she had made from a big pile of dung cakes. She was always uttering the name of Vitthala and remembering his name while preparing the dung cakes. The sound of God's name was absorbed by the cakes so it was possible for her to hear it from every dung cake that she had prepared. In the hearts of the devotees of God (Hari), as well as outside, the name of God is resounding. So, in every action, the name of God is repeatedly echoing. By their contact, the surroundings of His devotees become sanctified. That is how Muktabai said that she could identify her own cowdung cakes. What great Self-confidence she had! It is necessary that the devotee of the Sadguru should have such great confidence. Otherwise, there are some devotees who make a show of devotion to the Guru, but that does not help one attain the "Absolute State of Brahman." God is prior to the devotee. God is eternal. He already knows the hypocrisy of such a devotee. If the devotee is true to God, then God also is true to the devotee. So, one must say "God is mine, and I am of God." One whose heart is always echoing with His name, who knows Him, is "Liberated." He is like a cowdung cake of Muktabai, referred to in the above story. Nobody can steal it and burn it. He is liberated who knows that He is pure, unblemished, and free of doubt.

People are afraid in worldly life. There was once a man who was afraid because people used to criticize him, so he went to his Guru. The Guru gave him a Mantra (a name of God) to recite and said, " I Am That, I am the Self. You are the Self." Thus, it is said that he was twice born. He became a Brahmin (a knower of Brahman). The physical body is born from semen and blood, but by the Guru's advice and teaching, the man was born again into the spiritual life. Therefore, he is twice born, and he then puts on the sacred thread. A Brahmin becomes pure by receiving the *Gayatri-Mantra* from his Guru, and he becomes twice born. But, how does his wife become a Brahmin? How is she made pure? It is by the contact with a Brahmin (Brahman). Man is a "shudra" (a laborer) at the time of birth, but through initiation by the Guru he became a Brahmin. The Guru gives him a sacred name (Mantra) to repeat according to his tradition. When he becomes the "Son of the Guru," he becomes holy. He is respectable. "Although a Brahmin may be despicable in character, he is entitled to be respected in all the three worlds." The one who identifies with the physical body is the demon Narakasura. He was uncontrollable even by the Gods. In a way, that is the individual, the jiva. Lord Krishna slew Narakasura, and then he was absorbed into Shri Krishna. The Son of the Guru should never say that he is the body. When this is known, a man becomes free from all sins. The one who knows that he is Pure Knowledge becomes free from all sins. The jiva was harassed in the dream. The Self became the body although He is always only the Self. He came to know that He is Brahman, and therefore his dream was over and He was free. "I am Brahman, I am the Self, God" (Atmaram) was His Own Experience. First it was only intellectually understood that the very nature of Brahman is "Prajnana," which means Supreme Knowledge, and now that Knowledge is confirmed without doubt. All that is in existence is essentially of the nature of Wind (Vayu) which is one with the Life-Energy (Chaitanya), and therefore all is only Life-Energy. All Gods, even those who are subtly embodied and having some form, have come out of the Life-Energy. The Chaitanya has now been consciously known to be One in all creatures, and thus it is known to be "The Only Thing," everywhere.

There is a saying in Hindi, "You should remember the inner spiritual Rama and then the bondage of the cycles of births and deaths will be cut." Had Rama been aware of his essential nature as the Self, would he have gone to learn at the feet of Vasishtha? The Sage Vasishtha told him, "You are not the outer Rama, the body, you are the inner Rama." It was only after Shri Krishna went to the Guru Sandipani and realized that he is Lord Krishna, that he became fully powerful as an Avatar of Paramatman. Otherwise, he was just a simple cowherd. Only Rama can understand the inner Rama, the Self. The best way of devotion is to have the recognition of God in every being. Chaitanya is that God within, and it is He, who manifests in all beings. There is a saying in medieval Hindi, "Oh man, you should worship God who is living in man, why do you worship a stone?" The places of pilgrimage on the face of the Earth are beyond count. You may go to pilgrimage millions of times, but that merit cannot be equal to a fraction of a rupee when compared to Self-Knowledge. Laxman had marked a line on the ground in front of their hut and told Sita not to cross that line. Similarly, the Sadguru has put down a line for you. This means that you should not fall down from your True Nature as the Self, to the lower level of body identification by crossing this line. Here, your ego is the Demon-King Ravana who will put you in prison if you cross. Now your mind is like the Monkey God, Hanuman. With its help, you should become one with Rama.

There is a story of a man who was charged with committing a murder. He was acquitted by the "Grace of the Sadguru." That is all. "Then I was awake." Likewise, you are changed with committing the murder of the body, which has the duration of innumerable births. You are acquitted only when you become aware that you are the Self. You are Brahman. You are Paramatman, and that "You" is now awake. You must remain constantly in that awakeness. The jiva was harassed by sorrow and he awoke, and met Himself. He who has realized Himself in this way, became God. Such a one is the "Incarnation of God." Only He is victorious in this world. Only the one who is fully convinced that He is the Self becomes victorious. Only He is Paramatman.

Evening, 22-11-35

123. Saints are Incarnations of God

For those who were really incarnations of God, their power is undiminished even after the death of their body. Do they come back for this? No! It is not like that. They were completely liberated, yet people still get mystical experiences by their power, for example, at the places where they had visited, or where they had taken Samadhi (left the body). However, that does not mean that they have come back to this world. Even when these Saints were alive in their body miracles were happening. However, it is important to note that the Saint does not get involved in those miracles. People get experiences according to their faith or belief. It is true that God helps the faithful devotee. God is sometimes even seen in a dream. Similarly, many things and many animals also appear in dreams. If a man sees a train in his dream, will that train know it? Will the train decide that it should go into somebody's dream? No, it is not like that at all. Any person or any thing may appear in anybody's dream. That person or that article is not aware that it had gone into somebody's dream. However, the wise ones who know these things, tell us that some special occurrences happen even after the death of some Saints. Why do these things happen? Because those Saints have earned great merit, and by knowing God, they have become God. Whoever offers devotion to them by pure faith will get experiences according to their faith. In this case, doubt is gone and therefore you must have trust in the "One Thing." When one has firm conviction that one is the True Being, then one's power increases. People offer devotion to the man who has continuous "Unity with the Cosmos," and they may see many miracles.

You should be aware that you are Brahman by increasing experience and firm conviction. "I Am Brahman" (Ahambrahmasmi) is the greatest Truth. If all is Brahman, then why are you not Brahman? If all is God, are you not also God? If anybody will take your (Gods) name, his calamities will be removed. Therefore, you need not do anything. Do not do any jugglery of imagination. Everybody will get results according to one's own faith and belief. What do you have to worry about? One who does not demand anything receives pearls, while one who has demands does not get anything. Power cannot be gained by one who begs, but the one who says, "I do not want anything," attains all of the powers even though he has no desire for them. Those who are not devotees wish to have powers, while the devotee does not have need for them because he has attained wholeness of life. Do you become a Saint to heal another of his fever? Do you really care for the world? Have you become a Saint to increase the property or children of others? I do not lose anything if you get everlasting life, why should I worry if you become rich?

You should try to maintain and further develop your sense of being Brahman. Do not let your "Aloneness" be disturbed. Suppose the desired results are not gained, is that not also Brahman? All that your mind says is false. Whatever is being seen, and whatever will be seen, is all false. The Power of the one who has complete faith in the Self becomes very strong. You must have immovable faith in the Guru and in God. This means that you should have faith that you are Brahman, or at least you must have faith in your Guru. If there is no faith, all is in vain. Even if you attain knowledge about the Formless God, you should not cease to do meditation and worship of the embodied God (Saguna Brahman). Rather, it should be further developed in order to be thankful to our Guru, who has given us Spiritual Knowledge. Otherwise, there will be a state of mind where there is neither Devotion (Bhakti), nor Knowledge (Jnana). There will be only the pride that one is a "great man of knowledge" or of "spiritual achievement," and with this pride, one is thwarted in true progress. The repetition of mantra (japa), and meditation on the teaching given by the Guru (Manana), should not be stopped. The man who gives up the worship of the God with form becomes unsuccessful everywhere. Unless you repay (serve and worship) the Guru, your Knowledge is fruitless. The Knowledge of Brahman does not bring happiness to a man who gives up "Devotion to the Guru." The Sadguru very kindly gives Self-Knowledge and Power to the one who becomes His devotee. The one who gives up this devotion becomes a failure even though he may possess Self-Knowledge.

The Sage Kanva had to be an untouchable for half of the day and a Brahmin for half of the day because he obtained Divine Knowledge from his Guru by deceiving him. Other types of knowledge can be obtained by paying fees, but Self-Knowledge is given by the Guru freely. Therefore, one should not give up the devotion to the Guru. Devotion is the fee that makes you free from obligation to him. One will have experience according to one's faith, but the Sadguru is not concerned about all of this. He is faultless and stainless. Everybody gets the fruit according to their faith. The devotee of the Sadguru is certainly going to benefit. The singing of "devotional songs" (Bhajans and Kirtan) and the traditions of your particular school of instruction (Sampradaya) must be followed. Devotion to the Sadguru is the offering to God. If you have devotion, you will also get the food. If you keep God hungry by failing to do devotion, you will not get the ultimate fruit. It does not really matter if you forget to have your meals, but never give up devotion. You do not meet anyone who tells you to sing in praise of God and the Guru, but if you go without food, many will ask you to take some food. The one who sings bhajans remembers to do meditation, and definitely remembers the Guru. One who does service to the Guru day and night surely meets Paramatman. This is the strength of conviction.

Evening, 24-11-35

124. Conviction in Brahman Through the Path of Knowledge

Everything is really only Brahman. Name and form are false. All the creatures that are visible die and become part of earth. The wind swallows every particle of earth. That which moves is Wind, and the coolness of Wind is Water. The heat of the Wind is the Light, and the heaviness of Wind is matter, or the Earth. All human beings and other animals eat food of various kinds, but in the end, they all die. All become one with Wind. When water freezes, it becomes solid. "Prithvi" means to return. In Marathi there is a verb "Paratavi," which means "turns back." "Parat" means "pret," or "gone back to its original position." So, when all the elements become one, there is only the Life-Energy, Chaitanya. There is great speed to the Earth in its orbit around the Sun. There is nothing on the Earth that moves as fast as the earth itself. Our body is made up of the five elements which are nothing other than Chaitanya. The body requires food, water, air, etc., in order to have enough energy. Because our body is part of the earth, it requires part of the earth in its diet. The five elements and the one Self make a group of six, but there is a seventh, which is the falseness of all of these six.

Shri Shankara (Shankaracharya) while giving a discourse on Vedanta said, "One who says that Maya is real, is a fool." Maya means, "that which is nothing." Just as the games that children play with their toys are false, so is this theory about Maya being real. Equally "real" are those who argue about all of this. The ones who indulge in verbal arguments about Maya, are as much real as Maya is. Maya and greed are similar. Just as a visible piece of food becomes hidden in the process of eating, the scene that is seen becomes invisible in the process of seeing. The eating and those who eat, and the seeing and those who see, are all false. The argument and the arguer are both false. The concepts of "unity" and "multiplicity" are false. "One" and the "many" are false. There is only One, not a second. One and only One, is complete Total Existence. There is nothing other in it. It is not possible. Then how can that which is full and complete be false? Listen carefully. If it is understood that there is no other thing, and there is only "One Thing," are you not also "That Brahman"? Everything is contained in *your* wholeness, the one singular Brahman, but even the word Brahman is omitted. This is no poetry. There is no play of imagination. This imaginary individual, which is false, is not existing here. As we are not, similarly the second, or "other" also is not.

A clay pot found out what it is and knew that it is just a part of earth, and not a pot. Then the pot was free of worry. Similarly, those who know about the "Totality of Brahman" start to find out what they are and come to realize that only God is there. The physical bodies made up of bones and muscles are the abodes of God, "The Lord of the World" (Narayana). Where is God? You yourself are God. To hold on to a wrong concept is a fault, and having doubt is also a fault. To conceive of something else in place of Reality is a wrong concept. When you are God, Narayana, to conceive of yourself to be a man (Nara) is a wrong concept. Narayana is beginningless. Your calling him "man" is the wrong concept which you should drop. And, what is doubt? When you say, "I am only a man," and some say that "You are God," this is called doubt. To doubt about this, saying "How is it possible?" is doubt about Truth. If a picture of the sea that is painted on a wall is seen, how will the wall be there? There may be many paintings, but to know that they are in reality only one thing, "the wall" is Knowledge. Ignorance is the greatest of sins. To take the side of Ignorance is the greatest sorrow, but to recognize Ignorance is the highest happiness. To say that Maya is real is the meaning of sin, or to be mistaken. To know that "All is Brahman" is the highest virtue, the highest merit. To know that "All of this is of the nature of Brahman, of the nature of God," and to say so, is to speak the Truth. To say that this world is real is untruth. Lord Krishna spoke the truth when he said, "All of this is Myself, and all of this is Brahman." Although you may not accept the truth today, you will have to speak the truth eventually.

Suppose that by worldly standards, what Lord Krishna spoke was not true, but in his mind there was no duality of "true" or "false"? Would he be a sinner? For example, is not the story of the wedding of Hanuman false? One who speaks under oath, but whose statement is based on the wrong concept of thinking that the illusory appearance is true, makes a false statement. The one who speaks truth is the one who knows all of this world appearance to be untrue. All talk to the contrary is false. It is said that the moon drinks the milk of the moonlight. It is claimed that this is seen by a blind man, a deaf man swears that he heard the noise of the sipping of the milk, and the lame man walked to that place. Similar to this is the talk of one who says that Maya is real, just as all things that a liar says are false. If you are convinced about Brahman, only then will you be strong on the "Path of Knowledge." If you ask who has "Real Knowledge?," know that it is only he who is sure about himself being Brahman, and it is he who is the Great Yogi, the completely "Realized One." By ordinary standards, he might be a sinner and ignorant, but he has realized that "All is Brahman," and therefore he is "One with Brahman." Public opinion is not important, it is our own realization of the Truth that is important. The "Realized One" gets the powers of God. Whatever he speaks is proven "Truth."

Who is it that is to be considered under-developed? One who still harbors some doubt is undeveloped. He who has no doubt has become Brahman. The one whose doubts are gone has equanimity. What is his experience, and what is his conviction? He knows and feels Oneness with all things. He knows that everybody and everything is identical with himself, without a speck of difference. This is called equanimity. Those who have really understood that all is the Complete Brahman, have no need to question whether they are Brahman or not, or whether their state is raw or ripe. A donkey need not say that it is a donkey. He who says that another is immature, is himself immature. The one who really knows this, should be considered to be blessed by the Guru. After all, what is the meaning of the "Guru's blessing"? To understand that "You Are That," is the Guru's blessing. If you ask how lengthy the tail of Hanuman is, the answer is that it is as long as your doubt is great. Had one dropped all doubts as soon as he went to the Guru, he would have realized Brahman without delay.

The understanding of oneself as Brahman is called "Spiritual Knowledge" or "Brahma Vidya." When you actually know this, you have attained that wisdom which is profoundly important. Tell me, what is more significant? Are the visible objects and their enjoyment important, or is the eternal "Knowledge of Brahman," the Brahma Vidya important? Only the fault of doubt should go. When you have become Brahman, the Guru's advice is fruitful and there is the "Power of the Realization of being God." However, listen carefully! That "Power" does not belong to the human being. It is Brahman that is "powerful." It is Brahman that is the knower and possessor of this Power, and it is in this Power that Brahman is unattached.

No Date Given

125. God Incarnate

One who is certain that he is Brahman, gains power. First of all, he has to put to death, death itself. After dying to death, one is sure about what remains. By the word death, "time" is implied, and with that death, the word time also ends, and one remains without the dimension of time. A moment in time of Maya is equal to many ages. Consider the whole duration of four ages (Yugas) as one circle. Many such circles within circles appear and disappear in one moment of Maya. However, in Brahman there is no time even for a moment. Time says, "I eat the yogis, those who do japa (repetition of mantra), and those who do spiritual practice, but a man of Self-Knowledge (Jnani) goes beyond this world by using me as a stepping stone." Objects and the space in which objects appear should be considered to be the wife and children of time. Time says, "I cannot subjugate the Jnanis, as they do not give me any value." This is like sandalwood paste that is applied on the forehead. You may wipe it or not, but it is wiped off eventually in the course of time so one does not care whether it is there or not. Similarly for a Jnani, with the experience of time. It may be there or not, he is not worried about it. One moment of time is equal to the glimpse of the whole universe. If that moment is wiped out, this vast universe is gone with it. The Jnani remains steady in his Existence. It is time that does the work of all creation, as well as destruction. It is the work of time that a fetus develops in the womb. In time, everything is gained. All of this is the greatness of time. It is the artwork of time that there is creation, existence, and destruction. That is its power.

Time only increases the expanse of the world, but the Son of the Guru steps over its head and goes beyond. One step conquers time, another becomes deathless, the third wields power, the fourth becomes free, the fifth becomes non-dual, and with the sixth, one becomes complete, the "Total Whole." The one who realizes Brahman, is not the body of six feet or so in length, he is the Total Universe. Know that the "Root Self of the Universe," is the seed Self that is the "Egg of the Universe." That Self is as tiny as a speck of dust, or "atom like." In it is contained this vast universe. In it is contained all of the attributes such as "original," "natural," "with qualities," "beyond qualities," and "universal with endless qualities." However, the Jnani is beyond these. He who knows the "atom of the atoms" is endowed with Self-Realization. This is described in the 15th chapter of the Eknathi Bhagwat. One who remains quiet, understanding that all of this is whole and total, attains *all* Power. Do not concentrate on spiritual powers, because in that way, you lose the state of Brahman. To attain spiritual powers is like an illegal gratification, which causes an impediment on the path of Self-Realization. The one who pursues spiritual powers loses the state of Brahman. By spiritual powers, one gets honor, fame, and applause, but there is still a kind of cover on consciousness, a veil of pride, a snobbishness of Knowledge, and the seeker cannot have the strength to tear off this covering on Brahman. The seeker who may be attracted to any high state of experience that is short of Self-Realization loses the realization of the Self. Has it ever been experienced that Brahman has come, or that Brahman has gone, no matter whatever else may happen or not happen? No, that can never be the case. Will the "Real Thing" ever be destroyed? Why do you doubt about this and go astray from the Reality? Why do you fear public opinion and consider *your* Power to not be up to the mark, and thereby lose faith in your own strength? Never do anything to break your solitude. Here, solitude means having a fixed decision. Breaking of it means falling into duality. To maintain firmness in solitude is to be always in the privacy of our own Being. That is called solitude, being One, alone. That which does not get disturbed, is "Aloneness."

Now, there is another story, in which even though a seeker became the Son of a Guru, he had no firmness or conviction about the Power within him. He could not do anything, so he prayed to the goddess Divine Mother promising some offerings. The goddess was pleased, and bestowed upon him what he wanted. Thus, he became small and powerless. Perhaps someone may be possessed by some entity, and if a seeker worships him, or respects him, even though the seeker may be the Son of the Guru, then he becomes small, of little importance. His aloneness is broken. His firmness is loosened. One who has Self-Knowledge will never worship any spirit that possesses a medium or channel. The Self is the "Real God" and everything is done only by His Power. The Jnani would never lose faith in the Self. If after realizing the Self one becomes of the mind that he respects other gods, then he is the most unfortunate pauper, and he will never be liberated. One's faith should be so strong that it should not be disturbed even in the face of death. Trust should be there, whether it be in God or in the Guru. You should have enough faith to say, "My Guru is the greatest, and He does everything," or you should conceive that you yourself are Paramatman. The devotion to "God in form," in a body, is the real service to the Guru. This "Devotion" should not be neglected even if you know that God is formless and beyond faces or attributes. Self-Realization is only possible to the true devotees. The "Power of Knowledge" is increased in the man whose faith in the service to the Guru increases. The loss of faith, the loss of devotion, is the sign of the falling down of the fruit of Self-Knowledge. Lack of faith is the pest infestation of devotion. So, you must remain very keenly aware. The one who has left the "Devotion to the Guru," is deluded. Even if he has "word-knowledge," he is doomed because of egotistical pride. The man who leaves the devotion to the embodied God is truly luckless. You should never leave it.

Devotion is the fertilizer of Knowledge. It is the food that nourishes Knowledge. It is only by Devotion, that Knowledge is increased gradually. Blessed is the one who continues to do service to the Guru even after attaining Self-Knowledge. He is Paramatman. The sadhana should have strength behind it, and this will not be possible without devotion. There is a story about a moneylender who did a strange thing when his bull buffalo died. In the horn of that animal he put some gold, and he then threw the horn outside of his town. After one year, that horn with the gold inside was returned to him by someone. This means that everybody gets what is due to them. Faith is the greatest thing. The "Devotion to the Guru," and his "blessings" are the "Glory of Knowledge." However, the one who ceases to be a devotee becomes luckless even if he is full of Knowledge. We have been given a blessing by Samartha Bhausaheb Maharaj. He said, "I fulfill all of the needs of those who are My devotees and who attend the week long devotional program (Saptah). I am their support. I give my backing to them." One who attains knowledge and gains experience, and yet does not do devotion is unlucky, lazy, and unsuccessful. However great a man may be, he is not greater than his Guru, nor richer than his Guru.

Please do not be misguided by the circumstances of Illusion. Do not be proud because you are better off than another is, nor become afraid by worse conditions. Keep the Devotion to the Guru strong, and your faith and courage unmoving. Remember that Saint Tukaram has given his blessing to daily devotion, and singing of bhajans. I repeat that the success, fame and influence of the person who devotes himself to Guru, and to God continues to spread. Some call him God, some call him an Avatar, an "Incarnation of God," some call him a "great devotee." He is truly "God Incarnate."

No Date Given

126. The Grace of the Guru

When you have realized that you are beyond the attributes, the gunas, you are the Self. The intellect is like blotting paper. Just as blotting paper picks up whatever it touches, the intellect also picks up what it touches. You should give the intellect that which you really want. The intellect functions in the field in which it enters. Therefore, it should be occupied with the stories of Saints, "Incarnations of God," and other spiritual subjects. It is the sign of Paramatman that the intellect should not be occupied by any objects. It should be completely free, without any object. Devotion to the Guru is important. To feel love or to feel related to someone is the sign of Paramatman. To give respect to all is the sign of Paramatman. If the teacher is a graduate, then the pupil is likely to be a graduate. Similarly, only if the Guru is completely knowledgeable will the disciple be completely knowledgeable. The disciple should be totally faithful, desireless, and loyal. Without faith in the Guru the formless cannot be grasped. The signs of the understanding of the formless are a sense of apathy towards worldly life, an attitude of indifference towards relatives, and a confidence that "I am the son of my Guru, and my Guru is my God." One who is convinced about this, realizes Brahman.

Why is it necessary to reiterate that faith in the Guru is the most important sign of true realization? Because somebody who says, "I am One with Brahman. I have no need to be devoted to a personal Guru or God," is someone is called overly wise. The one who feels like this is basically wrong. He has lost both in the worldly life, and in the spiritual life. For a good disciple who is wise and knowledgeable, there is no higher thing in spiritual life than the Guru. The family man merely worships his wife. He loves her. A good disciple loves his Guru. The religious man who follows spiritual life behaves differently from worldly people. He says that if my life is saved, if I become Self-Realized, I will go on worshiping my Guru. Otherwise, it is better that I am dead. Such a disciple attains the highest Knowledge and definitely realizes Brahman. One should follow a daily schedule of singing devotional songs and observe a fixed routine. Do not be shy while worshipping someone greater than yourself, and do not fail to fulfill your duties. One who has no devotion does not gain the highest Knowledge, and one who has no Knowledge does not have the blessings of the Guru. If one has the blessings of Guru, clay will be turned into gold, and if one does not have the blessings of the Guru, the gold is turned into clay.

There is a story about what happens when one does not have the blessings of the Guru. A devotee of a Sadguru, having done good service to his Guru, went out into the world. In his travels, he entered a certain country. He was given grand receptions wherever he went. In time his fame reached the royal palace and the Prime Minister and the King came to hear about him. They came out to meet the disciple, and with great sense of honor they took him to the palace. In a short time, the disciple's fame had spread very far. The Guru came to know about this and went to the palace and showed himself to the disciple in front of the full assembly. The disciple was seated there in his personal glory. He saw his Guru at some distance, but puffed up by the honor that was being bestowed upon him, the disciple did not get up, nor did he bow to his Guru. The Guru observed this, smiled, and then disappeared from there. Even then, the disciple did not care. Considering that the king had greatly honored him, the disciple put a garland on the king spontaneously as a show of respect. As soon as the garland was put around the king's neck, the king's whole body became hot. The king requested the disciple to give him some relief from his trouble, but he was not relieved, in spite of all the efforts made by the disciple. The king threw him out of the royal hall, and when the people came to know of this incident, they chased him out of the country. All of his power and his glory were gone. Because of having attained name and fame he insulted his Guru. He dropped his Devotion to the Guru, and instead became proud of his body.

One should never drop the "Devotion to the Guru," no matter what may happen. If one gets honor, one should surrender that to the Guru. There is a story that illustrates having the feeling of the Self in all beings. A devotee of a Guru once struck the king with a shoe. At that time, a deadly snake that was hiding in the royal head-dress of the king came out, and the king's life was saved. The devotee of the Guru was then honored and the king became a follower of that disciple. In the kingdom there was a man who was outspoken against that disciple, and he was punished. The meaning of this story is that since the Guru is fully supporting all, the disciple has no cause for any fear. However, if the Guru is not one's support, nobody can say what calamities may befall one. By the blessings of the Guru, the disciple in the story was victorious. In the story of the Ramayana, monkeys conquered Shri Lanka, but by whose grace, by whose power? Of course, it was by the power of God, Shri Ram. Such is the greatness of the blessing of the Guru. The power of the Guru's blessing is vast. It is not difficult for a man blessed by the Guru to go beyond this ocean of the world. The Guru is the giver of that "Divine Power" by which everything, including all sin and merit, is burned and turned into ashes. Those people who are always doubting, will not get the Heavenly Abode, or Liberation. The truth is that one who attains Self-Knowledge does not have any lack of faith. In fact, his faith gets stronger day by day. He is the real devotee who cries out of love as soon as he remembers the Guru. One must give due respect even to the breeze that comes from the hometown of the Guru. Even the dog of a great man is given respect by all. Similarly, the pet dogs of the Guru's house must be honored.

All of one's fame, success, and influence over others are dependent on one's devotion. There is nothing comparable to "Desireless Devotion" when it comes to spiritual practice. Devotion with desire is the devotion that is done with a certain aim in mind. To promise some offering to God in exchange for some benefit is devotion with desire.

Desireless devotion means to be devoted only for the sake of the attainment of Brahman. What is real Power, real Strength, in this world? The one who does not want anything is the greatest and the strongest. Those who want and strive for power, are but beggars. One who does not demand anything is the giver to all. Spiritual powers and riches are his servants. Such unselfish devotion is not possible without the seeker being very strong. If any devotee of the Guru thinks that to have a lot of money is the sign of the blessings of the Guru, they are still the slaves of Illusion. Great is the one who judges the worth of his Guru by whether he himself has gained any Self-Knowledge. Others judge the worth of the Guru by whether the devotees become rich and famous by his blessings. If not, they say that that Guru has no powers. Those people who think like this are bound by Maya. Their thinking is only of that type. The selfless devotee does not like selfish devotion. The devotees of Lord Hari (Vishnu) do not like the gratification of such selfish devotion. By unselfish devotion it is proved that the devotee is Prabhu, God himself. By selfish desire it is proven that you are but a petty beggar. By unselfish devotion you are able to have the Glory and Immortality of God's.

When there is "Realization of Brahman," all Glory is inherent in that. So, why should we become beggars? The "Son of the Guru" (Guruputra) has unselfish devotion and becomes one with the Guru, while others demand something, and only perform service. Service is service, and ownership is ownership. Become equal to the Guru by "Devotion to the Guru," and don't desire trifles. You should not perform selfish devotion. Only unselfish devotion should be done. Meditate on the Guru and on how best to serve him. Meditation on the Guru should be with the thought that the Guru is Paramatman, the Supreme Self, the Great Lord. You should always remain in the bliss of the "Knowledge of Brahman" (Brahmavidya). Be free of all worry by conceiving of yourself to be Brahman. You worship me, and give me various things, but instead you should offer those things to my Guru. I am happy in your doing that. If you want to give me food, you should follow the rules of conduct in devotion along the lines that I have explained. To do this is to feed me, to give me dinner. Those who do not follow the rules, keep me hungry. I always remember those who follow the rules laid down by me. If you remember me, I will remember you. When you remember me, it is itself My remembering you. "One who serves the Guru receives the fruits."

Evening, 28-11-35

127. The Comfortable Seat of the Devotee of God

The Knowledge (Jnana) of the one who neglects personal devotion to the Guru does not remain strong and durable. For such a one, desire embraces the objects and identifies with them, and accordingly, just like the objects, the Knowledge does not endure. By the daily glimpse (darshan) of God in the temple, the devotee becomes free of all objects. By uniting itself with objects, Knowledge becomes confused. Therefore, in order to give it some solid anchor, there should be the devotion to some form such as the Guru or an image of God, performing puja, etc. This kind of "Qualified Devotion" (Saguna Bhakti) should not be stopped. If unselfish devotion is accompanied with it, there is no equal to this type of devotion. To practice devotion unselfishly is called *real* "Strength." The desire for some fruit is the wish to get some result from devotion. The desire is identical to its object. Unselfish devotion does not even aim at gaining Self-Knowledge. The devotee who continues routine worship even after Self-Knowledge is truly great. If unselfish devotion is coupled with the "Knowledge of Brahman," then that devotee is even greater than Hari (Vishnu) and Hara (Shiva). All desires except for the desire for the "Knowledge of Brahman" are selfish. Some people outwardly do devotion saying that it is unselfish while desire remains hidden in their minds. When God gives a boon to such a man, he requests so many things! Such a devotee is definitely selfish. It may again be stated that the one who continues his worship, rituals, etc., as qualified devotion even after attaining Self-Knowledge is truly great. Only the truly strong devotee does this.

Some people, after attaining Self-Knowledge come to realize that there is nothing to be achieved as such, and therefore ask, "What is the need to practice 'Devotion to the Guru?'" Of course, nobody acts without some reason, but one who continues devotion even after Self-Realization is truly great. It is true that devotion with some desire brings about its result, but by selfless devotion one becomes united with God, which means that he becomes Paramatman. Please discern what the fruit is, who the creator is, and who produces that fruit. Know who is superior, and who the real owner is. We say that unselfish devotion or spiritual practices is superior. If it cannot practically be performed outwardly, at least one should do it mentally. Selfless devotion is real strength. Even if one possesses a mantra against a scorpion bite, that mantra has to be re-chanted in order for it to retain it's power. Similarly, one who has fully realized Brahman continues with devotion to the Guru. One cannot say definitively how much strength one has, so, how can we say what the limit to the Power of God is? That Power is beyond imagination. God's Power is such that He can do or undo anything, and He can do anything that is contrary to what is considered normal. Whatever has been created is over. This means that whatever was utilized is over, and yet still after all has ended, still more Power is there. How much more is there cannot be surmised. All that Strength, all that Power is attained by selfless devotion. Lord Krishna was asked by his devotees, "Lord, how much is Your Power?" God said, "I cannot tell. I do not know. Only My devotees know that. My devotees have given Me the knowledge of My Power. When My devotees are having calamities, My Power becomes known. My Power becomes manifest only by the force of My devotee."

The Knowledge of Brahman has already been prescribed. One cannot say who will rejuvenate it and to what extent, or when in the future. It cannot be surmised. It is not definite who will use it and in what manner, or to what extent. As one will use it, accordingly, he will have the experience about it. However, one thing is certain, the Devotion to the Guru, or the Saguna Devotion (Devotion to God with qualities) is its nourishment. Only then, will there be the Power of Knowledge on Earth. The strength of the devotion of each devotee is different. It depends upon the firm determination and devotion of each person. Although there are many barristers (lawyers), each barrister has separate fame and popularity. The selfless devotee has no need to make any efforts to make his strength evident to others. God Himself gives the devotee fame. Only that which is incomplete has a desire to express itself. "That," which is totally complete, has inherent deep peace and happiness. The state of the One who is perfect, is complete and without any desire. All of His devotional activities are desireless.

There is a story of the Sage Mahipati. It is told that his wife took his robe and put it on the dead body of a man, and that man became alive again. Because of this miracle, the fame of Mahipati spread greatly. You should increase your "spiritual" awareness daily and constantly. Do not accept puja (the act of being worshipped) from others, because the sea never dries up, but the water in a small can is finished quickly. If anybody gives you honor, think of it as honor to your Guru. Your capital (wealth) is small, so increase it by recognizing that everything belongs only to your Guru. When the capital is full (with the fullness of the Guru) there is no problem. Those who have attained Sainthood have no such concept in their mind that there is any particular individual. Their existence is very naturally formless, and completely beyond the reach of the senses. For them there is no difference such as beneficial or not beneficial, useful or useless, or in the results of doing or not doing. Those who have transcended the senses are beyond all karma, and beyond all religion. Others may be forced to go to jail, or to be punished even if they do not take part in any mischief, or perhaps they may get hurt somehow in mind or body.

For those people who have by some effort attained some "spiritual knowledge" only to show off their greatness, it is necessary to admonish them about daily discipline, rules of conduct, good behavior and bad behavior, control in sense enjoyments, to be aware of their actions, etc. They put their confidence only in their mental and intellectual understanding and believe that now they have intimately understood "Totality." They create an atmosphere that they are one with "That," as if putting their hand on its shoulder, and make you believe that they are equal to "That." However, when some question of profit or loss comes, they are very much disturbed inside. This shows that they are not free of the experience of slavery to the Illusion. Therefore, the Saints, who are kind hearted, tell them, "Hold fast, let go, go away, stop, sit down, don't fear, etc." The people of this world are very clever at making you a fool, but you who are likely to be a fool should be very careful. Both the simple and the clever should think about this very keenly. Do not be carried away by the applause of other people. Do not stop your personal routine of daily qualified worship. Each gets his position according to his worth. Paramatman has already arranged for a comfortable place of happiness for those who are devotees of God (Vishnu), and of the Guru. Those who have Self-Knowledge. Had it not been so, this Earth would would have surely been topsy-turvy.

Even in spiritual matters, there are definite rules. Only the one who is the medium by which Paramatman gets his work done, is able to achieve Him, not anyone else. That is why you should always follow the rules. As the Sun is not hidden by darkness, likewise, the devotees of the Sadguru do not remain hidden. Always continue to do worship on the personal level, the saguna devotion. Your action is always with you. The study of the Self is like the light of the Sun. Darkness cannot approach the Sun. Similarly the one who has realized Brahman is Shiva in person. Calamities do not come in his way. There is no need for Him to pray for his own welfare. Such is this "Knowledge of Brahman." Calamities never turn their attention towards such a man. To check, to examine to see whether you have spiritual power or not, is also a desire. This is selfish devotion.

You see, before you say anything your work is done. You need not say that you should be successful. You have no idea that if someone puts the dust of the path upon which you have just walked to their forehead, that their wishes are fulfilled. This is not noticed by you. Unless there is full confidence in the awakening of the Self, your concept is futile. If this awakening is there, what is there to be astonished about if some work is done? In due time, the mango tree becomes full of fruits. Similarly, in due time, you are sure to be fully powerful. However, for now, let it be definite in your mind what you are, and where your attention is focused. Then you become as vast as the universe. You become unlimited and immeasurable. Why should there be any anxiety about whether you, who are God, will get any food or shelter? You will get anything you want. You are the whole world, but wait until that inner conviction becomes strong. Do not be too eager. Wait until your mind, which is only attuned to the Self, becomes itself "The Totality." By devotion to the "Personal God," unlimited power is attained.

Just as a mother is always wishing for the welfare of her child, the Guru wishes for the welfare of his disciples. The Sadguru, who has taken the responsibility for your life, definitely has your care and welfare in his heart. The Sadguru wishes that you should have more strength. Even Death should not turn towards you, he should be afraid of you. That is the Sadguru's blessing to you, so your devotion should be completely desireless, without any selfish motive. If you are worshipping with some motive, your motive becomes the fruit. It is the nature of the fruit that when the fruit is ripe, its stem becomes loose. You should remain as the stem. It is the natural process, that from the stem, the fruit is born. God was pleased with one of his devotees and offered him some boon, but the devotee said that he did not want anything. God said, "Behold, this is one devotee who does not demand anything. I will see to it that his every need is fulfilled." The jiva in the womb does not know anything about itself. It is only a fetus, a being of Objectless Knowledge. It is Consciousness without any object to be known. Everything that it really needs is provided for. All the care for it's development, growth and it's feeding is taken care of, as well as whatever is necessary in it's worldly life after birth. The whole body machinery, the food, the whole structure and its function, is provided for. Who does all of this? Of course, it is God who provides for everything in the life of one who is not conscious of oneself as a separate body. Therefore, the Sages and Saints say, "The Goddess of Fortune becomes a servant to those who do not make any demands, but makes beggars of those who make demands."

Be "That," and reside in "That," which is most natural. Wipe out all imagination. Paramatman provides for the total comfort and happiness of the one who by virtue of Knowledge does not even imagine at all. So, have faith. In short, one who demands, never attains perfection, or completeness, and one who does not demand never feels want for anything. Therefore, you should be unselfish devotees. Just as a tree grows and bears flowers and fruit when sufficient water and the right fertilizers are given to it, so should you give the fertilizer of unselfish devotion to the Personal God. Then all Glory is added to you. The preparations for the achievement of perfection by the unselfish devotee are already made. Be desireless and wait as the casual witness. What is so surprising in this? God is the devotee, and the devotee is God. When the "Knowledge of Brahman," and "Saguna Devotion" are combined, what more could you want? You attain such capacity that you become the giver of the "Fruit of Liberation" to others. It is you who frees the jiva from the jaws of death. Why should the one who has the power to make death run away, care about "others"?

Remain with firm understanding that Existence is one without a second. In the body, the doer and the receiver are both only the One Self. The food you eat is His food, His dinner, His grand ceremonial dish. Actually, it is He who demands, eats, and in fact, *does* all activities. You are in vain adopting the role of an imaginary "me," the one who identifies with the body that digests the food which is eaten, and who becomes proud of the body. Subtract this, and you will realize that it is only God, who has by His own Power of Maya, descended into the body and is performing all the activities and is receiving all fruits. You are nothing and it is only God who is doing all. Whatever it may be that one who realizes this may speak, is only the praise of God. One who understands this is complete, and the one who is very grateful to the Sadguru, who has bestowed the Knowledge of Brahman, has tremendous capacity.

Now I have told what needed to be told. How far your light of intelligence goes, that much is going to be your understanding. Do not let it be that I am telling you one thing and you are doing something quite different. For example, if the gutter to the sewer is covered, and you are told not to open it, but thinking that there must be something important hidden there you open the cover anyway. Please do not do like that. Have trust in the advice given by the Sadguru. You should be very careful to stay away from bogus people and teachers. Some people give up sadhana because some members of their community say something or other against the spiritual practice and beliefs of the seeker. You should ask yourself the question when you are dying, "Do the people of my community save me from death?" As your faith is, so is the result. Each one rightly receives according to his capacity. What is right for you will not necessarily be what is proper for others. Spiritual practice and devotion bring in their wake success, fame, and influence over others. Have steadfast determination that you are the Supreme Self, Paramatman.

Evening, 29-11-35

128. The Fruit of Happiness and Joy

All of the bodies and the entire world are nothing but our own Existence. The one who has such full understanding, gets all of the pleasures and joy of this world. Lord Krishna has said, "The one who knows that all of this world is oneself is the Incarnation of God. I am in all beings, and all are my own Existence. That one is really God, whose conviction is that all beings are 'Myself.' He is the Self, the knower and the director of everything in existence. The world is an idea, a concept. If your concept, your feeling, is that you are the world, then you are Brahman. Success, fame and influence, Knowledge, and desirelessness are all the riches of God. This world, this entire universe, is called the "Immeasurable Form of Brahman," or Saguna Brahman. Thus, the body of the Jnani is as vast as the universe. The gross physical universe (Virata), the subtle universe of concepts and pranas, etc. (Hiranyagarbha), the causal body of the universe (Avyakrit), and the Consciousness body (great-causal body) of the universe, or Moola Prakriti (Moola Maya), are the four bodies of the Jnani. This entire universe is his body, and this visible world is part of his body. The five objects of the senses are in his body. This vast body of his has limbs, arms, legs etc., and, just as food eaten by the mouth gives energy to all the sense organs and various parts of the body, whatever a Jnani eats, reaches God. One who realizes this is the "Incarnation of God."

The Knowledge given here transforms the individual, Jiva, into God, Shiva. Even a woman can become a barrister by being educated with worldly knowledge. However, what is contained here, is the Knowledge of Brahman. An ignorant fool can be treated as God, but it is a rule that the Knowledge of Brahman should not be given to just anybody. Even Lord Shiva and other Saints and Sages kept this Knowledge secret. After some time, it was given to a worthy person who served the Guru. Later, some were pleased with certain good and worthy people and this Knowledge was given to them, but it was given to only one man in each age, or "Yuga." Seldom was there one who became fully Realized. Now, the time has come when I have come to teach this Knowledge again. Thirty-three hosts of Gods shower flowers on the one who teaches this Knowledge to others. The significance of this Spiritual Knowledge is recognized only by the knowledgeable and the "Realized." At this time, I have fully explained this philosophy to you. Up until now, this Knowledge was not given in this manner by anybody. There is a saying by Saint Kabir, "Japa (repetition of mantra), strenuous penance, and other types of rituals or sacrifices are not necessary," and this is really true. The Self is the light of the Sun. To "know" Him, is to worship Him. One who knows will be victorious wherever he may go. "The word of my Guru is written over the writing of providence" is an appropriate saying. This means that the Guru is truly beyond God in his greatness. The one who says so is always fearless, brave, and victorious. He is "God Almighty" in any situation. Although he may be doing anything in any circumstances, he is only Paramatman. All the comforts and happiness in this world are at His service. In a way, the world is a mansion that is constructed by Him, for his own pleasure. The entire world is his house, his own garden. It is his playhouse, meant to entertain him, to amuse him.

Just as rats abound only where there are grains, and a tiger eats goats but does not eat the sun, similarly nobody can ever disturb or harass the man of Self-Knowledge. The "Man of Self-Knowledge," the Jnani, is always fearless while the individual, the jiva, is always afraid, terrified, and worried. In short, where there is God in his "Totality" there is success, fame, and riches everywhere. However, everyone gets experience according to one's belief. When Brahman is realized, what more is wanted? In the same way that Lord Krishna was worshipped, such a "Self-Realized One," a Jnani, will also be worshipped. All the Vedas and Scriptures have declared very specifically that "Wherever there is a man who has realized Brahman, all of the gods come and crowd together."

Totally drop the idea that you are a separate jiva. Be the Totality, be Brahman.

My blessings are with you all. Let this "divine wealth," this Glory be received by you, and may you enjoy it fully. Never leave the service of your Guru. His name has full capacity of achievement. That will be surely experienced by you. Only God is standing in front of you and behind you. He is in all forms. Now, with this Knowledge, nobody, or nothing such as the planetary influences are able to give you trouble, and their life span is limited. Never cease to do the Saguna Devotion. When you are steadfast in your way of worship, your determination is naturally stronger, and you say, "I am God. What undesirable things dare trouble me?" When by real solid faith, you are sure about the Absolute Brahman, only then does the Realty really shine. Who will not offer sweets to such a man? For My dear devotee, the sweet thing in his mouth will never be finished. On the contrary, if anyone receives the blessed food from him, his ailment will also be cured. Why not?

The most important thing is that the rules of this Knowledge cannot be broken by anybody. The Jnani is honored by all, and is full of all Powers. There must be the immovable faith that "I am Brahman." This Knowledge, this conviction, must be tested severely and made very deep and steady. All Saints and I stand as the witness that you are considered as God by virtue of this Self-Knowledge. We are responsible that if by following the rules of this "Knowledge of Brahman," realization does not take place. But to whom are we responsible? To those who have faith in the word of the Guru, and who do not fear death. We are responsible to those who never worry about death and are steadfast and determined. We are responsible to those who are faithful, and who consider the teaching of the Guru unquestionable. We have no responsibility towards atheists who are not devotees. May their welfare be all right, in this we can be happy. But, if one who is a "true devotee" does not realize God, then we are responsible.

There is a story about a Saint who declared as a place of worship, the tomb of a donkey. There once was a donkey, and when it died, a Saint dug a ditch without anybody noticing and buried the donkey's dead body. Then he constructed a nice tomb over the grave and erected a beautiful temple above it. He even gave the tomb a nice name, as the "Shrine of the Donkey-God." People started to come to the temple with faith in their hearts, and prayers for the fulfillment of their desires. Slowly their prayers were answered and it gradually became a famous place of pilgrimage. The Jnani is free from all sorrow, and all laws. Those who have realized Brahman wield all of the Power, and whatever they say is definitely going to happen. There is no limit to what they will do. They are unconquerable. Where such a man puts his foot, the eight spiritual powers reside. If the Sadguru, the "True Master," and the sincere disciple come together, they can achieve anything they wish. Similarly, if Self-Knowledge is coupled with the regular personal worship, there is no measure how far one's fame might reach.

This teaching is like a pouring out of "Immortal Nectar" only to those who lead a spiritual life. This realization of Brahman will not leave the devotee even if he may not want it. The one who disrespects the personal worship, actually insults the Sadguru, and even though he may well achieve the Knowledge of Brahman, it will not be useful or conducive to him. If personal worship and Knowledge are together, what is the limit of praise that can be attributed to such a man? How can one describe his greatness? The pen cannot write about his powers. Such is the powerful "Son of the Guru" (Guruputra). Paramatman in person is the Sadguru, and we, as His devoted disciples come together in this great "Yoga of Knowledge" that we experience, and which is self-existent, without a beginning. "That" must be attained.

No Date Given

129. My Only Capital (Wealth) is Devotion to All

Because I know that "I am in all beings as their Essential Existence," I enjoy the state of the Supreme Self, Paramatman, in them. I enjoy my status as God on that "Capital." On "My Own Being" I have created the entire universe. I know that whatever is seen, is of My own nature and is My own body, and therefore, I have become Paramatman. If you wish to attain My Status, you must have *this* Knowledge. Only then will you reach My Status. It is only on this strength of Paramatman, that I dissolve the earth millions of times, and then create it again millions of times. Those who understand this "Great Principle," become one with Me. The Sun never has any pride that it is "the Sun." The Sun dries up bad smells and purifies with it rays, and it may even dry up sweet nectars. The Sun is not concerned with whatever good or bad that may happen. Similarly, the vastness of Existence never takes pride in doing anything. Because of the vastness of Existence there may be a loss or gain of thousands or millions of rupees, but that vast Existence is never happy or sorry about any of it. It is because of the vast all-pervading Paramatman, that this world appearance naturally comes into existence and will be dissolved. Suffering or enjoyment is each person's destiny in life, and therefore Paramatman who is the cause, yet not the doer of all, does not become liable and is not to blame. Only that which is non-Paramatman takes the blame upon itself. Paramatman is unstained and unmoved by anything. He, who causes all to suffer or enjoy, yet remains aloof and untouched, is Paramatman. One who knows Him, attains His Status.

The Almighty God has nothing to do with sin or merit. On the strength of that Knowledge, I am the doer yet not the doer, of all things. He who knows Me as his own nature, is only Myself. That devotion is the greatest by which the devotee does not consider Me as separate from himself, nor considers himself as separate from Me. That devotee becomes one with Me, and knows Me as such. Before creation, I did such devotion myself. My own son, Brahmadev was faltering while creating the world. He was tremendously moved by compassion at the sight of so much sorrow, as well as pleasures, and he said, "Nobody abides by the rules made by me. So, I do not want to create this world." At that time Vishnu said, "Why do you bother about all of this? Your job is to envision only. People will reap the fruit of their actions, so you need not be concerned with that." Having heard this, Brahma was free of anxiety. He created the universe, but remained aloof.

Lord Krishna said, "Dear Uddhava, why are you afraid? How big is your family? You have five or six members in your family why do you take pride in them? See how vast my family of the universe is. I am not worried about it. I do not lament about it. It is all only conceptual. Why do you identify yourself with it? Without the one Self, this entire world is like a dead body. It cannot move. He who knows that all of this is the play of the Self, is really the greatest Jnani. Let people do any austere practices and learn the Vedas, without the Knowledge that is given here, all of that is futile. Many people do yogic exercises and perform various sacrifices, but all of that is meaningless without the Knowledge of Brahman. I learned this from my Guru Sandipani. There are many sons of cowherds, but only I could achieve this Glory through the blessings of my Guru. This is the flower of 'Devotion to the Guru,' that all worship Me calling me 'Almighty God.' Without meeting My devotee, My 'True Nature' (Swaroopa) will not be understood. Therefore, only they receive this Knowledge who do service to My devotees, and only they become united with Me. My devotees are the sacredness of the Ganges and the essential sanctity of all the places of pilgrimage. They bring you into themselves and then make you one with the "Ocean of Godhood." Therefore, one who does everything by way of devotion as instructed by his Guru cannot remain without attaining the realization of Brahman."

Evening, 1-12-35

130. Brahman Consciousness (Chidghana Brahman)

If you try to imagine Absolute Brahman, it is not possible because Brahman is non-conceptual. If you try to conceive of what Brahman is, you get only a zero. Concept, or imagination, is dark. It is Ignorance. Spiritual science says that there are three types of joy. When you get something which is liked, that gives you a kind of joy. For example, when a snake charmer gets a snake, he is happy because his concept is like that. That type of joy depends on the objects for which there is some liking. Another type of joy is the joy of Knowledge, or the joy of understanding. The third type of joy is the joy that those who are indulging sensual gratification get from those objects. These are a kind of demons. Those who enjoy Knowledge can also have Brahmananda, which is the great joy, or "Bliss of Brahman." That "Joy" is experienced by our own inner conviction that "We are Brahman," but that Joy is also an attitude or state. The attitude should be one with "That."

One can never be identical with God. The scriptures say that one can be identical with God, but it is not so. To become identical is an attitude. We do not become identical. Then how do we experience joy? The answer is that it is the "Joy of Knowledge." The Sadguru, by his words makes you aware of that Joy. The limit of this "Joy of Knowledge" is up to the Nirvikalpa State, the state where there is no concepts or doubt. However, Brahman is beyond that state. If a man, basing his efforts on the description given in the scriptures, tries to grasp the idea of Paramatman, what he grasps is an imaginary concept. As we have decided that He "is" according to our imagination, He is colored by our intellect. As we insist that He is, we will get the experience according to that concept, and this is only a God that is created by our imagination. Brahman remains beyond all concepts. It is not seen by the eyes, and the mind cannot comprehend it. So, how then can one realize this? Light can be seen, and Sky (Space) can be perceived, but "Brahman," is beyond these. How can "That" which is not visible or perceptible be recognized? How can "That" which is inconceivable, and beyond meditation, be gained by meditation? How can one attach oneself to that which has no attachment? How can one comment upon That where words do not reach? If one tries to meditate on it, there is duality, and being afraid of duality, one leaves the very will to meditate, and all goes in vain. This approach leads nowhere.

Therefore, it is necessary to do what the Guru has taught us. If very keen discrimination is not used, one only becomes confused. Discard the world with the help of Knowledge. Anything that is "second," or "other," the imaginary person, the individual, etc., all of these things, are worldly and based only in Illusion. The imaginary person who is of this world must die. The ego must be dissolved. The concept that I am a separate individual, a jiva, must be destroyed. To do that is the "True Spirituality." It is not necessary to recognize what Brahman is. Only remove the "I" that is in between. It is enough if this "I" is gone. This "I" is itself the imaginary person. In fact, there is no such thing as "I" at all, yet it comes into being. Brahman is something quite different from this "I." Those who have only studied scriptures get confused when they try to understand Him. Those who understand through a state or concept only get deceived. There is no purpose of using examples here, because in that way, the triad of seer, seeing, and seen comes into existence. "That" which exists without the seen, the seeing, or the mediator remembering it, is Brahman. It is natural, it is the withdrawal state, or Nivritti-Pada. As long as there is desire that we should know our Self, the missing of it takes place. The God who is in your own home (the body) is to be worshipped when you do the puja of SatyaNarayana. That God is not to be brought in from outside. He is your own "Original God." You should do the worship (puja) of only that. In fact, everything is only Brahman.

Then what is false? Only imagination is false. Imagination is perceptible only in relation to what is untrue. That which is True is never disturbed. The king does not need to declare every now and then that he is King. Brahman *is*. It does not say that it is Brahman. What is, surely is. It cannot speak anything. Without saying so, it is Self-Existing. If a husband keeps on repeating, "I am the husband," people will start doubting him. If he is in fact the husband, why does he need to say so repeatedly? He is the husband without needing that expression. Brahman is God, the Self. You should know this once, and let it go at that. Then, only Brahman is. Without meeting it through duality, it is perpetually only One. If you try to "meet It," that act brings in separation. Such is the Brahman to which there is no path. It cannot be cut apart, and it cannot be separated, no matter how you may try. It is, and it "Exists" as it is.

Had it ever disappeared, then its name would not be Truth. This is unfathomable without experience. One who says that he has understood has not really gone to "That" town.

When the projecting or holding of any attitude, state, or concept is gone, the state of "Complete Withdrawal" comes into being. How can we meditate upon That which cannot be thought of in meditation? Attitude is limited. It cannot grasp "That." It is not contained by mental attitude. Devotion is like a jar that went to bring an elephant inside of itself, but instead of its bringing in the elephant, it lost it's life. Likewise, in devotion, the jiva thus dissolves itself. If you make a pun and yet you say that you do not understand, then you are lying. If you do not know the cause of death of a person, does it follow that he was not alive before death? Only the one who has been given instructions by the Guru really knows. If you do not understand, hold fast to the teaching given by the Guru with complete faith. The mind has a habit of projecting imagination, but Brahman is not a thing of imagination. Mind is born out of ego, and unless the ego is dropped, Brahman cannot be realized. When the ego goes, it is Paramatman that remains, automatically. The doubt about "What am I?" is itself the ego, or the sense of "I." That ego sense cannot be burned, and cannot be cut by any effort. This sense of "I," swallows the person. Even the desirelessness of one who has ego is useless. Only the one whose ego is dissolved, gets real contentment.

The key problem is how to drop the ego. There is a way for this. It is through discernment, or "Discrimination with Knowledge," that it goes. What have we understood by listening to the teachings of Vedanta? We have understood that there are five elements and the one Self. We have understood that we are nobody. We are not in this physical body but we have believed that we are in the body. That is called the wrong knowledge, or imagination. When this "I" is gone, whatever is, is. What remains is "That." If you say that it is, then it is not, and if say that it is not, then it is. "That" which is described by "Not," (Neti) is existing. Ego goes off by understanding this, and when this imaginary "me" dissolves, then millions of ideas are all only part of Brahman. Nir means "not," or "not existing." Nirvikalpa means "no concept," or "no imagination." When the imaginary person goes, what remains is only Paramatman. He is the living, speaking, walking, active God. Great is he who worships without the sense of "I." One who has not realized God should worship Him, but whom should God worship? Be Brahman, and experience Brahman. The joy in the sense objects is equivalent to the Jiva. The Joy in Knowledge, is Shiva, and the Joy in Brahman, is Paramatman.

The world exists according to our concepts, our ideas. There is a story about a farmer and a widow during the lifetime of Sadguru Shri Bhausaheb Maharaj. It was the time of sowing the seeds in the field, so the farmer ascertaining an auspicious day according to his knowledge went to the field taking with him the yoke, the bulls, and the bags of seed. However, no sooner did he get out of the house, he saw a widow going by the road just in front of him. This was considered by him to be a very bad omen and he felt very depressed and uttered an exclamation, "Oh God! What can be done now?" Exactly at that time, Shri Bhausaheb Maharaj was going by that path after finishing his morning bath and he heard that exclamation of the farmer. He quickly went ahead and asked the farmer, "What has happened?" He said, "Oh, Sir, I started out for sowing my seeds in the field and at that time I saw that widow." Maharaj said, "My dear sir, You are so stupid! Actually, this was a good omen. Go straight ahead and sow the seeds now. You will have crops as big as a head! Why do you think in vain that this was a bad omen?" The farmer was well acquainted with Bhausaheb Maharaj, so he was encouraged by the Saint's words. Having faith that those were the words given by a Saint, he went to the field and did the sowing with great hope. Some months passed, and the season came to an end. Once, after that time, Saint Bhausaheb Maharaj was passing by the farmer's house and he met the farmer by chance. He asked the farmer, "How was the crop?" The farmer said, "It was all right sir, but the head of that widow became as small as the cob!" Actually, the field had yielded very big cobs according to the word of Maharaj, so accordingly the farmer said this. Bhausaheb Maharaj just smiled, and went away.

What is the moral of this story? The jiva becomes worried by his own concepts. So, instead of worrying, if the devotee conducts his life with the faith that "all is auspicious, all is good, all the world is God's own town, all is of the nature and religion of God, it is God who is active everywhere, there is nothing other than God, all profit and loss is for God only, and it belongs only to him," then he will be happy and have contentment. Therefore, nobody should raise unnecessary demons of doubt, and become miserable. We should listen carefully to what the Saints and Sages tell us and ponder over their advice. By understanding the Essence we should make our life happy. We should not behave with false pride. Please believe that there is nothing in our power. God does all, and gets all things done. It is God who is behind us, and in front of us. Do not cut your separate existence out of the wholeness of life. Drop that nonsense. Whatever is happening is exactly perfect. When you project an imaginary person, it all seems to be unstable. Actually, there is neither high nor low. Both the sides are equal. Everything is fixed perfectly, and undisturbed. If the ego is dropped, all Existence is perfectly still, nothing is unstable. At the bottom, as well as over and above, the experience that one has is that there is something that is utterly stable and very solid. That is the state that is the "Alive Consciousness of Brahman" (ChidGhana Brahman). There is a small trifle of a ripple in that Consciousness that appears to be unstable, but that small unstable thing appears to the jiva to be having such upheavals that the jiva is completely terrified. This is the strange phenomenon of this world appearance. Nobody ever thinks to find out what is at the root of this upheaval. However, what do you experience if but for a short time you take a pause in your habitual thought process and just observe?

It is no doubt a very good wish that we should be always happy with all pleasures and riches at our command, but it this desire that is at the very root of all misery. It is true that our life should be fulfilled, but what are we, whose fulfillment is sought? We never question this. If we give this some thought, then we will find out very clearly what and how we actually are, and what is absolutely necessary for living and for fulfillment. Then the problem that confronts us, that we should have a completely happy state, will be solved instantly. There is a scheme of things which guarantees complete happiness for us, but we never bother to look at it. In vain, we set out to destroy it with our ignorant and insane concepts. Truly, we need not raise even a finger to provide for our real happiness. However, in an effort to destroy our sorrow, we try through our misconceptions to produce a mighty club. What an insane concept this is. If by leaving this madness aside, you give full attention to the "Moment of Divine Experience," and find the subtle realization in that moment, you will enjoy complete happiness and joy and the dissolution of all sorrow.

Oh great people, by your own awareness and insight you should discern the truth of this. Since some time in the past the name and fame of real Saints has been completely turned into ashes. Some people who have heard and learned the words of Knowledge, and were able to repeat them, have earned public applause, and have adopted the names of real Saints for their own benefit. This has become rampant in society. Such people have already degraded themselves by superimposing topics of their own liking upon devotion to God and the fame of the Saints and Sages, with the purpose of enjoying the sense objects of their choosing. This has resulted in a state of affairs in which people are not ready to pay heed to what the ancient Saints have told, and what any real Saints in the present are saying. Thus, the very wealth of all the true Happiness that those Saints have left behind for us is left undiscovered and unused.

My dear wise people, try to get the best of this teaching. In the whole infinite universe that God has created, He has for his own pleasure, created man. This form of the human race is his most dear possession, his most valued treasure. He has created the human form by using his maximum skill and made a provision that the human being is by very nature, a being full of Knowledge. You do not have the experience that you have no Knowledge at all. You are very certain that you have Knowledge, and that certainty is quite correct. God has ordered this for the human form. You have the power to select what is true and false, good and bad, right and wrong in this world. Use it, and find out who is the true Saint and who is false. By finding the right person, learn from them what the Saints have said, and their innermost compassionate teaching. Do not discard all teachings by saying that all people are bogus, that all are charlatans. You should be in the natural and easy state of Self-experience. Remain there, and drink this "Nectar of Divine Understanding" and enjoy the great "Bliss of Supreme Knowledge."

Inchgiri, Sunday 8-12-1935

The End
of
Master of Self-Realization

www.ingramcontent.com/pod-product-compliance
Lightning Source LLC
Chambersburg PA
CBHW031054080526
44587CB00011B/676